This book is dedicated to Michael Martone
the Ur-Midwesterner

In the Middle of the Middle West

Literary Nonfiction from the Heartland

Edited by Becky Bradway

INDIANA University Press

Bloomington & Indianapolis

This book is a publication of

Indiana University Press
601 North Morton Street
Bloomington, IN 47404-3797 USA

http://iupress.indiana.edu

Telephone orders   800-842-6796
Fax orders   812-855-7931
Orders by e-mail   iuporder@indiana.edu

The paper used in this publication meets the minimum requirements of American National Standard for Information Sciences—Permanence of Paper for Printed Library Materials, ANSI Z39.48-1984.

Manufactured in the United States of America

Library of Congress Cataloging-in-Publication Data

In the middle of the Middle West : literary nonfiction from the heartland / edited by Becky Bradway.
p. cm.
ISBN 0-253-34375-5 (alk. paper) — ISBN 0-253-21657-5 (pbk. : alk. paper)
1. Middle West—Description and travel. 2. Middle West—Social conditions. 3. Regionalism—Middle West. 4. Middle West—Biography. 5. Group identity—Middle West.
6. Pluralism (Social sciences)—Middle West. I. Bradway, Becky, date
F355.I5 2003
977—dc21
2003010771

1 2 3 4 5 08 07 06 05 04 03

In the Middle
of the
Middle West

Contents

TRANSIT

CALIFORNIA, MIDWEST

WORKERS

ARTISTS

HOUSES

REWIND

Introduction

BECKY BRADWAY

Write an essay about a place—it sounds so easy. A place where you lived or once lived. Place is all around us, right? The container of our lives, the irritating wrapper that keeps us cellophaned. There's no escape. You can leap, you can get high, you can be in a song, you can paint your way from Boonieville to France, you can study your way into philosophy, but when you're done, there you are—in a place.

As limiting as it is, place invariably becomes a disappointment. Falling into a place, flying into an ethereal place, the moment of enlightenment and astonishment will pass, and there you will be with your feet on the ground. Damn. In a house, an apartment, a hotel room, on a sidewalk, an escalator, grass, dirt. You look up, you situate yourself, move in a specific direction—all aware—and you try to remember again who you are. Surrounded by place.

You find your place, stay in place, run away. Settle down. Take a trip (inferring:return). If you contemplate where you came from and where you are (right now, this moment), you might feel ambivalent, possibly even turbulent. Or grateful. Or glow in the light of good feeling as you keep to the well-lit corridors. If you are from the Midwest, you will probably be a little embarrassed. You may not want to think about it. You may instead watch a movie about Los Angeles or a documentary about New York City. The places of dramatic events.

The Midwest. Isn't that where they grow . . . corn? And wear bib overalls? Isn't that where everybody is happy but bland?

You might ponder the relevance of considering place at all. Given the ease of mental flight into entertainment, the quick leap into electronic realms, the availability of cheap plane tickets to any-flipping-where. Maybe the only relevant places are the bed, the chair, and the plains and galaxies in our individual heads. In a time when people (Americans, anyway) rule—having conquered all space and land—perhaps place no longer exerts its demands.

Unless you're a nature girl or boy, you probably only go outside to get in your vehicle (or catch a vehicle), or maybe to mow the lawn or sweep the pavement or take the occasional stroll around the lake. Animals, weather, geographic formations, even neighborhoods mean nothing when you are always inside.

But only the staunchest and most insular hermits can truly maintain their lives in airtight boxes. And even they usually have to go out to work.

Then we go into the outdoors, getting into our cars (place A) to go to our jobs (place B) to go to the grocery store (place C) and maybe a restaurant or a movie or a coffee shop then home (place AAA). There may even be a nature stopover at a jogging path or lakefront (unusual and exotic place X). Between buildings we see places fly past. People-packed neighborhoods, most likely, in their permutations. Or fields. Or mountains. Towns. Created terrains, with the occasional errant brushy, free-willed natural spot that asserts a separate force.

We are influenced. We create place and are shaped by it. We are manipulated by this place where we have come by choice or been drop-kicked by accident and fate. It eases into us, despite our intentions—or we welcome it, obliviously becoming part of the great shoe carnival or the prairie grass. If we are artists, that place creeps into our art, whether we choose to represent it realistically or to abstract it. As the place creates us, we create back at it.

The place is people. What we build, destroy, and let be.

This book is about the Midwest. The place between the two coasts—that place not the South—that place not the West (or the Plains)—and not Appalachia, either. We don't have mountains here. You're right: we have corn.

We seem to fall away, ill-defined. Ignored, mostly, a kind of joke. The place you'd want to leave.

It isn't what it used to be.

Most of us don't walk into the cornfields. We don't even drive past them much. The small towns and farms have been whittled away.

Most people live in the cities or their suburbs. The biggest and best, like Chicago, St. Louis, and Indianapolis, each with its own quirks and energy. Others live in the many scattered in-the-middle cities. Government cities and college-town cities that rise up because of an industry. When the farm kids go, they go to these, and each is a network with its particular touchstones and feel.

When I put this book together, asking writers to create something about the Midwest or set in the Midwest, I didn't know what I would get. I didn't know whether there would be any similarities between these pieces. I thought they might, in truth, prove that place was no longer relevant—that there was no distinctive "Midwest." I thought I might get anti-heartland tirades, exegeses on the need to flee. The writers had few surface similarities in background and style: some defined themselves as poets, others as novelists, a few as filmmakers, and more as journalists. Some were born in the middle of the country, but most were migrants. Some stayed—others left. Writers of varying ages, races, gender, class background, and sexual orientation. What in the world could these people have in common?

What I got wasn't what I expected.

Most pieces intersected and merged one or more of these foci:

home (or houses, or rooms in houses)
family (as children, as parents, as spouses)
geography, weather, landscape
identity and/or sense of being lost (see home)

rejection and/or isolation
fear and loathing (self-hatred as Midwestern trait)
direction or lack thereof
the strange similarity between the Midwest and California
myths, illusions, and dreams
disappearance

Forty writers took on the imposition of this Midwestern place and the ways they have adapted to it. Far from being disconnected from their surroundings, the writers have no choice but to be shaped by them. Most pieces don't praise or condemn, but show a moment, a cross-section, a situation in a life. The Amish, gay-bashers, poets, wise old men, firemen, reflecting women, busy women, accident victims, grieving parents, homebuyers, new parents, rappers, and lonely children all make appearances. All carve out some place for themselves in this place that used to be called a heartland.

Prairie carving has never been easy. The isolation, the sheer flatness, leads to struggle despite all good intentions. Most writers decided that staying was worth the fight, and claimed their homestead here in the land of corn. Even if you are not from this place, it's true—we're all from the same place. A place that is never easy, but can be beautiful, nevertheless. We all have to find ourselves somewhere.

Outskirts

Midwest

STUART DYBEK

A week after the ground has thawed enough to turn, Snyder, our landlord, knocks at the door.

"Got some bad news for you, Sturt," he says. "You're gonna have to pen up your chicken or get rid of him. He's scratchin' up the garden."

It's really more my wife's chicken than mine, as those things go—not that she brought it home or looks after it, but she's more inclined than I to see the chicken's side of things. I worry she'll be angry when she comes home and finds it gone. She rides the school bus home each afternoon as it meanders from rural stop to rural stop, from her teacher's aide job at the middle school—not an arrangement that puts her in the best of humor.

But Snyder has an unassailable point. I've seen the chicken working over his newly seeded furrows myself. We're living on food stamps and grad student incomes, and Snyder is renting us the lopsided, drafty little farmhouse that's still haunted by the ghost of its former resident, Grandpa Snyder, for only $85 a month. So I go out with him into the fields.

I hang back watching Snyder's technique, figuring to learn the right way to catch a chicken. This one is wary. It's a rogue chicken, a chicken run amok that hit the road on its own. Beside whatever private demons it's run away from, it has since been made even more skittish by constant ambushes from Jumbi, our Siamese cat. The cat lives up to his name, Jumbi, the word for ghost on the Caribbean island where we acquired him, a beautiful island where for two years we both happily taught at the local high school before moving here to Iowa.

The chicken has been with us since the dead of winter, our first Iowa winter, and, according to the *Des Moines Register,* the coldest in twenty years. There were nights we huddled under so many covers it was difficult to budge: sheets, blankets, quilts, bedspreads, cat and child balled between us like a couple of hot water bags. We could hear the wind, tinged with Northern Lights, rushing across Canada and the Dakotas toward its first collision—our farm house. Each night, all night, wind clawed obsessively at the shredded, fogged plastic stapled over the windows. We could feel an arctic jet stream boring through the uninsulated walls. One night it dropped to thirty below. We stacked newspapers and dirty laundry between the

walls and mattress, and went to bed wearing our coats, our feet bundled in gym
socks, and lay shivering while waves of wind surged across the prairie and the
' house creaked as it lifted and settled like a wooden ship on a pitching sea.

Next morning, in the old stable Snyder had converted to a garage, the Chevy
wouldn't even turn over. A service station truck driven by a hippie-looking kid
with STAN on his coveralls, his acne pitted purple in the cold, finally made it out.
When he connected the jumper cables, the frozen battery exploded in our faces.
We staggered into the house to wash the acid out of our eyes. Then, for the rest of
the morning, Stan and I sat sliding the whiskey bottle between us across the
chipped enameled kitchen table Grandpa Snyder had left behind. I was able to
pick up a station out of Chicago, not that it played anything different than the station in Des Moines, but Stan liked its station breaks better. He said he was going
to try living in Chicago after a hitch in the Army. When the whiskey was gone, I
put on a pot of tea and Stan pulled out a baggie full of homegrown dope.

Later, still a little buzzed, I walked across the frostbitten field. The verdant landscape of pasture and vegetable gardens heavy for harvest and towering cornfields
with seductive, shady aisles that had beckoned us in September when we arrived
in a U-Haul truck was now transformed into a lunar surface of nodules and craters
under icy snow that crunched beneath boot soles like a mineral dust. It was a slow,
head-down, wind-slashing trudge to Snyder's big house, a half mile away, the only
other house on the horizon.

One of his dogs was lying dead next to the stairs. Another whimpered in the
doghouse.

Snyder answered the door, invited me in.

The kitchen exhaled steam and the warm, sweet smell of baking bread. Huge
pots of boiling corn rumbled on the stove. The kids were all sitting around the
table, ready to eat. A&W root beer mugs of milk brimmed beside each plate. Enid,
the oldest, who always flashed the peace sign at me from the back of the school
bus, blushed as I stepped in.

"Cold enough for you, Sturt?" Snyder asked.

"I see it got one of your dogs."

He caught what was in my voice and looked at me. "Cold alone wouldn't kill
'em, Sturt. I always had dogs. Never brought 'em in no matter how cold. He got
hit on the road and drug hisself back. I woulda put him in the basement had I
knowed. Ailing dog ain't gonna make it through this kinda weather, that's for sure.
How's the house?"

"Pretty cold."

"That's a good furnace in there."

"It's working all right but there's drafts everywhere."

"Yeah, well, Granpa Snyder used to complain every now and then." He laughed
in the direction of his wife. "He was a tough old coot. Used to sleep in the bathroom when it really got bad. Said it was the warmest spot in the house."

"My car is dead. I wondered if I could borrow your truck just to get into town so
I could buy an electric heater."

"Well, Sturt, I got a heater downstairs we don't use, except when we're playing ping-pong, be happy to let you borrow."

So that night and the rest of the month until the cold spell broke, we slept with the electric heater on a chair pointed at the bed, its coils grilling on and off in the dark, our faces the color of fast-food french fries under a light. It stayed subzero for nearly three weeks, and during that time the chicken showed up.

My wife saw it one day, approaching our house across a field, a flurry of sparrows twittering around it. At first we thought they were attacking, that things were so bad the sparrows were after live meat. But it became clear that the chicken was scrabbling through the snow and must have been turning up something to eat. I went out and threw it some popcorn kernels and it moved in.

There was a scooped depression on the lee side of our house where a sunken sill half-buried in dead leaves and festooned with sooty webs framed a small cellar window. The pane was smoked from the oily heat escaping the cellar, and it must have made for a warm nook. Snow melted before it could accumulate there. Drifts scalloped around the house like paralyzed white waves pocked with chicken tracks. In the mornings we'd always check, and the chicken would be there pointing east like a weathercock, staring sidelong across the fields, perfectly still—meditating, my wife insisted.

We concocted stories about how it was a soul in transmigration—a seeker on a pilgrimage who'd stopped to pray through winter. We felt it was superior to other, sedentary chickens, tucked in their coops, sitting on their little nest eggs. Our chicken had renounced the constricts of such comforts the way that Hindu writing distinguishes between wandering monks and householders, the latter being not up to the former.

The only thing that distracted the chicken's meditation was the cat. The bird would remain perfectly still, bunched and fiercely meditating while the cat stalked along the side of the house. When the cat crept close enough to pounce, the chicken would explode into a undignified fit of squawks and flapping, racing in crazed circles on its scaly yellow legs across the snow.

And that's what happens when Snyder tries to catch it. I'd thought there was some finesse way to catch a chicken that every farm boy learned. But Snyder is after it as if he's in a pig-calling contest, waving his thick, stubby arms over his head, yelling *Whooooeee Whooooeeee* as the chicken bolts from its nook, feathers flying.

We give chase across the newly plowed field, our feet sinking in, leaving footprints as if we're running across a freshly painted floor. The chicken jukes back toward the house, across the yard, under the clothesline, and we trap it for an instant against a rusted skeleton of a reaper. But when Snyder reaches for it, he gets a pecked hand instead, and the chicken squirts between his legs.

"Almost had the sonnabitch, Sturt!"

The bird is putting up a good fight, and I begin to admire it again. As soon as Snyder suggested getting rid of the chicken, I realized how down I was on it—that, for me, the chicken had become emblematic of all that seemed wrong about having moved from the islands back to the Midwest just to pursue degrees. Snyder keeps calling it *him*, and for all I know he might be right. When it first showed up we'd had a vision of fresh eggs, some small promise from the countryside of the bountifulness people must endure such winters for. But it's eaten its way through two plastic bags of Jiffy popcorn and is on its third drum of Quaker Oats, and not one egg. I've been out every morning for the last month scattering feed into the nook, then carefully checking the nest of flattened leaves against the sooty windowpane, but nothing, no token of gratitude.

When I complained the chicken wasn't laying, my wife said she'd mentioned that at school and was told by the farm kids that one could test for eggs by inserting a finger into the chicken.

"If that's what you're suggesting, no way. I'll knock down yellow jacket nests, I'll clean the decaying mice out of Grandpa Snyder's stove, but I draw the line when it comes to feeling in a chicken for an egg." It wasn't squeamishness; I was afraid of hurting the chicken. That kind of intimacy wasn't something a city boy should be attempting without guidance.

I'd begun to suspect that the chicken was no free spirit at all, but rather some drone driven from the coop for its lack of productivity.

"*Whoooeee!* We got him now, Sturt!"

With the entire horizon in which to escape, the chicken circles the garage three times and darts inside.

We swing the doors shut. The chicken almost blends into the gleams slatting in through the warped wooden siding. We can make it out, banded in a sunbeam, like a trembling mop head beside a barricade of boxes.

The garage is full of boxes I've learned by moving to save for future moves. I select one of my prized beer cartons—its handholds and solid construction make it great for hauling books—and I flap it open. It's Snyder doing the watching now. The chicken doesn't even struggle as I fold its wings to the side and set it in the box.

"Why don't you butcher him, Sturt? Get some good outa feeding it."

"Nah."

"Want me to wring its neck for you? That's an authentic what they're calling free-range chicken you got there."

Instead I'm driving the dirt back roads with the chicken clucking next to me in the Pabst Blue Ribbon box. I'm looking for a farmer who wants it. First I try a place down the road, but they don't keep chickens anymore, the lady tells me.

When I tell her it's just one chicken that needs a home and won't be any work, she insists on taking me out back, through their empty coops. Whitewash bright droppings crust weathered wood. Speckled feathers float up as we swing through the doors. It's odd how an empty chicken coop throws a kind of silence.

"Used to keep hens, hundreds—Leghorns, Andalusians, Rhode Island Reds, Sussex, you name it. Don't pay anymore with this economy."

"No money in chickens?" I ask, just trying to make small talk.

"You sure ain't from around here," she says.

The next two places don't want it either, and I don't bother with a sales pitch.

For a while I just drive, thinking maybe I should pen it, should drive into town for sticks and chicken wire. But I know that's crazy, that as soon as it gets warm we'll move into town, closer to the university. We've learned the hard way that, even at $85 a month, students can't afford country life. We can't afford another winter like this last one. Our country dreams seem pastoral, naive, a version of the American Midwest learned from musicals: sheep in the meadow, corn high as an elephant's eye . . .

The roads wind into one another, bounce over railroad tracks, past endless stretches of bare fields. In hollows where snow is still melting, enormous quantities of waste paper emerge, yellowed, flying about, plastered everywhere, against barns, stuck on barb-wire fences, and in bare branches.

Finally, I'm lost. I reach a farm I know I'll never find again. A farmer in gray coveralls stands among grunting swine as I grind up his rutted driveway.

"Does she lay?" he asks suspiciously after grilling me as to just where I got this here chicken.

"No," I admit.

"Well, she's an old one. You can tell by them spurs," he says, grabbing it by the legs and slinging it over his shoulder. "She'll be tough."

I keep driving till I hit a highway. By the time I get back it's nearly twilight. The lights are on in the house, and my wife and daughter are home. I wonder if they've noticed it's gone. I pull the car in the garage where the chicken allowed Snyder and me to finally trap her. Looking at the spot, I notice how that ground is littered with dried white droppings, and above, in the corner, that the straw packing sticks over the lip of one of the cartons I keep for moving my stereo. Inside the stereo box, where the straw is scooped and flattened, a glow: three eggs.

That Glorious Time of Old

MARY SWANDER

Squeezed together on the hard wooden benches in the meeting room of the country schoolhouse, we sang Christmas carols, a slow, modal sound echoing off the plain pine walls. *It came upon the midnight clear.* Outside, the storm cocooned us in snow, the flakes swirling through the darkness, covering the horses at the hitching post. It was the night of the Christmas program in my neighborhood, a rural Iowa community where I am one of the few "English," or non-Amish. Several families were delayed, their sleighs inching over waist-high drifts. Mahlon, the minister, kept us singing, his hand moving up and down with a steady rhythm. *That glorious song of old.*

Then some older boys extinguished the kerosene lanterns hanging from ceiling hooks. Our voices hushed. A chorus of young voices arose from the basement steps, the notes pure and clear. Thirteen Amish children and their teacher—who couldn't have been more than eighteen years old—wound through the meeting room. Each child carried a single white candle, the light glowing in the darkness. *With angels bending near the earth.*

The candles were snuffed, the lanterns re-lit, and the children went into a sing-song rhyming recitation of a poem dedicated to "Grandma." Just one grandma? I thought. There have to be others here. The room was packed with older women, their shawls draped over their shoulders, their white hair pulled back into buns. But when the poem was finished, just one grandma stood up and bowed. She was the ancestor of all the children, these siblings and cousins smiling out at us with the same grin that swept across the old woman's face.

Outside the window of this one-room schoolhouse, the wind swept across the pastures and cornfields where this same ancestry, this same sense of community, keeps the face of the land intact. Here, near Kalona, Iowa, the largest Amish settlement west of the Mississippi, the farms are small, averaging around a hundred and twenty acres, the houses nestled into the rolling hills, one close enough to another to hear the voices of children carried through the clear air from one farmstead to the next. The farmhouses are large, white boxy structures with wraparound porches and room for at least ten people at the dining room table. Most farmsteads have "Grandpa" houses, smaller structures that quarter elderly relatives; a loom or quilting frame is often set up in the main room. The well-kept barns are painted bright red, their lofts filled with hay, their stalls with Holsteins. Every

Monday morning, clothes flap in the breeze: a chorus line of denim pant legs dancing in the wind.

When the snow melts, the gardens are tilled, their rich, composted soils planted
with peas, lettuce, and spinach. Earthworms wiggle through the dirt dotted with
plastic milk jugs, or mini-hothouses, encasing cabbage and broccoli seedlings. The
manured fields are plowed under, teams of draft horses or old tractors preparing the
land for a four-crop rotation of corn, beans, oats, and alfalfa. Hay is still baled in
squares with binders dating back to the 1950s. The wagons wobbling down the
road on their metal rims are piled high with their bounty. Oats are stacked to dry
in shocks before threshing, and in mid-summer the play of light across the bun-
dles creates a mirage of earth tones that rivals a Monet painting. During fall harvest, you can still find whole families picking corn by hand or slaughtering their
own hogs and canning the meat, the pressure cooker steaming on the stove.

During any season, one can immediately grasp the health and prosperity of the
region. Bankruptcies from debts for purchases of large machinery and additional
tracts of land are virtually nonexistent. No beer cans litter the ditches. No old cars
or washing machines trash the creeks. Instead, the grid of gravel roads carries
buggy, buckboard, and sleigh travel, the horses trotting along through dust, mud,
and snow. The grid of human relationships carries a five-hundred-year-old agricultural way of life, its successes trotting through depressions and farm crises. The
farms, like the families in this region, are tightly knit together by a set of spiritual
beliefs that embrace the sustainability of the land and the importance of community.

The Amish, a conservative sect of the Christian Anabaptist Mennonites, originated in Switzerland during the Protestant Reformation. From their beginnings,
the Mennonites believed in adult baptism, non-violence, and non-conformity as
a response to the materialism of the world. The Amish held all these same beliefs
but desired an even stricter, more ascetic existence than their fellow Mennonites.
They modeled themselves after the Benedictine monks and nuns of the Catholic
Church, living a life removed from the outside world. The Amish, like the Benedictines, emphasized days filled with work, prayer, and dedication to community.
But unlike the Benedictines, the Amish allow themselves to marry, raise children,
and work within separate family units, each farm striving for self-sufficiency. Unlike many other Utopian societies, the Amish are capitalistic, not communistic.
They do not hold common land or businesses or eat together like the settlers of
the Amana Colonies in Iowa. Yet they do pool their money in mutual assistance
to pay for high-cost items in times of crisis. The Amish allegiance is to the group
as a whole and not to the strivings of the individual.

Why don't the Amish drive cars? Why do they have such small farms and little
machinery? Why do they drive tractors without rubber on their wheels? Why can
they use a phone but can't have one in their house? Why don't they have electricity? Why can they use a kerosene lamp? Isn't that using as much fossil fuel?
And what's wrong with televisions and radios? Why don't the Amish go to school
beyond the eighth grade? Do they vote? Do they pay taxes? Do they receive So-

cial Security in their old age? Disability or Medicare? Why happens when they get sick? What happens if their barn burns down?

These, some of the most commonly asked questions about the Amish, are a real mystery to most "English." Yet, all of the answers to these questions can be found in the Amish sense of community. Instead of prizing the accomplishment of the individual in a competitive society, the Amish prize the good of the group. They value humility rather than pride, the ability to work cooperatively rather than standing out in the society for some special talent or skill. They choose to live apart from the corruption and temptation of the "English" world with its emphasis on independence and self-development. For the Amish, the center of their life is their home, family, and community. Any idea, invention, or experience that takes away from the sanctity of their monastic life is shunned.

So why no large farms? Large farms necessitate large machinery, which creates both debt and greed. The more money one makes, the more money one desires, the more taxes one pays to the government to wage wars. Large farms also spread families apart, destroying a sense of community. Small farms lessen rural isolation and encourage neighborliness. Cars allow one to move more quickly, their speed taking one farther away from the farmstead and family. Rubber tractor tires serve the same purpose. A person could drive to town on a tractor and stay there for days separated from his family. Amish don't prohibit all technology or labor-saving devices. I have seen some of the most inventive foot-pedaled chicken-plucking machines and horse-driven sorghum presses. When the telephone was first invented, some Amish were allowed to install them, but the Amish quickly found that they were spending too much time talking to people at great distances and not interacting with their families close at hand. Soon, for the good of the family and community, telephones were banned.

The Amish can use generators and kerosene, but their homes cannot be connected to electric lines. Again, the Amish feel that even this kind of connection would violate their sense of separateness from the outside world. The commercialism of television and radios would distract them from their purpose. A higher education would inevitably carry them away from the home and farm, leading to a job in the outside world. While they pay taxes, they do not draw any aid out of the system. Instead, they find jobs for their disabled, take care of their own elderly, and pay for their health care out of their own pockets. If their barn burns down, they have a "frolic," a gathering of neighbors who work together for a couple of days to erect another one.

The Amish, like all other cultures, have their own inner rivalries and tensions. "Now isn't that just like a Yoder," I've heard members of the Miller clan pronounce when assessing the idiosyncrasies of a neighbor. But overall, the Amish have a deeper, more developed sense of cooperation than the "English." They turn the drudgery of repetitive tasks into social occasions. Once a month the women in my neighborhood congregate at one home and as a team do an attic-to-basement housecleaning, bake bread, cookies, and pies, sew new curtains for all the windows, or whatever else needs to be done. While they work, they catch up on gossip, discuss problems, joke, tell stories, and support each other through the joys and sorrows of living.

And when the Amish work together, they coordinate their actions with an uncanny synchronicity that achieves an astonishing efficiency. One winter night I found myself at a quilting bee hosted by my neighbor Fanny. Without greeting or chitchat, ten Amish women took off their wraps, then filed into Fanny's sitting room, assuming their places around the quilting frame. Needles were threaded, thimbles pressed onto their fingers, and soon the quilting commenced: the women bent over the frame, heads down, wrists cocked, the needles dipping down into the batting four times before the thread pulled its way through the blue cotton cloth. Fanny's teenage daughter Lydia reached up and refilled the kerosene lamp that hung from the hook overhead.

"Thread, please," one of the women called, her eyes fixed on her corner of the quilt. Lydia snatched the spool of thread from one side of the frame and danced over to place it in the caller's palm.

"Wiggle," Fanny said, and then, as if it were a choreographed ballet, the women on each end of the frame rose in unison and undid the clamps, rolling the quilt underneath the frame. For the next two hours, the women never glanced up, never stopped to stretch, their energy devotional and upbeat, driving forward, their conversation spotlighting one quilter, then the other, their hands moving in deep muscle memory, their fingers so many beautifully executed steps across a stage.

"But you have to understand," an eighty-five-year-old Amish man once told me, "when I was a boy, everyone had quilting bees, threshing crews, and barn raisings. No one had cars or electricity or telephones. Most farms were small and farmed with horses. Everyone had a manure spreader. No one had heard of synthetic pesticides. The Amish didn't invent these things. Rural people joined together and helped each other. The Amish didn't become 'quaint' until around 1930, when the old ways began to fade."

At the turn of the millennium, the Amish are a blast from the past for most of us who have no concept of one-room schools and a gathering of people with a common ancestor. Yet, many Baby Boomers are on a quest to find a better way of life in our society. Our postmodern culture has given us more career options, more education, more mobility and independence than our grandparents enjoyed, but it has also left us with a malaise. We are weary of moving from one job to the next, from one city to the next, where the only constant is the familiar McDonald's sign. We are frantic with the responsibilities that have funneled down to us, trying to single-handedly care for our own growing children while at the same time caring for our aging parents. We distrust institutions and dread turning over the end of our own lives to nursing homes and assisted living centers. We long for a stronger sense of community and connection, a desire to at least know our neighbors' names.

So, co-housing and intentional communities are springing up all over the United States. Clusters of people are founding communities addressing a variety of special needs: gays, disabled, artists, and organic farmers. Whether in rural or urban settings, people are attempting to reckon with their isolation and loneliness, trying to cope with their lack of extended families. The Boomers want to create a sense of community with more organization, structure, and continuity than the "communes" of their youth. Most of these intentional communities are filled with entrepreneurs who desire to interact with their neighbors in a cooperative way. When you click on the websites of a sampling of these successful communities, whether a chic enclave in Santa Fe or a cluster of trailers parked in the Monzano Mountains in New Mexico, you discover threads of the Amish philosophy. These communities are stitched together by common values or spiritual beliefs. They often pool resources and undertake cooperative tasks. Many of these communities are urban and simply desire a saner way to live together in clusters of families. Others are rural communities involved in raising organic livestock, in truck farming, and in CSAs. The "quaint" Amish with their nostalgic window into the past have become a model for the future.

The Amish are capitalists just like the rest of us. And the Amish are greedy just like the rest of us, but their spiritual values attempt to temper this basic human instinct. On their farms, the Amish tread a bit lighter on the land, using more horses for field work, fewer fossil fuels, and fewer synthetic fertilizers, pesticides, and herbicides. As a whole, they have fewer confinement operations, and experience less soil erosion. The Amish know that they are working not only to provide for their immediate families but for generations of future Amish. Their farms are passed down through their families, and it is a rarity to find one "up for sale" to the English world. In their quest for self-sufficiency, they grow and put up much of their own food, and in their small way eliminate a portion of the wasteful American practice of shipping produce from afar.

The Amish also renew the countryside by supporting small towns and keeping the local economy thriving. The Amish community provides products and services necessary for their own growth and survival as well as the enjoyment of the English world. In addition to running their farms, the Amish run wheelwright and blacksmith shops, bakeries and general stores, shoe and small engine repair businesses, quilt, rug, and yard goods stores, and vegetable and fruit stands. They have become a force that stands in the face of urban sprawl, of the Wal-Mart stores and Wendy's that have gobbled up farmland across the country. Take a ride through the Kalona area and notice the integrity of the landscape. As changed as it is from its native ecology, you can still capture the feel of the majesty and openness of the prairie.

Take a seat on a wooden bench in a one-room schoolhouse at the Christmas pageant and listen to the words of Mahlon the minister. "We kept our gifts to each other small this year and gave most of our money to a needy children's fund," he said. He handed his sons and daughters and nephews and nieces small packages wrapped in old grocery bags tied with bright ribbons. The boys received a pair of pliers, the girls a comb or handkerchief—enough to make the occasion special, but not too much to create desire. Most of the money for gifts was spent on the larger community, not even the Amish people, but a global cause.

The writer Gene Logsdon has predicted that the global future of farming belongs to the small producer and not the large agri-businesses. In his essay "The Future: More Farmers, Not Fewer," Logsdon points out the obvious economics: it's cheaper to grow a zucchini in the backyard garden than on a mega-farm. Logsdon continues with the sociology of the times: people are beginning to understand what they are really eating and demanding high-quality food that mega-farms can't supply. Logsdon cites scores of small producers, from angora goat, to urban squash blossom, to hydroponic spinach farmers who have filled niches left vacant by the heavily subsidized corn, bean, and wheat growers. If agriculture is indeed rethinking its sense of scope, it would also do well to rethink its sense of community. If the "new" farmers hope to carry the light of single candles into the darkness, they must also renew their relationships with their neighbors. The Amish way of life can provide an example of an agrarian tradition that through the cohesiveness of its people has done much to preserve the land.

Your What Hurts?

JAMES McMANUS

Excuse me, but you're goddamn right I live in the suburbs. I was born in the Bronx in 1951 and since then have lived in about a dozen suburbs and cities and towns—in a villa in the Alps, a rooftop duplex overlooking the Arno, a Winthrop Towers studio down the hall from a pimp and a heroin dealer, a three-room apartment upstairs from a plumbing company in Winnetka, as well as in ranch houses and cottages and coach houses. Right now I'm living in Kenilworth, albeit on the wrong (west) side of the tracks. And I'm here to report—getting creakily up from my Naugahyde La-Z-Boy, hitching my Loose-Fit Gap denim over my whitebread, Clintonian gut—that I've been both enlightened and bored, titillated and frightened in *all* of these places, and not necessarily the ones or the ways you might expect. Because all too often such expectations are based on naive stereotypes about poor, soulful, ethnically variegated cities vs. affluent, vacuous, lily-white suburbs. But anyone who's been paying attention of late knows that neither cities nor suburbs, villas nor manors, nor three-flats nor dives have a monopoly on one kind of *frisson* or culture.

My impatience stems from just having read a special section of *F*, the School of the Art Institute's student newspaper I founded thirteen years ago, in which my colleagues on the writing faculty sound off on the suburbs. "Pretty boring" is their general gist. "This dreamscape where everything was clean, fresh and white." While city dwellers have high-minded concerns such as crime, unions, and social justice, all this while frequenting authentic blues bars after sampling nightly the indigenous cuisines of the world's many cultures, "suburbanites' main problem"— as the editor of the section alleges—"was how to get their neighbors to quit using ChemLawn." Having been on sabbatical, I wasn't asked to contribute, but I was startled to read one of my colleagues of color complain: "Whenever my mother and I sit at a table in a restaurant, usually in our suburb, the service is always bad. The waitresses are often mean. My mother thinks it's because we have the appearance of bad tippers. I have my suspicions." Another of my colleagues, this one a famous novelist, testifies proudly: "Whenever my husband and I decided where we wanted to live, it was always in cities or small towns, never the amorphous in-between." Even a short story writer who lives in Evanston insists that "suburbia, for my city-born characters, is where people go to escape history. Though the notion sounds restful, it's too spooky for most of them—a tad too much like death."

Like death. As opposed, one supposes, to the uniformly unamorphous life to be found the minute one strolls south of Howard Street. Where the waitresses are always so friendly.

The prevailing impression among my colleagues appears to be that cities are the singular repositories of civilization, suburbs where you go to close off body and brain from the world while raising your children to complaisantly atrophy, vegetate a tad, and then die. Pathology-inducing population densities and godawful transportation systems apparently combine somehow with museums and coffee bars to boost one's overall level of sophistication. Whereas a two-car garage plus anything more than a square yard of "manicured" lawn equals death—or, worse, an unedgy squareness.

Plenty of city folk subscribe to this view, as we know, not just these ex-hippie art-school types. And over the years I have noticed that those who resent the suburbs the loudest have often spent a miserable adolescence ensconced in a six-bedroom split-level on a tree-lined cul-de-sac and are still, decades later, without the emotional intelligence to stop associating their pimply emotional frustration with *where it took place*. They prefer to believe they'd be better adjusted if only they'd been raised on food stamps up on the seventeenth floor of a housing project, or mucking stalls down on the farm. Where it's real. Where it's natural. Anyplace where the bourgeoisie patriarchy would have had less of a chance to oppress them. Meanwhile the fatherless folks in the actual projects are aching to move out to Schaumburg.

Are duskily endenimed CTA passengers on more intimate terms with madness and death and creation, or with any existential conundrum, than the average Soccer Mom? Most of my colleagues would sure love to think so, but perhaps they should get their narrow, brittle minds around the fact that Soccer Moms have reason to patronize ICU's and asylums and galleries and crematoria, too. Maybe more of a reason, in fact, since the suburbs are primarily about parenthood, the human condition *least* likely to spare one from the pressures of history, dread, or biology.

So, no, we are not unacquainted, up here, with the night. Nor do our jumbo mortgages insulate us from the *nada, la nausée,* narcotics, the serious novel, nonets, or from getting bad news from the neonatalogist. Precious few of us are gamboling barefoot across organically fertilized lawns without a real care in the world. Yet we still have the energy and resources to patronize, sometimes lavishly, orchestras and jazz clubs and architects, opera and theater and dance companies, women's hospitals and art schools and medical research foundations. And it's mainly our daughters and sons keeping the gangsta and indie and triphop artists (and art schools) in business. These gritty urban spirits gots to get pizzaid, after all. We pizzay them.

Besides, how long would a list of heathenish, even Gacy-ite city dwellers or of urbane, Nobel-caliber suburbanites have to be before it was clear how reductive any blanket pro- or anti-suburban prejudice is? One list of Eminent Sons of the Suburbs might begin with James Joyce, Albert Einstein, Samuel Beckett, John Cheever, John Updike, Thomas Pynchon, and take off from there. Another list would note that Virginia Woolf wrote Mrs. *Dalloway* in the same London suburb Mick Jagger was born in, that Todd Solondz wrote *Happiness* and Junot Diaz *Drown* in suburban New Jersey, Cynthia Ozick *The Shawl* in New Rochelle, Seamus Heaney the Glanmore Sonnets just south of Dublin. Still another would show that Miles Davis, Jimi Hendrix, Public Enemy, Busta Rhymes, and D. L. Hughley all hail from outside the hood.

Plus, aren't Berkeley, La Jolla, New Haven, Cambridge, Ann Arbor, and Princeton all suburbs? It wasn't even very long ago that Hyde Park, "The Lake Forest of the South Side," was officially considered one, too. Lotta brain cells to rub together in *those* places.

Closer to home we have the variegated likes of Liz Phair, Leon Lederman, Aaron Freeman, Lisel Mueller, Scott Turow, Michael Jordan, Hillary Rodham, Garry Wills, Jim Nutt, Jane Hamilton, Bob Chinn, Alex Kotlowitz, Eddie Vedder, Sam Prekop, even the late great Leon Forrest and Walter Payton and Mike Royko—movers and shakers of the body politic, purveyors of high and low culture, yet card-carrying suburbanites all. And last time I checked, Fermilab was still in Batavia, the Baha'i Temple in Wilmette, the Chicago Botanic Garden in Glencoe. Much of Frank Lloyd Wright's strongest work rings the city, as do our best zoos and farmers' markets and casinos. One of the baddest blues bars around anymore is FitzGerald's, in Berwyn.

So I clench my fist and extend it aloft—*Power to the Kenilworthians! Right own!*—when I say that my kids go to school in this suburb, my wife Jennifer has her garden and easel and teaches her cooking classes here, and this is where I write essays and novels and poems. We have no back yard to speak of, and our side yard needs work, but I still don't use ChemLawn or listen to J.Lo or Celine or Shania—who are huge in most cities, I hear. I do coach baseball and softball and basketball teams for the park district and listen to Koko Taylor and Lucinda Williams and read Jeanette Winterson, Gilles Deleuze, Michel Houellebecq, Edwidge Danticat, Zakes Mda. Like most of our neighbors, we subscribe to *The New York Times, The New Yorker, Harper's,* plus Jennifer's two dozen food magazines—a habit, I'd like to point out, that she picked up while living in Ravenswood. Three days a week I commute on a Metra train into the Loop, where I teach writing and literature at SAIC. When I get back home I watch a heck of a lot of TV, click rather too often on pornographic web sites, never go to church, seldom barbecue, drink too much tequila and red wine and scotch, frequent casinos in Indiana and along the Fox River, shop and often dine at Old Orchard. That's right, at a *mall, motherfucker!* No gritty, immigrant-run, bars-on-the-window authenticity for *moi,* at least not every time I go out. I even drive a—*gulp!*—BMW. But does having a 328is (arctic white, black interior) as my ride, or craving the Olive Mountain's chicken shwarma, or buying my boxers at Nordstrom's make me colorless, amorphously inbetween, depoliticized? Certain of my colleagues must think so. And in my less patient moods I'm likely to let them know how welcome they are to kiss my Royal Hibernian three-bedroom-red-brick-ranch-in-Kenilworth-residing posterior, twice.

But not now. Calmed by a glass of '85 Biondi-Santi brunello, I'll simply respond, "Shucks, I hope not."

Kvetching about the dull, whitebread suburbs, of course, isn't new. When Hemingway handed down his famously withering "broad lawns and narrow minds" verdict on Oak Park (and by extension Evanston, Kenilworth, Flossmoor, et al.) in the early 1920s, the observation may well have been dead-on. Compared to between-the-wars Paris, where he and his wife Hadley were living courtesy of her *trust fund*, any town on earth would have seemed culturally circumscribed. Yet Oak Park et al. today are home to some of our most enlightened citizenry, persons Chicago or any metropolis would be only too happy to claim as its rightful sons and daughters, including not only Payton and Rodham and Mueller and Kotlowitz but a sizable fraction of my creative and scholarly colleagues. While some of the narrowest, most reactionary minds you'll ever encounter sport nose rings and 606 zip codes.

There are broad lawns in Kenilworth certainly, these to go with minds of all breadths and proclivities. The landscape resembles much of America, a fact that often surprises our friends when they visit. From my desk I can see a Pee Wee baseball diamond, two apartment buildings (one in considerable disrepair), a Korean laundry, a playground, a half dozen houses, and four lanes of traffic along Green Bay Road. Our neighbors include a pair of piano teachers, one of whom is also a jazz pianist with an active performing and recording career. Within a block of our house live a salesman, a painter, a gallery owner, a real estate contractor, a trio of software designers. There are two homosexual households, two burgeoning families of color. There's also a bike shop, a dry cleaner, three doctors, a dentist, and a physical therapist's office. Lots of kids. Levels of education among the adults range from sixth-grade and proud to post-post-doctoral. Most of us regret Kenilworth's exclusionary past, its current lack of stores and restaurants, its relatively bland demographic. At the same time, we relish our easy access to Chicago, Wisconsin, the Skokie Lagoons, and O'Hare—and our privacy. The lake not only tempers the temperatures, it cuts the population density roughly in half. We are twenty-two minutes by train from the Loop, a shorter commute than many of our friends in Brooklyn or Santa Monica or Kenwood. For our children, the schools are world-class. Though this hardly guarantees them a good education, just as no underfunded school by itself can preclude it, the absolutely stellar public grammar and high schools are the principal reasons to live here. We pay for these schools with our exorbitant property taxes.

And hey, let's be honest. We envy our friends in the city—their proximity to offices, restaurants, live music venues, ethnic and cultural variety, the superb public library system. But everyone has to make trade-offs. In Kenilworth the deal is boring but safe: great schools/no restaurants, high taxes/low crime rate, jumbo mortgage payment/high resale value, bogus faux-Scottish town name/zero street credibility. I'm also willing to stipulate that Kenilworth remains unideal for sowing wild oats or meeting one's mate, let alone as a site for a sunny, dynamic retirement. And that once the kids grow up and move out, it may well be time to relocate downtown, up to Wisconsin, or for that matter back to Connemara or Como.

My own little nest should be emptying around 2019, when I'll be only sixty-eight and a half, all set to get another tattoo, pierce my scrotum, sample some daring cuisine. I also look forward to exchanging opinions with performance artists and taxi drivers, union organizers and aldermen. In the meantime, however, you're more likely to find me nestled back into the Naugahyde with a ball game on low and a book in my lap, hoping the dishwasher's loaded and the homework's about to get started.

Fag

BEN ALVEY

I was wrestling with my brother the first time I ever said it. My mother heard us scrapping outside the window, loud enough for the entire trailer park to hear us, and screamed for us to come inside. She asked me if I knew what it meant. I bowed my head, puddled up, and squeaked out a "no." She told me it wasn't a nice word and certainly not a word to call a family member. I was forced to sit in the living room chair and was forbidden to play outside the rest of the day. Part of me was relieved I wasn't spanked. In that chair, I stewed and fumed for what seemed like hours. I didn't understand what I had done wrong. It was just a word, and I didn't even know what it meant. I hadn't even cursed. She never even asked me where I had heard it from, and I guess it didn't matter. I was never to say the word again. It would be years before I would actually learn what the word "faggot" meant.

In the 'nam of junior high school, I learned that faggot was a "no-no" way of saying homosexual. It meant queer, and I knew what that implied. I can't be for certain when I learned it, since so many slurs and fat mama jokes were shoved into my repertoire that the time of its assimilation into my vernacular is impossible to detect. The first time I personally was called faggot is fuzzy to me, too. It was most likely in junior high, flung by a thick-necked ball boy or a red-necked Deere driver who meant it more as a slam to my quiet disposition and lack of outward manliness than to my sexual preference. I was "that kid." "That kid" who lost his books every day to the ass-kicking antics of attacking eighth-graders and sometimes lost his lunch in the bathroom afterwards. Even then the word made me sink into myself. Echoes of what my mother had told me after the fight with my brother reminded me that these boys didn't think too highly of me. The funny part was that neither the asshole boys nor I were aware that I actually was a faggot. I still had two years of baby fat and low self-esteem to wade through before realizing I had another brick to hold me under small-town waters. At that time I had one night of truth or dare that I desperately tried to erase from my memory because it made me fear what pubescent boys could do if the rumor mill got turning.

In retrospect, it was a common occurrence for many young boys (or so I've read in a dozen coming-of-age commentaries). In the spirit of the game, a friend and I had ended up touching each other in a more than friendly way. What started out as a night of gross-out humor and fart jokes had turned into a sleepover of naughty adolescence. My mother picked me up from his house the next day, and I never talked to him again. I worried myself until I became physically sick, crying myself to sleep and feeling guilty during even the slightest of daily activities. I convinced myself that I had been brainwashed that night. My overnight pal-cum-incubus had tainted my Kool-Aid, and I was unaware of what I was really doing. This explained my actions but not my guilt. I was sick because, I realized, I did know what I was doing. I was sick because I realized that part of me enjoyed it.

I returned to school and avoided him with relative ease. For being such a freak in junior high, I had a surprising number of friends, so at least I could ignore him in good company. A few weeks later, though, I would be punched in the stomach, not by thick necks and their fists, but by blackmailers and their words. A friend of a pal of a buddy had gotten word that I had done something naughty with my partner in crime. I certainly hadn't told anyone (no one—though my mother could sense that something was wrong, as mothers always do) and couldn't understand why he would tell anyone, either. I suppose he felt angry that I had ignored him, but at that point it was easier for me to lose a friend than to deal with shame. One day while sitting in social studies, a boy I could hardly call a friend (thin as a rail with a penchant for Hawaiian shirts and percussion) came up to me and told me he had heard "a very interesting story about me." I knew exactly what he was talking about. My stomach caved and clenched, and I must have physically flinched, because he asked me if I was all right. I played it surprisingly cool for about five minutes.

"I don't know what you're talking about," I replied in the most sotto of voices.

"About you and _____." He half laughed when he said this.

"I have no clue."

"I heard all about it." I was resolved. I wasn't going to admit to anything. Nothing. Then he said the most unbelievable thing for a thirteen-year-old. In a moment that made me realize how evil junior high school is, he said, "If you don't get me ten dollars by the end of the week, I'll tell everyone you fucked him."

I hate crying in public, especially in school. I bit the inside of my mouth so hard to keep my bottom lip from turning up that I started to taste blood. I said nothing, but I knew that I would do it. I would pay him. Whatever he asked. I was being extorted, and I hadn't even finished puberty. Worst of all, the "incident" had been exaggerated tenfold. There was no fucking. I was thirteen; fucking was a word at that point, and I certainly didn't know how to do it.

I went to school the next day and paid him his money. Some of it was in change, because my allowance was only ten a week and I had spent some of what I had saved. I started to walk away relieved. It was over and I could put this behind me.

"Do you collect baseball cards?" All of the color in my face dropped to the floor. I never even looked him in the eyes.

"I don't have any more money and I don't collect baseball cards." I finished my weak decree and stood there motionless, staring at the tiling. The bottom of his oversized Hawaiian print hit just above his knees. The edge of his shirt was frayed, and the white threads had started to gray. It was the same shirt he had been wearing all week. His sneakers had a hole in them, and I could see his socks poking through. I had always heard he was poor, but never realized to what extent. Poor kids don't pay notice to other poor kids. It was then I realized that I had more in common with him than I wanted. What little I did know about him centered around his father. A man any child would fear. In junior high, kids' personal lives are like currency. You could share dirt on someone else to gain a foothold. I had heard about his father, how horrible he was and how suddenly he wasn't there anymore. At the time, I remember feeling sympathy for him and could more than relate. While my father was never a monster and most certainly never physically harmed me, he had a wonderful talent for never being present when he was needed. By the time I was in junior high school, I hadn't seen him for years. Staring at this boy now, his knees shaking (was he nervous?), his brow creased, I felt no sympathy for him. I was glad he was poor, and a very ashamed part of me was glad his father was so awful. Wishing death on someone when you're thirteen can occur almost daily.

"Well," he started, "I need something, so why don't you bring whatever you can."

I nodded. I ran a fever that next morning. I worried myself sick and missed the next three days of school. I lay around all day crying with my head underneath my pillow while my mother was at work. By the end of the week I had no choice but to return. I was going to offer him some Dungeons and Dragons dice and old action figures. It was enough. He took them with little notice to what he was doing to me. He had no clue how my stomach felt.

"Next week, faggot"—and this time he meant it—"I want twenty dollars." He laughed at me while fingering his new acquisitions. I agreed and left the hallway before my eyes would spill over. In the bathroom I bawled/puked for longer than the passing period, which lasted five minutes. Outside my stall I heard two boys giggling at what I could only assume was me. My fears were validated when one of the two said with a giggle, "Listen to that faggot. He can't decide if he should puke or cry." I opted for the nurse instead of a tardy for class. I cried for a whole period and cradled my stomach, hoping to warm the worry out.

That afternoon in English, which I unfortunately shared with him, I told him it was over. I was tired of puking between classes and tired of paying him money I couldn't spare and tired of wondering how many people he'd already spilled my secret to. I told him more. That I didn't care if he told everyone, and that I knew my closest friends wouldn't give two shits or believe him. He was flabbergasted and sputtered for a moment.

"I'm tired of you invading my nightmares." It was all I could do to keep talking. "I used to wake up sick after dreaming of my father. Now I wake up sick after dreaming about you." He never asked for anything else again. He could have told everyone, but I had a contingency plan for that scenario. I spent the rest of the day telling my closest and loudest friends that this kid had picked a fight with me and was going to spread nasty rumors to get back at me. My friends told me no matter what he said they would back me up. My safety net was set, and for the first time in over two weeks, my stomach unclenched.

My blackmailer regarded me with quiet bitterness for the rest of the year and only ever cracked the word "faggot" in my direction once after that. In my mind, by defeating the blackmailer I had defeated the possibility of being gay. I could force the whole ordeal from sleepover to Dungeons and Dragons dice behind me. My extortionist had become my shame. A walking version of the word "faggot." He made me sink into myself and hate myself more than I loathed him. My mother had told me never to hate another person. I assumed it was all right to hate myself.

In high school the word popped up less frequently but with increasing vehemence. Boys were becoming men, and a pecking order was necessary. That line between a simple swipe at my esteem and really meaning it was decreasing with each slam. I wasn't a feminine-acting teenager, but I certainly wasn't manly. My voice wasn't high-pitched, and I was more clumsy than swishy. I dressed in funny t-shirts and ripped jeans and drifted toward the outside of the social circle. I wormed my way out of the pecking order by being different. A few swipes were made in my direction, but rarely enough to draw blood.

The kids in my high school ranged from upper suburban pre-fab richies to raised-on-the-backroads-value-of-the-dollar farm kids. The city itself was the same amalgamation. One half was a farm town that had outgrown its fields and no longer wanted the name of "Corn Country." The other half was factories, industrial parks, and one of the largest diesel engine companies in the world. That company had made its headquarters dead center in downtown. If you were a pre-fab richie, you lived in the city and grew up in large housing developments with tennis clubs attached, and your parents spent their workdays in the industrial park. If you were a farm kid, you didn't actually live in the city but in one of the many "not on the map" blips ten minutes outside of the city limits, and your parents most likely owned twenty acres and two barns. I fell moderately in between. A raised-in-the-trailer-park-on-the-back-roads type of kid. My parents labored at the factories the pre-fab families were managing. I didn't live in the city, but I didn't live in a blip. I lived on the highway between the two.

Most of my friends were moderates, like me, that lived in the city. I had met them after I began doing theatre. Theatre is one of those high school extracurricular activities that lets you either fall off the radar or fall under intense scrutiny. I, the consummate moderate, fell under both at different times. Only a small group of people felt it necessary to let me know I was a faggot. Most people assumed I was straight and that I was probably dating one of the girls I was constantly seen with, or some may have thought I was gay but could have given two shits. Regardless, most people had no clue that the word "faggot," even in passing, could cause such inner conflict.

The word itself wouldn't have been so damaging, but it was at this time in high school that I could no longer escape the shame of not being like the other boys. The last girlfriend I had had was in eighth grade, for two weeks, and it ended as it began, with a note passing. As I got into high school I had faux crushes on the girls who made me laugh, but I never once thought about kissing them, and certainly never about having sex with them. I wasn't one of those anomalies who didn't have sexual desires. I very much had them. I just didn't want to admit to myself that they were about boys. Regardless of how many times I pictured the baseball team naked, I still wasn't gay.

It wasn't until after my freshman year that I found a compromise. One night while lying around in my best friend's bedroom, I made the comment that I liked certain girls but didn't like them enough to want to date them. She asked me if I had ever been attracted to guys. It was the first time anyone had ever actually asked me that question. It was alarming how quickly the answer came to me. Yes, I was attracted to guys, but to say it made my stomach crawl. I eventually murmured an "I don't know." She responded with, "I've thought about what it would be like to be bisexual, you know?" Bi? Bisexual. Bi-sexual. I had never thought about liking both sexes. That seemed far safer than lusting after guys only. I was sold. I wanted her to sign me up. I admitted to her that I thought I might be bisexual, and she admitted the same to me. We had come out together—to each other—and no one else. But even then I knew that part of me was lying to myself. In the coming years our stances would change, hers to a more socially acceptable choice and mine to the type that led to bloody noses.

With the bi-sexual world at my fingertips, I found it easier to fantasize about guys. I convinced myself that it was okay because I still liked girls. The shame factor had decreased immeasurably. Not that the twinge of guilt was gone, but at least I had something prideful to counterbalance it with. I was "half okay." I could be "half honest" with myself publicly. A need grew to seek out other gay and bisexual people in my hometown. If not an actual person, then at least some gay culture. Problem being, to the young, untrained, agro-inundated eye, there were no gay people. So I turned to the only source I had: the video store. I bought so many entertainment magazines that I knew every movie that was coming out and who it starred and who directed it. Not that I would ever see these films (my hometown usually played the movies in which things blew up or Jim Carrey farted), but I knew of them. So I trotted my happy bisexual ass into town to the video store where my mother had put me on her card and left me with no viewing restrictions. I walked up and down every aisle looking for something that just might have gay people. I had read in a magazine that there was a documentary film about gay cinema and was bound and determined to find it and rent it. As luck would have it, my video store had one copy of *The Celluloid Closet*. This was to become my guidebook for bisexual life. I marched up to the counter and handed the clerk my card and just as promptly took it right back out of his hands before he could even scan it into the computer. I had one film. A GAY film. I went back to the aisles and rented two teen comedies and a shoot-'em-up to hide the contraband.

For two days I ended up watching everything but the documentary (the shoot-'em-up wasn't that bad). Finally I put it in and watched one of the most absorbing films of my life. Every time a movie came up that I wanted to see, I wrote it down.

After the documentary was over, I watched it again. It showed men kissing, and I had never seen that before. I convinced myself I was just being thorough. Halfway through the second time I was fast-forwarding through the boring interviews and lesbian stories. The next day I was on a mission to go home from the video store with something gay. The next gay film I rented was *My Own Private Idaho*. Within five minutes I was not only in love with River Phoenix, but I was dazzled that gay people could be so gritty and edgy. I had heard the joke people had made in English class, and the gay people on this movie didn't talk or act that way. My only real exposure had been fairies on TV or limp-wristed impersonations in bad watercooler jokes. The entire time I was watching the movie I thought, *How great for him that he can express his love for another man*. I never took into consideration that the characters in *Idaho* were prostitutes.

Over the next year I rented *Dog Day Afternoon* (I was more riveted by the acting than the gay culture), *Cruising* (for two days I swore I was straight), *Making Love* (I never made it to the end of that one; I realized gay didn't mean good), *Love! Valour! Compassion!* (then subsequently found and devoured the play), and countless others. Every time I watched a new movie, I thought how wonderful it was for them to be gay and open and honest. It dawned on me then. It was okay for anyone else in the world, especially Hollywood, to be gay—but not me. The movies only made me feel lonely. All of my friends had, not so surprisingly, started dating. I most certainly had not. Girls had expressed their interest in me, but, as I told my friends, they weren't my type. The type I was attracted to sat in the back of English class and made jokes about breasts and girls. Some of these same boys occasionally could be heard "joking" about plans that entailed two-by-fours up the side of "some queer's head." I had resigned myself to the fact that I was the loneliest teenage bisexual in the world (or at least the Midwest). I didn't see the absurdity of this idea—as if I were the only closeted boy in all of Indiana.

Then something strange happened. It was suddenly fashionable to be bisexual. Every kid with black hair and ripped jeans could say they were bi, and their popularity, within the skateboard-savvy group, went through the roof. (Although it only gave the boys in the back of the class ample fuel for two-by-four fantasies.) I was stunned. What the fuck was this? I was convinced that most of them weren't actually bisexual; it was just cool to say it. I became outraged; my best friend had fallen into this web of bi, and I could only watch from the sidelines. I refused to let them initiate me into their faux-sex cult. Part of me wanted to join in, but I didn't have the security of goth clothes and Sloppy Seconds albums. I was so pissed: here I was an actual "bisexual," and I could do nothing about it. I watched my best friend strut around cuddling with random guys and girls, laughing by the bus stop or in the cafeteria, and wanted to scream. But like all fads, the bi wave died out, and only a few hangers-on remained firm in their decision. I suppose I should have found it comforting to see such support in my school, but it only made me feel more separated. I paid more attention to the side comments from the onlookers and the glances shot my way because I associated with one or two of the "bi's."

Time went on, and I gradually accepted my life as a closeted "bisexual." I could talk about it with my best friend and not cringe if I actually muttered the word "gay" or "boyfriend." I felt no shame in renting a gay film (partly because the clerk had little clue what any of the movies I was grabbing were about). It was shortly after this breakthrough that I admitted to my best friend that I really didn't like girls. Casually over nachos and Coke, I mentioned that I was more attracted to guys and that actually, I had no inclination toward girls whatsoever.

"So you're gay?" she asked. Gay? What the fuck? Gay? Bisexual was one thing, but gay? I mustered my courage and, with my eyes down on the nachos, muttered a very weak "Yeah." My shame spiral resurfaced and grew bigger. I was now gay. I had signed a new list and there was no going back. I was a faggot.

I noticed how accepting she was, or rather, I noticed how unfazed she was. She neither flinched nor, as I truly feared, jumped up onto the table to point and scream, "Faggot! Faggot eating nachos!" In her face was a quiet acceptance, and maybe a glimmer of pride. If she could be so prideful of me, why couldn't I? I went home to mull my closet over for several hours. I had no religious convictions holding me back from liking myself, and I certainly had no moral qualms with other people being gay. Maybe I could like myself and be gay at the same time. It sounds simple to say, but that thought had never entered my mind. I was too busy thinking about blackmailing fuckers with Hawaiian shirts and prick asses with two-by-fours. I could only remember that stupid joke from *Philadelphia* about how faggots fake orgasms. I was more concerned with how gay would affect other people. I had already accepted that I could never be out in a town like mine. The daily torture at school and the backlash from a half backwoods/half porch-sitting family would be more than I could handle. But I had never planned on staying in my town. I was going to move out to a big city and leave it all behind. Then I could be gay. Simple. Set. Done.

I had decided to go to a small liberal arts college in Illinois because it had a strong theatre program, was far enough from my hometown, and gave me a lot of money. I wasn't on campus for two days before I had met more gay people then I had ever met in my life. I also wasn't on campus for more than two days before everyone started asking me if I was gay. It terrified me. I wasn't afraid that these people were going to beat me in the head, but I was afraid of the candor with which they asked. They weren't asking to ostracize me; they were asking because they were interested and because it was relevant. College and dating go hand in hand, so at the beginning of every year, students are weeding out their options.

I had planned to come to campus and be as gay as the day was long. I was going to be out and everyone would know. After being assaulted in a barrage of gay words before I had even finished unpacking, I froze. I told people for about two weeks that I was straight. I was starting it all over again. The lying, the shame, and this time I didn't have a secret friend to tell my woes to. But wait a minute. That was what I needed. A secret friend. I was making fast friends with a girl in my acting class. She was openly gay-friendly and loved the atmosphere of the university.

So over nachos, yet again, I opted to exchange my gay woe for her story involving a party woe. I came face to face again with the same acceptance, or rather face to face with the same non-fazement. So I was set; I had my secret gay woe friend, and now I could date other closeted men. That was the second catch. In college, most of the gay men aren't closeted. My plan wasn't working out. And this new friend wasn't letting me wallow in the self-pity to which I was accustomed. She wanted me to tell. She knew that this environment was safe (safer than my previous one), and I knew she was right. So I took baby steps. I stopped answering the sexuality questions and told people it wasn't their business. Then I told people one by one that I was gay. I started another closeted relationship, with a guy who was out but willing to make the sacrifice, but after a month I realized it wasn't working out and that it wasn't fair to him. He had earned his acceptance. He had been brave. I hadn't. So as time went on and the rumors spread, I was out. Everyone knew and no one had two-by-fours. In fact, I hadn't heard the word "faggot" since I had arrived on campus. My plan had worked. I was living in Mecca and had found my people.

It was a few months later when I realized that my campus wasn't Mecca and that I didn't like all of "my people." I realized gay people could be annoying just like straight people, but it was still nice to have that comfort and honesty. A week later, someone spray-painted on the wall of the performing arts center on campus:

"Go home fags. Go home."

Weeks later a girl was assaulted on campus because she had been seen at a table for the gay organization. She was a friend of the fags, and someone wanted to teach her a lesson. That's when I realized that no place was safe. Industrial park, corn country, Chicago, or a liberal arts campus. People said "faggot" everywhere, and they meant it. There was, is, and always will be the possibility that something could happen. I had planned on coming out back home; I had planned on being out to everyone I would ever meet. I weighed the joy of being honest with myself with the joy of being one hundred percent safe. I didn't know which was better.

The word "faggot" was thrown my way one night when I was seen kissing my then boyfriend on a street corner. We parted ways, and as I walked home, two guys I had seen on campus before started following me and calling after me. *This is it,* I thought. *This is when I become a headline.* I began to walk faster as they yelled after me and crossed the street to the side I was on. They were drunk, and "faggot" was the only word I could make out. Luckily I made it to my dorm in time. I was too scared and too scatterbrained to even think about calling security. I lay in bed for hours, brain flooded with the first time I had called my brother a faggot, the extortionist who had made my junior high school hell, the bisexual club, the two-by-fours, and the joy of honesty and the joy of safety. There is no such thing as safety.

Over the course of my college career, I went through the gamut of gay rites of passage. I came out to my mother with no consequence and told my friends back home, who were surprised but more than supportive. My cousins had found out from a girl who I knew from home. She had gone to school with me for a semester, and word got around. They weren't extremely happy about it, but I knew they wouldn't say anything to me. And I didn't care. They were my family. They had to accept me. I accepted them for their weirdness and loved them for it, so they had no choice. I started to recognize gay people and gay life in my own hometown. For some reason, I discovered that all the gay people had migrated to the video store and wore their hair big and painted their nails. Why not? If my hometown couldn't grow anyone else normal, then why should the homos be different? There was an ease with home and with school that I hadn't felt before. There was nothing hidden when I was out with my friends, and I could finally join when they talked about dating. I could now go through life on my terms, and I knew that I wouldn't have to be lonely. There is no guilt. There is no shame. But my stomach still clenches when I hear the word "faggot."

Little Man in the Woods

JAIMY GORDON

for Herb and Shirley Scott

Ein Männlein steht im Walde
ganz still und stumm . . .
Sagt, wer mag das Männlein sein,
das da steht im Wald allein?

I feel at home in a town that hates itself. After I left it, Baltimore came up in the world and in its own eyes, but for me it was too late. I gravitated to another city rich in self-disgust, Kalamazoo, whose burghers sneer at its mistakes and whose youth can't wait to get out, or say they can't. If they are still here in their thirties (they usually are), they slouch around in jeans and flannel shirts, smoking cigarettes and grinning sheepishly. They blame no one else for their troubles. I like them, these good-natured volunteers for their own defeat.

If you want to meet the living creatures of a place, naturalists say, go to the edge of it, the wet meadow between pond and forest, the strip of brush between the last yard and the first farm. And this is how I've happened to meet orphaned deer in Kalamazoo, on the overgrown property of the old Home for Boys—three of them, milling about in confusion near the still-warm body of their mother, who had been hit by a car on Oakland Drive—or a puff adder on my jogging path, nervously spreading its *faux* cobra hood; or, in the bog called Kleinstuck, with his back up against the largest bald cypress in Michigan, a scared little man masturbating. The *modus operandi* of this man's pleasure was to make women joggers run screaming out of the woods at the sight of his naked penis. And I make him the hero of my story, for an exhibitionist is the very flower of self-hatred, its extruded, visible sexuality. In showing his sex to you, he asks not for your love, but for your loathing. Kleinstuck, his chosen backdrop in this case, is what is left of nature in Kalamazoo. A leftover scrap of nature in the city is all edge. In such a place, neither this nor that, or rather this but also that, self-hatred, like wildlife, feels at home.

No city can have always hated itself, you think; but once a town begins to have that habit of mind, it colors the water, rusty and styptic, like tannin in an old cask. A self-hating town like Kalamazoo will long ago have buried the living stream it built itself on. Kalamazoo sank the wild Arcadia, which must have run amok in the mud streets of the pioneer town once too often. And when, in the restoration-minded nineties, the downtown authority decided to let the creek out again, they confined it like a bear in a zoo to a concrete trench so deep you have to stand at the railing even to see it. For acts of faint heart like this, Kalamazoo has nothing good to say of itself. Why? It still has handsome old neighborhoods, natural ponds, so many big trees that, flying over in summer, you might not know a town was there. It has history: an old railhead once on every self-respecting hobo's list, it gave the world the Checker cab, the card game Flinch, the Upjohn "friable" pill, and the Gibson guitar. Abraham Lincoln slept here.

Nevertheless, Kalamazoo prefers to hate itself. Dan Mancilla writes that at a wrestling match put on by some low-budget promotion in a gym near the airport, the visiting "heel" tried to heat up the sparse crowd by telling the folks they were all losers for living in Kalamazoo. The people nodded their heads serenely. Hating itself is second nature to Kalamazoo; it has forgotten its first nature, whatever that was. True, Checker closed, Gibson went south, Abraham Lincoln never came back, Flinch sold out to Milton Bradley. The great paper mills shut down one after another, leaving Superfund sites behind them. Maybe all that closing, all that submissive coming down in the world, poisons the mind of a town forever, as the paper mills poisoned the river. Still, some towns love themselves. Grand Rapids, fifty miles north, thinks well of itself, though it sports the fishy brand name Amway on its Grand Hotel. Ann Arbor, one hundred miles east, loves itself, and what does it have over Kalamazoo? A thousand restaurants. Houses cost half as much in Kalamazoo. Those who sneer at themselves in Kalamazoo are sneering in mansions, while those who gloat in Ann Arbor gloat, like as not, in shacks.

In Kalamazoo, as soon as a former paper plant hand—now a jail guard, or laundromat attendant, or pest control technician—is two thousand dollars to the good, he buys himself an acre of the county. A self-hating town like Kalamazoo can't squander its green outskirts fast enough in its haste to run away from itself. It spills over the city limits into cheap farm land, putting down dinky cottages and mobile homes, one or two to an acre. Then self-hatred returns with a vengeance, for here is only more Kalamazoo, Kalamazoo looking more defeated than ever, stripped out here of all character, now down to pastel boxes stranded on big bald lawns, concrete birdbaths and plastic pinwheels spinning in the wind, fake-wood woodsheds from K-Mart, and one sad little mohawk of piss-elms and blackberry briars waving in a culvert where the lawn mower won't reach. It's no use anymore, from Kalamazoo, to try to get out in the country. Those who must have nature, first nature—the joggers, the bird watchers, the sex criminals—are stuck with patches of woods in town.

When I first got to Kalamazoo, cautious people told me to stay out of Kleinstuck. I paid no attention. It's true that a small piece of nature in the city has more perils than nature at large, but only because humans are near and humans are always trouble, even in a piece of nature the size of Siberia. "In the Ussurian *taigá*," wrote the explorer Arseniev, "one must expect at all times to meet with a wild beast, but the most dangerous meeting of all is *with a man*." As soon as I saw the man on my running trail in the bog called Kleinstuck, I knew he was trouble. But

I corrected myself. What was wrong about him, if reason was applied? He was smallish; his dust-brown hair was thinning in front, and he wore a drooping Fu Manchu mustache that was somehow more pathetic than scary. He looked maybe thirty. His jeans and denim jacket were ordinary and respectable in these parts where university professors dress like loggers into their forties, and I recognized his vaguely swashbuckling gait, knees bent out, as an unfortunate cowboyism affected by half the white boys west of the Susquehanna. So what was wrong about him? He looked furtive, cartoon furtive, despite the bowlegged do-si-do in his walk. He looked caught in the act when I gazed at him, and at bay, his face twisted in a crude fearfulness that most of us, even if we felt it, would try to hide. That face made his clothes, which could have been a graduate student's, look like a crazy person's. He looked shabby, cornered, out of work, and fearful, and he was walking, not running, walking alone in Kleinstuck, in the woods, at midday. What is that guy doing out in nature? I asked myself, and that was when I corrected myself. Even if he's all that he looks like, why should he need nature any less than you? With his troubles, probably he needs it more.

All the same I had to pass him on the dirt trail that circles the bog, and so I made the usual calculations: Were people near enough to hear me if I screamed? Yes. Could I make myself scream? Doubtful. Yell? Maybe. My tired old dog, who had fallen a few feet behind me, would make the man think twice before he laid a hand on me, despite her grizzled chin; in fact she would bite him, I was pretty sure, if he touched me and I yelled loud enough for her to hear through her deafness. And anyway, as soon as I was past him, I could outrun him. I was in better shape.

By now he was behind me, and my thought, the usual *Oh well, nothing will probably happen,* with which I head into danger, drained away, leaving its usual residue: *You're a slob, you always were a slob, and you'll always be a slob,* I told myself. For in a certain way I don't care what happens to me enough to change my route for such a person. I take a chance. That's why I belong in Kalamazoo.

I belong in Kalamazoo, but as soon as I got myself stuck in Kalamazoo, I gravitated to Kleinstuck, on account of its name. What better marker for a scrap of nature inside the city limits than *Kleinstück,* which means "little piece" in German, Kleinstuck being fifty acres of raw edge, an unfenced peat bog whose greatest asset is its uselessness. No one swims here, no one fishes, no one boats. A would-be wader is still twenty feet from the water when she sinks up to her thighs in muck.

The name Kleinstuck is surely apt, but not, it turns out, by anyone's design. The bog was deeded to the Michigan Board of Education for one dollar in 1922 by Caroline Hubbard Kleinstuck, daughter of one of Kalamazoo's great paper barons, Silas Hubbard. Before he came west to the new state of Michigan in 1838 and made his fortune buying up failed homesteads, lending money, and finally organizing the Kalamazoo Paper Company, Hubbard had been a country schoolmaster in upstate New York. Though he had little formal schooling, he taught himself proper syntax from a Murray's *English Grammar* that he bought with the first few coins he earned—a story he liked to tell. He was partial to educated women and seems to have consoled himself for his own meager education by surrounding himself with females who had all that he lacked. He was an elder of the Unitarian church that brought Caroline Bartlett to Kalamazoo as its minister in 1889, and he donated $20,000—a fortune in those days—to build the first People's Church for her congregation three years later. Caroline Bartlett Crane, writer, reformer, scourge of the Kalamazoo slaughterhouses, was the age of Hubbard's own daughters. The Hubbard women, starting with Silas's wife, Mary Olivia Loomis Hubbard (A.B. 1847), and oldest daughter, the Caroline Hubbard Kleinstuck of the bog (A.B. 1875), as well as Caroline's daughter Frieda (A.B. 1909) and granddaughter Dorothy (A.B. 1937), were the first to receive degrees from the University of Michigan for four successive generations. Caroline of the bog was the first woman to earn a master's from Michigan. It was in mathematics.

Caroline and her next sister, Mary, were liberally educated heiresses of the American Midwest, Republicans, suffragists, in no hurry to wed, who finished their degrees and lived for a time in Paris and Geneva, perfecting their French under the wing of one Miss Julia Beerstecher—they sound like Henry James heroines. On the grand tour in 1879 with father, mother, and sisters, Caroline met a Prussian military officer, a Saxon. They married in 1883 and settled in Kalamazoo, on land given to Caroline by Silas Hubbard; their estate, Saxonia, ran from Oakland Drive (then Asylum Avenue) a long way east, and included my peat bog, which Caroline later named the Kleinstueck Preserve, in her late husband's honor.

Carl Gotthold Kleinstück had been a little man with a pinched leathery face, an immense, voluptuous set of handlebar mustaches out of all proportion to his size, and, in the one photograph of him I have seen, a voluminous greatcoat with astrakhan collar, cuffs, and hat, and a dachshund under his arm. He was secretary of the National Humane Society and president of the National Peat Society. He is said to have died of a broken heart (in the form of a stroke; or some say he shot himself, discreetly, in Florida) a short while after the sinking of the *Lusitania*.

He had long dabbled in the scientific study of the utility of peat as fuel: perhaps he thought our American peasantry should be deprived of none of the miseries of its European counterpart, including a choking, smoky peat fire in the *Stube*. He rigged a hand trolley on the slope behind the manor house of Saxonia (which still stands, the noblest house on Oakland Drive) and hired Potawatomi workers to cut blocks of peat from the bog and haul them up the hill to the drying shed. Luckily for me this was a gentleman's rather than an entrepreneur's occupation, and in due course the bog passed to Western Michigan Normal School, eventually WMU, where I teach. Oddly, the university policewoman whom I eventually had reason to drag to Kleinstuck, on police business, so she would understand what I was talking about, claimed never to have heard of the fifty-acre preserve in the middle of town. On the way in and out, she huffed and puffed, for despite her presumably risky profession she was forty pounds overweight, and Kleinstuck requires a brisk five-minute walk even to arrive in it. In short, I might be in better shape than the little man in my woods, but he was in better shape than Public Safety Officer Holleran.

The next time I saw him in Kleinstuck—and from then on, it was remarkable how often I saw him—the little man with the Fu Manchu mustache was walking that same clumsy swashbuckling walk, only now a brown paper bag the size of a half-pint of whiskey dangled from one hand. After that, he was in Kleinstuck in the early morning, in the darkening afternoon, at any time of day at all, not every time I ran, but every second or third time. Maybe twenty times he showed up, often enough so that I asked myself what hole that fellow had crawled out of, considering that he didn't look well traveled, he looked like a creature of grimly local habit if there ever was one, but I had lived ten years in Kalamazoo without seeing him, and now I saw him all the time.

Prison was one hole that occurred to me. Although the university where I teach has 28,000 students, I sensed he wasn't one of them. And although in the last ten years the great and gloomy state hospital in Kalamazoo has disgorged most of its chronic cases into the town, I was pretty sure he wasn't one of those, either. In Kalamazoo the ambulatory mad don't take to the woods. Summer and winter they walk the streets, restless, carrying all they own, having nothing to do and nothing to hide, asocial yet gravitating to the outlines of human habitation like moles; and all the runners in Kalamazoo know all ten of the walking mad by sight, with their makeshift carts and lumpy backpacks, their Rip Van Winkle beards and running shoes, in one case a Day-Glo vest and CAUTION ROAD WORK blinker flashing on the chest. *They* are in good shape, though missing most of their teeth, lean and leathery men of thirty-five whose faces look fifty. Not my little man in the woods, who looks soft as well as fearful, baby-faced as well as grotesque in his Fu Manchu mustache. I once complimented one of my students, an ex-convict, formerly a bank robber, for looking younger than his age, and he told me, "Jail preserves you." Maybe likewise this face, so tense and yet unworldly, for all its fear.

Summer passed into fall, and a curious thing happened with the little man: nothing. Nothing, but now I had seen him so many times—eighteen or nineteen—that I decided I kind of knew him. He was tortured-looking, led a strange life, no doubt, but he seemed to be harmless. He was a part of Kleinstuck now, an uneasy part, like the roots that floated to the top of the peaty soil and tripped me from time to time. When I passed him on the path, I would slightly nod at him. *Should you be nodding at him?* I would ask myself. His face was always skewed and fearful. He did not nod back.

In winter Kleinstuck fills with snow that takes its time to melt on the well-shaded trail. For three or four months, runners go indoors or take to the slushy streets, cursing all the while, for Kalamazoo, a self-hating town with lake-effect snow, doesn't shovel its sidewalks. In early May I was back in Kleinstuck, and I had forgotten the man. I was cursing nevertheless, cursing myself for coming here too early, for Kleinstuck was bone-cold and dripping, gray with rain that didn't get around to falling but webbed the air and my hair and eyeglasses, and my dog was filthy, caked in sand and peat. Of course I was the only runner, the only person. No one was running, and I didn't feel like running either, but then I never feel like running. I am not a natural runner. I have a long back and short legs; I was built for flexibility, not locomotion. I hate to think of what I look like when I run, with my short legs and big shorts, my chickenyard gait, my big hair and small, severe face. I can't even think when I run: the tom-tom percussiveness of it doesn't suit my style of cogitation. But I run because my father ran, because running is a rite of minimal self-love in my family, so we all run, because as a woman who likes to be alone I need a dog and a dog needs to run, because I tell myself I'm prepared for trouble since I could outrun it, although I'm not at all sure I could outrun it.

I was running, but I was in a rotten mood, and so was my dog, who never much liked running and now, at age eleven, stiff and tired, wanted to fall a few more steps behind. But I wouldn't let her. Come on, Tschotschie, I said crossly, you can do better than that. She sped up a little, but as soon as I stopped glaring at her, she dropped back again; she was old, and she was not a natural runner either. *You're a bully too*, I told myself, guilty and disgusted, and just then, there he was, the little man in the woods, leaning back on one elbow on a stump or a rock some fifteen feet off the trail, and though the view into the wet woods was cross-hatched with branches, and I didn't exactly want to stare, it was obvious what he was doing, the flashes of white, the bucking trunk and hunched shoulders and the angled hand.

I ran on. I had run only the first mile of five; I didn't want to leave. The lower my spirits, the doggeder I am. I had things to do, a tedious event at the university at four. To call the cops would take time. There was no need, I told myself, to do anything about this. I could ignore the man, run my three loops whether he leaned there on a tree showing me his penis or not. *Nothing will probably happen.*

I wasn't angry right away, the way I had been the first time a man exposed himself to me, tapping his erection softly against the steering wheel of his low-slung Cadillac like a big fat cigar as we idled side by side at a red light in Pimlico. A moment later, as he knew we must, I turned left and he turned right, but I made an illegal U-turn on Reisterstown Road and chased after him uselessly in my pickup truck, trying to get a view of his license plate, and his face. Even at the time my anger surprised me: What's this all about? What do I care if some chubby middle-aged freak in a Cadillac shows me his upright dick?

That was twenty years ago, and if I wasn't mad now, it was, at first, because I knew the man. (In truth I was far from knowing him; we had never spoken, I had never heard his voice, and he had always looked beyond unfriendly—skulking and downright scared of me.) Between then and now I had acquired the common wisdom, specious as it might be, about exhibitionists—that they do what they do again and again, as rhythmic in their compulsions as masturbation itself. That the more they do it, the more they do it again, all the more so if they've once been caught. That usually they do no more than that, but once in a while they do. That most of the time they shrink in horror from touching a woman, but not always. And now, remembering the exhibitionist's vocation to repeat, repeat, repeat, same act, same park, same tree at the same fork in the path, I did at last get angry at the little man in the woods, because I realized that if I didn't get rid of him I would lose my running loop, my little piece of nature, my edge, my Kleinstuck. I wasn't afraid of him, but if I expected him to be here every time I went running, I wouldn't come back again. He needed a shadowy place deep in the woods, but so did I. It was him or me.

I would call the police. I like to believe that summoning the constabulary to my aid on small provocation isn't my style, but on this occasion, I assured myself, ratting was my civic duty. Third-grade nature classes trooped through Kleinstuck regularly, three by three behind their teachers, and coed gym classes from the junior high ran here, if you could call that running, on the bog path in the late spring, the boys and then the girls, panting and flirting and straggling far behind. I could describe the man in every particular. I was sure the police must have had other complaints about him. I couldn't believe that, if he exposed himself to me, he hadn't exposed himself to any number of other women in these woods. I had a sudden jealous suspicion—since I had, in a manner, known the little man already for months—that I had only got treated to this display today because the weather was miserable and no other woman would come out of her hole, no one younger and silkier, and dogless, with a less forbidding face. As it turned out, I might have given him the benefit of the doubt. It was women's forbidding faces that my little man loved best.

I would call the police—and I now began to word his attributes as I would relate them to the cops, the duck-footed walk, the balding crown and stringy Fu Manchu. *I'm positive I could identify him; I've seen him there a lot, maybe twenty times, just walking, never doing anything, walking in this bowlegged* faux *cowboy way he has*, and I demonstrate. *His pants weren't down, they were open, not down. He had his penis out and his hand around it; I saw it from the corner of my eye. Well, I know that's what it was, although I didn't stop and look. No, I wouldn't say he showed it to me, I'd say he held it so I would see it. His face was turned away. He was sideways to me, leaning on his elbow in some bushes fifteen feet off the trail, with his legs sprawled out; there was thicket between us, branches. I saw something white. I didn't want to stare. I saw the way he was moving. I knew what he was doing, I knew it was for me, but I didn't want to look. I didn't want to give him the satisfaction.*

The first thing the police would ask me, I realized, was what exactly I had seen. Had I seen him masturbating? *You're an idiot,* I reminded myself, for I had gone to some trouble not to see. He had turned his face away, and I had done the same. It was a weak case, very weak. I would find it so myself. The little man would probably say he was only urinating. On what evidence could I contradict him? I needed details. I ran past the sandy stream bed I usually follow up the hill and out of Kleinstuck, and started around my loop again.

It was a strange five minutes, then, jogging in the wet woods, looking all the while for the flash of a man's white penis in the brush, the way a hunter looks for the flagged hind end of a retreating white tail deer. I doubted he would stay in the same place in the sopping woods as long as it took me to come all the way around the path again, but for once I didn't wish him gone. This time, I wanted him there. I wanted to see him and see him exactly, so that I could start the process of getting rid of him, getting him out of Kleinstuck once and for all.

I think he wanted the same. By then he must have known me as I knew him. He must have said it to himself: now she'll know. He must have wanted me to do something about him, to help him get rid of himself. He had not left. He had come out of the thicket and onto the trail and stood in full view, with his back propped against that famous bald cypress, a giant, ten feet around, planted by Carl Gotthold Kleinstück in 1885, and now his cowboy slouch had a new meaning, a true meaning, of making a bowstring of his arm to his crotch, his jeans bloused a bit around his hips and his half-hard penis bunching up in his hand, as floury pale in the wet light as a roll of unbaked dough. I ran past less than a yard away, and still he pretended not to look at me: his face was turned at an odd angle, toward the woods, as if he had heard something there. He watched me in profile, out of the side of his eye, the way a nervous goose does. You're going to get in a lot of trouble for doing that, I said to him as I ran by. I hadn't planned to say anything, and my voice in the rain-heavy air sounded hollow and sad. He said nothing.

I found out that, nowadays, if it's a town of more than twenty thousand and it's not a Sunday, you are likely to speak with a woman officer if a sex crime is involved. Without thinking, I had called the Kalamazoo police, and they didn't quibble about Kleinstuck being university property. The detective who came to my house had a whip-crack twang and a Wild West Show name: Annelee Oaklie. Was she related to *the* Annie? We spell it different, she said. Maybe somebody just couldn't spell, I said.

Detective Oaklie had a checklist: hair color, eye color, facial hair, exact time of day, northeast or northwest corner of Kleinstuck, closer to the Y or the perimeter trail? Standing there with his pants undone or masturbating? You mean some flashers don't masturbate? I asked. Around half and half, Detective Oaklie said; I take it this one masturbated? I ran back around to make sure, I assured her. You went back to observe the individual a second time? Detective Oaklie lifted her eyebrows and leaned over her clipboard, making a note. Well, you've got to realize I sort of knew him already. I mean, I'd seen the guy in Kleinstuck twenty times before, and nothing had happened. I wanted to be sure I saw what I saw. Twenty times, she repeated, writing it down. Maybe eighteen times, I said. The point is I saw him so often I thought he must be normal after all. Why didn't you think he was normal in the first place? Something about his face; he might have been scared of me or my dog—a feeling I had, it's hard to explain. He looked kind of down on his luck, but why shouldn't a poor man walk around by himself in nature? You should follow those hunches, Detective Oaklie said. Follow them where? I said. I wasn't going to give up my running loop. Anyway, I never saw anything, but I bet you have other complaints on him by now. I'm not the only woman who runs in Kleinstuck. Detective Oaklie called in to the station. There were no other complaints.

I was late for the tedious affair at school. Sorry, I whispered to the dean whose event it was, a man exposed himself to me in Kleinstuck and I had to talk to the cops. The dean, Shirley, looked at me strangely. She said: Was he a little guy, stringy-haired, with a mustache? Fu Manchu mustache, I said, balding on top, and he walks like *this*. I saw him last October, Shirley said, or wait, I think it was November, my sister-in-law was in from St. Louis for a visit, we were walking the trail and he stepped out in front of us, masturbating. We went the other way, and he cut through the woods and came out in front of us again. I charged him. *I wasn't going to hurt you*, he said. *Really? Well, I'm going to break every bone in your body*, I said, and he ran away. Did you call the cops? I asked her. I made a report, she said, but I never heard anything. I gave up running in Kleinstuck after that. Herb says it smells like dog shit in there anyway. It does not, I said, in case she was implying something about my dog. All bogs smell like that.

Two days later I went back to Kleinstuck with Tschotschie. Slowly and warily I ran the trail through the leafless woods where every tangle of branches showed a faint rouge, the first sore flush of spring, and at the end of my first loop my partner Peter came running the other way around the bog path to head me off. I saw him, he said. How do you know it was him? Jeans jacket, dangly mustache, everything exactly like you described it. Are you sure? Peter glared at me. It was him, he said. He walked into Kleinstuck right behind you, going the same way. You mean he's in here now? You'll see him on your next lap, he said.

We ran up the hill out of the bog, and this time I called the university police, while Peter ran back to Kleinstuck with his camera. But the little man didn't show himself. When Public Safety Officer Holleran said she didn't know what Kleinstuck was, let alone the footpaths into it, I offered to show her, and when she didn't take me up on it, I said a bit testily: When can you go? We arranged to meet later that afternoon, on an angle of city street where a metal guardrail marks the edge of the woods. There is a sign, *Welcome to the Kleinstuck Preserve*, with a few words about Caroline Hubbard Kleinstuck and her husband Carl, and just beyond it the sandy stream bed slopes down a long hill to the bog path.

The king of the birdwatchers in Kalamazoo is a stocky, black-haired, smolderingly handsome man who looks more like a mambo band leader than a Midwestern ornithologist. The first time I saw him, from behind as it happened to be, drifting slowly down the bog path in the smoke of a summer eve, wearing red bathing trunks and a dark blue polo shirt, alone and bare-legged in the buzzing, hissing, mosquito-rich twilight, I feared him more than I ever did my little man. On my next pass he was standing to one side, looking into the woods, and I saw his dangling binoculars. That had been years ago. By now we nodded at each other when we brushed by, and I always wanted to tell him that I loved birds and hated running and was sorry if I had startled the thrush or cerulean warbler he was watching. Although I never said anything, he didn't seem to despise me on sight as many birders do joggers. He had been alone that first night, but later I came to realize that he had a kind of harem, women and even a man or two, in drab, with clipboards and binoculars, who took the avian census for him at dusk or dawn.

Now I saw him ahead on the rutted sand track, and he saw me, walking, not running, into Kleinstuck with a policewoman by my side. We had never exchanged a word. We both began at once: Have you seen a little man—? I said, and he said, Every morning, every evening; doesn't this guy ever go home? I've had to keep a close eye on my ladies. Officer Holleran asked the king of the birdwatchers for his telephone number. I listened, staring off into the woods, and practicing to be a creep, I memorized it.

The next day Detective Oaklie telephoned. A man who might be the one who had exposed himself to me in Kleinstuck had been picked up in a backyard next to the preserve, on a peeping tom. He had been looking in a window, she said. The woman of the house had seen him from a different window, hid behind a curtain, and watched him. He climbed into the children's tree house. She called the police. When a patrolman found him crouching there, he said he had only wanted to get out of the rain.

Detective Oaklie was hoping to bring some photographs by my house. Possibly I could pick the man out of this group. Suddenly I worried that every gray-faced, guilty-looking thirty-year-old male with a mustache in this claustrophobic, self-allergic town would look familiar to me. Hadn't I seen them all by now, the red-eyed private snowplow drivers and the sullen minimum-wage garbage men and the bad-tempered, pony-tailed young father of four who had pushed the cart in front of me in the checkout line at Meijer's last week? But when Detective Oaklie showed me six faces, I knew only one.

His name was Joseph Roy McCatty. He was twenty-nine years old, and he had never been in anything but trouble, three times already this year, twelve times between the ages of twenty-one and twenty-four; and the same back into the mists of his juvenile record. Just before his eighteenth birthday, he took a Honda three-wheeler, for sale for $300, on a test drive and did not return. He was picked up and eventually placed in a K-PEP (Kalamazoo Probation Enhancement Program) residence for young men on a busy avenue a few blocks north of Kleinstuck, from which he strayed repeatedly. At first the court was patient with him, but now the charges of indecent exposure began to show up, and plainly his probation officer no longer knew what to do with him: "The People recommend 18 mos–5 yrs," the record states, and he went to real jail for the first time, the whole year he was twenty.

None of this was big trouble, all of it small trouble, all of it within a half-mile of where I live. Joseph Roy McCatty sneaking into garages and churches and stealing food and liquor, crouching in the children's playhouse, or lurking, the bottle in its brown paper sleeve as often as not in his hand, by the two marshy ponds each in its little woods near Oakland Drive: Kleinstuck to the east, or Woods Lake just behind the liquor store at Parkview. When he was twenty-one it was always Kleinstuck: always that same brushy slope behind the bald cypress, always coming closer, with each loop of a woman jogger, until she finally saw him at his frantic exercise with his sad, pale manhood in his hand. Even back then, one woman had taken note that when she ran by, he turned his face away from her. Three times, too, he had been warned away from the YMCA, from the asphalt tennis courts that stretch into the woods toward the northeast corner of Kleinstuck. One day he had held on to his bare dick for dear life at a plate glass window, behind which a roomful of middle-aged women were doing aerobics. That time he had been sent away for two months. When he reappeared it was at Woods Lake, at the little town beach where the lifeguards knew him by face, and even by name, as *Joey*. In June, Joey showed himself to two college women in bathing suits and was taken away again. He spent his 24th birthday—in mid-August—in the Kalamazoo County Jail. He was back at Woods Lake in October, when the lifeguards were through for the season, and, groaning with misery or delight, worked his naked penis in his hand before a mother whose two small children were splashing in the shallows. She thought, when he turned his face away from her, that he was look-ing at the children, and though she might have been mistaken, the judge took the thing on its face: after that he was gone a full five years. That was the nowhere he had come out of last year, when I first ran into him in Kleinstuck.

Detective Oaklie didn't tell me much of this, of course. Once I had a name, I could search the public record. For the last ten years, after each conviction, the *Kalamazoo Gazette* had run his sentences: Joseph Roy McCatty, *of Cherry Street*, it would always say, Cherry being a steep hill of well-kept unassuming little bun-galows that runs along the northern edge of Kleinstuck down to the Y; always Cherry Street, no matter how many times he was sent away or for how long. Joseph Roy McCatty, I told myself, was no homeowner, not even in dirt-cheap Kalamazoo. His mother must live there, I surmised, or his grandmother, some wreck of a middle-aged woman with a small fixed income, who lets the boy come and go, wringing her hands, probably nagging helplessly from time to time, not knowing what else to do, knowing his record. Not even an address on Cherry Street quite explains why Joseph Roy McCatty comes back to the same woods time after time and watches sweaty women in baggy shorts out of the side of his eye until he can keep it to himself no longer—he has a lonely and terrible date with Miss Michigan (as young men of Kalamazoo sometimes say, pointing to their open palms) and lets the guilty, wondrous truth burst out of his pants and wraps his hand around it.

The guy can't stay out of the woods where women go jogging no matter what they do to him, I said to Detective Oaklie. He can't help himself. What's going to keep him out of Kleinstuck again next week?

He's in the county jail for now on the other charge—the tree house thing, De-tective Oaklie said. He's used to being in jail. He won't post bond. He'll sit there a while and do his sixty days, and meanwhile we'll be working up a bigger case against him, you follow me?

I just want my running path back, I told her.

But two weeks later I saw him in the far distance, a good two hundred yards away from me in Kleinstuck. At least I thought it must be McCatty, the denim jacket, the dusty boots and shaky cowpuncher's walk, rounding the curve at the northwest corner of the preserve where another footpath runs off to the Y. I saw him from behind, before he saw me, and I stopped running and held my dog, for this time I was scared—scared because he had to know that I was the one who'd turned him in, *You're going to get in a lot of trouble for doing that,* and just as I stopped, he stopped—alerted not by noise but by some animal inkling he must have had; after all, he had lately had an unpleasant experience, like me, resulting in a hunted feeling, like mine, and he, too, was jumpy—and he turned completely around, at bay, and faced down the trail toward me. I didn't wait to meet his eye, ran straight up the hill through the pathless woods, and across Saxonia Lane, to Oakland Drive, hurrying my dog along, to a payphone near the liquor store. Detective Oaklie hadn't heard that McCatty was out, if he was. I'll be amazed if it's not him, I said. I ran home again, and Detective Oaklie telephoned me: McCatty had posted bond.

Jesus, he must have gotten out of the can and come straight to Kleinstuck, I said in disgust.

But we're about ready to make the other case against him, she told me. We'll pick him up in a day or two and he won't get out again.

I saw Joseph Roy McCatty for the last time three months later, in a courtroom in the county courthouse. Neither of us looked much like nature lovers anymore, if we ever had, I in a tweed suit and pantyhose, he in an orange jumpsuit from the county jail, styrofoam flip-flops on his very white feet. With skinny arms sticking out of his jumpsuit and a thin tuft of hair waving on his crown, he looked at once naked and barely there, hardly a match for his persecutors, the twenty-four witnesses and complainants whose names appeared on the cover page of the court case, and who included a university dean, a woman columnist from the *Kalamazoo Gazette,* the mother of two from Woods Lake, the owner of the tree house, the king of the birdwatchers, and Detective Annelee Oaklie and me.

Indecent exposure is an obstinately persistent but not exactly a serious crime in our society. The weaselly little man holding apart the flaps of his trench coat is a figure of wincing comedy, probably more funny than disgusting as long as you are hearing about it instead of seeing it in your favorite park. It is not a crime that men usually witness, unless by accident, a fact which doubtless makes it all the funnier in our culture. In any event the exhibitionist sits uncomfortably in the one broad category of Sex Offenders with the rapist, and yet exhibitionist acts make up one-third of sex offenses on the books in most American cities. The offense itself is generally a misdemeanor, punishable by less than a year in prison—and more often a routine sixty days—if it is a first offense. But with this compulsive act the first offense is soon lost in the stammering echo of its repetitions. What to do with such men? No one seems to know. When people run out of patience, at least in Michigan—if enough women are complaining—if the court can be persuaded that the offender is a "sexually delinquent person," then the man can be sent away for an indeterminate sentence, from one day to life.

I said that Joey McCatty's pleasure was to make women joggers run screaming out of the woods, but in truth I'm not sure he had any pleasure from his act, or even the brief untidy release of orgasm. There was no mention of an end of the act in all the twenty-odd cases, although one sees again and again the futile stipulation:

$100 bond. Do not go to Woods Lake or Klinestock [sic] Preserve or property other than his own w/o permission. No Alcohol.

Even if the actor has no pleasure in the act, for some reason the unwanted surprise of his erection declaring itself in full view—so very white in your eye (exhibitionists are almost always white)—awakens a punitive anger in a lot of women, as I can attest, and especially when the refuge of some last bit of public greenery, some Kleinstuck, is at stake. And even though the brief sight of the woman's shock and anger is all that the exhibitionist craves in return, the matter can't end there. The satisfaction women want is the removal of that spectacle from possibility. They want the banishment of the creep from nature. Nothing less will do.

When I saw Joseph Roy McCatty in court, I couldn't locate any part of my anger. *I know this poor clown*, I kept thinking, irrelevantly and incorrectly. I'd been living, clearly, in this self-hating small town too long. All the same I felt like a bully among so many other well-dressed, well-established burghers of the town, twenty-four of us ranged against McCatty in his flimsy orange jumpsuit, but my resolve to get back my running loop was firm. I was ready to testify. As it happened, I didn't have to. None of us did. Joseph McCatty was more preternaturally defeated than anyone had foreseen. He didn't care to fight. He didn't want to talk at all. He was willing to be named a sexually delinquent person by the court, *nolo contendere*. The judge reminded him that he was giving up the right to a trial of any kind, the right to be presumed innocent until proved guilty, the right to question the witnesses against him, as well as the right to testify in his own behalf or to be silent. McCatty did not change his plea. The judge asked:

With the no contest plea do you understand that for purposes of sentencing, if that plea is accepted, I would be treating you as though you were found guilty of being a sexually delinquent person?

Yeah, McCatty replied, or so the transcript reads, although I never heard him say the word.

It's no small thing to send a man to jail for life. Not that I give myself so much credit: let us remember that he managed, in the few months he was out, to expose himself to one English professor, a dean of the Graduate College at WMU, a woman columnist for the *Kalamazoo Gazette*, and a whole roomful of women doing aerobics at the YMCA after work, bouncing wearily in their sweatshirts. One look around the courtroom made clear it was the bitchier women's faces, after all, that enticed him. Or perhaps it was education that he prized: There was scarcely a woman in the room without a college degree or two.

True, Joey McCatty was eligible for parole the day he was sentenced; and it's doubtless true as well that, were he to be paroled, he would be back in Kleinstuck, frantically working his sex in front of some sweaty, well-educated woman in shorts, as fast as his legs could take him there. He could have been out any day since September 30, 1997, if he had struck his captors as a changed man, and more than fifteen hundred days had gone by. He might also be in prison for his natural life, although I have read that after the age of forty most flashers lose the urge to flash, and are perhaps as baffled, once they are fifty, by another man's compulsion to drop his trousers in front of a woman in a park as other people once were by his.

I wanted Joseph Roy McCatty out of my nature, but I find that I think a lot about his nature, his nature and his crime, a crime of warm weather and broad day, for which he wore no disguise, no gloves, no woman's stocking over the face, no ski mask, although he did—discreetly, or god knows why—turn his face away. He didn't threaten to kill me if I told, and when I warned him, obliquely, that I might call the cops, he didn't chase me with a stick or protest. He never touched me or any woman, as far as I know. He didn't hide. Even most flashers swiftly depart the scene of the crime, though they soon come back, with their penchant for repeating themselves. Joey McCatty never left; in a sense, he lived at the scene of the crime, one green spot by water or another, before there ever was a crime, at both Woods Lake and Kleinstuck; he was as much a part of the shady landscape as the gnats, the woodpeckers, the birdwatchers, and the joggers. Straitlaced prairie towns where strangers were unwelcome sometimes used to tolerate, and even shield, a village idiot. What about a village exhibitionist? I've heard no report.

I've read that exhibitionists sometimes turn in other exhibitionists whom they've spotted on their beats, less to keep the coast clear for their own pursuits than to protect civilization from others like themselves. Somehow it's no surprise that this model of self-hatred has no pity for his own kind, sees the poor schnook in the grip of compulsion as deserving whatever he gets. But even the nature of the flasher's crime protects civilization from someone like himself. His show of desire repels its object, and that is the whole point of its iteration: the O that blooms in the woman's face proves indubitably that he has a sex, an amazing and disgusting organ, and guarantees at the same time that, however many other penises have worn that O like wet warm silk, his won't be one of them. She's safe from him, and he's safe from her, and if she should turn him in, why, he only gets what he deserves.

Eventually it got to me that, other than his record of convictions, I knew nothing about Joseph Roy McCatty. There had been a time, after all, when I felt I kind of knew him. If the little man had been able to keep his tortured nature in his pants, we might have shared Kleinstuck forever, though uneasily. He could not, and so we wrestled for Kleinstuck, and I won. I am a person of consequence in this town, and he isn't. But woods, by water, are my resort as well as his, and so, to his misfortune, we ran into one another.

All the same, it got to me. At last I went to the county clerk's office, sifted again through the court records, found the exact address on Cherry Street, and, finally, on a bond release authorization form, a man's name, Edward Winterhalter, and a telephone number. On the way home from the courthouse, I drove by the house. It was a modest one-story, built, probably, in the fifties, of concrete block painted slate blue, but it struggled valiantly, in a sort of budget Usonian manner, to meld with the rhythms of its landscape, a little westward dead end of Cherry Street I had never noticed before, on the blind side of the Kazoo School, a lot chipped out of the woods of Kleinstuck itself and looking, from its back windows, down the slope into it.

When I get home, I telephone. An elderly gentleman answers, slow of speech, but precise and clear. I ask for Mr. Edward Winterhalter. That's me, he says. I was involved in that 1997 case against Joseph Roy McCatty, I tell him, and I came across your name and telephone number in the court records. It wasn't clear if you're a friend or . . . ? Grandfather, he says firmly; are you a lawyer? No—I was a jogger, I explain, feeling ridiculous. I was one of the people named in the case, and I would like to ask you . . . I don't know anything about that! Mr. Winterhalter barks. Not about the case, I say, I don't care about the case, I'm interested in . . . in Joey, if you can tell me anything about what kind of person he was. He always seemed—I hope you won't mind my saying this—so scared and broken to me. I'd like to understand what kind of person he was. You see, I used to see him all the time in that park, Kleinstuck. I saw him there so many times before . . . before it happened, I'd like to know why he was always there.

You're an idiot, I think to myself—as if it isn't all too obvious, by now, why he was always there.

Something interesting! the old man offers, amazingly enough, in a tone wholly different from the one I had expected of this conversation—for this is a voice of self-confident idiosyncrasy and family pride: Something interesting! Joey's great-great-grandmother, he says—my grandmother, Caroline Hubbard Kleinstuck—owned all that land that became the Kleinstuck Preserve.

Did you know Caroline? I say dumbly.

Oh, yes! She was a determined lady. She was strong for that woman suffrage, you know! She got what she wanted. But then she was going to move to Canada if Al Smith was elected! We were all FDR haters in those days. Hello? Hello?

I sit speechless a moment. So Joey McCatty is the great-great-great-grandson of Silas Hubbard, backer of the Kalamazoo Paper Company and builder of the People's Church, financier of that pioneer generation that bought up the trees and the early homesteads, and buried the creek and dug a root cellar for the city jail in the Indian mound outside the courthouse—the one who gave all the land that later became Kleinstück's Saxonia—and with it, my peat bog—to Caroline in the first place. I feel rather put in my place, but I like this claim of Joey McCatty's. Thanks to a three-minute telephone conversation, he has been transformed from a homeless, landless, jobless, weightless person into the relict of a baron of industry, well-spring of that self-hatred, or, more precisely, of that innocence in despair of itself, which is Kalamazoo, one last Hubbard who wanders about the erstwhile family estate warding off female intruders (suitors?) with a sexual show that is the last stutter of a family curse, the curse on himself and all his sons of the well-meaning old Hubbard whose paper company made of the Kalamazoo River the longest flowing Superfund site in America, "a ribbon of rancid waste," as one resident called it in the fifties. Though he may know little of this history himself, Joey McCatty needed me to locate him in it. Now we're almost square, I think.

Did Joey have any particular talents or interests? I ask Mr. Winterhalter.

None whatsoever! he shouts. He went to that Loy Norrix High School for just one day and never went back, he says. Couldn't stand all the crowds, he said. He had an aversion to it and walked out the first day.

You seem to be the closest person to him, I say—could it be that his own parents have given up on him?

His father died in a motorcycle accident when Joey was ten, Mr. Winterhalter says. I predicted it! He was a rouser—big, strong—proud of being Irish.

What did he do for a living? I ask.

He was a factory worker—worked in that Fisher Body plant in Comstock. Went to a roadhouse out there and rode his motorcycle into a tree. After that the boy spent a lot of time around here. His mother didn't know . . . just didn't know what . . .

What she could do to help him? I ask.

Yes.

I don't quite see, I say, why they would put Joey in a maximum-security prison twelve hours' drive north of Kalamazoo, in Baraga, where it snows ten feet a year and no can possibly visit him.

He wanted to be in a cell by himself, Mr. Winterhalter says, and that's where they said they had one.

We are silent a moment.

Can you tell me anything of what Joey was like as a kid?

He was a nice enough boy. He couldn't talk to people and didn't want to be around 'em. He could talk to me all right. He meant no harm. He never had any sense. He couldn't see the consequences of things. You know, if he was a normal, intelligent person who committed crimes, robbed banks, and such, I wouldn't have any sympathy, Mr. Winterhalter says. But I do for him.

You would think that a self-hating town like Kalamazoo would have a special institution for its exemplary cases, its most disfavored and self-disfavoring sons, a sort of sibylline cave of self-hatred, inside of which Joey McCatty, safe behind glass before a file of female spectators in athletic *déshabillé*, could perform his apotropaic rite of sexual desire and avoidance in a single act. Surely there is a building free on the vast, mostly abandoned campus of the old Kalamazoo Regional Psychiatric Hospital—where Mr. Winterhalter tells me Joey once was sent, for just three months, when he was seventeen, between the Honda three-wheeler and the failed

Probation Enhancement Program that was the beginning of his downward slide. WMU owns the state hospital property now, as well as Kleinstuck. Surely there is an edifice on the grounds for an oracle of self-hatred who says not a single word.

Or perhaps now and then he will utter: What's this *life*? What's this *life* you give me? Which is what Joseph Roy McCatty said to the judge when he was finally sentenced. I just did what I always did and now you give me life! They were the first words I ever heard him say.

WORKS CONSULTED

Christoffel, Hans. "Male Genital Exhibitionism." In *Perversions, Psychodynamics and Therapy*, edited by Sandor Lorand. New York: Random House, 1956.
———. "Exhibitionism and Exhibitionists." *International Journal of Psycho-analysis* 17 (1936): 321–345.
Cox, Daniel J., and Reid J. Daitzmann, eds. *Exhibitionism: Description, Assessment, and Treatment*. New York: Garland STPM Press, 1980.
MacDonald, John M., *Indecent Exposure*. Springfield, Ill.: Thomas, 1973.

Geography

Mid: One Tentative Taxonomy of a Region

JANET WONDRA

> A vast expanse of level ground; unbroken save by
> one thin line of trees. . . . A tranquil sea or lake
> without water. . . . It was lonely and wild
> but oppressive in its barren monotony.
> —Charles Dickens on Illinois, 1842

ORIGINS

Being a pure product of California as I am, the Midwest is both strange and familiar to me. When I was asked with a slight sneer by a prominent Southerner if I was one of those Californians who speaks of herself in terms of generations—this from a fellow who happily trots out his own heritage without invitation—I responded "Absolutely": third-generation, card-carrying, dyed-in-the-wool. Wherever I am, I am Californian, although not, I hope, an ugly American. Now I find myself living in Chicago, casting about.

HISTORY

Though my maternal grandfather was born in Pasadena, I learned recently that his parents, my great-grandparents, whose camelback clock graces my bookcase, married in Michigan in 1879. Momentarily I will be in possession of five Michigan-made, curved-back, cane-seated hardwood chairs presented to the happy couple on their wedding day. After the UPS man buzzes my doorbell in Evanston, I will be sitting in Michigan, a state I have never visited, where I have no remaining kin.

GEOLOGY

More than once, the Midwest was an inland sea, although a shallow one, unlike the Pacific, my definition of significant water. Ordovician, Silurian, Devonian, Cretaceous—the stately names of geologic periods parade by as the Midwest fills up with sand and shell, then, as the waters retreat, sandstone and limestone; plant and animal, then coal, peat, and petroleum. In the Carboniferous period, the Equator cut across northwestern Minnesota, how or why I do not know. As the region passed through the ages, the climate altered from tropical to temperate to frigid. Ontology recapitulates phylogeny, as my Long Beach–born mother says: right now my windows are closed against the heat and humidity I know best from my graduate school days in tropical Louisiana, a weather pattern I was unhappy to rediscover in Chicago. And I haven't yet had a chance to store my mufflers and gloves, dry-clean my burgeoning collection of winter coats, check my snow boots for last traces of salt. I join the ranks of Midwesterners praying for the temperate, dry breezes of spring and fall. May the moderate seasons linger immoderately!

HISTORY II

In the late 1880s, Harrison Gray Otis, owner of the *Los Angeles Times*, allied himself with the great transcontinental railroads, especially the Southern Pacific, to entice thousands of Midwesterners to invest their cash in Southern California real estate. When the fare from Chicago to Los Angeles was reduced to one dollar, who could resist the promises of unlimited sunshine, a piece of the Mission-style, Mediterranean dream, and freedom from tuberculosis and a medical encyclopedia's worth of other ailments that afflict those living in harsh climates? Otis was a native of Marietta, Ohio.

A prime narrator of the Southern California dream was journalist Charles Fletcher Lummis, who in 1884 spent 143 days walking from the Midwest to California in search of better health and gainful employment. Upon arrival, Otis made Lummis city editor of the *Times*. In 1880, Los Angeles ranked 187th in the census, with only eleven thousand residents, but thanks to Otis, Lummis, and other boosters, by 1920 the city was the largest in the West, and the city and county combined boasted nearly one million residents. Lummis was from Chillicothe, Ohio.

As early as 1890, thirty-four percent of Los Angeles's population had been born in the Midwest. In the 1930s, according to my father, the joke was that Long Beach equaled Iowa. Every year in Bixby Park, which overlooks the Pacific, there was a huge Iowa picnic, with tables organized by county so one could meet up with kith and kin and reminisce about home and the endless sea of cornfields.

My hometown, one small part of the vast City and County of Los Angeles, was founded by Edgar Rice Burroughs, who supplied the new community with a myth of origin, complete with a Moses-like stranger who wandered out of the mountains to proclaim that the town would be named Tarzana. In his earlier years, Burroughs was known for his half-cocked, even disastrous business ventures in Chicago and his native Oak Park. I don't know how Tarzana worked out for him, but from my childlike perspective he seemed to have done well, leaving at his death in 1950 a ranch house atop a small hill, surrounded by pine trees, sheep, and a magnificent view of the Santa Monica Mountains. His writing studio, a little adobe structure with dark crossbeams, was across the street from the Bank of America on Ventura Boulevard, and while my father cashed his paycheck, I would ponder the life of a writer.

It is no wonder, then, that I feel at least partly at home in the Midwest, since I grew up with those steeped in Midwestern values and my city was shaped by Midwesterners—both the hardworking, salt-of-the-earth folks and the hucksters and wheeler-dealers. In an article in the *Des Moines Register,* after his return from graduate work at the University of California at Irvine, Iowa writer Michael Borich claimed, "There is a sanity about life here in the midwest that is unique. The people and the seasons have something to do with that. I've come to realize that conservatism is more than a political label; a midwest conservative is a caretaker of time-proven beliefs. We are less trend setters than trend evaluators. If we are rednecks, it is because we work hard. If we are traditionalists, so be it. To be narrow-minded is not to be intolerant, but to focus our energies." Yet the people I was raised by and those I grew up among fit this description, and it's no wonder. As I look more closely at the family tree, I discover that most branches spent at least one generation in the Midwest. My paternal grandmother was born in Gerlaw, Illinois, before moving on to Santa Ana, then Los Angeles, where for a time the family rented a farm at 9th or 10th and Broadway, a piece of land now occupied by the foundations of downtown skyscrapers. My maternal grandmother was born in Lincoln, Nebraska—beyond the Midwestern pale for some, I know—but her sister Nina was born in Penfield, Ohio, so has impeccable Midwestern credentials. The bedrock of Heartland values is as unbroken in California as anywhere else; the Golden Rule was always part of the Golden Dream, although these days you may have to dig deeper through the drift of glitz, produced in part by émigrés from the Midwest, to find those core values. Those who are "just folks" have a tendency to keep their values to themselves and live quietly, often in California bungalows, not so different from those of Oak Park or Chicago, although they are made of wood, not brick. Brick and mortar are, after all, the worst possible construction materials for an area prone to earthquakes.

GEOLOGY II

When it comes to earthquakes, the Midwest trumps California in at least one instance, although this is a game no one wants to win. The New Madrid quakes of December 16, 1811, and January 23 and February 7, 1812, are the most severe on record, although they predate modern scientific techniques of measurement. The earth shook horizontally and vertically; it rolled and cracked; great fissures, some several miles long, opened and slammed shut as dirt, rocks, coal, and carbonized wood (perhaps from the Carboniferous era) were thrown in the air. Whole forests were demolished as trees cracked down the middle, were tossed about like pick-up sticks, or sank as the ground fell, sometimes as much as twenty feet. The Mississippi roiled, its banks collapsed, and at times it ran backwards as whole floods of water were sucked into caverns in its bed and water spouts spewed up debris from its bottom. Much of the river's course in the lower Midwest was redefined by this quake, and new lakes were created throughout the Mississippi Valley. On land and water these occurrences were accompanied by explosions, earsplitting roars, and mysterious hisses, flashes of light, and noxious sulphurous odors. No wonder the region experienced a religious revival and preachers flocked from miles around to take advantage of the inhabitants' new, if temporary, fervor.

The December 16 earthquake shook twenty-seven states, from Canada to the Atlantic, from the Gulf of Mexico to Kansas and Nebraska and probably even farther west. Seismologists estimate that the quake was felt moderately in an area of one million square miles. The San Francisco quake of 1906, in contrast, was felt moderately over about sixty thousand square miles. One reason for this disparity is that the earth's crust west of the Rockies absorbs energy more efficiently, while east of the Rockies the crust tends to transmit that energy, broadcasting the damage of potential earth shaking. Midwesterners are wise not to swap the Mississippi Valley for California, though, since that would be like jumping from the frying pan into the Ring of Fire. Still, they may want to reconsider living in brick homes, at least in southern Missouri, Illinois, and Indiana.

URBAN LIFE

Said my sister, "Who wouldn't want to live in Chicago? It's one of the great American cities." I retorted, "Who said I wanted to live in a great American city if it's not Los Angeles or San Francisco?"

CULTURE

My family never considered leaving California or exploring the almost invisible filigree of our Midwestern roots, although my sister eventually earned a Ph.D. at the University of Chicago. We were too busy enjoying our Mediterranean pleasures, far more than a dream or a marketer's pitch. In Tarzana, I walked to school through orange groves heavy with fruit, and the blossoms would scent the evening air. "When I was a boy," my grandfather would tease, playing off our fears of exile to other, less fortunate regions, "I had to walk miles to school, down the hills, struggling through the snow"—patiently we awaited the punch line—"in Pasadena."

GEOGRAPHY

How can I define the region when even the experts are still quibbling? According to the author of *The Encyclopedia of the Midwest*, who declines to justify his delineation of a perimeter, the pertinent states are Illinois, Indiana, Iowa, Michigan, Minnesota, Missouri, Ohio, and Wisconsin. An equal number of *I*s and *M*s, with an *O* and a *W* for spice. The editor of *Growing Up in the Midwest*, just as evasive about his own definitions, simply states that the region has been defined as "the land between the mountains: between the Alleghenies to the east and the Rockies to the west; between the Canadian forest to the north and the Ohio River to the south, projecting westward along the northern Arkansas and Oklahoma borders. Others would place the Midwest between the eastern Ohio border and the approximate line of demarcation between wet, humid conditions and the dry, high plains—the one hundredth meridian of longitude. Some would rule out Michigan's Upper Peninsula as more like the Old World than the New and the Boot Heel and Ozark regions of Missouri as more Southern than Midwestern." I ask friends and acquaintances: Kansas? Probably not—more the Great Plains. Nebraska? Maybe. North Dakota? South? Probably. What is the defining principle? How will I know when I am turning Midwestern? Or am I already?

GEOLOGY III

Then there's the lake—Michigan, but just "The Lake" to us in Chicago—rather tame for those reared on the Pacific, but nonetheless a vast body of water where I can bathe my homesickness as it shifts from blue to green to gray. It provides a horizon toward which to yearn, but because the unbroken line is to the east, toward the state of Michigan, I must constantly reorient myself, a movement that stirs up the very feelings of loss I'm attempting to calm. Still, its quietness is mysterious, how it can lap gently, patiently, at the sea wall along the curve of Sheridan Road where Chicago ends and Evanston begins, without the impetuous insistence of the ocean, although it can whip up a decent-sized wave when the winds are high. Usually, though, the lake is in no hurry; it learned its tempo from the glaciers that dredged its shallow bed.

CLIMATE

Snow: you want it, we've got it. But I don't know what to do with it. By virtue of my heritage, I have no idea how to play with snow, or in it. I need a tutor, perhaps a young child, someone adept in fort building, snowball warfare, and ice skating backwards. The idea of ice skating outdoors is completely novel to me, a wonder to stare at. And after I've made a snow angel and thrown one snowball, I'm through. I've heard of snow cream, but I don't have the recipe. (I know, though, that the ice cream cone is believed to have originated at the Louisiana Purchase Exposition in St. Louis in 1904, so if I had some snow cream, I could slap it on a cone and have a distinctly Midwestern treat.) I take a walk and find a large black dog rapturously plunging in two feet of white powder and think, "Even the dogs know better than I." But there's little novelty in that.

Now in Evanston, I walk in the snow down the slight hill from Ridge Avenue to the "L" to go to work. (My sister tells me Ridge marks a fault line, but I haven't had time to investigate the geology.) When I moved to Chicago, I imagined the winter would be Antarctic. In fact, I'm still far from earning my polar credentials.

EDUCATION

I learn the local *bon mot:* In Chicago, there are two seasons—winter and road work.

URBAN LIFE II

Said Lezlie, my Francophone friend, "There are only three American cities the French care to visit: New York, New Orleans, and Chicago." I thought, "Good enough for the French, good enough for me." Then I faltered. Being a tourist is a far cry from putting down roots.

HISTORY III

First U.S. president to serve also as Chief Justice of the Supreme Court (1921–1930): William Howard Taft, born in Cincinnati, Ohio, 1857.

First major U.S. auditor to be convicted of a felony: Arthur Andersen, headquartered in Chicago, 2002.

First modern typewriter: Christopher Latham Sholes and Carlos Glidden, Kenosha, Wisconsin, 1869.

Invention of chiropractic medicine: D. D. Palmer, Davenport, Iowa, 1895.

Invention of the common frame house: George W. Snow, Chicago, 1832.

First skyscraper: Home Insurance Building (ten stories), Major William le Baron Jenney, Chicago, 1884.

First mixed-use structure: Auditorium Building, architects Adler and Sullivan, designed when Frank Lloyd Wright was their apprentice, Chicago, 1889. Today, it is the downtown campus of Roosevelt University, where I teach, climbing the staircases whose elegantly subdued lines helped define modern architecture.

Tallest building: Sears Tower (110 stories or 1,450 feet), 1974 (unless you count those upstart Petronas Towers in Kuala Lumpur, which we don't).

First modern automobile: Elwood Haynes, Kokomo, Indiana, 1893.

First changeable parts for automobiles: Henry Leland, president of Cadillac, Detroit, 1896.

First assembly-line production of automobiles: Olds Motor Works, Detroit, 1902. First moving automobile assembly line: Henry Ford, Michigan, 1913.

First automobile race: From Green Bay to Madison, Wisconsin, 1875, won by a steam-powered car. Average speed: six miles per hour.

First U.S. dirigible meet: St. Louis, Missouri, 1908.

First Ferris wheel: George Washington Gale Ferris, World's Columbian Exposition, Chicago, 1893.

First American astronaut to orbit the earth: John Glenn, 1962, born in Cambridge, Ohio, 1921.

First man to walk on the moon: Neil Armstrong, 1969, born in Wapakoneta, Ohio, 1930.

First American woman in space: Sally Ride, 1983, my classmate at Gaspar de Portolá Junior High School, Tarzana, California.

First American woman to walk in space: Kathryn Sullivan, 1984, my classmate at William Howard Taft High School, Woodland Hills, California.

CONCLUSION

The Midwest is a mystery, even to those in whom its roots run deep. Its nature, its genus and species, its boundaries, its force—all conspire to hide themselves, even from those who are defined by them. The region sits in the middle of the country, in the middle of the continent, silent, keeping its own counsel.

So I find myself both qualified and underqualified to consider the question of the Midwest. I lack the understanding of the native; paradoxically, however, I bring both the outsider's perspective and the sympathy of one steeped in Heartland values. I am midway in my understanding—not midway in terms of time, perhaps, for who knows when I'll return to my native region? I am in process, in the middle, amidst.

Big Trees, Still Water, Tall Grass

SCOTT RUSSELL SANDERS

Maps tell me that my neighborhood of low hills and shallow creeks belongs to Indiana, a state bounded on the south and southwest by the Ohio and Wabash rivers, on the northwest by Lake Michigan, and everywhere else by straight lines. The lake and rivers mark real edges, where you can wet your feet or row a boat, but the straight lines mark only human notions, inscribed with rulers on paper. The soil knows nothing of those boundaries. Birds glide over them. Deer browse across them. Winds blow and waters flow through them. Thunderstorms rumbling by make no distinction between Illinois and Indiana, between Indiana and Ohio. Monarch butterflies laying eggs on milkweed plants in our meadows pay no allegiance to the state. Raccoons and coyotes prowl through our woods and fields wherever hunger leads them, indifferent to survey lines or deeds. Sandhill cranes trace their long journeys high overhead, guided by the glint of water and the fire of stars. These wild creatures are oblivious to the names and borders we have imposed on the land. They belong to a grander country, one defined by sunlight, moisture, soils, and the tilt of earth.

For years I have aspired to become a citizen of that primal country, the one that preceded all maps. I find myself wondering how this region looked 200 years ago, before it was called Indiana, before it was parceled out by straight lines. How did the rivers run? How did the air smell? What color was the sky? What would an early traveler have seen in the forests, the wetlands, the prairies?

Trying to answer those questions, I spent the fall searching out remnants of land that have survived in something like their pre-settlement condition. And they truly are remnants, for less than one percent of the territory that became Indiana remains in our day relatively pristine, unaltered by saws and bulldozers and plows. I'll speak here of three such places—Donaldson Woods, Loblolly Marsh, and Hoosier Prairie. For shorthand I use their names, in case you wish to go look at them for yourself. But these refuges shrug off all titles, for they belong to an order that is far older than language. They remind us of our original home. They give us a standard by which to appraise how good or wise, how beautiful or durable is the landscape we have made from the primal country.

/ / /

In 1865, just as the Civil War was ending, George Donaldson came from Scotland to a spot in southern Indiana near Mitchell, where he bought a stand of old trees, built a house he called Shawnee Cottage, and soon earned a reputation for eccentricity. What the neighbors considered most eccentric was that Donaldson permitted no hunting in his woods, no felling of trees, no collecting of mushrooms or ginseng roots. He didn't clear any ground for farming, didn't quarry stone for building, didn't charge admission to visit his caves. He made no use of the land at all, except to walk around and admire it.

What Donaldson set out to preserve was a scrap of the primeval forest which in 1800 had covered some twenty million acres of the Indiana territory, but which by 1865 had already become rare. In two-thirds of a century, nearly all the forest had been cut, the prairies plowed, the swamps drained. No wonder the official seal of Indiana features a man with an axe chopping down a tree (and a bison fleeing). One scientist estimates that between 1800 and 1870, settlers must have cleared away one and a half billion trees, an average of 7,000 acres per day. Most of those trees were never used, but merely killed where they stood by the peeling of a ring of bark around the trunks, after which the standing hulks were allowed to dry, then felled, rolled into heaps, and burned. For decades, the smoldering piles must have made the countryside look like a battleground. Earlier civilizations, from China and Mesopotamia to Greece and the British Isles, had stripped their own land of trees, exposing the soil to erosion and extinguishing much of the wildlife, but none had ever done so at this dizzying speed.

Resisting the advice of neighbors and the appeal of lumber merchants, Donaldson held onto his big trees. After his death near the turn of the century, a combination of good stewardship and good luck kept the woods intact until they were incorporated into Spring Mill State Park in 1927. The park map now identifies the 67 acres of Donaldson Woods as "Virgin Timber," a quaint label that joins a sexual term for an unviolated female with an industrial term for board-feet. Measured in board-feet, many an oak, maple, walnut, or hickory in these woods is worth as much as a fancy new car. Measured by their historical significance, by their contribution to air and soil and wildlife, by their dignity and beauty, by their sheer scale of *being*, these trees are priceless.

I have gone to visit them often, in all seasons, never without thinking gratefully of that eccentric Scotsman who refused to turn his land into money. As part of my search for glimpses of primordial Indiana, I visit Donaldson Woods on a bright, warm, nearly windless day in late October. Viewed from a distance along the park road, these might be any Midwestern woods, fringed by sumac lifting its scarlet seed heads like torches, but up close they reveal their age, with fat trunks set far apart, scant undergrowth, and a canopy rising 150 or 200 feet. Stepping from the parking lot onto the trail at the edge of the sanctuary, I cross a threshold not merely from pavement to dirt but from the realm of mechanical hustle into the realm of organic, planetary rhythms. It takes a few minutes for eyes to adjust, for heart to slow down, for mind to arrive in this company of giants.

Not far inside the woods, I approach a huge tulip tree, lean into it with open arms, and press my cheek against the trunk, seeking to absorb some of its mighty stillness. The bark is so deeply furrowed that my fingers slide easily into the crevices. Even if a friend were to reach toward me from the far side, we could not join hands around the girth of this tree, for it is perhaps four feet in diameter at the height of my chest, more than twelve feet in circumference. After a spell I turn around, rest my back against the trunk, and gaze upward. Frosts have changed the leaves from supple green to brittle copper, iron, and gold. In summer, the shade here is so dense that only woodland flowers, ferns, and the most tolerant of saplings can thrive. Today, however, beneath a tattered canopy, the sun shines through with a beneficence of light. The most abundant saplings are beeches and maples, which will eventually supplant the oaks and tulip trees and hickories. The other common trees in the understory will never grow large—sassafras, with its mitten-shaped leaves; colonies of pawpaws, with leaves the size of mules' ears turned tobacco brown; and hornbeam, with narrow trunks reaching up like sinewy arms.

I walk on down the trail, passing among the giant columns, laying my hands in greeting on one great flank after another, seeking a blessing. Even the smoothest of trees, the beeches, have been roughened by age. Their gray elephant-hide bark has often been carved with the names and initials of lovers. Tony & Jill. Betsy & Bill. I wonder how many of those couples are still together, years after they left their marks. At least the beeches have remained faithful.

The fall has been dry, so the leaf duff crackles under my boots with every step. As I walk, spider webs catch on my forehead like stray thoughts. Several times I hear a ruckus in the leaves just over the next ridge, without spying what made the noise. Finally I surprise a deer perhaps fifty feet ahead of me on the path—a yearling that gazes at me curiously for half a minute, twitching its delicate muzzle, until it catches a whiff of man and then with a flash of white tail goes plunging away. Otherwise, I hear only the hammering of woodpeckers, the fussing of blue jays, crows guffawing, squirrels scolding, and the distant drumming of traffic.

Even in drought, the ground feels spongy, for this land has been covered with forest since the retreat of the last glaciers, 10,000 years ago, and during all that time the soil has been gathering its dead. Many of these trees have grown here since before Indiana became a state, since before the American colonies became a nation. I come across fallen trees whose prone trunks rise to the height of my chest, their roots thrust skyward still clutching rocks. They remind me of stories from early travelers who often heard, even on windless days such as this one, the occasional thunder of falling trees. It must have been frightening to close your eyes at night in the ancient forest, never knowing when a massive tree, tipped over by the weight of so many years, might come crashing down on the spot where you lay.

There is nothing to frighten me here today in Donaldson Woods, no falling trees, no bears nor wolves, no poisonous snakes, no enemies of my tribe. I know how the fear would feel, because I've traveled in wild places where I understood, from moment to moment, that I could die. Such places hone your awareness more sharply than any small refuge ever could. Aside from caves and cliffs, where you can still break your neck, and aside from rivers, where you can drown, the only dangers left in Indiana are all in the human zone, in cities and schoolyards, on highways and factory floors.

Safe though it may be, I still relish this sanctuary of tall trees. I rejoice that there are no stumps here from lumbering, no straggling fences, no moldering foundations. This patch of woods is like a country that has never known war, a land where all the citizens can hope to die a natural death. The trees stand for years or centuries, until succumbing to wind, shade, drought, ice storms, insects, disease, fire. Even after such assaults, the big ones often hold on for a long while, as you can see by the number of fat trunks bearing healed-over scars from lightning strikes. Of course we have left our own marks on these trees—from acid rain, alien pests, warming atmosphere, thinning ozone layer—but so far the obvious damage has not been of our doing. On leaving Donaldson Woods, I realize this is one of the attractions for me of primal country—that here one may taste the flavor of innocence.

/ / /

Since there is water enough everywhere in Indiana to grow trees, the only places that would have been clear of forest in 1800 were those where there was too much water, such as lakes and rivers and bogs. Even swamps grew trees, the species that don't mind getting their roots wet—red and silver maple, black and green ash, American elm, bur oak and swamp white oak, swamp cottonwood, willow, sycamore. On a misty morning in early November, sycamores lifting their creamy branches above the pathways of creeks are the clearest landmarks I can make out as I drive to the eastern border of Indiana, near the town of Geneva, to see what's left of a great swamp.

In 1889, a new bride whose first name also happened to be Geneva moved to that town with her husband, who ran the local drugstore. As business prospered, Geneva Stratton-Porter designed and oversaw the construction of a two-story log house with ample room for children, on a lot not far from the swamp. Against her husband's and neighbors' advice, she began to explore the 13,000 acres of wetland forest, braving the snakes and mosquitos and desperados that flourished there. If her husband was worried about her safety, she told him, he was welcome to tag along. He often did, carrying her specimen boxes. Fascinated by the secret life of the swamp, Gene Stratton-Porter taught herself the newfangled science of photography in order to record the moths, butterflies, and birds; she painted the marshy landscape on canvas; and she wrote a series of books, including *Music of the Wild* and *A Girl of the Limberlost*, which would eventually carry the name of this place to millions of readers around the world.

Limberlost Swamp was a gift of the glaciers, which leveled out this borderland between Indiana and Ohio, covered it with rich soils, and left it soaking wet. Such flat country is a confusing place for water. Some of it flows northeast toward Lake

Erie, and thence by way of the St. Lawrence into the Atlantic; some flows south-west toward the Ohio River, and thence by way of the Mississippi to the Gulf of Mexico; much of the water simply stays here, not inclined to go anywhere. At least, much of it would stay here, had the contemporaries of Gene Stratton-Porter not dug so many drainage ditches and laid so many tiles, leading the water into one or another of the many rivers that pass through this region—the Wabash, MississenewaMississinewa, Salamonie, St. Mary's, Flatrock, Maumee, Beaver, Whitewater, White, and St. Joseph, among others.

The draining of the Limberlost had only just begun when Stratton-Porter ar-rived in Geneva, yet by 1913, when she left there for another small town in north-ern Indiana, the swamp was all but dry. She grieved over that loss, even years later when she moved to Hollywood to oversee the translation of several of her novels into films. The destruction of the swamp made many people rich—from cutting timber, pumping oil out of the drained land, and farming the deep black soil—and you can still see evidence of that wealth in the size of the houses hereabouts. Strat-ton-Porter herself grew rich from film contracts and the sale of her books, the best of them rising from that rank, fertile, mysterious wetland.

On the damp November morning of my visit I expect to see nothing of the grand, primeval swamp, but instead look forward to seeing a small vestige of it called Loblolly Marsh, a 428-acre preserve where the ditches have been dammed, the tiles plugged, and the waters have begun to gather once more. Today they're gathering all the more quickly, because the mist has turned to drizzle. "Loblolly" comes from a Miami word meaning "stinking river," a reference to the sulphurous smell of marsh gas. The only smells I notice on climbing out of my car are the per-fume of decaying grass and the meaty aroma of mud. My boots are soon black from the succulent mud as I make my way into the depths of the marsh along a trail pocked by the prints of horseshoes and deer hooves.

On such a morning, with the grasses on either side of the path bent down by rain, bare trees looming on the horizon like burnt matches, and the calls of geese filtering down from the gray sky, it's easy to imagine that the glaciers have only just withdrawn. There is a damp chill in the air. The earth yields beneath my feet. This might be tundra, rolling away far to the north, browsed by musk oxen, woolly mammoths, ground sloths, and elk. Even bent over by rain, the tawny foxtail grass reaches higher than my waist, the rusty big bluestem reaches above my shoulders. As I walk, my elbows brush the curled-up heads of Queen Anne's lace, the spiky crowns of thistles, the drooping fronds of goldenrod. Here and there, burst milk-weed pods spill their downy seeds. The wet kettle holes are choked with sedges and rushes and blowsy cattails. In a few months these holes will ring with the mat-ing calls of spring peepers and western chorus frogs, but right now they yield only a few, forlorn chirps from crickets. The sound of drizzle stroking the lush vegeta-tion is soft and caressing, like a brush in thick hair.

As I come within sight of a shallow pond at the heart of the preserve, I startle a great blue heron that has been feeding there. With a squawk of alarm and a fran-tic beating of wings, the stately bird rises into the mist and flaps away, its neck drawn back into a tense curve, its long legs trailing. I am dismayed by this undignified haste. I want to assure the heron that I mean no harm. Yet my kind has been harming its kind for hundreds of years, not by hunting so much as by destroying wetlands. Here in the Limberlost, just over a century ago, a great blue heron could have fed anywhere among thousands of acres of prime habitat; now it must wade in ditches laced with agri-chemicals, in scattered kettle holes, or in rare ponds, like this one I stand beside in Loblolly Marsh.

Rain dimples the surface of the pond between tussocks of willows and sedges. Beyond a palisade of cattails on the far shore, beyond a rolling expanse of grass, the horizon is rimmed by a line of trees, their branches reaching like frayed nerves into the leaden sky. My own nerves are soothed by the rain, by the prospect of water lingering here, by the resilience of this land.

In the mud at my feet I find the four-toed prints of a muskrat, the neat line of paw prints from a fox, and the splayed tracks of a raccoon that resemble the tiny hand prints of a crawling child. There are many other scrawls I cannot make out, for these wet places attract whatever flies or creeps, whatever hops or runs. I see no beaver tracks, but I know that refuge managers have recently had to dismantle some beaver dams in the drainage ditches, to keep the nearby fields from flooding. I imagine that Gene Stratton-Porter would be cheering for the beavers. I imagine she would be delighted to learn that part of her beloved swamp is being restored, that herons and muskrats are feeding here, that wildness is returning to Loblolly Marsh.

/ / /

Wildness alone would not have sustained the third sample of primordial Indiana that I visit, a prairie in Lake County, up in the northwestern corner of the state near the steel mills of Gary and the skyscrapers of Chicago. At some 500 acres, never plowed nor paved, Hoosier Prairie is the largest remnant of the grasslands that once covered a few million acres of Indiana. Prairies out on the Great Plains were kept free of trees by a drier climate, but here in the humid East they were kept open by fire. Lightning might account for some of the fires, but others were deliberately set by the native people—in this region, mainly the Potawatomi, Kaskaskia, and Miami—who knew that clearings improve hunting.

The only hunter I meet on my visit to Hoosier Prairie is a red-tailed hawk, which spirals high overhead with barely a tilt of its wings. This day in late November is unseasonably mild and the sky is clear, so the sun beating down on these russet fields heats the soil and sends up a column of warm air, and that is what the hawk is riding, on the lookout for a meal. I pick up a handful of soil and stir it in my palm, a grainy mixture of sand and loam the color of bittersweet chocolate. Where I'm standing was underwater until about 9,000 years ago, when a vast inland sea formed of glacial meltwater gradually shrank back toward the present shoreline of Lake Michigan. The sand most likely descends from bedrock in Canada by way of grinding glaciers and pounding waves; the loam is a legacy from countless generations of prairie plants.

The plants I see on my walk today have lost their sap and most of their color. Aside from the golden leaves of willows and cottonwoods and the carmine leaves of blackberry, the prairie is now a medley of buff and bronze. From the stems and seed heads I can make out downy sunflower, blazing star, leadplant, rattlesnake master, wild quinine, wild indigo. In the low spots that stay damp year round, I find cattails and cordgrass and sedges. Observers with far more knowledge than I possess have counted some 350 species of plants in this vibrant spot. As at Loblolly Marsh, here the tallest grass is big bluestem, which even this late in the season still rises higher than my head. At mid-summer a traveler in this tall grass would be able to see no more than a few feet ahead except by climbing a tree.

The only trees stout enough to hold a climber at Hoosier Prairie are oaks, mostly black oaks with a scattering of white. The big ones grow in clusters with a throng of saplings crowding their trunks, and the clusters are widely spaced over the prairie with grassland in between, creating a distinctive type of landscape known as oak savannah. The leaves clinging to the black oaks appear to have been cut from old leather; the white oak leaves are the ruby shade of cooked cranberries. It's clear from the abundance of saplings that the savannah would soon give way to dense woods if it were not periodically burned. These days the fires are set by crews from the Department of Natural Resources, usually in late fall or early spring. A charred swath perhaps ten feet wide between the prairie and an adjoining field shows that preparations have begun for a larger burn. The big oaks can survive periodic fire thanks to deep tap rootstaproots and thick bark. The other prairie plants are likewise adapted to fire, drought, hot summers, cold winters, and grazing, because they store their vitality underground, in roots, rhizomes, bulbs, tubers, and corms. Roots may extend more than a dozen feet down, and they may stretch out horizontally ten or twenty feet from the parent plant.

By midday the heat has made me peel down to a T-shirt, and I am having trouble believing it's nearly December. A brisk wind from the southwest rattles dry leaves on the cottonwoods, like a fluttering of bangles. The hawk spins round and round beneath the implausible sun. Much higher up, the silver needle of a jetliner pierces the blue. Nothing else moves in the sky except blown leaves, crows, and a scarf of starlings. In spring I would see yellowthroats, goldfinches, tree swallows, swamp sparrows, woodcocks doing their sky dance. For now, in spite of the heat, the land is locked down, the migrants have flown south, the crickets and cicadas have fallen silent, the juices have been sucked back into the earth. Today the hawk will have to make do with white-footed mice and meadow voles.

Earlier frosts have curled the fronds of bracken and the bushy sweetfern. These are northern species, hanging on since the retreat of the glaciers in this damp, fire-prone land. I crush a handful of sweetfern and tuck it under the shoulder strap of my pack so that I can smell it as I walk, like the clean fragrance of dried hay. I need this reminder of earth's own potent smell, because the longer I stay here in Hoosier Prairie, the more I taste the murk of steel mills and refineries on the breeze. Even from the center of the refuge I can see, beyond a scrim of trees, the gleaming white tanks of an oil storage depot. During my visit I never cease to hear the grinding of heavy machinery, bulldozers and trucks and trains, as relentless as any glaciers.

In the gravel parking lot I start up my own machine to drive home, adding my fumes to the air, adding my bit to the global warming that may well account for the crazy heat of this late November day. Every lot I pass on the road bordering the refuge is either listed for sale, torn up for construction, or already occupied by pavement and stores. So much dust blows across the road from new building sites that many cars approaching me shine their lights. I turn on mine as well. It's 3 P.M. The only clouds in the sky are ones we've made.

/ / /

Off and on this fall during my search for remnants of primordial Indiana, a muscle in my chest would twitch. The sensation was not painful, not especially worrisome, merely a light tremor as if a bird were shivering under the skin. When the twitching recurs this morning, the last day of the twentieth century, I wonder if the troubled muscle might be my heart. Cold weather has come at last. I look out on a fresh snowfall—barely an inch deep, but enough to renew the complexion of things. I welcome the change, even though the white coating can't hide a history of loss.

In 1800, the grasslands that we glimpse now in tiny scraps would have stretched westward to the Great Plains; the glacial wetlands that we've almost entirely drained would have stretched north to the Great Lakes and beyond, up to the ice-gouged vicinity of Hudson's Bay; the hardwood forest that we've reduced to rare pockets of big trees would have stretched eastward all the way to the Atlantic and south into the Appalachian Mountains. Bison, bears, lions, wolves, passenger pigeons, Carolina parakeets, and countless other animals dwelt here in astounding numbers. This original abundance, thousands of years in the making, we have all but used up in two centuries.

I admit to feeling dismay over much of what we've done to this country—the clear-cuts, strip mines, eroded fields, fouled rivers, billboards, smokestacks, used car lots, scourged rights-of-way for power lines, junk yards, animals flattened on roads, pastures grazed down to bare dirt, microwave towers looming on the horizon, dull box-buildings painted garish colors plopped down in the midst of parking lots, tattered plastic blown against fences. I know I am party to this havoc. I live in a heated house; I burn coal to write these words. I could recite apologies for this human landscape, naming the energies and appetites that have brought it to pass, but it already has more than enough defenders. What so many people call progress will get along fine without any praise from me.

I speak instead for the original country, on which our survival and the survival of all other species ultimately depends. Our bodies, our families, our communities cannot be healthy in the long term except in a healthy land, and we can't measure what health means without looking at places like Hoosier Prairie, Loblolly Marsh, and Donaldson Woods. I seek out patches of wilderness because they represent an order, a beauty, an integrity from which everything human and nonhuman has descended. These fragments of primordial Indiana are refuges not only for the plants and animals that occupied this land long before we came, but also for us. I've kept a token from each of the places I visited—a curl of sycamore bark, the furry spike of a cattail, a handful of sweetfern. Touching one by one these talismans of the primal country, I think of those roots lacing through the black soil of the prairie, beneath the swamp, beneath the woods. I remind myself of all that buried strength.

A Walking Tour of the Chicago Lakefront, with Detours

REGINALD SHEPHERD

I

Having lived most of my life in the Northeast, one of those people who con-fused Idaho and Indiana, Iowa and Ohio, I moved to Chicago in 1993 and lived there for six years. Though that may not seem a very long time to some, it's twice as long as I've ever continuously lived anywhere else in my adult life; Chicago was the first place I'd lived since 1986 that I ever came to think of as home. Though I've been gone for several years now, I still think of the city as home, and I long to go back. Before coming to Chicago, I spent almost two years doing an MFA de-gree at the Iowa Writers' Workshop. Iowa was my first experience of the Midwest, and it had no large bodies of water, though Iowa City had the Cedar River, from which the town drew its undrinkable water, so full of the chlorine used to treat the fertilizer run-off from adjacent fields that fumes rose up from the taps. Everyone drank bottled water. Iowa also had Alberta clippers, freezing winds sweeping down the plains from Canada that made the windows of my little shotgun shack shake and rattle. But those weren't enough to keep me there. After several years of liv-ing in assorted college towns I was ready to get back to a real city, and Chicago was both the closest and the most real city available. Indeed, it may be one of the most real cities in America.

Chicago calls itself "The City That Works," or at least that's the city's official motto, and in one sense it very much is. Despite its ongoing efforts to remake it-self as a postmodern information hub, Chicago is still an industrial city in a way that New York, the American city its physical presence most closely resembles, has not been for a long time. I think of Chicago as a city with an exposed ex-oskeleton: its workings are visible on the surface, the gears and pistons apparent to the naked eye. The scaffolding is always up in Chicago; indeed, the city some-times seems to be one ongoing construction project. Even downtown in the Loop, the aging "L" (whose circuit defines the downtown rectangle within which nest so many corporate skyscrapers, its tracks and platforms hastily thrown up out of surprisingly durable sheet metal and wood) reminds one of the rusting mechanics (what Nelson Algren called the city's "rusty iron heart") underlying all the virtual numbers traded on the various exchanges. It feels significant that Chicago has retained its elevated trains while New York and Boston have torn theirs down: the machinery is all out in the open.

Walking along Fullerton (one of the North Side's major east–west thorough-fares) from the yuppie neighborhood of Lincoln Park to the once-depressed and now gentrifying neighborhood of Bucktown, one passes condos and factories directly abutting one another. Some of the condos used to be factories, and some of the factories will be condos soon, but the sense of the material underpinning of the city, of the physical embodiment of social relations (and even of means of production), is palpable. You can even smell it. It's not a pleasant smell, but it's very real.

In the movie *Candyman*, an affecting exploration of race and sexuality in America, one of the characters lives across the "L" tracks (the Brown or Ravenswood Line) from Cabrini Green, a sprawling public housing project now in the process of being torn down. A friend tells her that her apartment building and several others immediately adjacent are identical to those of Cabrini Green, built as part of the same construction project; only the windows and the interiors are different. When I first rode the Brown Line after seeing the film, I realized that the movie hadn't lied: the only difference was that Cabrini Green was literally on the wrong side of the tracks. That, of course, and the fact that it was falling down. This was disturbing but oddly comforting: in Chicago, even the poverty is kept in plain sight, or was until recently. So, besides wondering where all those poor people (mostly black) will go, have gone (no one has seen any sign of the "scattered site" "mixed income" housing to which they are supposedly being relocated), I am also disturbed by the effort to put poverty out of sight, represented by the demolition of Cabrini Green. The presence of a public housing project on prime North Side real estate served as a salutary reminder of the realities of oppression and exclusion on which Chicago's newfound prosperity rested.

As the photographer David Plowden writes in his book *Industrial Landscape*, Chicago "is built on an absolutely level plain, which spreads away from the lake surely to the edge of the western horizon. Because of its flatness everything that Chicago has built stands in bold relief against the sky. There are no hills behind which to hide its works, or valleys along which to take shelter. Everything is laid bare. The relationship of man and mechanization is dramatically played out. No other city that I know of reveals the industrial world on such a stage" (xi).

Chicago presents a topographical paradox, a city of towering landmarks built on a featureless and seemingly endless plain, yet it is uniquely defined by the massive presence of Lake Michigan, an utterly other kind of plain, of fresh water stretching out far past the limits of sight. Chicago presents a social paradox as well: forgetful to the point of amnesia of social history (indeed, such social history feels as if it's been repressed, as is the ever-present but almost never-mentioned social and racial tension), it is replete with physical memory, despite the myriad of notable buildings that have been carelessly demolished over the years (as Plowden writes, "Parisians and Londoners do not throw away their buildings as readily as Chicagoans and New Yorkers"). I remember walking through downtown one afternoon on some errand or another and realizing that I was walking past the Monadnock Building, the last and tallest masonry skyscraper in the world (masonry was soon superseded by the development of steel-frame construction). I'd just read about it in an architectural history; appropriately enough, it was co-designed by Daniel Burnham, to whom the city owes so much of its physical character. Chicago is, of course, famous for its architecture, and almost the whole course of modern architecture can be traced just by walking around the city.

Despite the presence of such a massive edifice of architectural history, for me Chicago has always meant the lakefront. Perhaps this is a reason why I always lived in the neighborhood called Lakeview—besides, of course, the fact that that is where the boys are and were. My first roommate, a native of the area and a local history buff, explained to me that much of Lakeview had been swampland or even underwater until it was drained and filled in. (The lake landfill process started with the construction of Grant Park, the site of which was built up out of rubble and debris from the Great Fire of 1871, two hundred acres' worth, though the park wasn't completed until the early twentieth century.) This is a similar history to Boston's, in which the neighborhood called Back Bay had actually been a bay until the mid-nineteenth century, gradually filled in year by year until the waters were driven completely back. Even now Back Bay's buildings all rest on sinking pilings, because the bedrock is far beneath the landfill, and the landfill won't bear the weight.

Boston and Chicago are very similar in some ways, in their intimacy with the water, in their segregation and their ethnic patchwork of largely self-contained neighborhoods, in their carefully planned garlands of parks and green spaces and their grand boulevards, in a certain proud parochialism that is nonetheless always looking over the shoulder at the competition (New York, mostly). Both owe much of their landscaping and extensive parks to the famous architect and city planner Frederick Law Olmsted, though Chicago owes even more to Daniel Burnham and his visionary 1909 Plan of Chicago, from which emerged Lake Shore Drive (not finally built until the 1930s, under the WPA and the Public Works Administration), the twenty-something miles of park along Lake Michigan (including my beloved Lincoln Park and the landscaping of Grant Park), Northerly Island (now the peninsula on which Meigs Field is located), and Navy Pier. Boston and Chicago are also similar in that both are cities well suited to walking, Boston because of its diminutive size (46 square miles, more than a quarter of that water), Chicago (massively larger at over 588 square miles) because of its utterly logical street grid and the string of parks along the twenty-nine-mile lakefront that allows one to walk from Rogers Park on the far North Side almost continuously to the Loop.

Besides the six years I lived in Chicago, my next-longest stretch of continuous residence was in Boston, where I lived for three years and returned for another year. For part of that time I worked at the Boston Public Library, and when I worked in the rare books department I was fascinated by the city maps showing the gradual retreat of the bay, the grand avenues like Boylston Street extending a bit farther every year, stopping abruptly at the water's edge. Likewise, the original marshy shoreline of Chicago (the swamps and bogs extended as much as twenty miles inland in some places) is today unrecognizable under the skyscrapers, museums, and parks that have been constructed on the five and a half square miles of landfill (comprising 57 million cubic yards of fill material) built up since the 1800s. Man-made alterations and additions to the lakefront include piers, breakwaters, beaches, peninsulas, and even changing the course and direction of the Chicago River, which now flows upstream, away from Lake Michigan, bestowing its gift of treated sewage effluents and industrial wastes on Missouri. In 1955 the American Society of Civil Engineers declared the reversal of the Chicago River to be one of the Seven Wonders of engineering in the United States. Chicago always thinks big.

II

Water. Since I was a small child growing up in Bronx tenements and housing projects, I have been fascinated by water. Even the word enthralled me: I recall once walking around repeating the word "water" over and over until it had lost all meaning, had ceased to be a word at all, had begun to break down into a collection of sounds. I got ear infections constantly because I was always submerging my head under the bathwater, pretending that I was a deep-sea explorer (Jacques Cousteau, perhaps) instead of a little boy in a chipped clawfoot tub in a tenement bathroom. During our infrequent trips to Orchard Beach, or Archie Beach, as I always thought it was called, New York's poor people's beach, I would stare at the water for hours, wading along the surf, paddling in the shallows. Strangely enough, I didn't learn how to swim until considerably later, so I never went in farther than I could stand. I just admired the ocean from the safety of its rim. But I admired greatly.

My poems are full of water, replete with it: rivers and streams and ponds and lakes and oceans. For years I lived without the ocean or any equivalent body of water (there was certainly nothing like it in Iowa, for example). When I went to Chicago and saw Lake Michigan for the first time, stretching off into the distance as if there were no opposing shore (the first body of water I'd encountered in many years that reached all the way to the horizon and didn't stop), it felt like home. The lake made Chicago a place I recognized, a place where I belonged. I lived in Milwaukee briefly before moving to Chicago, and though the two cities share the lake, their relation to it is totally different. I always felt that Milwaukee had turned its back on the lake. From the bluff of Juneau Park (a notorious gay cruising spot, and too scraggly and ill-maintained to be good for much else), one could look down and out and see the lake from a distance, but immediately beside the lake was a highway called Lake Shore Drive, a pale simulacrum of Chicago's, and as far I could tell one couldn't actually get to the lake. From the rest of the East Side of Milwaukee (the nice part of town; they kept the black people on the West Side), one would hardly know Lake Michigan was there at all. But, as befits the only American city whose entire waterfront is dedicated to public use and recreation, in Chicago it felt as if everything led to the lake, as if to Rome.

When I first walked the lakefront, which I used to do quite often when I lived in Chicago, frequently all the way from Lakeview to Michigan Avenue just north of the Loop, the beginning of the Magnificent Mile, I was struck by its obviously man-made quality: the huge stones were all squared off and dressed, and alternated with giant cement blocks, some with rebar sticking out where the structure had been undermined and begun to crumble. You could look down over the edge and see rusted corrugated iron girders reaching up from underneath the water. There were stretches where the graffitied rocks (natural and artificial) had collapsed, sloping down into the surface waves the wind made; I had to pick my way carefully, or at some points resign myself to walking on the grass, take a few steps back from the lake itself.

This interpenetration of the natural and the man-made fascinated me and still does: it was a physical embodiment of the interrelation of man and nature, the social and the natural, and of man's will to master and remake the natural environment, just as the soaring skyline was the physical embodiment of the capitalist enterprise which always felt more palpably present in Chicago. But there was also something virtual, almost unreal, about the lakefront's obvious artificiality. This struck me most visibly in the way people lie out on the cement in bathing suits, on towels (I always think of them as yellow terrycloth), or even on the bare cement, perhaps with a fanny pack to cushion their heads, soaking up the summer sun, as if the cement would turn back into sand, the pavement turn into a beach, if they just willed it hard enough. Chicagoans believe in the power of positive thinking.

I remember one overcast Memorial Day, my first in Chicago, when I went to the Belmont Rocks with a new friend, a resident at the VA hospital, to watch the gay boys picnic, party, barbecue, and cruise. (Men have sex in the bushes there, too, but that's a bit more out of sight.) Two guys in bright, almost fluorescent bikinis clambered down the wet rocks, slick and slippery with algae, to swim, their footing always precarious, hanging on with their hands as well. The way up seemed more dangerous than the way down, the chances of falling onto a jagged rock, or just a hard one, even greater, but they treated it as a lark, as if danger were just a rumor they'd never heard. I considered trying to swim, but thought it better to remain a spectator, on the sidelines but unbruised. But then, that's been much of my experience of life, though bruising has often ensued nonetheless.

In fact there are several beaches spaced at various intervals along the north–south lakefront stretch. Some, like Oak Street Beach, are natural beaches, though much enhanced by human action, including the constant replenishment of sand

washed away by erosion. Most are artificial, the sand shipped in (much of it from
the southern end of Lake Michigan, scooped out of a huge sandbar called the Indiana Shoals), an artificial slope created, and beyond that a severe drop-off into
deep water. At North Avenue Beach there's a submerged steel wall about a hundred feet offshore that helps contain beach sand that would otherwise wash away
in longshore currents. In summer, the only time when it's legal to swim, and only
on the beaches (people swim all the time anyway, and everywhere, despite the
ubiquitous "No Diving Submerged Rocks" painted on the cement blocks, on the
rocks), teenaged lifeguards in bright orange vests sit in little rowboats to keep people from even approaching the rusting corrugated steel that marks the end of the
man-made slope, the beginning of the real and dangerous lake.

Though I have written many poems about the Chicago lakefront (my books
Angel, Interrupted, Wrong, and *Otherhood,* all written in Chicago, are overflowing
with lake poems), my poem "Maritime" encapsulates much of my sense of the
lakefront and its interface with the city, as well as my sense of the city's physical
embodiment of social relations (and the poem's end implicates the reader both in
the urban landscape and in the social system it stands in for). I suppose that the
poem should have been called "Lacustrine," but "Maritime" had a better ring to it
(and I was listening to a song of that title while I wrote the poem). It captures
both the lake's impression of endlessness and the feel of the poem as a kind of
periplus or navigator's guide, mapping out the coastline of this vast and mysterious body of water. The poem is dedicated to my friend Jocelyn Emerson, a wonderfully talented poet one of whose poems provided the opening gesture for this
one. The old woman asking for spare coffee is real, by the way; she used to stand
outside Tower Records on Clark and Belden in Lincoln Park, a store where I used
to spend all too much of my time and money.

MARITIME

For Jocelyn Emerson

There's always been this dream that reason has, shearing off
from the conceivable like pollen or Sahara dust: a windy day
along Lake Michigan, cold water, cold war won. The ferroconcrete
lakefront where yuppies jog with dogs and clouds of midges
hover mating is a second nature, like the city it defines
by excluding it. People sun themselves on yellow
terrycloth across cement, water too clear
to be clean. The mind, unable to rest in such fragments
capital has shored up or left behind (man-made rock
fissured to exposed steel rods, absence filled in with lichen
and a sudden fear of heights: the undertow
of Lincoln Park a marsh, contradiction
buried in an unstable foundation), would be an inland gull or kite
convenient to the lowest clouds, flat roofs

of residential high rises across Lake Shore Drive
and lunchtime traffic: crippled by a rising wind,
untimely car: tethered or tangled there. Would be a sign, NO DIVING
SHALLOW WATER SUBMERGED ROCKS. Enlightenment
comes later, or not at all, lampposts flaring on in orderly rows
in summer, when days are long and promise
stalls like a gull against prevailing currents and falling
barometric pressures: every third bulb dead, burned
out. Would be anywhere, almost. Over there, the real
world of elevated trains and the Chicago school
of architecture rises into the sphere of possession,
claims the view south: the Carbide and Carbon Building
or U.S. Gypsum tower. Market fluctuations and assorted
human rights violations are duly noted in the ledger, cement
that holds society together, the concrete world
of what's smashed in order to make other things
whole. That's what this afternoon America tastes of, floating
tar particles and pulverized quartz on the tongue, wet sand
trucked in from building sites to make a beach, closer to mud
without the salt to desiccate and keep it fresh: silicates
and contained local conflicts, the debris disposed of
carelessly (a rusting corrugated breakwater, collapsed causeway
green-yellow algae plashes over, a drifting Fritos bag
or this old woman asking if anyone can spare some
coffee), also called the Third World here at home, but not in this
neighborhood. The wind employs each cardinal point
in turn, or pushes a low-pressure zone across the Great Divide:
of which I thought I caught a whisper, echo, or response,
anchor, answerer, or worse. Also, you figure.

I'll close with the words of the visionary planner Daniel Burnham, whose highly influential though never fully implemented Plan of Chicago is responsible for so much of the glorious lakefront that Chicagoans take so much for granted, a lakefront declared "forever open, clear and free" by an 1836 act of the Illinois Legislature, but kept that way only through constant struggles against insensitive "development," struggles mostly forgotten today. Burnham's words are a bit high-flown and sentimental (he was a Victorian, after all), but they are nonetheless true for all that:

> The lake has been singing to us many years, until we have been re-sponsive. We see the broad water, ruffled by the gentle breeze; upon its breast the glint of oars, the gleam of rosy sails, the outlines of swift gliding launches. We see racing shells go by, urged onward by bronzed athletes. We hear the rippling of the waves, commin-

gled with youthful laughter, and music swelling over the Lagoon dies away under the low branches of the trees . . . A very high purpose will be served if the Lake shore be restored to the people and made beautiful for them.

Lake Michigan is singing to me still and always will, no matter how long I'm away from it.

Back Home in Indiana

SONIA GERNES

I have a complicated relationship with the state of Indiana. In one of the first poems I wrote on this soil, I said: *Nothing is wrong in northern Indiana, / and nothing is particularly right.* That about summed it up for the first few years. The flat, fertile land seemed dull, insipid, compared to the bucolic undulations of my childhood bluffs along the northern Mississippi or my six years of grad school in Seattle, where Mount Rainier bloomed above the horizon on clear days and flowers seemed to rise endlessly in the soft fall of rain. When I flew to South Bend and back for my on-campus interview at Notre Dame, friends asked me what South Bend was like. "Bleak," I said. "Bleak."

"It's February," they said. "Every place is bleak in February."

"Not *every* place," I said.

I needed the job, however—it was by far my best offer—and when the little South Shore train brought me the last leg of the journey, green fields surrounded us, and the sun was a lush red disk sinking into the corn. Despite that, and despite ND's lovely campus and the proximity of Lake Michigan, I was slow to convert to the virtues of the prairie. In one of my first years here I found a cartoon in *The New Yorker* and taped it to the refrigerator door. In the first panel, a man with two suitcases climbs down the steps of a Greyhound bus. In the second panel he looks to the left but sees nothing; in the third he looks to the right with the same result. In the final panel, he puts his suitcases down with a slump. The caption read: *Back Home in Indiana.*

I thought it was hilarious, but my best friend advised me to take it down. "People who can't adjust are immature," she sniffed.

So I adjusted, or tried to, though my poems were mostly about Minnesota or the Pacific Northwest. Over time, I discovered the farmers' market, auctions, Amish settlements, orchards and wineries just over the border in Michigan, paths that twine along the river in the center of South Bend. I soon understood that living here allowed me to afford travel, since my rent was among the lowest in the nation, and I realized, slowly, that for a writer, a love-hate relationship is not all bad.

What makes the Midwest different, I think, is that women and men here are not part of an elaborate and lengthy social heritage as they often are on the East Coast, nor are they posed against a grandiose landscape as they are in the West. Things are elemental here—stripped down, flattened out, in plain sight. Life can be harsh at times and, yes, bleak, but a certain robustness keeps emerging. Midwesterners have the ability to endure not only the country's most violent change of seasons, but often a sameness, a landscape monotonous as truth. There's not much here that I can sentimentalize, and not much that I can overlook. I am forced, day after day, to admit the solidity, the tenaciousness, the simply assumed sense of survival that holds those of us who live here to this flat and fertile earth.

During my first year in Indiana, I saved every penny for a two-week return to Seattle. In my second summer, New England called. For my third, I planned a trip to the British Isles with a close friend, and when she suddenly decided to marry, I went alone, beginning in Ireland. As often happens to the solo traveler, companionship presents itself, as it did one evening when I walked along the river Lee in Cork to a restaurant in a castle. The sign on the door informed me that the restaurant was closed, but as I turned away, the proprietor, a young man who had recently spent time in America, hailed me, let me in, and fed me salmon from the river. He said he felt indebted for all the kindness and hospitality he had received in America, and volunteered the next day to show me some of County Cork. It was an irresistible invitation and a lovely private tour along streams and lakes and ruins, culminating at Gougane Barra and the ancient monastery of St. Finbar.

We didn't fall in love, alas; we didn't even vow to keep in contact, but meeting him was a small adventure nonetheless. When I returned home, I found myself wondering what I would show him of Indiana—were he to come here, were we to become lovers. At first there seemed little, aside from Lake Michigan, that could compare to County Cork, but when I tried to ferret out the essence and nuance of the place I now called home, I realized that the music of northern Indiana was already in my bones; I had already learned the rhythm of the landlocked heart.

BACK HOME IN INDIANA

for Ciaran O'Carroll

Were we to love in Indiana,
I would teach you
passions of the landlocked heart.
Groundswells would be swift
but languid. My body would part
from yours and level like a plain
where half-expected roadways curve.
Trucks would hurtle through the night.
The towns, when we came upon them,
would lie prone—sleepers unnerved
by a vast bed, unfiltered light.

Love,
far from glen and hawthorne tree,
you would shoulder the air

differently; would learn the trick
of the steady wheel; how to wear the heat
like a canvas glove, running miles
through your fingers like so much wheat.

You would go south
through an alphabet of towns
where children toss voices
from hedge to hedge at dusk;

westward, where Gary's great mouth
tears at the heartland's seams,
spits flame by night, steel by day.
You would learn that searing message well;

at every river's end, the sway
of corn leaves rasps out the dusty swell
of plump barns, well-fed sameness, the husk-
less truth of what we would be.

Were we to love here,
our coming would leave
no cleft in the day. Simple
as sheaves, our limbs would weld
nothing to this tempered land.
We would bed in the forge itself;
we would be the fired clay.

What You Can See Mid-Winter in the Midwest

SHERYL ST. GERMAIN

Today, three years sober, eyes burning with a white as cold and unforgiving as an unwritten poem, I walk into my backyard. Snow, snow, and more snow. What's new. White, white, and more white until I think I will die of this whiteness, this unwanted guest that will not leave.

But wait.

Wait. Look harder. Stay longer, I tell myself. The dark brown bones of the swamp rise to the south out of reach of snow and then fall back, clean, pure, and budless as a good line of prose. The brown stalks of coneflowers still stand; the elderly of the garden, they will fall with the first wind. Their stalks look like dark lines that have forgotten where they're going. Stripped of petal and color, dark seed pods hold on like iron; it's the way I find myself holding on to the days as they stay white and cold and do not change.

Thistle and black sunflower seeds pepper the ground under the feeder, proof of the frenzied feeding the birds have done these last days of subzero temperatures and thick snow cover, a small piece of chaos in all this sobriety. The bird bath stands, useless, a sad gray monument filled with frozen water, snow on top like icing on a cake you cannot eat.

I can barely tell the location of the garden, which is also covered with snow, though I can guess it because the butterfly bush and stalks of mint are still visible. I mark it out and know that when the snow melts I'll plant three kinds of basil, parsley, peppers, tomatoes. I know that mint and four kinds of thyme will come back in the spring; their roots still live under the snow. Like me, they're just waiting for sun.

A sea of green along the back side of the house: junipers, mint green, blue green, silver green, water green, the green of Lorca, lines the western border of the yard. I planted it this summer. To the north, pine and spruce, the green of Christmas.

The cottontail that ate my lettuce this fall sleeps, curled near the back of the house. I see a feather, dark blue against the snow. I see tracks of squirrel and rabbit and dog, silver-blue and blazing on the snow where they've melted and refrozen, melted and refrozen. I see the weakness of the structure of my house—how all the snow falls off the steep roof to one part where much of it turns to ice and swells the gutters, melts and refreezes on the back porch where I cannot open the door because of the ice. I'm sure my gutters will soon fall from the weight of the ice.

All of this I see, and I see it because of the snow and its dark sister: a kind of brutal cold that stings and slaps you awake when you walk out into it, a cold I swear I can also see, the way you can sometimes see the cold water someone splashes on your face to wake you from a drunken reverie.

For just that moment you can remember everything.

Walking the Prairie Rail Trail, Thinking about Loss

SHERYL ST. GERMAIN

> The art of losing isn't hard to master.
> —Elizabeth Bishop

I watch reruns of *ER* some evenings, and at least once an episode they have to shock a heart back to life. This is the stuff of drama. Sometimes it works, sometimes it doesn't. And once in a great while they have to crack someone when it's really serious—they crack the rib cage open, I guess, and then it's usually the med student who is least experienced who gets asked to put his or her hands inside the chest of the victim, grab the heart, and try to massage it back to life. It doesn't always work, but what a metaphor for intimacy! To hold a heart, literally, in your hands, to open someone so fully, to have someone touch you so deeply—

I'm walking along a place I like to hike, the Prairie Rail Trail, a ten-meter swatch of Iowa prairie that follows an old railroad track and is sandwiched between two endless cornfields. I'm trying to recover from some small rejection from a man that feels huge—though I'm no newcomer to these things, this one feels like *my* ribs have been cracked open, maybe in front of a huge television audience, and the inexperienced, fumbling Dr. Carter is manipulating my heart before he drops it on the floor. I understand, for the first time, how one could die of sadness; at some level a certain kind of emotional loss becomes physical and invades your body like a virus whose job is to make pain.

This trail is pitiful, a skinny swatch of prairie grasses and flowers, a thin habitat for wildlife squeezed so tight between the corn it's hard to know how it might breathe. The cornfields, like omnipotent gods, dominate the landscape; the prairie walk is like a wound, a bright scar joining the two fields. I've been walking an hour carrying my cracked-rib self along and have only seen one bird and one pheasant feather.

This is a landscape about loss. The grasses and flowers only remind you of what is not here. Like a thin-lipped, skinny man who gives just a little, and the little he gives makes you sad instead of happy because you know how vibrant love can be.

Last week, suddenly and without a lingering, warning sickness, I was struck deaf in my right ear: Sudden sensorineural hearing loss, the doctor said.

Sorry to tell you that you won't hear in that ear again. We don't really know what causes this; we have theories, but there's no treatment. It's fairly common; two people a month come into my office with this type of hearing loss.

This is boring, not like the excitement of *ER* when someone comes in blue-faced and bleeding, IV's hanging every which way, music pumped up in the background, doctors shouting at each other. And there's no kind Nurse Hathaway to look on, and the silence of the sky doesn't suggest the kind of trauma the *ER* music does. Truth is, they probably wouldn't even do an episode on sensorineural hearing loss on *ER*; it's just not dramatic enough.

But isn't that the way it is with matters of the heart, too? Somebody you felt as part of your body rips themselves away, and you're left with cracked ribs and hearing loss and no Dr. Benton with his scalpel to come in all seriousness and make it right again. Dr. Benton doesn't even get called.

People leave one another for lots of reasons, some good and some bad and some unknown. Things happen to your body for no reason sometimes, too, even though you take care of it. I know this, and I also know why there's so little wildlife on this trail.

Maybe we don't perceive the loss of prairie as a loss because we've filled it with something else, something apparently useful: cornfields. Why should we miss what's not here? Bluestem and Indian grass, coneflower and compass plant. Butterflies, birds, foxes, moles, rabbits; why miss these useless things when we have corn—we're feeding the world, right?

The thing about one loss is that it makes you feel other losses, makes you see loss everywhere, and maybe that's not so bad, for a while. Maybe it's not so bad to want everyone to feel what we've lost here, to feel it so deeply your ribs crack open, to feel the quiet, birdless sky as a deaf sky, to enter that deafness and our own thin-lipped soundlessness, enter it fully, and acknowledge the pain, make a sound to mourn the loss of the prairie, of your hearing, your lost love—to feel it shock your heart, your ears, your eyes, back to life.

Transit

Railroad Crossings

BONNIE JO CAMPBELL

On the morning of **March 10, 1993,** Nicholas Bakhuyzen approached the tracks in a truck containing 780 gallons of liquid propane. As Nicholas chatted with his wife on his cellular phone, he coasted down the hill and toward Balkema's private railroad crossing. When he attempted to brake, he found that the previous night's snow had made the dirt driveway slippery. The Amtrak *Wolverine*, en route to Detroit, hit him at about 60 mph, exploding the truck like a gas bomb. Nearby Comstock, Michigan residents said they saw a fireball rise into the air. The heat from the blast melted a nearby streetlight. "Oh, shit" were the last words Bakhuyzen said into his cell phone.

Seconds before the windshield exploded in his face, Amtrak engineer Jimmie Childs of Chicago spotted the propane truck sliding toward the tracks. Childs was within weeks of retirement, and he'd been hoping he wouldn't kill anybody before then. He knew it was too late to brake, knew he'd collide with the truck. He also knew that if he moved from the controls, it would be the equivalent of letting go of the dead man's switch, and the passenger train would slow before clearing the fire, and passengers might die. Propane flames burned his whole body, but he kept the train speeding through. Afterwards he was taken Bronson Hospital burn unit in Kalamazoo.

The tracks run north of and parallel to the Kalamazoo River, and sandwiched between them is Michigan Avenue. If you want to see Comstock Township's new development—apartment complexes, superstores, a five-lane shopping road—you have to follow 26th Street off to the north. But just south of where 26th crosses the tracks lie the important old centers of commerce: Comstock Beer Store, the post office, Boer's service station, and the Riverview Café, where all the working-men gossip at a big center table. From the café you have a view of Merrill Park, where President Clinton once delivered a campaign speech. Farther south lie hundreds of acres of black mucklands that used to be the biggest celery field in the universe. In the 1930s, train cars were loaded with white celery destined for Chicago, Detroit, and New York. Now trucks are loaded with petunias, impatiens, and begonias grown in greenhouses erected upon the old celery fields.

Not long after the propane truck fatality, somebody hiding in the scrub near Balkema's Sand and Gravel tossed a brick at the front of the eastbound Amtrak

Wolverine. The brick went through the windshield without harming the engineer, and the train continued to Detroit.

August 25, 1993, Jacob Ranney drove his dump truck along Michigan Avenue, speeding to keep ahead of the westbound Amtrak *International* out of Toronto, destination Chicago. The engineer blew his whistle at Ranney when he saw the truck turning to cross the tracks at Modern Septic & Sewer, just west of where the propane truck had been hit. Ranney felt pretty sure he could make it. Perhaps Ranney forgot that he was pulling an eighteen-foot trailer with a backhoe on it. His truck cleared the crossing, but the train, which was traveling backward, with the engine pushing, could not slow quickly enough to avoid hitting the trailer. The train lifted the backhoe from the trailer and snapped off the hydraulic arm. The big yellow steel arm slid across the top of all five passenger cars until it thudded against the back of the engine. The trailer was crushed beneath the wheels. Ranney, age thirty-five, got out of the truck unharmed and yelled obscenities. The Amtrak engineer picked up a length of pipe and chased Ranney.

The north–south roads that cross the tracks in Comstock have numbers for names: 26th Street, 28th, 30th, 33rd, 35th. In addition, there have always been a dozen private rail crossings, plus Worden Street, a narrow road just east of 26th, winding around Comstock's two ponds. Accidents have occurred at every crossing—nobody knows just how many, because government records of the accidents at public crossings, such as 26th or Worden Street, are only kept for five years, and there are no public records whatsoever of accidents occurring at private crossings. Fatalities such as Bakhuyzen's are not classified as traffic deaths.

Not long after Ranney's accident, an empty gravel truck pulling a *pup*, an attached trailer, was leaving Modern Septic & Sewer. Joseph Applegate drove that truck onto the tracks in front of the eastbound *Wolverine*. Thirteen Amtrak passengers were injured. Joseph Applegate was killed.

A few months later, representatives from the Michigan Department of Transportation (MDOT) and the Federal Railroad Administration attended a Comstock Township meeting. A few months after that, James VanBruggen, longtime township supervisor, had good news: there was money for a new road north of the tracks. This road would eliminate all the private crossings. Fortune had struck Comstock with the randomness of a tornado touching down. Because Comstock's stretch of rail was along the route of a proposed fast train between Detroit and Chicago, money would come from a special federal fund: Section 10-10, funding improvements in support of high-speed rail. And this would not be a gravel access road—this would be a class A road without weight limits, stretching most of the way from 26th to 35th, at a cost to Americans of $1.8 million before overruns. Construction of the new road, K Avenue, has since been completed. The Worden Street crossing has been closed in addition to the twelve private crossings.

Today, the sign at the tracks at 26th Street reads "Railroad Crossing. Stop on Red Signal." In a picture from the turn of the last century, the sign reads "Danger. Look out for mail pouches thrown from trains." A mechanical arm used to reach out and grab Comstock's outgoing mail so the train didn't have to stop, even back then.

Another picture belonging to the Comstock Historical Society, dated 1912, shows ladies in big hats, gentlemen with canes, and wide-eyed children strolling near 28th Street, alongside a derailed train whose cars, still joined, lean off the tracks, some toward the north, some south.

My hometown of Comstock has made the national news twice. The first time was **May 1939,** when a tornado destroyed or damaged the majority of houses in the south part of town, all around the celery fields. People came from as far as Chicago and Detroit to marvel at dwellings reduced to piles of busted lumber. That was the same month and year that my mother Susanna was born in Comstock. Tornadoes still touch down regularly, but they don't usually devastate more than a few houses, garages, and trailers. As children, my siblings and I never hid from the tornadoes—we ran outside to watch the sky turn gray-green, to feel the air tug at our clothes, to hear the roar like a freight train.

The second time Comstock made the news was **September 1995,** when President Clinton came to deliver a campaign speech on the south bank of the Kalamazoo River. He arrived in his own train.

July 26, 1948, George and Cora Hudson of Comstock kept a cow at what some old locals still call the Snow house, north of the tracks, east of Worden Street. The Hudsons were returning from milking one evening when the westbound *Twilight Limited* encountered their car on the Snows' private crossing. Mrs. Hudson, the driver, aged seventy-one, was torn to pieces, while Mr. Hudson, seventy-nine, was crushed and then thrown a hundred feet through the air. *Kalamazoo Gazette* photos show a row of boys and a few girls standing and staring at the wreckage. The paper also supplied a fiftieth wedding anniversary photo in which the septuagenarians were frowning and facing slightly away from each other. The article included the following description of the car:

> The wrecked automobile, which was a 1936 Chevrolet two-door sedan, was picked up by wreckers in a score or more parts. Nearest the impact were found seat covers, then demolished fenders, rear wheels, rear framework, a section of the body framework, transmission, fuel pump, water hose, front wheel, gears, cylinder head, pistons, and small pieces of the motor and metal parts of the body.

In **1961,** George and June Boney closed on their house, the second house north of the tracks on Worden Street. The Worden Street rail crossing was steep then, and narrow, just a little wider than a car, and there were no gates or lights. George Boney tells a story: "The realtor, she came to pick up the down payment from us and take away the for-sale sign, but when she was leaving she got a wheel off the road. The 26th street signal started, so she got out with her kids and they all stood there and watched the train take her car down the line. Then she grabbed hold of a cop because it turned out she had our down payment in an attaché case in the car, a thousand dollars cash. That was a lot of money then."

"After we moved in," George says, "there was one car a week that got hit on that crossing for six weeks. But nobody was killed." He seems proud when he says, "Nobody was ever killed here."

June Boney remembers the morning in **1964** when she was watching her neighbor Carol Zimmerman's kids for just twenty minutes so that Carol could drive her mother home. Carol and her mother were in the car talking, perhaps arguing, when Carol drove onto the tracks at her private crossing between Worden Street and the Snow house. The train struck them from the east, killing both mother and daughter. "We were out in the back yard when it got hit right there," says June Boney. "It took them clear down the line." She lets her finger travel west. "I took my kids and her kids into the house."

A few hours after the accident, Janie Boer and Joanne Liggett, Comstock high school students, were on lunch break. The school was just north of the tracks on 26th, but students were never supposed to walk across—instead they were supposed to go under the bridge on a concrete path. But Janie and Joanne walked on the tracks anyway, as usual. The train, police, and ambulance were all gone by then. The girls poked around until they came upon a clump of wet, gray stuff lying on the railroad stones some hundred yards from where the accident occurred. The girls used little sticks to push the mess onto a flattened paper bag and carried it back to the school, to their biology teacher, Miss Bernadine Mott, who agreed that it was probably part of a brain. The police later came to reclaim the tissue.

Two decades later, Janie Boer moved in with a man whose house was beside the tracks. Sometimes when the Amtrak approached, she went outside and took off all her clothes, stood naked in the yard, and waved at the passengers. The engineer nearly always blew his whistle.

On New Years Eve, **1967,** five high school students were on their way to toboggan at Comstock's Echo Valley. They saw the eastbound train approaching from behind, running parallel to them as they raced along Michigan Avenue, but they were certain they could beat it to the 33rd Street crossing if they accelerated. They didn't notice, however, that a westbound train was also approaching. Their car, as it turned onto 33rd, was grazed by the eastbound train, and the boys probably heard a sound like the middle of a tornado right before the westbound train wadded their car into a metal ball and tossed it in the direction of Chicago. Two boys were crushed within, and the other three ruined and busted bodies were cast off beside the tracks.

My father Rick is a *Kalamazoo Gazette* photographer, as he was in 1967. He and my mother had finally gotten us kids to bed, and the New Year's party at our Comstock house was just starting to swing when Rick got called to the scene of the accident. He was a little worried about having alcohol on his breath. By the time he got there, they'd thrown sheets over some of the bodies. Rick doesn't remember if it was snowing, he says, but it was cold.

The five of us kids grew up in the house my grandfather built just north of the upper pond in Comstock. Every day during the summer I was eight, some of us kids walked along 26th Street, then crossed the tracks to go to the Comstock Beer Store to get candy. Sometimes we took our dog Brownie, a black and tan mixed breed. I don't think we ever used a leash. As we were coming out of the store one day, Brownie bolted. She ran head-on toward an approaching train and disappeared under the cowcatcher. My sister Sheila screamed, and my brother Tom's mouth hung open as the train clattered over the bolted rails, ka-chung, ka-chung, ka-chung. After fifty-five cars passed, Brownie lay still between the rails right where she'd disappeared. We approached cautiously. The tracks were hot. Brownie's eyes were open and glazed. The top of her head was bleeding. We carried her home, and after two days she was able to recognize us. After three days, she stood up. She never regained her hearing.

Some weeks later, my brother Tom was delivered home by a policeman who caught him throwing rocks at trains across from the Beer Store.

One summer afternoon in **1975,** a man was driving his brother-in-law's five-yard dump truck, full of gravel, and he thought he had time to cross the tracks at 30th Street in front of the eastbound *Wolverine.* He got halfway across, then depressed the clutch to shift, but somehow couldn't get the truck into gear. Though he began to roll back toward East Michigan, toward safety, he could not roll as quickly as he could run, so he jumped out.

When my mother Susanna saw the driver, he was standing beside what was left of the truck. The front wheels were still in place. The truck's engine, however, lay smoking in the road some yards away. The hood and front fenders lay in the field north of the tracks. To the west, the train was still braking. Mom pulled to the side of the road to see if he was okay. The truck's windshield was gone, but a pair of sunglasses still lay on its dashboard. "My brother-in-law's going to kill me," the guy kept saying. "He's just going to kill me."

In **January of 1978,** a woman driving along Michigan Avenue went home and called the police to report a long-haired, bearded man dragging a bloody body on the north side of the tracks near Lobretto's private crossing, just east of 30th Street. Officer Dan White of the Kalamazoo County Sheriff's Department followed the trail of blood through the snow to the partially remodeled office building of an old construction yard, where Chris Dondero lived. Officer White found Dondero in tears, bashing at the ground with a round-end shovel, surrounded by what was left of his dog Dominick. The dog had run off down the tracks that morning after the scent of a female in heat. Years before, Dominick had lost a leg in a farming accident but had survived. "He died of love," Dondero told the cop.

As a teenager, I used to sometimes make out with Roy Hill. He and my brother Mike used to moon the trains from the first house on Worden Street, between the Boney house and the tracks. After surviving twenty-five trains a day running right next to his bedroom window, Roy moved to Florida where he died in a car accident. The Hill family's house was one of two houses torn down to build K Avenue.

Levi King used to hang around the Comstock Township compactor, watching people throw things away. If he saw something good, he'd grab it out of the pit before it was crushed. One day in 1982 he turned north off of Michigan Avenue onto the private crossing leading to Lobretto's Welding Service, and was struck by the eastbound *Wolverine*. The impact killed King. The train pushed his car down the tracks and then off to the north.

In the mid-1980s, Conrail removed one of the two pair of tracks running through Comstock, scrapping out the metal. Ever since the single-track system has been in place, people here have been awaiting the head-on collision of two engines. Perhaps one would be pulling a passenger train, the *Lakeshore Limited* out of Chicago, and the other train would be a freight out of Detroit with fifty graffiti-covered boxcars full of soybeans and scrap metal, and some of those piggyback semi trucks on flat beds, and a couple cars full of squealing livestock. The people of Comstock do not consider any system of warnings and signals foolproof. An MDOT representative says there are "preliminary plans for returning the double tracks as part of high speed service."

When a train approaches, children who live by the tracks sometimes place pennies on the rails and then run for safe ground. After the train passes, they return and look for the coins. Sometimes the pennies are pulverized and disappear; sometimes they are knocked clear and the kids can't find them. The best pennies lie a few yards away on the railroad stones, flattened to twice their original diameter, as thin as a chip of lead paint, only a hint of Lincoln on one side, a ghost of Lincoln's monument on the other.

The K Avenue project in Comstock involved erecting a chain link fence all along the tracks, to prevent pedestrians from crossing at any place other than gated intersections. My mother Susanna bought that old construction yard near Lobretto's Welding, and so she was one of the people who lost a private rail crossing when K Avenue was put in. She initially fought the new road because it required her to sell an acre and a half of land to the county at market value. At one Comstock Township meeting Susanna told the assembled group, "Nobody was ever killed at our crossing."

When Susanna came upon Township Supervisor VanBruggen installing a road sign, she asked him, "Where will my grandchildren learn to flatten pennies?"

VanBruggen doesn't live by the tracks, and he doesn't think about flattening pennies. He thinks about progress and commerce. He has told the *Kalamazoo Gazette* that he imagines Comstockians riding the proposed new fast trains to good-paying jobs in Chicago or Detroit.

In **September 1996,** the Clinton campaign train rolled west along this Detroit–Chicago corridor. People living in trackside houses in Comstock waited in lawn chairs all morning for the president's train. Some of them took the day off work. When it finally came, it must have been traveling at 79 mph, which is the fastest a train can legally travel on that stretch of rail. Three Secret Service helicopters flanked the train, close to the ground, tearing up the air like black tornadoes. Comstock children ran into their houses terrified, and dogs laid down their ears and whimpered. The train itself was decorated red, white, and blue. "Moving into the 21st Century," proclaimed a ruffled banner flapping madly at back. The platform from which the president and Chelsea had waved on the TV news was empty.

The train continued to Kalamazoo, and then Clinton was brought back to Comstock in a motorcade to Merrill Park. Boats appeared strategically in the river, and the muscular men with earpieces pretended to fish without baiting their hooks. The only bridge across the river for miles in each direction was closed off, with a collection of vehicles and barriers that reminded locals of the scene of a train wreck.

If Amtrak doesn't go bust altogether, trains may someday be flying through Comstock at 110 miles per hour. MDOT analyst Jane Wievers says, "We have a long-range plan to eliminate all grade crossings and at the same time improve the road system."

"Every single one?" I ask. "How can you eliminate every single road-track crossing?"

"Overpasses, underpasses, and consolidating crossings," she says. "We know it's an ambitious goal."

Who could even imagine such a thing? No crossings, no gates, no signals. How could the road not meet rails?

Given the cost of tunnels and bridges, the consolidations are bound to make up the vast majority of closings. Wievers doesn't deny this. As an incentive to communities, the fast train fund awards money for the closing of each public crossing. Comstock Township received five thousand dollars for closing Worden Street.

But how many crossings can be closed without radically changing life along the tracks? Without greatly increasing the distances people must travel? Without trapping people on one side of the tracks or the other?

Because of all the accidents that have occurred in Comstock, the engineers start blowing their whistles when they enter the township, and they blow them all the way through. Susanna's four big dogs hear the sound, and they get up from where they're lying and they howl. They're not howling in pain—the sound is too lovely to be that. Since it's just after 4:30 now, this train is the *International*, eastbound to Toronto. Each of the four dogs howls in a different key, perhaps to make their little dog pack sound bigger than it is. Mom has just returned home from working at the greenhouse. She pours herself a glass of cranberry juice with a dash of vodka and says to me, "You know who's the leader of the pack?" No, I ask, who? The dogs continue to howl even after humans can no longer hear the train's whistle. "It's the train," she says. "The train is the leader of their pack."

Connections

S. L. WISENBERG

HOWARD LINE, WASHINGTON AND STATE

Rush hour you stand on the platform and guys with a cello are singing, "Yoo-oo send me, yoo-oo send me," so that you want to sing along, even move a bit. Harmony. You put a dollar in their box of bills.

At the end of the song no one claps, but the performers aren't nonplussed. (This is different from being plussed.) They say, "Thanks for the standing ovation."

Everyone laughs. The group starts up again. They know that like every captive audience, this one must be won over. They have a specific kind of coyness—for public mass flirtation. The singers hold a note when the southbound comes. When the northbound arrives they say, in a slow nasal unison: "This train will be running express from Washington to Howard Street." Everybody gets the joke. Howard is the end point. This is a ploy to keep the commuters from leaving. Everybody laughs. In unison.

Most of the audience boards.

#22 BUS, ALONG LINCOLN PARK

A couple of guys are talking to everybody—yups without much city in them yet, or so much of only one part of the city that, still natty in their suits after 5 P.M., they think the whole damn town belongs to them. They start singing and talking to women about drinking, telling jokes. Just about everybody on the bus is as well-dressed: Same colors, creases in the same place. Same tribe.

Possible conversation ploy: Who does your laundry?

HOWARD LINE, JACKSON AND STATE

Your students are always so amazed, their own personal discovery. It happens in the fall, freshman year. First time away from home. They say: "It's so weird, did you

---

This was written before the advent of the Red and Brown lines, formerly known as the Howard and Ravenswood lines, respectively. The fares have increased, also, since. Some of the initials of real persons (and they are all real persons) have been changed to avoid confusion. An earlier version of this piece appeared in the Chicago *Reader*.

know that when you wait for the subway downtown, the blacks all go one way and the whites go the other? There's nothing like that in New York"—or Cincinnati or San Francisco or wherever they're from.

HOWARD LINE, JACKSON AND STATE

M. the storyteller met E. on the Howard el. She was reading *Newsweek* and he was reading himself in the *Tribune*. He asked to trade. Or maybe it was vice versa.
It lasted as long as he stayed in town.

When K. was still living in Lakeview, he met L. on the bus. They got on at the same time in the morning. She was reading Natalie Goldberg's *Writing Down the Bones*, which he'd thought about buying. They went out for a while. You assume that during their romance they sometimes took the bus together in the morning. Maybe they reenact the opening scene: "Hello, miss, I couldn't help noticing the book you're reading." Or: "Excuse me, ma'am, that's a mighty interesting book you've got there in your handsome little hands." Or: "Darling, I must have you. I've always dreamed of meeting a woman who reads the work of Natalie Goldberg." Now he sees her every once in a while at the gym. She often runs into the boyfriend she had after that, the one she doesn't speak to anymore.

HOWARD LINE

This was the idea. J.'s friend the graduate student liked it. Like a cruise ship, a singles bar. Have everyone on the el who's willing to talk to strangers wear something obvious—a red scarf, for example. Then you would know. Could converse with impunity. While you're communicating. But what if the person who wanted to talk to you wasn't the same person you wanted to talk to?

HOWARD LINE

C. tells you she doesn't have her final paper because of what happened the night before. A strange man on the subway told the guy next to her he had to take his seat because C. was his wife. The sitting man complied. The other man started screaming at C. and grabbed her rough draft and stepped all over it. Finally someone told him to leave her alone. The conductor did nothing. C. was afraid to get off at her usual stop, scared he would follow her. She did it anyway.

HOWARD LINE

Morning rush hour you can stand there in the car, body touching three people you don't know, and hear two lawyers you've never seen before talk about this guy

P. who was the best man at M. the storyteller's wedding—where she married R., two boyfriends after E., the one she'd met on the el.

And here are these two young lawyers who don't even care when you repeat P.'s full name and say, "I know him! I met him at the wedding! He has curly hair, blue eyes, maybe late thirties."

They look at you blandly. "Yeah." Their eyes are hooded, give nothing away. They are lizards. They tell you the name of the firm he works for. They ask, "Do you know his wife?"

"No," you say. "Tell him," you say, "you met someone who met him at this wedding in Connecticut. He was the best man! It was his best friend. From college, I think."

"Yeah," they say.

They turn back to one another.

These young lawyers are not awed by coincidence.

HOWARD LINE, CHICAGO AND STATE

A Sunday on the platform with B. from Fort Lauderdale, and you see this student coming toward you. She's been waiting for the train so she can drop off her paper at your house.

HOWARD LINE, MONROE AND STATE

You say hello to the student originally from Romania. He's getting off the train. You're about to walk down the stairs. He calls you from the other side of the turnstile. He has his paper. One day late.

Two days later, you see him again, on the platform this time, both of you waiting for the train. You tell him his paper's in your box. Waiting for pickup. He gets it the next day, turns in the rewrite on time, in class.

RAVENSWOOD LINE

You like looking at women who look like you, your coloring. Is this so strange? This one has dark wavy hair and a skirt and blouse. Nice clothes, not too tailored, not too boring. Neat. At least not a suit-hose-socks-and-athletic-shoes combo. She's carrying new-looking shopping bags. You try to imagine what's in them. Is she going to Crate & Barrel at 8:30 A.M. to try to return something?

That afternoon, you're at the historic house where you give tours, and she walks into the bookstore attached to the house. A. the linguist is working at the bookstore and asks if you two know each other. The woman remembers meeting you months before. "I saw you on the el this morning," you say. You find out that in the Crate & Barrel bags were clothes for A. to take to a shelter for battered women near her house. The woman has lost a lot of weight, had big clothes to give away.

Such satisfaction to know. Like having the answer to a riddle walk smack into your life.

RAVENSWOOD LINE

B. the rosy-cheeked student says sometimes he just knows things. Like the time he saw this guy get on at the Merchandise Mart and just knew that he had a manuscript inside his briefcase and had just come from a meeting where it was discussed. And he engaged the man in conversation and found it was true. Did he tell the man? "No. I didn't want to freak him out."

EL VS. BUS, PART ONE

On the train you often don't ever see the conductor, so if knowing what the authority figure in charge looks like is a priority, then you are headed for anxiety. On the bus you always know who's driving. On some lines, the drivers know the riders, especially the older women, who walk up slowly, as if on the plank of a ship, sit up close, vigilant. In dreams of community, there are bus drivers like this, who know you, who place you. They are like familiar bartenders or waitresses who smile when they see you and ask, "The usual, babe?"

#8 BUS

The driver will stop for you at Halsted and Roscoe and give you a free ride a few blocks to Diversey, where he turns, because you thought this was a bus that went all the way to Fullerton.

If it's cold and nighttime, and you are carrying a bicycle helmet, and the bus is nearly empty, he will ask you the obvious: "Where's your bike?" And you'll say, "About 2600 north," and he'll talk about his bike, and his family, so you'll think: a family man, not trying to pick me up, just being friendly, taking me to my own means of transportation, so that I'll be closer to being able to pedal on my own power, how nice that everything in the city all fits together.

EL VS. BUS, PART TWO

While the el gives the illusion of directness, not varying, the bus gives the illusion of freedom; anything is possible because there is no track to veer off of, only open road, the apotheosis of middle-class (economic) freedom: let's take a road trip, go places—all is wide open.

#29 BUS

On State Street downtown, you decide at the last minute that this northbound bus is as good as any. You tap on the doors just after they close. The driver opens them for you. You ask for a transfer. She frowns: "I don't know if I'll give you a transfer." Can't read this stranger's face. She waits. Her mouth turns to a laugh.

"Oh," you say, "I forgot in your contract you can give them at your own discretion."

"Where does it say that?" she asks. "I haven't read it yet. Have you?"

"In the fine print," you say.

This guy in a seat at the front looks at you and says to the driver: "Doesn't she look like a high-powered lawyer?"

You're wearing a striped Indian cotton skirt and a blouse and a black vest, sandals, backpack. You think they probably don't dress this way even at the People's Law Office.

He, on the other hand, could fit the part: early thirties, maybe, short-cropped reddish beard, dark suit. You get the transfer. Of course. Just playing with you.

But the bus itself betrays you, turns east on Grand, toward Navy Pier. You pull the cord to get off, say good-bye. It's only polite.

HOWARD LINE

You can't hear on the subway, but it's easy to forget this if you usually travel alone. But then if you sit next to a friend you end up shouting things like "He has a pea-brain. I feel like biting him." Looking around furtively, though you know the pea-brain takes another line in another direction.

Even when you're not underground, you find yourself embarrassed when on a crowded night el train, a friend—acquaintance, really—says in a regular voice: "I'll spend two whole days thinking I should be back with her, and then a few days thinking the opposite. Is it like that with you, too?"

And you start to answer, then you wave your hands, brushing your protoconfession aside, because—maybe it's just that you're on the el, maybe not—you don't want to inject this damage from the past into this conversation that's moving, moving forward.

BUS/RAVENSWOOD LINE

On the bus you can't write—except in big loopy scrawls. It's harder to read, too. Lines wriggle, jolt. But you can look out the windows and remind yourself why you came to the city in the first place.

Same with the Ravenswood, the view part. You met A. the linguist's aunt waiting for it. She talked to you because you were holding the new Louis Sullivan biography. She said she always takes the Ravenswood so she can look at the buildings. You didn't know she was A.'s aunt until you saw her at a party a month later.

B. the rosy-cheeked student, late to class one hot spring morning, says: "It was such a pretty day I had to take the Ravenswood instead of Howard."

HOWARD LINE, BELMONT

The prematurely gray-haired ticket-taker guy seems to know you. You think so by the little flicker in his eye when you say hello or hand him the money.

The newsstand guy always says "Good morning," even though you hardly ever buy a paper from him. Sometimes he burns incense. He looks East Indian, wife, son with him. Sometimes he talks into a powder blue phone. In your maudlin moments you think you are spreading such joy to him with your regular "Good mornings," then you think *he* probably thinks *he's* adding a smidgen of warmth to *your* miserable, solitary life by *his* regular "Good mornings"; *he* probably takes joy in thinking how he's making you feel you aren't just some faceless commuter in an endless gray stream of commuters.

HOWARD LINE

You are more likely to run into colleagues and exes on the el than the bus. Colleagues are also more likely to run into your exes on the el. Like C. the poet, who came into the office that morning, maybe two days after you and N. had broken up, and, oblivious to it, said, "Oh, guess who I saw on the el." They'd had a light guy-to-guy conversation about leagues and pennants.

H. (one of M.'s exes) also ran into N. once on the el. They probably talked about torture (political).

You never run into a current lover on the el or the bus. Or N., either. You've crossed paths twice on North Broadway and twice in Rogers Park. (The worst was when he just got up and left the counter at the Japanese restaurant. The next worst was when you saw him with his new girlfriend at the Heartland Cafe and you threw a crumpled-up napkin on their table just to be funny, and missed, and so they saw you just standing behind their table, looking embarrassed. The napkin landed somewhere behind the partition in the smoking section, probably in the middle of some smoker's stir-fried tofu.)

J. ran into your other ex, B., on North Clark, or so she thought. He was wearing a jogging suit, like the one he'd worn in a dream you had. She looked and looked, walked on and then glanced back, not sure if he was indeed B. You've never run into him. Yet. Though you keep seeing men everywhere with similar bald spots. His could have spread by now. The el, the bus, the cafes, bike paths, restaurants, sidewalks, theaters, cars, stores, lobbies, in this town are all filled with balding men.

312-836-7000

Occasionally they will lie to you about the schedule when you call the free number, but they are always pleasant, and the men at least joke with you. Things like: "Yeah, I guess I could tell you when the next bus leaves. What's it worth to you?"

And you think: If I were a foreigner, if my English were weak, I wouldn't know what he was talking about. I would be lost.

HOWARD LINE/EVANSTON LINE/212 PACE BUS

Just think, for $1.50 you can go from Belmont and Sheffield to the corner of Waukegan and Willow in Techny in less than two hours. By car in the same time you could go there and back and partly there again. But you don't have your own car anymore, so sometimes you rent one for $15.85 (including tax) and take the streets, not the Edens because you don't like taking $15.85 cars on the freeway, and sometimes you go too far and end up almost in Glencoe or west of Glenview, among anonymous fields and low buildings.

If you have to take the bus from Davis Street in Evanston, you have to walk 0.8 miles from Waukegan and Willow to the Divine Word Mission, where you meet your therapist, who takes you to the belfry, which she rents, and you can look out and see cornfields and almost feel you're in the country. Afterward, downstairs, you can put a quarter in Max the upright stuffed Russian bear, and he will move his head up and down and tell the history of the town and the mission, and you can buy postcards to show your friends: This is where I go on Wednesdays. You can walk next door to the Techny post office and buy stamps, usually without having to wait in line.

You walk back to Waukegan and Willow to wait for the bus, and now that you have a Walkman, it's not too bad. You can still hear WBEZ. It's only bad when it's about five degrees with a wind or when men pull over and offer you rides. Insistently. You never see anyone else walking that 0.8-mile stretch.

You feel like a doctor, taking Wednesdays off, and then you stop at the Evanston library or Northwestern and usually run into people you know. They think Evanston is awfully far away from your home.

For you it's midway, your entry point into civilization.

HOWARD LINE

He's in radio. Has lived in Chicago seven months or so. Says when he carries tapes in his shoulder bag, he never sets the case down on the floor of the train because he's afraid the magnetic power of the third rail will reach up and zap them blank. He seems to enjoy this fear. Keeps him alert. Reminds him where he is.

#212 BUS

You can get on or off at any intersection along the way. This is the way of the suburban lines. And the stop-requested pulls always work. But there are never *Streetfare Journals* to read, help wanted ads for a hardware store.

You can leave your poncho on the bus and get off at Davis Street and realize it a few seconds later and go back and get it. The man sitting in your seat will hand it to you.

HOWARD LINE, MONROE AND STATE

On the train you cannot get a free ride. You even have to pay to change your mind. If you walk in and pay your $1.25 and five minutes later decide you don't want to take the train after all, you won't get the $1.25 back. Not even a transfer, even if you said "Good morning" to the ticket taker or made an unforgettable comment. Except maybe sometimes. Depending.

EVANSTON EXPRESS

You tap him on the shoulder. Haven't seen him in a year or two. Tell him you are looking for a new job. He says to call. You think it's a sign, that a month from now you'll say, "If I hadn't run into him on the el, this never would have happened." But you don't send him the resume. You stay where you are.

HOWARD LINE

On the el you can fall in love—like that.

With a profile—something about it, as beautiful as architecture or sculpture. Nice round forehead, perfectly balanced chin. Your reaction is visceral. Like wanting to touch terra cotta. *I must sweep back your straight, straw colored, poufy-but-not-too hair.*

He is talking to two women, laughing. You think one of them was the one who introduced the Palestinian speaker that time when you were still seeing N. You don't remember much the speaker said except he came across well—an intellectual, a Man of Sense. Could you now say to her, "Oh, I've seen you around, don't you do solidarity work?"

He turns, full face, just before Belmont. Not like a sculpture at all. Not at all.

Call *Guinness:* the world's shortest self-contained love affair.

#36 BUS

On the bus you see part of the city you haven't seen before because of the angle. On the Near-North, on second and third stories: a spa, a school of dance, a globe in a window, plants balanced on a row of books, a guy looking over his balcony in front of a sun umbrella, pink shirt, smiling.

Crayon drawings of brown-and-white rabbits in the window of the Cathedral School. It's just past Easter.

A huge sign advertising a lawyer. The couple behind you make fun of the sign, saying things like: "'Hire me—I'm a hardass." "He must be advertising for criminals." "Who else would hire him?"

The city wants to present itself as if from a bus on a sunny Sunday, glass filtering out the smells, showing only what you can see above street level.

HOWARD LINE

You were standing on a platform with L., the summer she lived with the Board of Trade runners and knew all the bartenders in town. Sex was on her mind. Two trains arrived in opposite directions at the same time. She said: "Simultaneous. It's really rare." You still think of that. Always. Have stolen her joke. A pretty obvious one, anyway.

IN TRANSIT

You tell your students to write in their journals as much as they can. You have them write down conversations they overhear. Most of them do, but some are self-conscious about it. One of them is berated by a couple whose argument he transcribed. On his birthday yet. Not P. She's undaunted. Unsinkable. This is what she tells the class: She always writes in her journal on the train. One time she saw that the man next to her was reading her every word. So she wrote: "When the man finishes this sentence he will drop dead."

A Chicago Story

ROSANNE NORDSTROM

A long time ago, on June 14, 1991, I rushed out of my Hyde Park condo with Miguel, the dog. Earlier that Friday morning, I'd met a friend for a lakefront walk followed by breakfast, so I was an hour behind schedule with the walk. Miguel was desperate to be outside.

From previous neighborhood experience, I knew that Miguel's appearance would not go unremarked. He hadn't reached the first tree south of the apartment building before he and I were surrounded by a pack of unruly kids on their way to the public school on the next block. "Miguel! Miguel! Hey, look, it's Miguel. Miguel's a good dog."

"Hey, lady, can we pet the dog?"

"Will he bite?"

"Miguel doesn't bite. He's a good dog, aren't you, Miguel?"

Because so many members of Miguel's fan club were talking at once, I didn't even try to answer the questions. I stayed close to his head so he could see me, lean up against me if the onslaught was too much.

Miguel was half Newfoundland and half black lab. He weighed at least ninety pounds and had long, wavy black hair. I suspect that he was born calm. He was also loved, well cared for, and secure. Miguel was friendly and the kids flocked.

As an adult, I've never been drawn to children. Babies don't make me coo. Children's voices, especially if they're yelling or crying, make me feel like screaming. I never looked forward to interactions with the kids Miguel attracted. At the same time, I had vivid childhood memories of the comfort and joy I'd felt around dogs and cats. It was an experience I would deny no child.

On that long ago morning, I'd had a good walk and breakfast. I was wearing a favorite outfit, a blue blouse with matching Capri pants and dark blue sandals. I was relaxed and content to let the kids hug and pet Miguel. I smiled. I showed the fearful how easy and wonderful it was to pet a dog.

After a while, the kids dispersed, leaving Miguel and me to proceed. We did so in the company of four boys. As soon as all of us crossed the street, Miguel stopped.

"Wow, look at all that dukey!"

"Yes," I said, "Miguel's a big dog. He eats a lot. He poops a lot."

"What does he eat?"

"Dog food."

"You don't give him table scraps?"

"No, but you know what? He loves grapefruit. Have you ever met a dog who eats grapefruit?"

"Yuck. I can't stand grapefruit. It's too sour."

When I started pulling bags out of my pocket, I heard for the first time from the smallest boy. He was dark-skinned, and his hair was about a month past a haircut. He wore black jeans that were about two sizes too big and a black striped aqua blue shirt that was missing several buttons. Both his shoes and his book bag were dirty and torn up. What I noticed was this kid's big, dark eyes. It'd been a long time since I'd seen such beautiful eyes. "Hey, lady, you aren't really going to pick up that dukey with your hands, are you?"

A ways into the walk, Miguel dove into some bushes and re-emerged with a beat-up old tennis ball in his mouth. "Oh," I said, "Miguel's found another ball for his collection."

"His what?" Big Eyes, who I later learned was named Paco, asked.

"His collection. Every time Miguel finds a ball, he carries it back to the apartment. He won't drop the ball until he's inside. Miguel has his own toy box, and it's full of balls that he's found on his walks."

"How many balls?"

"The last time I counted there were more than twenty-five."

"More than twenty-five? Are you kidding? Can we see them? Can we count them?"

I looked at my watch and noted that the bell for school would ring in about ten minutes.

A few days after Paco's tenth birthday, my husband Roger and I took him and his friend Reed, who lived down the street, to the Indiana Dunes. There a maple syrup festival was in progress. People were gathering sap from the trees and then boiling it in huge pots. A breeze blew, and steam from the iron pots billowed like fog around us. The pots were big enough, black enough, and smoky enough to belong to witches. I felt like I'd stepped into a fairy tale, but I wasn't aware of fear.

Paco and his friend Reed ran all over. They looked at the pots, the horses pulling carts, the barn, and the woods that were covered in a light layer of fairly new snow. The boys couldn't resist the snowy woods. Neither could Roger and I. At one point, we turned a corner in the path and saw Paco and Reed squatting in front of a fast-moving creek, intent on watching the broken sticks and clumps of snow they sent into the running water.

The picture of Paco and his friend was so boy ordinary, so kid in the woods happy. I smiled, and my heart clenched with dread. Instead of the winter scene in front of me, I saw Paco and Reed running Hyde Park's west end streets. From time to time I remembered that image.

Three days before Christmas 1999, the phone rang while I was sipping coffee and turning the pages of the morning paper.

"Hey, Rosie."

"Hola, amigo mio. It's so good to hear your voice, but what's wrong?" To my ear, Paco's voice sounded heavy, too heavy to talk.

"It's Reed. He's dead."

"Oh, kiddo."

"He was shot in the head. In Rockford. Over a $25 drug deal."

"Oh Paco, that is so sad."

For a couple moments both Paco and I remained silent. "Paco, do you remember the day Roger and I took you and Reed to the Dunes?"

"Yeah, I've been thinking about that day. It was a good day."

"So you know for sure that Reed had one good day during his life. That doesn't seem like enough, does it?"

"Nah, Rosie, one good day in sixteen years isn't nearly enough."

In 1993, Roger and I moved to the far north side of Chicago. Paco visited us on weekends, and we quickly established two rituals. One was breakfast at the A&T, a restaurant on the southwest corner of Clark and Greenleaf, a few blocks from our house. The A&T is an ordinary sort of neighborhood restaurant. It is square in shape and lined with booths. Roger, Paco, and I always had the same waitress, who knew to bring Roger and me the Village Omelet, a feta cheese/vegetable mixture, and to bring Paco a waffle with strawberries and whipped cream and a hot chocolate with whipped cream. The waitress was generous with Paco's whipped cream, which made him feel special. Every time before we left the house, Paco complained about the great and terrible distance of the walk. On the way home he was infinitely more cheerful. He skipped or hopped between Roger and me with a hand on each of our shoulders. Many times he'd challenge Roger to race, and then I'd walk the rest of the way home alone.

The other ritual was that of tea and night reading. If Paco slept overnight in this house, he, Roger, and I would sit in the living room before bedtime. While I read, Roger and Paco would drink herbal tea and eat fruit or sweets. Then Paco would put his head on my shoulder, and I'd continue reading until he fell asleep. I found this ritual comforting. No matter what troubles had filled the day, the nighttime reading felt like a promise to me that there would always be good days.

Abracadabra

SHARON SOLWITZ

For Jesse (February 10, 1987–January 31, 2001)

Once upon a time a woman gave birth to twin sons.

They had enough fingers and toes, and sweet-smelling bald heads and, eventually, wide, toothless grins, and she loved them.

Thirteen years passed, then one got sick. In the year that followed he was sick and better, then very sick, then a little better.

He died.

His mother, however, remained alive.

Those are the high points. Interesting (maybe), but not searing, not devastating. It's what I can write, that or aanhhh! James Joyce wrote a cat's cry not meow but mrrgniaouw, satisfying in its phonetic precision. Arrnyanghh?

Perhaps it needs back story.

The boys came in her forty-first year, after five of doctor-assisted trying. Pregnant, she sometimes referred to herself (mostly ironically) as biblical Sarah, Judaism's first first lady, blessed with child when she was (almost) too old to conceive. Like Sarah, she was hospitable. Her Hebrew name was (really) Sarah. She called the boys, among other things, angels, devils, and little wild men. She called them her miracle babies.

These words, general and distant from me, come easily to mind. But other words clump together down somewhere, caught as in some internal oil spill, slimy-billed, gasping for air, feathers stuck to emaciated wing-bones. A few bedraggled words break loose. *Aaaaanrg!*

I once wrote an essay about turning life into fiction. One's own life. Pit your enraged self (for example) against your obsequious self. It strikes me now as frighteningly obtuse. Writing one's secrets and fears? Dare to do it! In service of literature and one's psyche! Yeah, right, I say now to my relentlessly perky younger self, to whom the worst that ever happened was walking in on her husband screwing another woman. Now I scream at her (not my ex-husband's lover but my earlier self): That was nothing!!

How do you write about a hole in the world, a loss that renders everything you still might have, see, feel, pointless or at least continually, repetitively painful? Yes, transformation is necessary, of dire experience into something by means of which life becomes more than a series of increasingly dire losses. But can writing transform? Will it make me feel better?

DIALOGUE BETWEEN TWO HALVES OF A BRAIN

X: I can't think straight. I want to die. It's like I'm already dead.

Y: Oh, shut up. By its nature, self is in bondage to death. Find a purpose apart from your desire to "feel better." Write for teeming humanity, in which every household has suffered loss. *Om mani padme hum.*

Lost in the sea of bad feeling, X will try to follow the advice of the more rational Y. Will the swimmer make it to shore? Will the swim be beautiful?

In my grad school days a fellow student, excellent poet, had a baby with a problem who died at six weeks. The woman dropped out of the program, went on to have another baby but, from what I've heard, couldn't write another poem. Now, maybe she wasn't supposed to write poems; maybe the world is happily free of her poetry, and she is happy in law or medical school learning how to save physical lives and make money to boot. But maybe, dissecting her cadaver, she looks into the abdominal cavity and stumbles into the empty place in her that words might fill nourishingly. Can words nourish? Can they replace, redeem?

I write to know, and so that you can know. Oh, lapsed M.F.A.; oh, exile from the kingdom of poetry, in your pea-green scrubs following chick-like after the attending physician, this essay—attempt at essay—is for you.

ADVICE

Describe your state of mind. Make it concrete, an object to look at, a piece of writing by, about, someone else.

Then you can step back from it, take in something new.

My mind is sludge; undifferentiated. No feelings, thoughts. No images even, of friends, family. I'm sorry, Seth, my other son. Remaining son. Twin, untwinned. Now his face comes, fleshy (he fattened up while Jesse shrank). It means nothing to me.

But I can breathe, am breathing. Hear my voice talking to people. I speak, therefore I am. Downstairs during shiva I sat on a low stool, liking the lowness, the non-necessity of making sense, of squeezing back the hands that squeezed mine. People's legs passed, clothed in fabric, I saw from my stool. Thinking: I like this stool—Bubby's mahogany footstool, salvaged by my mother from her mother's estate. I like this vantage point, reflecting exactly my sense of my state in the world. From now on, to dinner with friends, I'll bring my stool, and show, at table, the top half of my face. I'll walk to class with my stool under my arm. Teach from a low stool. No reason anyone should listen to me in that abject station, but I don't mind not being listened to. Let me stay here in this abased, overlooked place.

Then a thought, and it's bad. Hold still, stiff, for what's coming. His last breath. I heard it. In bed beside him I was listening to him breathe, fast and shallow (as he'd been breathing the past three days), and I was breathing in time with him, *in unison,* silently instructing him how to breathe better. He took a long, deep breath. A pause, maybe fifteen seconds. I held my own breath, open, alert that quarter of a minute for a squeeze of maybe hope, the thought of healing; from now on he'll start breathing normally again. Remembering the monitors over his hospital bed, the rise and fall of his respiration, varyingly sized troughs and crests, shallow, erratic, and me willing them into mountain peaks, an even row of crags, the breaths of someone who doesn't have to labor at it, who can climb a mountain on the fuel of his calm deep breaths. And voila!—not even a miracle, the normal expected—the boy up and out of the hospital, back to school, talking to friends on the phone, all things eternally possible . . . Another breath now. I taste it in my mouth, work to extend it in my mind. Another long pause. I wait, breathing shallowly, so as not to miss the next sound, however frail.

At some point I stopped waiting. For a reason I don't know even now, nine months later, since I am not an observant Jew, I rolled against him, breathed in his ear, *Shma yisrael adonai elohenu adonai echod. Hear O Israel the Lord our God, the Lord is one.* If the soul lives even ten seconds after death, he had to have heard me.

And now? Nine months later, the period of human gestation. I have cried. I have had sex. I have eaten in restaurants. Talked with friends. Taught classes. Played bridge. Petted my cat. Cut my fingernails. I've taken Seth to the doctor, to the orthodontist, and to Air Wair for new boots. I've had fights with my husband Barry and made up with him (sort of). But how I am? Adjectives galumph about: Depressed? Lost? And nouns: ache, anguish, agony. Piercing wound? The sound of his name twisting a place just above my belly button? Sentences resist completion. Jess. Jesse?

ADVICE

Think about Jesse, then. What do you remember?

I remember how he looked in his Johnny Jump-Up. He was less than a year, and I have no pictures of him in the spring-driven harness, but I remember his grinning mouth and how quickly he learned to bounce. He couldn't walk yet, but he could bend his knees, then straighten, sending himself high into the air, euphoric in charge of his own pleasure.

I remember how he'd nurse, frantic, seeking his rhythm, hands flailing, then finding my face, my mouth. Sucking evenly now, fingers in my mouth, calm with the full sensory load. A few years later, playing catch with a tennis ball, he'd daydream and miss. When we added a second ball to the game, he hardly ever missed.

His first written word, his name, on a piece of construction paper brought home from pre-kindergarten: ESSJE.

His first recital piece, "The Wild Swans," from the John Thompson book. Lots of triplets. He learned to play quickly and with flash, with dynamics—in part, I think, to best brother Seth.

Karate. He'd daydream or start a conversation and have to apologize to the class. He liked the loud, wild boys, cohorts under the flag of anarchy. He loved to laugh, to talk out of turn, to fall in a heap on the floor.

Table manners. The kindergarten teacher said that some of the other children were offended. That he was "inappropriate."

My father offered him twenty dollars for an essay on table manners. He was nine or ten. He wrote a remarkable essay, detailing the table rules, discussing their purpose, their possible origin. On his third grade statewide writing assessment test (IGAP) he got a 26, perfect score, highest in the school. And still ate with his hands, from the box, the serving plate, roaming the house dropping crumbs.

He couldn't sit still in a chair. Drove his grandparents crazy. "Put your feet on the floor. Why do you keep turning?"

He and Seth walking together along the sidewalk, bumping into each other, not as a dominance game but as an unconscious joining, a return to their junction in utero. In a room they'd gravitate toward each other till they were leaning on one another, a proximity that most other pairs would have found irksome. As if, for nourishment, the bodies needed physical contact.

Walking, he'd bump into me; he'd walk leaning against me. If I was seated, he'd sink into my lap as if my lap were a chair continually offered him.

He signed a mother's day card, Jesse "the Bomb" Silesky.

He told his widowed grandma, "If you smile nicely, you'll find a man to be your husband."

A girl's birthday party. He walked in a little shy, and she called out, "Chase me!" His face, changing from uncertainty to joy.

Some kids on the bus told him he smiled too much. He felt bad. But it was hard for him to stop smiling. If he'd lived, he'd have worked, at least for a while in junior high, to turn himself as cool as boy society required. I'd have watched aching from afar, hoping that he'd find the part of himself that was unassailable. Hoping he'd learn to love the self that loved the world to the point of self-negation, and wanted to be loved equally back.

Stretched out on the living room couch where he spent most of the last three weeks, he told my good friend, who was reading to him, "I love you, Joyce." He thought further, smiled: "I love all my Mom's girlfriends."

That same period Seth said to him, "God, don't you just hate this," referring to his sedentary state, or maybe the ongoing tedium of the illness (not, I think, to future terrors). And Jesse, on morphine but awake, alert, shrugging: "It's not so bad."

He used to be afraid of death. At times, age eight or nine, he'd curl up on the couch in the den, under a blanket, TV off. He wasn't afraid to talk about being afraid. He was easy to comfort. I told him, yes, he would die, everyone died, but it wouldn't be soon. He was young, his years stretching out and out.

A couple of years later, I asked him if he was still afraid of death, and he said no. He figured that without death, life had no meaning. Really? Where did that idea come from? Him smiling, knowing it was a cool thing.

I think of the woman lucky enough to marry him, the joy of her awareness of the depth of his love for her, a capacity burgeoning the last year of his life. His fascination with her mind, his eagerness to romp with her on the playground of ideas. Nothing in the mind verboten. He said he wasn't sure that Hitler was a sinner. If Hitler believed that Jews were demons or robots, then for Hitler killing them was like killing bad guys. That's what Jesse said. When Hitler learned that Jews were human, he probably "felt so sorry."

His last night I lay beside him in bed reading *When Bad Things Happen to Good People*. The theory didn't soothe me, but I was drawn by the author's personal tragedy, his son dying slowly from age three on up. I read about the country of the afflicted, a place I was determined to avoid. When Jesse made his awful fast gasps (sleeping? is that sleeping?), I thought of the acupuncturist I'd found for him, scheduled for ten the next morning. Ten was not far away.

Better describe his handwriting. On his old homework, turned in and marked *100% but write more clearly*. His letters were small, open in odd places, bouncing off the lines. He made honor roll his last semester, no checks for behavior. No irritated comment: He has trouble staying *on task*. The grades came, A after A after A. Jesse is an outstanding student. A pleasure to have in class. He was working at home then with the teacher mandated by the Chicago Board of Ed for homebound kids. He said with a smile of rue, "They think I'm great when I'm not there."

THIS IS NOT MAKING ME HAPPY

Or sad in a good way. I'm sad in a scared and empty way, and haven't you heard enough? Aren't you (you must be) tired of this? I am, in a way that hurts the back of my neck.

ADVICE

Forget what I said before. Write for yourself, not for other people.

But I fear madness without my audience, my readers, however imaginary.
Hey, anyone out there who's lost, who feels lost, who feels what I feel?
Anyone out there?
I'm the babbler on the subway, lips moving at my reflection in the dark glass. I've lost my boy, anyone seen him?
It's not Jesse lost, it's me, lost without him. I was one of four, the one female in the family photo, my hand on a boy's shoulders, beside Barry behind boy number two. Four seats filled at the restaurant four-top. A carful: two in front, two in back. Four playing Cranium, hearts. We never got to bridge.
Three is stable, but barely.
For stability we build things, plant things, fill photo albums, arrange objects on shelves.

The last day at Camp Simcha, a weekend retreat for bereaved Jewish parents, we planted bushes for our loved ones. Tamped down the dirt. Watered.

There's a lilac bush in the garden outside of Newberry Math and Science Academy that will soon have a plaque with his name. There was a service, the gift of a quilt. Some girls cried. A song played: "I will remember you."

On his bookcase—along with the books he read, one he didn't get to. I bought it for him, read a few pages, hoping he'd pick it up himself—*The Amber Spyglass* by Philip Pullman. The last month he listened to books on tape, went to sleep to *Harry Potter.*

More on his bookcase: Chess trophies. An unwieldy purple-glazed ceramic bowl. Comic books in plastic sheaths. A magnetic toy from the hospital. These things are horrible to me now in their stillness, their refusal to give way to more adult mementos.

Most terrible: Our private "pieta" of his stuffed animals, Teddy—a knit rabbit, premier comfort icon, hero of the "teddy" stories. Teddy lies in the arms of Tigger, gift from his kind and hope-inducing doctor.

Is there a worthy monument? I think of the Vietnam Memorial, winding through its cleft in the earth.

I ordered his photo inset on his "memorial stone" at the cemetery, imagining people gathering round weeping. Even strangers. Even if they're not weeping for him but for a loss of their own. How can anyone help but weep for his luminous face, beaming in the enameled photo over those horrible dates (write it) 1987–2001. People stop, murmur to each other, "Beautiful. Sweet. And he died so young."

Other people's grief for Jesse, my link to them and the world.

Thus pain suddenly lifts. Mind irresponsible, footloose, slipping out from under its burdens. But, no sooner am I situated on the brink of pleasure or just the relief of surcease of pain, than it's back again. Tethered to me like a dog on a short leash, winding around me in tightening circles. Pulls up to the house and leans on the horn. We have a date, babe, did you think I'd forget?

ADVICE

Keep your date. Embrace what comes, even pain.

JESSE'S HAIR: A HISTORY

Newborn, it's fuzz on my lips. Smells of milk and something sweet, like flowers. (Love the present tense.) Seth's too.

At sixteen months, silky blond curls, color of new pine. Cut it myself. A snippet resides in an envelope labeled First Haircut May '88, J.A.S. I have one for Seth, too, identical.

Ages five, six, darkening. Earth brown, thick and straight, a shag rug, hard in your hand. Sturdy like his body, limbs, mind. He plays soccer, gets knocked around, never cries. First barber cut age seven or eight, for $8 (kids' special) at The

Hair Cuttery. He chooses a style from the barbershop catalogue, adult section. The result is nothing like the picture, shaved close to the sides of his head. His head looks scrubbed, face too open and vulnerable. He looks in the mirror, shrugs. On to the next venture.

First round of chemo, Topo-cyclo, two weeks. Hair intact the first week. We think, He's lucky. One of the lucky ones. It starts to fall but leaves a thin layer, lank and fine, pale brown all over his head. I touch gently, so as not to dislodge.

Round two: Adriamycin, in hospital, forty-eight-hour drip. He's bald unto the eyebrows and eyelashes. Even the nose hairs are gone. Nose continually runs. I love his bare scalp, warm to my cheek and lips. Alive and warm.

Remission: in time for his bar mitzvah, June 27, 2000. Hairs sprout, hard prickles all over his scalp. Seth's is long and thick, enough hair for two.

Late summer, an inch of new hair, curly. He looks like a little Jewish boy. At Camp Simcha, two weeks with Hassids and Jewish cancer kids, he learns to love Torah and believe in the Jewish God. He will keep Kosher, place money in the Tsedakah box. His hair is strong and wiry on his scalp; you can grab, yank it. An observant Jew, he won't die.

For school he wants blue hair; a friend (Franco?) dyes it for him. His hair fits with the hair of the other smart eighth grade dissidents: Franco's Mohawk, Nick's crayon red, the gelled lavender peaks all over Seth's head. Jess is sensitive to looks from adults on the street, but bears it (he says) for the school camaraderie. Noticing how style bands you with one group and alienates you from others.

Recurrence, late October. Largest tumor is golfball-sized, operable. Chemo first. Doctors reassure us: Chemo will be light, killing cancer but not hair cells. But doctors are wrong. In three weeks the hair begins to fall. I pat his head. Hair sticks to my hand like cat hair.

Can I quit now?

His last good day. I type with my eyes closed, fingers keyboard punching—he went with Avi and Seth to Dave'n Busters, though he was already peeing blood. No more curly blue hair. He wore a derby hat I bought him for Chanukah. He looked like a Mafia accountant, small, shrewd, bright-eyed. Still animated, interested in his life, going to school, and out after school. At Dave'n Busters they played laser tag, and Jess so tired he could barely move, but he trained that fatigue into focus and got his man, every man, his score twice as high as the next closest. But the next game he lost, got wiped out by his laser-armed enemies, and the day after he was in the hospital with hemoglobin 7, half what it should have been, a wonder he could speak, let alone stand and shoot.

OH, JESSE

I want other people to miss him, to be affected, hurt, overwhelmed by the loss of him. Nick cries in his room, Meesouk's grades have gone down, my friend Sheryl has upped her Zoloft. Good. Good, good, good.

ADVICE

You sound angry. You can write your anger.

I HATE

Grocery shopping, the process of selection that I used to love even in Jesse's last days when I thought flax oil or raw organic garlic or taro root ground up and mixed with ginger would start the long process of restoring his health.

I hate buying clothes, remembering the pleasure of buying him something that in his new thin state would look good on him.

I hate airports, remembering the last ride we took, Jesse in a wheelchair scared of a new pain in his chest, and me trying to hide how scared I was. Mom, is a tumor growing in my heart? Your heart, Jess, is loud and strong. On the plane we sat next to each other holding hands and agreed not ever to cry in each other's presence but always to be happy.

I hate Florida, my parents' house on the fifth hole of the golf course that I used to love because of how alive and well we all were there—every year before this last year—radiant in the warm, flowery air and the possibility of fun. The boys learning golf, at sunset hitting balls across the empty fairway. Scowling at bad shots. Ignoring well-meant advice: Keep your head down. Beaming at Grandpa's rare and moderate compliments. Pleased at something well hit, scourging each other with looks of triumph. I'm a better golfer.

I hate other people's young children, especially boys running down aisles at Wrigley Field or skateboarding down Clark Street. I hate mothers with two boys. Remembering driving back in the night after an evening at Sara's house, the boys wanting mother comfort in the back seat, and me glad to oblige, sitting between them with a head on either shoulder, the smell of those two thick beautiful heads of hair, and the feeling of being blanketed, of swimming in boy love.

I hate waking up, feeling something wrong and not knowing; then knowing. Passing the temple. Getting mail from the temple. Getting mail, usually a credit card offer, addressed to Jesse Silesky. His bank statement: quarterly earnings from his bar mitzvah money, $88.27. Finding old medical supplies: a needleless syringe or the red top to a syringe swept out from under the fridge. A prescription bottle for Diflucan, anti-fungal agent, 50 mg., (1) refill, never filled.

And what he said in the hospital as the nurse came in to irrigate his bleeding bladder: "Here's someone with another useless, pain-causing procedure."

I'd fight God if I believed in God. During a "bereavement weekend" at Camp Simcha, a feisty woman in my group said that she and He or She were going to have "a little chat" when she got to heaven. An Orthodox feminist. But my enemy is random chance, a guerillero, a spirit. Shrugs when you ask a question; dissolves when you raise your fist.

I hate the little box of memory. Contents depleting, fading. Or circling—coming back and back, a tightening, strangling rope around you.

ADVICE

Write what you can't remember.

I CAN'T REMEMBER

The play of expressions on his face, the sound of his voice. High, low? He's disappearing into his face in his photographs, tapes of his Torah portion, his piano recital (*Für Elise*). Oh, this is frightening. Wanda leaps onto the desk, lands silently, displacing nothing, sdfg,.l; walks across the keyboard. m,;p Down, girl. Wanda was Jesse's cat. Who's the cutest kitty in the world? Jesse said that. Or was it Seth? Sometimes I say it.

Is this enough? It's excruciating, memories fading even as I write them into words that don't call up the boy at all but just the fact of his absence. Alive in me only in the sear of each eroding image, mangy ravens cawing nevermore.

ADVICE

I'll bet there are things you're afraid to remember. That you don't want to remember.

I don't want to remember that a kid spat on him in pre-school. I'd just walked him in, a little late, stayed to watch him "integrate." He'd run smiling to the jungle gym on which the kid was perched. The teacher made the boy sit down at an empty table. He had an older brother, she tried to explain, who bullied him. I tried not to show her or Jesse how angry I was. And hurt. Hurt, even though Jesse's hurt was mostly surprise, and vanished as he climbed onto the jungle gym.

I don't want to remember Jake. He and Jesse were wrestling, and he bit Jesse's ear. Made it bleed. I still hate Jake, asshole Jake, not for the biting but for the fact that his mother wouldn't let him play with Jesse after that, as if Jesse had incited the violence.

I don't want to remember his voice the last three days of his life, high and breathy, not like him. But it didn't quit. Gallant soul, hardly the breath to speak, and talking, talking, opinions on politics; oh, what did he say that impressed the rabbi and cantor? I sat next to him in bed, facing the visitors and their delight and amusement, their relief at him so sharp and feisty. (He'd rebuked his surgeon for having voted for George Bush.) Don't give flowers in honor of Jesse, or money or cards; just tell me what you remember he said. It makes me ache and feel good at the same time, more root to this plant that will never bloom again, but what a plant! His unpredictable, earnest, witty, joyous, outraged, hurt, scared, terrified, loving, honest, searching ideas and feelings and declarations: "Mother, you're golden inside. Mother, I don't want to die because I don't want to be reincarnated in another family." (Looking me in the eye) "I don't want to have another mother." The afternoon I stopped making him eat mashed-up cloves of garlic (then what can I do? how can I make him well?) he kissed me. "Mom, you're being the good mother again." I still ground up taro root, mixed it with ginger as a poultice for his swollen belly. Sorry, Jess. I know it itches.

I don't want to remember the color of his urine in the tube that led from his bladder to a removable bag, hues from pale pink to bright blood red. Sometimes, between the clots, the liquid was pure golden yellow. A sign of hope, from which hope could be derived, wrung (yield continually lessening). I don't want to remember dumping the bag, rinsing it, red to pale pink to water clear. Or the words of the resident (discountable on account of his inexperience), "He'll be wearing a bag for the rest of his life." The two implications of which—neither do I want to remember.

His last morning he woke up with yellow eyes. I called the doctor. He's been jaundiced for a while. We've noticed that. Oh. Does that mean it's okay? Afraid to ask.

His leg, one of his legs, one only, was swollen. Raise it up, said the doctor. It's already raised. He's lying on the couch. Should I raise it higher? I rubbed his feet, both of them, not looking at his one meaty-looking thigh, massaging in the hospital hand lotion, the new pink squeeze bottle that came with each hospital stay.

His last night, in bed upstairs, he called down to me—"Mom?!" I ran up, led him to the bathroom. He'd pooped in his pants and Yay! Who cares! He'd been constipated. Now his stomach was flatter, his pain less. (Still weak, though. Still talking high and thin, breathing fast and shallow.) I said, "Jess, the pain is gone from your face. You must be feeling better. This is what we've been waiting for. This is the beginning of healing." Me feeling the very slight loosening that might become, if it lasted, relief. And tomorrow the acupuncturist . . . We hadn't tried acupuncture. And he (hoarse but himself), "Don't overdo it, Mom." That his second last speech, ever. His last, interrupting my flow of crazed murmurings, "Jesse the best and sweetest boy that I'll love forever, darling amazing personthing . . ."

"Shhh." He put his arms around me. How can he get well with arms like that? Not looking at his arms. "Good night, Mom."

I don't want to remember . . . But there's nothing I don't want to remember, or feel—not even the pain of the biggest loss, the knowing that what I know now of him is all I'll ever know. I won't see him falling in love, to be dazzled, hurt, and dazzled again. I won't see him furious, tender, amused at the antics of his children. Would he have worked to serve the world or give himself joy, or both? Would he have developed his precocious intimacy with the life of the spirit into something to sit in the shade of? How can I take in that I won't know this—witness, even tend a little—the beauty and wonder of his becoming? His absence, an unredeemable, unfillable hole in things.

MAGIC

As a child I wanted a doll with shiny red hair and eyes that opened and closed, and instead of asking, since the gift-giving holidays were over, I tried to obtain it through magic. At that point in my life, the wall between life and imagination was full of holes, and I, not fully but almost, believed that if I pictured something hard enough, it could materialize. So I called to mind, sharply, for a good span of time, both the doll and the exact place where the doll would be—on the floor in the den between a certain armchair and our television set. I was at school then, early afternoon. To further ensure the desired outcome, I performed an uncharacteristic and daring act, rising from my desk and circling it three times, unusual for me, normally shy and rule-abiding. (God knows what the teacher thought, if she saw me.) But I came home from school, my heart pounding with hope, and ran to the place where my new doll was supposed to be . . .

And I know, as sure as my eyes are tearing up again (yet again), that I'm writing to make the same magic. To conjure the object of my desiring. If I can sing like Orpheus, I'll get permission to retrieve him from the land of the dead.

I'm not afraid. Abracadabra. Open sesame. I want him back in my house, in his room, at the table eating food I've cooked, fighting with his brother, talking on the phone, drawing his teddy pictures, doing his homework or not doing it, even playing video games, which I discouraged, or upstairs asleep behind the protective wall of his stuffed animals. I can almost see him on the futon in his room, I'm looking in on him, kneeling to kiss his cheek, or maybe just standing there, breathing the air of his sleeping . . .

And feel an absence bigger than the empty place at the table. Get me to a nunnery. Or med school, where I can maybe learn enough to be part of something that might accomplish someday the magic that failed for us. Because—didn't I know before I started?—writing is always about loss, is always a failure, an attempt that must fail, to bring back what can't be brought back. This attempt to memorialize Jesse only points to a double loss. Says Jacques Derrida, "Language, unable to recreate the world, only points to its absence." Abracadabra? If words can't raise the dead, if they can't restore what—if goodness or justice had any sway in the scheme of things—would never have been lost, what's the point of them?

TRANSFORMATION?

At Camp Simcha the rabbi told us grieving parents to seek, in our grieving, a way to turn loss into something else. He didn't say what else. He did not mention "meaning"; I liked him for that. I think of Mother Jones, who lost her husband and children to yellow fever, then four years later her possessions to the Chicago fire; who spent the rest of her hundred-year life fighting for labor and child welfare.

We are fields cut down to be sown again.

I will not be sown! Acid hot, rocky and dry, I shrivel any seeds that flutter down here. I am so angry that words combust as they mount to my lips. Jesse, where are you? Jesse, do you hear me?! (I'm screaming) Jesse (he was always absent-minded, selectively deaf, upstairs reading or playing Quake), get down here this, this minute!!

BEYOND MEMOIR

A couple of weeks after he died, I dreamed about him. I'd been going to bed in hopes of a dream. Friends had mentioned clear sharp dreams of departed loved ones that were almost "visits." I wanted a visit. In my dream Jess was standing on a sunlit path alongside a house. A white house, nice house. He was smiling at me, a little uncertainly, but smiling. His hair had just started to grow back in little prickly dots all over his skull; the beginning, the return, again, of life. I walked toward him slowly, as if he were a half-wild animal, and stood before him. I didn't touch him. I was afraid he'd disappear. We stood facing each other, beaming at each other, with clear though tentative joy in each other's presence. And I wanted to say something encouraging, health-affirming, like "You look so well, honey," or "Your hair looks really great." But I was afraid to speak, as if something in my words or tone would destroy the frail magic of his presence.

Now I'm back where I started from. I stand before his image, straining, clawing for words, my link to other human beings and myself and sanity. But the words that come lack the essential unpredictability of Jesse, the shimmer that surrounded him that was in part his potential, the becoming he was in the process of. I'm locked in a room with no windows. I'm lost in the shadowy caverns of memory.

ADVICE

Why limit your writing to what you think actually happened? Embellish. Invent, lie, write fiction. A story that centers on Barry, whom you fault (still fault) for his self-indulgent optimism. Or give Barry's traits to the mother of the sick child; it's she who overlooks the problem's seriousness.

Or you can mimic the voice of your sister in Cleveland, who seems to have it all together but who you know is jealous of you; wouldn't that be fun? In invention lies shimmer!

You can even pretend to be Jesse.

"UNTITLED"

A soccer morning, cool and sunny. Seth is in the back seat with you, wanting to see your Game Boy. He lost his own and he'll probably lose yours, just put it down somewhere and leave it, or take it apart, or chew on it, leaving teeth marks. "No way, José!"

"You're not even playing it."

"So?" You put the Game Boy under your butt.

He kicks you. You feel it through your shin guards. "Quit that!"

"Quit what?"

He does it again. You know better than to kick back. He'll shriek, and Dad will blame both of you. But the terror Seth can conjure in you—Seth your twin, your second self— like how you feel in the middle of an escape dream in which your legs are weakening, too weak to keep running—has no outlet but violence. You bend your arm, jab in his direction, hard and sharp.

Even before your elbow bone hit flesh, you knew it was a mistake. Frozen, you watch blood gush from his nose. (You were aiming for his ribs; how did his face get in the way?) Blood drips from his chin onto his shirt. He shrieks, "He just killed me!"

"Shut up," you whisper, and hand him the game. He throws it on the floor.

"I'll give you my allowance."

He smears blood onto his hand, wipes it on your soccer shirt.

"Don't," you cry, glad for the retaliation." Cut it out, Seth!" The shirt is dark blue. The blood hardly shows. But you yell at your brother, for Dad to hear.

Dad drives faster, then pulls to a stop at a gas station. You think, by the stiff back of his neck, that he's going to grab you and Seth by your opposite ears: "Do you want me to knock both of your heads together?" A lame threat, but creepy. But he surprises you. He hands Seth a tissue and lets you climb in front. You and not Seth!

In front, though, in this comfortable seat that leans back, it's not as good as you expected. There's Seth behind you, kicking the back of your seat. You like sitting beside Dad, and you like your small victory over Seth, but Seth hates it; his hate burns the back of your neck. You turn, hoping that by the time your mouth opens you'll have words to fix things a little. He gives you the finger.

You watch the road. And then you remember: After the game you're going to the doctor. You won't be getting a shot, Dad said, but there are things Dad doesn't know; you've noticed that. You think of Mom, two hours away where she's just started teaching. For a second you wish she were here, though she's lots more nervous than Dad and sometimes makes you nervous. She came to your practice yesterday, and you ran at the ball and completely missed, and kids laughed and the coach said, "Earth to Jesse," which she had to have heard. Back home she made you walk up and down the sidewalk to see if something was wrong with your legs. But nothing was wrong with your legs. It's a little hard to breathe, maybe, but maybe not, maybe that's how breathing is. You don't see the point of this doctor appointment except to make Mom feel better. You close your eyes, recline against the seat back. In your mind kids are running around the soccer field in a million pointless directions, kicking balls, bumping into each other, falling down, and you far off away somewhere. It's a new perspective. A little scary.

I wrote this on the computer with my eyes closed, to get it down without experiencing it, like placing an aspirin tablet on the back of one's tongue. Could barely skim it for typos. But I think I see where it might go.

His last December in Florida, when Bubby yelled at Seth for driving the golf cart into the mailbox, Jesse shed tears for his brother. Jesse, so weak he was in and out of a wheelchair, accosted me, weeping. "Seth feels so bad." At the funeral, Jesse's cousin, who plans to become a rabbi, spoke of the progress of Jesse's soul that tormented but weirdly blessed final year, Jesse's gentleness and wisdom and humor and courage, "all of that on top of the wildness and wholeness of being and of personality and of spirit. . . ."

Jesse doesn't need to be a sage to make him merit remembrance. But illness was a fire that seemed to purify him. Can I look out from his brightening eyes? What can be seen?

Wanda's back on my lap with her ever polite retraction of claws. You're a sweet cat, Wanda, but I can't type with you here. I lift her to the ground. She jumps back up, and settles in the same place. Purrs aggressively. It buzzes my skin. Alive, alive-o.

So dim the lights. Bring up the background music, *Für Elise*, his last recital piece, played quick and competent, and him afterward suspicious of his teacher's praise combating his own shame at his two or three goofs. His face, screwed with self-disgust but eager to eat her cookies, laugh at someone, preparing to be happy again.

His beautiful, sad, smiling face.

California, Midwest

Michael Jordan's Lips

MAXINE CHERNOFF

In Chicago, where I was born and lived most of my adult life, people worship Michael Jordan beyond the adulation offered him in other cities. This includes people who in life have never spoken to a black person. Michael Jordan is king of what was once called the most segregated city on earth, a city which, judging from where black and white citizens stand waiting for buses and trains from work downtown to home, might well have a stated policy of apartheid. Yet when the new basketball stadium, United Center, was built, a poll revealed that most Chicagoans thought it should be named after Michael Jordan.

My twin sons, who had always attended scientifically integrated magnet schools in the city, who had friends named Hakeem and Tolu and Ryan and Amir, whose first sleepover party was at the home of a Nigerian child, were bewildered when my job took us to California, where we settled in a beautiful small town outside of San Francisco.

"Where are the black children?" Philip asked the first day of school as he surveyed playground demographics.

"Why, there's one over there," I said with some chagrin, noting that their city-trained eyes were pointing out a lack I hadn't calculated.

Their further displeasure with the first impression of their new surroundings was brought out in two different incidents. After a week at their excellent new neighborhood school, one boy said, "I didn't know kids can behave so bad."

"There weren't bad kids in your old school?"

"Today a kid swore at the teacher, Mom. He said the F word."

Elton had been famous in Chicago for using the F word in class.

About a week after we settled in, we attended an event at a bookstore in Oakland. Glancing down integrated College Avenue, my sons looked animated. "This looks like Chicago!" they both announced.

And they were right to a degree. Chicago is a city with a deep black culture, a city where you know that other people live, if not among you, alongside you. I recalled a time when my daughter, who attended an 85 percent black junior high program in Chicago's Hyde Park area, was invited to a graduation party aboard her friend's yacht. I drove her to the far South Side and left her at a house identical to ours in a neighborhood identical to our far North Side one except for the fact that it was all black and ours was mainly white.

When we first got to our mountainous, peaceful California village, I kept remarking to my children, "Isn't it beautiful?" I thought that the physical appeal of the hills and mountains and curving roads might serve as an antidote to all the personal miseries that moving had unleashed. I imagined the freedom they'd enjoy in a small town and the adventures they could have on bike and hiking paths that offered a new meaning to the word *vertical*. I thought the huge redwoods, California cypresses, and breathtaking vistas would offer solace to the boys, who missed so many things about their former home: their tire swing in the magnolia tree; their "forest," a small stand of trees between our yard and the neighbor's; their good friend B.J., the Korean proprietor of the local video store; their safe, completely horizontal bicycle path around the block.

"I like Chicago better," Julian protested. "I like pretty and ugly together."

Philip added to the chorus his disdain for the pastel stucco houses on the avenues of San Francisco. "Whose idea of beautiful is *this*?"

Julian is an excellent artist and for his classroom newspaper did a portrait of Michael Jordan, who had retired from basketball after his father's death. Jordan stood alongside Magic Johnson, and both men held their retired jerseys in their large, capable hands. We both agreed it was one of the best cartoons he had ever drawn before he took it off to class.

Several days later he said to me, "I made their lips smaller."

"What are you talking about?" I asked him.

"The principal told my teacher that maybe someone would be insulted by my drawing."

"And why would someone be?"

"Because someone might think I was making fun of Michael Jordan or Magic Johnson."

"Because of how you drew their lips?"

"I guess so," he shrugged.

Who would this someone be, I wondered to myself, while counting to ten and practicing controlled breathing. Who in our all-white enclave would protest the rendering of Michael Jordan's lips? And for what reason would he or she protest?

I looked at my son, who seemed unconcerned about the issue. I wondered what a confrontation with the principal of a new school might accomplish. I thought of all the places in our society where race is read and misread and longed for a place where a realistic portrait of black men wouldn't need to undergo social engineering. Where would that place be? Chicago? Oakland? Surely not my new village, which I hated very much at that moment.

This past Christmas we went back to Chicago to visit, and my sons spent an afternoon with the two Ryans, their best Chicago friends, one white, one black. So far beauty hasn't won out over reality. At the end of the trip, both said unequivocally, "I'm moving back to Chicago when I grow up."

Not From Here

ERIN McGRAW

> A person with a bad name is already half-hanged.
>
> —Proverb

Call it a family trait. My aunt Barbara, christened Imogene, changed her name when she was seventeen. Her sister Inez began with a different name too, but she changed it so early no one can recall the first one. Their brother, my father, struggled under Clarence Thomas, then got tired of his friends' teasing and went by Tom.

Terrence Thomas, my brother, briefly tried to follow my father's example, going through most of high school as Tom before reverting to Terry. At about the same time, in another stab at personal re-creation, he tried to train himself to be ambidextrous. He would take ten minutes to comb his hair or brush his teeth with his left hand, and his attempts to eat sent the butter dish skittering across the dinner table. I don't suppose he stayed with the experiment for more than a month or so, but in my memory he kept it up for years.

I admired his attempts, understanding even as a ten-year-old why a person would want to re-sculpt the clay of his identity. The whole business of personality preoccupied and troubled me. Everything I did, it seemed, served as a clue to other people that I was a certain sort of girl—tenderhearted because I liked animals, snooty because I liked ballet, rebellious because I liked John better than Paul or George. Choices apparently added up and told the world something about me. But I wanted to tell the world nothing.

I resented how freely relatives and neighbors claimed to know some "me" who always struck my private self as brassy and unsubtle. No sooner would an aunt predict that I would grow up to be a baker, since I had made cookies the last time she came to visit, than I would deliberately botch whatever was in the oven. To the neighbor who bought me a one-piece bathing suit, remembering how I'd criticized certain showy girls (we lived near the beach in southern California, and swimwear was a constant topic of conversation), I coldly said that I only wore bikinis. I'm embarrassed now at having been so surly with these kind women. But their assumptions made me feel trapped in a tiny box, and I couldn't stop myself from scrabbling back out.

The best way I knew myself was by negation: I was not who other people thought I was. And so I cheered my brother on as he spent hour after hour teaching himself to write with his left hand, just so he'd be able to startle his friends the day he casually took out his pen and signed his name with a back slant. Ha! his action would say. You thought you knew me so well. You don't know the first thing about me.

I lacked his obsessiveness, but not his impulse, and like my Aunt Barbara I waited until I was seventeen to make my move. Seventeen is an age for urgently trying out new identities, the last year to make changes before college, that portal of adulthood. Many kids I knew, people who had walked home by the exact same route for eight years, were rearranging their friends, their habits, their look. Over thirty of the girls in my high school class of six hundred elected to have rhinoplasty the summer before our senior year. They presented their pert new profiles at the beach a safe month after the surgery, when the bruising wasn't too noticeable.

Equipped with a nose that polite people have told me lends character to my face, I could have used rhinoplasty myself. And for a solid six months before my senior year, as my mother reminds me, I pestered my parents for the surgery. Just as they started to waver, I backed off. A change in appearance, especially one that would require general anesthesia, wasn't what I wanted. Surgery would only trade one concrete source of identity for another. I was secretly proud of my profile, which recalled Ethel Barrymore's. But still I felt the itch to step outside of myself, whatever myself was. And so, like my father and brother and particularly my aunts before me, I changed my name.

The procedure was surprisingly simple. I wrote to the Los Angeles County registrar for an affidavit to amend my birth certificate, adding a middle name where before none had existed. I went to my parents' bank and got the form notarized, unsure what "notarized" meant but proud of the word, which I worked into conversations for weeks. Then I sent the paperwork and ten dollars back to the registrar and left plain Susan McGraw, that contrary girl, stranded in 1974, little remembered and not much missed. Instead, I became a new thing, though no less contrary. S.E. McGraw. Erin.

If I had been able to read the poll of sexiest female names published a few years later in *Playboy*, I would probably have chosen differently, or not at all. Susan was ranked number three on the *Playboy* list, behind only Cheryl and Sandra—sibilant, insinuating names. Beside them Erin sounds ungainly. But in 1975 the poll wasn't out, and I didn't know anyone named Erin, and that was the point.

I knew a lot of girls named Susan. I'd gone through grade school with three of them, all, like me, diligent but not brilliant students, lousy at sports, nice girls who weren't invited to the best parties. Anything but centerfold material, no matter what *Playboy* said. So far, personally, I had seen nothing to recommend being a Susan.

Erin, on the other hand, had immediate attraction, not the least being its Hibernian lilt. Although "McGraw"—from, probably, the more forbiddingly Gaelic "McGraugh"—sounds Irish enough, my branch of the McGraws are a little shaky on their identity. My father's father's family emigrated from Donegal, in the north of Ireland—or possibly Cork, in the south; the stories vary—in the mid-nineteenth century. They settled in Michigan, then immediately fanned across the continent, resisting the pattern of some immigrants to cluster and cling to the traditions of the old country. The McGraws had gone to considerable trouble to relocate. The last thing any of them wanted to do was re-establish the impoverished, clannish selves they had left behind.

The other side of my father's family tree looks, at first glance, as if it might have been a little more attached to its Celtic roots. His mother's mother was actually named "Ireland." But her family, despite that name, had lived for generations in Lyons, a town located at the time of my grandmother's birth in Indian territory. Now it's in Kansas. If her forebears had ever come from Ireland, none of the family knew when, or cared. So my claim to Irish ancestry, all the leprechauns and toora-loora-looras that "Erin" suggests, was attenuated, though not quite inaccurate.

If I had wanted a cultural identity, I should have looked on the distaff side. My mother's parents emigrated from Croatia to Rock Springs, Wyoming in the 1920s. From the house where I grew up in southern California, my mother spoke in Croatian—she called it Slav—to her parents every week on the phone; I remember reading the comics while she talked to them, and feeling not the slightest bit of curiosity about what she might be saying, even when I heard her say my name. ("Ja, ja, Susie—" and then the pretty, incomprehensible jabber. I assumed she was telling them that I was fine. I was always fine.) I didn't wonder about my mother's story, or ponder what might have pushed her to quit the immigrant, coal-mining town that she knew, and come instead to a split-level house with a husband who couldn't pronounce his mother-in-law's maiden name.

Her parents were real immigrants, making their own wine and curing their own garlicky sausages, re-creating their Croatian lives in a community so saturated with other émigrés that when I visited for a resentful week every summer, I could walk four blocks without hearing English spoken. I didn't think about the fact that my mother hadn't taught me to speak Croatian, although it had been her first language.

Taking her subtle cue, I held that potent, valid heritage at arm's length. The foreignness was too raw for me, something that could smother me against its garlicky bosom. Besides, what child in the 1960s had ever heard of Yugoslavia? The Balkans had no cachet then. Posing on the narrow stage of my last name, I pronounced myself Irish.

It wasn't hard. I'm scarcely the first person to notice that a broad, sentimental sympathy for Ireland exists in this country, anchored on one end with St. Patrick's Day pub crawls and on the other with *Riverdance*. To that sympathy I attached myself like a barnacle. Although my family knew virtually nothing about Irish history, I somehow knew about the legendary leader Brian Boru. Although for years I pronounced Yeats to rhyme with Keats, I could recite all of "The Lake Isle of Inisfree." And although we had no Irish records, my family still knew "Danny Boy," that cliché of Irish clichés that still makes my throat tighten, even though the tune is hackneyed and probably inauthentic. If "Danny Boy" happened to come on the radio or TV, we all, even my mother, stopped to listen. I didn't have to look to know that my father's eyes shone with a film of tears. "Danny Boy" was our secular hymn, a filament tying us to a past that had no tangible claim on our lives.

In precisely this spirit did I embrace shamrocky "Erin McGraw." I liked its hint of the brogue, its suggestion of fey humor and a certain wildness at the core. I encouraged in myself behavior I thought of as Yeatsian—including, I am embarrassed to admit, a fling with automatic writing. I was big on republicanism. Never having stepped foot in the country, I didn't think about Ireland's chronic unemployment, nationalist defeatism, or alcohol dependence. I made an Ireland to suit myself. Why not? I had already made a name to suit myself, and that seemed to be going all right.

> A true man never frets about his place in the world,
> but just slides into it by the gravitation of his nature,
> and swings there as easily as a star.
>
> —E. H. Chapin

It's probably just as well that at seventeen I didn't realize that by fiddling with my identity I was clinging more firmly than ever to my roots—following the custom not only of my family, but of my native place. Like my father, I was born and raised in Redondo Beach, California, a suburb southwest of Los Angeles. This fact is a point of pride for me, since proportionally few inhabitants of southern California were born in the same town where they grew up, and far fewer can boast a family line that stretches all the way back to 1920.

In most areas, to have a family history and lineage tied to a specific place connotes something in terms of personality or values or habits. Regional stereotypes still have currency—the laconic Vermont farmer, the chatty Mississippi hairdresser, the hearty Texan. But the traditional Californian is harder to figure, since the traditional Californian tends to be someone who started out as a laconic Vermonter or hearty Texan, somebody who left the home place in order to start again. Since 1960, when the immense wave of ex-GI's coming to California for aerospace jobs petered out, most of the state's newcomers have hailed from Mexico or Central America or Asia, but the pattern holds. The regional trait that identifies Californians is the sense of possibility, that life is infinitely renewable, that the past can be shed as if it were a coat.

My paternal grandfather, the first Clarence McGraw, was the sort of ambitious, restless man who populated the state. A high-school dropout from Michigan, Clarence wound up in Los Angeles building cracking plants for Western Oil and Refinery, one of the dozens of start-up oil companies that were making overnight millionaires in the 1910s and '20s, though my grandfather wasn't one of them. Still, it was not Clarence but his wife, my grandmother Bess, who set the bar for creating a new identity.

Bess outlived Clarence by twenty years, and I remember her clearly—an impatient woman of needle-sharp intelligence who did not pretend any interest in topics that bored her. Medicine, my father's profession, bored her. Neighborhood gossip bored her. Children bored her profoundly, and she would only pay attention to me if I would converse at an adult level. For her clear belief that I could be a grown-up if I would just try, I adored her.

On summer mornings when she visited, we watched TV game shows together. I tried to impress her, watching *Jeopardy!* without complaint, calling out answers on the rare occasions I could, usually a U.S. president. She accepted these contributions without comment. From her side of the couch she burned through the other categories—politics, fashion, even great books, although my father claimed he'd never seen her with a book in her hand. She kept track of her winnings in her head and smoked ten cigarettes in half an hour, looking with scorn at the TV contestants whom she outscored. At the end of the program she told me how much she would have earned. Usually she came in close to the winning contestant. I think her scores were honest. "People come on the show without knowing anything. To play this game you have to *know* something," she said.

It's easy to imagine how such a restless brain must have been frustrated by the long, blank horizons of her Indian Territory home place, where there was no library, and no schooling past age twelve. Lyons was pure prairie—sidelined, barely inhabited, as peripheral to both the coast and the heartland as some ancillary artery. Easy country to forget, if a person didn't happen to live there.

Like a lot of impulsive girls of her time, Bess married when she was fifteen, to get away from a father who slapped her around when he was in his cups. She married the first man who asked, a Mr. King. Too late she discovered that he also would slap her around when he was in his cups. By the time she was seventeen, that fraught age, she found herself the mother of two daughters, more thoroughly chained in place than ever.

Anyone who has read Kate Chopin's *The Awakening* knows all about women trapped by expectation and circumstance. But apparently nobody told Bess Cates, now Bess King, that she was supposed to feel trapped. One day she dressed the girls and took them over to her mother's house, asking her mother to look after them for a little while. Then she went into town, bought a train ticket to Portland, Oregon, and headed west on the Union Pacific. Who knows where she got the money. The porter needed to help her up onto the train, she told me—the hobble skirts fashionable then didn't allow a stride wide enough to manage the steep train steps.

Onto the train was handed Bess King, wife and mother of two. Off the train came Bess King, single gal. I like to imagine that she debarked *looking* new, though I know that long train journeys around 1900 didn't leave passengers rejuvenated. But she was new now, fresh, having thrown off the weight of her short lifetime's bad decisions. Who knows? Maybe she cut her hair on that train, or smoked her first cigarette. I'm free to invent, since at this point the narrative becomes fuzzy. Maybe Bess had relatives in Portland, maybe she didn't. Maybe she stayed in a genteel boarding house, or a not-so-genteel one. We know for sure that she didn't contact her family or tell her little girls where their mother was. She meant to cut her ties for good.

My mother is always appalled by this part of the story; she can't bring herself even to imagine a mother who would leave her children, especially with a father who drank himself into violence. And of course my mother is right. Still, I see my grandmother's ruthlessness as a kind of courage. Having decided to start afresh, she did the job right. No one knows if she was ever overcome with homesickness, or dread, or the hunger to smell her young daughters' hair. She knew that a decision, if it's going to mean anything, must be kept. A large part of whatever made up my grandmother was steel.

We assume she supported herself in Portland as a seamstress, because by the time she made it down to Los Angeles—following what man, or hunch, or new name?—her skill as a needlewoman gained her a job in the alterations department of the Tony I. Magnin department store. Her skill with quick conversation and unstated promises gained her a new husband, Clarence, the up-and-comer with Western Oil and Refinery. With him she made a fine new family, featuring a daughter, Katherine—who actually remained Katherine her whole life, a McGraw record—and a son, Clarence Thomas Junior, called Tommy.

My mother and I often speculate just what kind of scene ensued ten years later, in the mid-1920s, when first Barbara (née Imogene) and then Inez (née something) materialized on the front porch and called Bess "Mother." When Clarence came home that night, did she sit him down on the couch and say, "Dear, there's something I've been meaning to tell you"? No one knows or remembers, and Bess and Clarence's marriage went on, with who knows what kind of resentments or paybacks. There was drinking. We do know that.

Their life may not have been perfect, but it wasn't Dickensian, either. Bess did not fling herself into the Pacific Ocean when her past came and rang her doorbell. She was *changed*, and her children got changed right along with her. Leaving behind their prairie roots, Barbara and Inez had careers as starlets in the 1930s, with Barbara memorably performing in the immense chorus of "Barbaric Rhythm" at the Paramount Theater, where she wore a few feathers and a pair of shoes. Inez, who could sing, was billed as "The Songbird of the Southland," a title that suggested, in typical Hollywood fashion, banjos and magnolias but literally meant the freeways, oil derricks, and tar pits of Los Angeles.

And Bess? She played the organ at her church, and as president of the Altar Society oversaw the laundering of altar cloths, a task that took two days every week, stretching and ironing the long linens across the length of the living room so they would hang without a crease on Sunday mornings. She was a member in good standing of the Redondo Beach Women's Club. She had become a respectable matron, a role she would never have attained back in Lyons, with Mr. King. And if it was a life that her flapper daughters would look at and mock, if rebellious Bess had come all the way to California in order to create the exact repressed, status-conscious life that many people fled the Midwest to escape, so what? We go where we have to in order to grasp happiness, a truth any Californian could tell you.

To be happy at home is the ultimate aim of all ambition;
the end to which every enterprise and labor tends, and
of which every desire prompts the prosecution.

—Dr. Johnson

All my life Californians have told me, "You don't seem like you're from here."
Even as a girl, I understood the accuracy of this statement. Something in the
agreed-upon identity of Californians—their sheen, their ripeness—eluded me, and
that suited me fine: I would rather be elusive than shining. I can get a good tan if
I want to, and I have a Californian's sense of the informality of public spaces; I'll
walk down a sidewalk in a bathing suit and flip-flops unless my husband stops me.
But still I don't feel at home in my home state.

I didn't comprehend my sense of out-of-placeness until I moved away. How
could I? If I'd thought about it, I would have assumed that everyone lived in a state
of tension with his or her home culture, always fending off people's insinuating familiarity, always finding ways to repudiate their assumptions of intimacy. Then I
came to Indiana.

I was twenty-three, and moved to Bloomington with my first husband to attend
graduate school. "Just wait till you see how people cluster around you at those California cocktail parties when you tell them where you're going," said my Indiana-
born friend Jeanne. Herself, she was moving to Hawaii.

I had no expectation of staying in the Midwest longer than I would need to get
my master's degree. While I didn't scorn the flyover zone, I didn't feel any pull to
live there, either. Life in the states from Pennsylvania to Colorado was one more
thing I'd never thought about, aside from watching presidential election returns
and making the occasional dim remark about America's Bread Basket, which I understood to exist in the Midwest someplace. It was a region that didn't seem to require thought. Had I been paying attention, I would have understood that to be
an attraction.

Although I had lived out of the country for a year as a college exchange student,
I'd never lived in a different state before, and at first I found the experience un-
nerving. Hoosiers didn't display the casual Californian sense of familiarity with
one another, but they shared with one another similar habits and turns of speech—
"Hello, dear," said sales clerks in the first four stores I entered. When a woman in
the office where I got a job broke her leg, all of her co-workers except me dropped
by her house the next day with casseroles and coffee cake. I still don't know how
they found out her address. They all seemed to be operating out of the same rules,
and because I didn't know what those rules were, I felt nervous and exposed.

I talked to people shyly, trying not to reveal my ignorance of the local customs,
but every time I stepped out the door I stumbled on something else I didn't know:
How the movie *Breaking Away* wasn't just about the annual bicycle race in Bloomington, but about the still fierce town–gown clash in the community; how college
professors scheduled exams around the NCAA Final Four but ignored the Oscars;
how I could not buy liquor on Sundays, an astonishment. The fourth or fifth Sun-

day that the same cashier at the grocery store plucked a bottle of wine from my broccoli and pork chops and set it behind the cash register, she said amiably, "You're just not right with this, are you? Where you from, dear?"

"California." My voice was an embarrassed croak, but at least nobody was behind me in line to witness my dunderheadedness.

"That explains it," she said, while the cashier at the next station looked over and said, "Huh. You don't seem like you're from California."

"Not everybody there looks like a beach bunny," I said.

"My cousin married a Polish gal. You look kind of like her."

"A lot of Poles in California," I said. "A lot of everybody."

"See, now I wouldn't like that," she said. "I don't like being around too many people."

"Me, neither," I said.

"Well, you should like it here," she said. "Don't worry about the wine. We'll look after you."

I left the grocery store with a light heart. The cashiers had offered me a new status: a transplant, whose definition was Not From Here. Any expectations about attitudes or behaviors could slide off me like oil. My actions, my opinions, my choices in food and pets and administrative representation didn't have to add up to anything—who could expect consistency from someone Not From Here? I understood that I was, in a sense, being written off, but I didn't mind that. What I loved was not being written in the first place.

I started paying attention to this place that I was not from. Like California, it had a car culture, but unlike California, which loved snug, sleek German and Italian cars, Indiana was all about Firebirds, Corvettes, Trans Ams—American models that were brawny and loud. They tore around the downtown square on summer nights, and people complained, but their complaints were indulgent. Race Day, the Indianapolis 500, was practically a state holiday.

At the local truck stop, I noted food as if I were an anthropologist, studying the immense pork tenderloin sandwiches, with their bubbled, deep-fried meat lolling over the edges of the bread, and the Big Red soda pop, advertised on billboards with the slogan It Just Tastes Red. "That about says it all, don't it?" said my neighbor, with an irony so profound it took me a while to recognize it. Once I did, I parroted him like crazy.

Parroting was harder than it sounded. The Hoosier accent is complex, inflected with the Appalachian sing-song that floats up from Kentucky to the south, but broadened in the Midwestern fashion—"pie" is neither "pah" nor "pah-ee," but something in between. I practiced, trying to get the distinctions. "Catawpa" for "catalpa." "Murder" for "murderer." I got to hear that one in my first year because the local newspaper, the Bloomington *Herald-Telephone*, was covering the trial of a woman who had killed her abusive husband by dropping a bowling ball on his head several times. Years later, on a trip back to California, I related this story to a journalist friend, thinking she would appreciate the bowling-ball details. "*The Herald-Telephone?*" she kept saying. "*The Herald-**Telephone**?*"

"That's not the important part," I said irritably.

I didn't understand yet what was happening to me. Having little experience with them, I didn't recognize feelings of ease and expansiveness, of fundamental comfort. What I did recognize was the new sense of spaciousness that surrounded me, and I responded to it by giving over my heart. To anyone who would listen, I defended the breaded tenderloin sandwiches, the strongly Republican politics, the culture—insular, yes, and self-protective, yes, but quick to see and respond to people's needs. Hoosiers, I said, knew how to demonstrate a personal interest without being intrusive. This was real sophistication, as opposed to the brittleness of fast-paced coastal culture.

Then and now, people who grew up in the Midwest hoot at me when I try to express these feelings. They tell anecdotes about how every gesture they make reminds family members of aunts and grandfathers, sometimes dead for generations, and how every word out of their mouths betrays one side of the family or the other. From birth they are scrutinized, classified, and categorized, and once they've been assigned a category, they are expected to stay there. "Why are you acting like your mama?" one friend of mine was told when she was a child. "That's your sister. You're your daddy's child." I understood her frustration and sense of enclosure, and understood why she wanted to go to New York, where no one knew her. But those rules don't apply to me.

At the same time that I was falling in love with Indiana, my first husband, a Minnesotan who had moved to California as a teenager and promptly cathected on the West Coast, was not. He was taking courses toward his MBA, and came home from his first midterm enraged. The professor, meaning to give the students an easy question, had posed a statistical breakdown involving the likelihood of a loss of temper by incendiary basketball coach Bob Knight. But in our first few months in the Midwest, my first husband and I had never heard of Bob Knight, a fact that brought gales of laughter from our neighbors—as it would now, from me. Never heard of Coach Knight? Never *heard* of Coach Knight? Where are you from, anyway?

At the time we thought it meant something about us—something to be proud of—that we didn't know the name of the basketball coach. And it did, of course. It meant that we thought it was important for our lives to mean something, whatever that meant. Our tastes and choices and impulses were part of an elaborate fabric of signification—not simply being indifferent to basketball, but being *the kind of people* who were indifferent to basketball. It took my first husband and me a while to figure out that our new friends and neighbors could give a rip about our fabric. He, disturbed by the dimensionless quality of such a life, went back to California. Feeling as if I had been set free, I stayed.

> Who hath not owned, with rapture-smitten frame,
> the power of grace, the magic of a name.
> —William Cowper

To live the life I wanted, I came to the Midwest from California. My grandmother did just the opposite, but I like to think that we were responding to the same impulse. As far as I'm concerned, I'm carrying out her legacy.

I was well into my twenties before I assembled the details I'd heard over the years about her young life and my aunts, and started to comprehend the story that had never exactly been told to my brother and me. It's hardly surprising that my parents never sat us down and said, "Children, your grandmother was a bigamist." But the part of her history that catches my interest isn't the husband left behind in Kansas, the one who seemed to care as little for her as she for him—from the evidence, he never troubled himself to look for her. What I weigh is how thoroughly she walked out on her past and gave herself a new beginning. The move was amoral, to say the least, but it still seems a little bit wonderful.

Like many Californians, I'm more in love with my future than my past. I have a hunger for fresh starts, and when I say "fresh," I mean "total." I don't gain a pleasing sense of connectedness when I think about my history, the little mistakes and little triumphs that have taken me to where I now stand. I still squirm about the day that I, age five, caught my brother's goldfish between my fat fingers and plucked its fins off. Terry wailed when he found his dead pet floating in the fishbowl, and my mother told me, "You won't get punished so long as you tell the truth."

"He must have tried to jump out," I said. The plucked fins, dried now to tiny transparent chips, were scattered around the fishbowl, and it occurred to me that I should have gotten rid of them. "I guess he wanted to get out of where he was." Five years old, and already the most plausible rationale I could imagine was the desire to start afresh.

Since I came to Indiana, I have relished the contrariness of the move—Frederick Jackson Turner had assured us all that populations moved *to* California *from* the Midwest—and the neatness of the pattern. Moving, the quintessential California act of reinvention, has taken me away from California.

I relish also the retrograde fashion factor. By any known scale, it is cooler to live in California than in Columbus, Ohio, where I have finally settled, close to my beloved Indiana. But any Californian can tell you that the coolest thing of all is to embrace that which had heretofore looked nerdy. With the smallest, most superior smile I can indicate that California coolness is *over*. And if you don't see the point of the Midwest—well, never mind. If you have to ask, you'll never get it.

The attitude isn't all an act. To the bemusement of my family, I derive unforced pleasure from my garden, from talking about the weather with my neighbors, from watching the dismal careers of the Bengals and Browns, Ohio's disastrous NFL franchises. Not only do these little acts provide pleasure, they give me comfort— the assurance of a reliable context. I can join in on things if I want, but nothing will be expected. *Nothing is expected.* If this isn't liberation, what is?

People don't so often say now, "You don't seem like you're from California." Instead they say, "You seem like you're from here," and it's a measure of how much I have changed that I take this as a compliment. But I'm still a McGraw woman, and sometimes when I make out tax or motor vehicle checks to the State of Ohio I can make out my aunt Barbara's stout figure, Aunt Inez's sweet smile, perhaps sniff out a whiff of my grandmother's cigarette.

My brother doesn't think I need to sever my California ties so completely. "You can have it all," he is fond of telling me, a sentiment that is Californian to the core. But he tried living in the Midwest—his youngest son was born in Cincinnati. After a few years the old restlessness seeped up in him, the yearning for a life that was different, and like his grandmother he took off for Portland, the place where middle-aged professionals such as he now go when they want to re-make their lives. When I mention Cincinnati to him, he looks pained.

I go back to California to see my parents, but not once have I returned for a high school or college reunion, not once sent anything but regrets and a present in response to wedding invitations. When my mother asks, in frustration, if I'm not even curious about my old chums, I answer her honestly: No. Those people knew someone named Sue, and Sue has been gone for years.

Displaced

CRIS MAZZA

On a snowy January evening in Elmhurst, a far western suburb of Chicago, I watched an A&E documentary called *California and the Dream Seekers*. But I didn't need to be reminded that the world reflects on California from the perspective of those who have yearned to be there. California's history is a linear succession of great migrations: conquistadors and Franciscan missionaries, gold-rush prospectors, Chinese laborers escaping their country's exhausted resources, Midwestern dust bowl farmers fleeing both environmental and financial ruin, movie star pipe-dreamers, and contemporary migrant agricultural workers. The state's growth into a region with the world's eighth-largest economy is credited to those and other pilgrim castle-builders who came to it as a place of unbounded possibilities. Over nearly a century and a half, hundreds of thousands of people elected to turn toward California for what they wanted or who they aspired to be.

But what of those who were born there? Jostling for space with the transplants and snowbirds and immigrants and "zonies" (a special word for those escaping Arizona's heat), we haven't really known a *wow-look-where-I-am* wonderment, an *I'm-lucky-to-be-here* glow. We're there because we've always been there. Media's depiction of the place may engulf or dupe us; but for many natives, it does not. We scoff at, even rebel against the notion of California as land of the ocean-view condo, land of the forever-young Coppertone beachbaby, land of the year-round after-work buffed-out executive surfer, land of the sunglassed convertible-driving blond aerobics instructor, land of the cult-of-the-month, of palm-treed boulevards made just for rollerbladers, of psychedelic black-lit drug parties begun in the '60s that have never ended, of drive-in churches and drive-through espresso bars, of crystalline blue cloudless skies sailed everlastingly by a hang-glider (and his dog), a vegetarian restaurant on every block, a guru on every corner, a Lana Turner on every drugstore stool. But if we didn't *choose* this enchanted place to live out or chase our visions, if we are a generation or two removed from those that dared to hunt a dream, does it mean we *don't* dream? Or don't have the same quality of dream? Or don't have the same fortitude because we're not *required* to uproot and resettle in this unique region in order to help make our dreams possible? Does it mean California, either the real or the fanciful, doesn't influence or put its distinct mythic stamp on our dreams—and on who we become?

In August 1993, a moving van left a small postwar slab house in East San Diego, followed by my white Mazda pickup, its aluminum shell packed to the roof. I was moving to Illinois. My fourth book of fiction had just been released, and I'd accepted a position as an assistant professor at the University of Illinois at Chicago.

I'd left California before, always for temporary stints, for a second graduate degree in Brooklyn, as a writer-in-residence in Tennessee and then Pennsylvania. At one time the reasons for these ventures, including the latest, had caused a bitter sentiment for my own state: Off to Brooklyn because, advisors told me, I couldn't be well-rounded if my education was concentrated in Southern California. To Tennessee and Pennsylvania and now Illinois because California had become so accustomed to being the aspired-for destination of so many, the state had developed a sweeping attitude that jobs could be filled with the highest-caliber candidate only when *not* filled by a native. "No man can be a prophet in his own land," someone advised, and it seemed especially true of California. It looked as if one had to either be educated elsewhere and/or gain experience elsewhere before expecting to come home and be given credit for accomplishments. Or just *go* elsewhere. Southern California and San Diego in particular—beneficiaries (or victims) of a literal flood of "new blood" that hasn't abated since the Depression—didn't give me a second look. There were so many exotic non-locals to choose from! But should my bitterness have been aimed at California, or the *people* who'd moved there, *then* turned it into their icon of Land of Banished Free-Thinkers-from-Elsewhere? Wasn't there another California that had, after all, given me a more subtle and priceless endowment?

Free-thinkers-from-elsewhere. Hadn't another population of indigenous people endured this kind of guest (who never went home)? I recall hearing of the Native Americans who once populated San Diego County as culturally uninspiring, "merely" nomadic gatherers without the imagination of more sublime native peoples who built pueblos or hunted bison. Was a new breed of "natives" now doomed to carry this mantle as well—had each passing generation's energy and hope and inspiration somehow been diluted? I don't know how this perception of the original people of California came about, but I can guess: it seemed the natives docilely accepted the new order imposed by Franciscan missionaries, became virtual slaves in the mission compounds, and, except for minor uprisings and skirmishes, were basically easily subjugated. Simply put, the native people didn't have an organized enough society to wage a *war*. Thus they have been generally regarded as fundamentally uninteresting, and were even classified as such by European anthropologists of the era.

When I arrived at Brooklyn College in the early '80s, a fellow student, upon hearing I was from California, responded: "Oh, California? Isn't everything really *laid-back* there?"

Laid-back? Of course I'd heard the term. But I had never been asked to apply it to myself or my experience, or even to give a particular example of its manifestation. *Laid-back:* chill-out, mellow-out, everything's-cool, go-with-the-flow, whatever-makes-you-happy, have-a-nice-day, find-yourself, get-in-touch-with-the-inner-child, take-it-easy, I'd-rather-be-surfing, hey-dude-whatever. Did my life fit on a bumper sticker? Was it laid-back to plug my ears during the detonation of the shotgun but keep my eyes trained on the falling bird so I could retrieve it, decapitate it, and drain the blood? To take away the hammer and hand my father the knife after he'd cracked a rabbit's skull? To throw not just balls, but sticks by the thousands and even rocks into the tumbleweedy, foxtail-filled canyon to be retrieved by a pedigreed dog whose ancestors had strutted in dog show rings? To spend teenaged afternoons marching with a trombone under an oppressive glare of sunshine, and spend teenaged weekends doing the same in full-dress wool uniform being judged on musical and military precision? To participate in family outings gathering the rejects of a farmer's harvest that's been dumped behind the trucking docks? To earn minimum wage spoonfeeding pureed spinach into a profoundly handicapped imbecile's mouth after you've changed his diapers? To hike miles up and down a Sierra creek bed with a rod and reel, engrossed body-and-mind solely in a contest with wily native trout? To watch one's husband, dressed in white tie and black tails, pace in a picket line outside Symphony Hall? To see the clear ripples of heat in the air, watch the rain of ashes, and stand in the current of fleeing grasshoppers as the yearly brushfire thunders up the hill toward our property line? To have one's grandmother drown in a swimming pool? To sit like a stone during sex therapy while a charlatan pigeonholes you as a puritan? To time and again attempt to make pets of lizards, crawdads, snakes, frogs, tortoises, horned toads, and other indigenous things that slithered through seasonal run-off creeks or crawled through the brush of the arid coastal scrub which the rest of the world doesn't seem to know *isn't* a lush, palm-treed tropical paradise?

I was, at first, dismayed that my state citizenship had been called to the test, and that I would fail, right out of the gate, to *really* be what the world seemed to hold so dear: a Californian.

I would evolve to realize that my non-laid-back experience has, in fact, been a variation of—my particular rendition of—the real thing.

During the 1998 World Series between San Diego and New York, the predictable scorn reined forth from the "superior" metropolis toward the one on the West Coast. New York newspaper columnists alleged that San Diego has no image and has nothing to offer but weather. They claimed that everyone except New Yorkers shops only in malls and considers Denny's to be fine dining, that everyone except New Yorkers smiles too much, and that San Diego doesn't even have enough infamy to make the city interesting or the citizens "smart." At once boasting of New York's diversity, then slamming a place that chooses to neither compete with nor emulate it. One columnist spoke of *our* jealousy that we don't live in New York. Don't bullies pick on other kids because they themselves feel uncertain? Would a truly superior place speak with such venom against another if it didn't feel some insecurity?

Moving to Chicago in 1993, I was not-too-obliquely informed that displaced Californians are presumed to be ashamed of where we've come from, and should only admit to missing the weather. During my interview, I was asked if I would "be able to" leave San Diego's weather. Eight months later, at a department reception during the first week of my first semester in Chicago, a senior member of my department sidled up to me to make introductory small talk. She politely asked where I'd chosen to live. With only slightly guarded verve, I informed her that I'd found a one-bedroom cottage with a big yard in Elmhurst, eighteen miles west of the loop.

"Why *there?*" she responded, not bothering or unable to conceal her disgust, "there's nothing *there* you couldn't find in *Southern California.*"

OUCH . . . in one breath she'd cast aspersions on not only where I'm now living but where I came from as well. Long after my stammered response (something about my dogs needing space), I realized that this person, who obviously had the stock intellectual's intolerant view of Chicago's suburbs, had an even dimmer stereotyped opinion of Southern California. Looking askance at the suburbs might come naturally for an academic in Chicago, but where might her view of California have come from? What sources *are* there except inane TV shows, magazines, and slick popular novels that depict Southern California as either a witless wasteland or a vast tract of bland white middle class with no deeper thought than what color stucco should houses in the community be made of, and no nobler pursuit than getting a tan during lunch hours? If this college professor seemed to actually hold pop media's shallow view, what does it reveal about *her* and all the tens of thousands like her: what must *she* have been reading or watching in order to *develop* such a view?

This attitude continues to be displayed in my presence. At a meeting where the business at hand was devising a flier to promote the department, someone described a circular they'd received from the University of California at Santa Barbara. Not only was it a slick, four-color brochure, but it dared to contain photographs of the coast. This information immediately won scoffs and laughter from several of the professors around the table, as well as a comment that Santa Barbara's faculty was likely out surfing. Our discussion, meanwhile, had determined that our brochure should show some kind of cityscape, to promote the fact that the university is in Chicago. There is no doubt that the city of Chicago with all its resources is one of the advantages of an education at the University of Illinois at Chicago. But why is admitting (or promoting) that your university exists in a coastal landscape automatically denotative of low intellect while a cityscape is indicative of important serious thought? Perhaps we should consider that the existence of the coastline so near the University of California speaks highly of its scholars' intellectual abilities, if they don't need to be locked inside a winter-bound city of concrete, steel, and glass in order to produce music, art, literature, scientific breakthroughs, or academic research of the same caliber as work completed in Chicago.

What indeed does Southern California possess that isn't found in greater Chicago and/or could be worthy of notice by an educated person—and could I possibly miss anything other than the weather? That's how shallow Californians presumably are: *Oh, dude, where's my sunshine?* (Admittedly a small sampling, but among the people I know, the only "California-beachy" types are non-natives.) So I must be just slightly more profound than that mythical Californian. Among the things I miss are canyons, hills, bluffs, and mountains, a soft tawny color most of the year, until days after a rainfall when a tint of fuzzy green begins to pervade, then overwhelms the brown. I miss the sharp scent and graceful silhouette of eucalyptus trees and the midnight caterwaul of a coyote pack making a kill. I miss ranch houses with walls of picture windows overlooking valleys or canyons or with views of hazy hills. I miss college campuses and museums built in red-roofed Spanish-style architecture, the dry furor of Santa Ana winds, and the zinging white streak over green grass of another Tony Gwynn opposite-field single.

Many of Chicago's suburbs, mine included, have maintained a small-town charm, with tree-lined streets, a town square, and storefront village shops—hardware, bakery, bookstore, jeweler, drugstore, shoe repair, library, town museum, and more. The suburbs shoulder the burden of their negative reputation among the city's "intellectuals"—called yuppie sprawl or plastic mommyhoods—by ignoring it. If I were in charge of boosting the image of these boroughs, I would eliminate the word *suburb* from colloquial speech. In San Diego, probably in all of Southern California, the vernacular doesn't use the word *suburbs*. In the city's vast geological area (in square mileage, San Diego has 320 to Chicago's 228), there are, as in Chicago, *neighborhoods*. The regions within the metropolitan area, but outside the city limits, are referred to as *North County, East County,* and the *South Bay,* even though it's all one big county. The word *county* in these cases is like *country,* a place you used to be able to keep livestock and poultry, even slaughter your own domestic rabbits in the back yard. At least until the little municipalities in the county began incorporating themselves into cities.

Of course I love my home state. But I love a different state than the image-hologramed place I left. And a different state than the one now being covered on every available flat place, and some not so flat, with big boxy houses, nearly shoulder to shoulder, or condos crusted like barnacles on sandstone bluffs. My feelings are for the state whose indigenous people were "a disappointment" because they didn't declare war over proprietorship of the fragile yet durable landscape. The state where you might have to go outside to get warm in December because the night's chill has refrigerated little slab houses without central heat. A state whose seasons are named *fire* and *rain.* The state in which there are parcels of land that were originally a "throw-in" free offer for anyone who bought a dictionary or encyclopedia from a Depression-era door-to-door salesman somewhere in the East. A place where the real value is a little harder to see.

A&E's *California and the Dream Seekers* said California is best represented and characterized by visionaries who had the boldness, vigor, and imagination to pioneer what would become great industries, great movements, great development, or just greatness. But that idea only seems to consider what it meant, fifty to two hundred years ago, to *become* a Californian or for California to *become* what the world thinks it is. And, of course, there's even a substantial amount of truth— truth that admittedly feels good—in the observation that no other place on earth has inspired so many different migrations of people seeking a better life, so maybe there's something to the Conquistador legend that said there was no other alloy there but gold.

For those of us who didn't have to *become* but *are*, understanding the state is not a task of expressing enough aggrandizement, but of locating the words at all, a delicate endeavor to extract the state *we* know from the romance and hoopla. Perhaps the indigenous people, overwhelmed with the pomposity of the Spanish explorers and missionaries, would agree.

I can't begrudge California to those who sought it as a source of hope, as the last romance of the last western frontier, or simply for its unrivaled resources, from agriculture to precious metals to recreation. After all, if my parents hadn't come— one with a family reeling from the Depression, the other as an implicit gesture of postwar personal independence for women—I wouldn't've been one of the fortunate, one of the upshots of someone's flight of fancy: to be born there.

But like those who have left hometowns and home states and now call themselves Californians—those who sit in the stadium in San Diego and cheer for the Chicago Cubs or New York Mets; those who dock their sailboats at Quivera Basin, De Anza Cove, or Shelter Island and send yearly contributions to orchestras or museums back east, tsk-tsking the bankruptcy of the symphony in San Diego— like *their* life-long allegiances to other "more worthy" places, no matter where else I am, I'll not ever *not* be a Californian.

Desperately Seeking Blue Mound

ROBERT GRINDY

I

> We teach our children all the stories
> of the blizzards and tornadoes,
> the droughts and the black deep soil,
> its grand slow rolls only idiots
> and easterners could call flat—
> how we love it, how we hate it,
> how it did not quite kill us young.
> —Jeff Gundy, "Where I Grew Up"

On a clear day from the top of Blue Mound, you can see four counties. That's what the brochure says. I'm not that impressed. Since the county-line road runs right next to the mound, you can see *two* counties from the parking lot.

Blue Mound is a small hill just to the west of the town of Blue Mound, a village of twelve hundred farmers south of Decatur, where I live, so centered in Illinois that the map folds on top of us. Officially the mound is in the Griswold Conservation Area, owned by the Macon County Conservation District and maintained as a park, with ball fields at its base and a small shelter at the top.

I'm on top of the mound thinking of Gundy's poem and trying my damnedest not to think like an idiot or an Easterner, neither of which I am. This March day is bright gray, and, of course, windy—not as windy as yesterday, with gusts of 50 mph, not as cold as the day before that, with temperatures in the single digits and blowing snow, not as warm as last week, when it hit 72. *Don't like the weather?* goes the standard joke around here. *Stick around a few minutes and it'll change.*

My eight-year-old boy and his friend do what comes naturally on a hill—they roll down it, gathering grass and mud. Raised in a flat country, they still know what to do, I'm pleased to see. When it snows, sledders of all ages come here for the long ride down the southern slope. How can you not love hills in this country when you are so deprived of their company? On our hikes in another conservation area in Decatur, my kids always ask to go on the trail with "the big hill," a small quarry with a short sharp slope to scramble up.

Though the land around here rarely goes up, it sometimes goes down—rivers and creeks cut gullies and dig out shallow valleys, so that sometimes as you drive back roads you might think you've wandered into hill country at long last, until you pop up onto the plane of the prairie once again. Next to all the freeway overpasses are "borrow pits," quarries now filled with water where construction workers dug dirt to build ramps. A few years ago a neighboring town tried to have one of these ponds declared to be "navigable water," which would've allowed a "riverboat" casino to be moored on it. Common sense prevailed, luckily. The borrow pits show that in this country "you can only go up as far as you go down," Michael Martone notes.

But I ache for real hills, the kind that go up and stay up, and even if the four-county claim is suspect, and even if I am not as high as the top of the grain elevators just off to the east, Blue Mound is still the best hill around. Its eighty feet of rise off the surrounding farmland makes me huff more than I should to get the top. And when you live in an area where there is no mount in Mt. Zion, no hill on Hill Avenue, no height in Maryland Heights, you have to appreciate that there *is* a mound in Blue Mound. Two mounds, actually—across the road to the south is a similar hump bristling with bare trees, "Long Mound" on the topographical maps.

This isn't to say that these are the only hills in my part of Illinois, oh no. Mt. Auburn, visible off to the west, and Mt. Pulaski, twenty-five miles to the northwest, are bigger—big enough for hardscrabble little towns to cling to their slopes, like prairie flotsam washed up out of the corn and beans onto isolated reefs. John's Hill Magnet School does sit picturesquely on top of a proper hill in Decatur. And just east of Assumption I came across a lovely long-sloping hill with a farmhouse and barns at the top.

But that's it. All the hills I have found in my neighborhood. Coming from California, I find it nearly absurd that I can count the hills in four counties on one hand. But more than absurd—it nearly breaks my heart.

Whenever I tell native Midwesterners that I am from California, the reaction is the same, and has been for nearly two decades: "Why in the world did you move *here?*" For seven years in southern Indiana and twelve years in downstate Illinois I have explained to them my story of graduate school and the job market and marriage and kids, and they nod politely but still shake their heads. "I'd kill to live in California," they often tell me, especially if they are young, or if they are older or more rooted, "This must be quite a shock."

Such comments are revealing but not unexpected. I found right off that the Midwest has a Canada-size inferiority complex. The movie and television equation that Midwest = Nowhere has been accepted as gospel, even by the natives. If California is the place you ought to be, as the *Beverly Hillbillies* song tells us, then the Midwest is the place you ought to leave. Or the place you *have* to leave: since 1980 my own blue-collar city of Decatur, a victim of rust-belt economics, has lost 12,000 residents, 13 percent of its population. Small Midwestern towns are drying up and blowing away, the younger generations fleeing to bigger towns or sexier states. Many rural areas of the Great Plains have lower population densities now than in the early decades of the twentieth century.

When Midwesterners ask me about my difficulties adjusting or when they start on how I must miss the beaches and palm trees, swimming pools and movie stars, weirdoes of all stripes, I tell them I am from the Midwestern part of California. When I describe the tiny towns where I was raised, they are usually surprised.

It's my throwaway line, my "Midwestern California" quip, designed to keep me on the inside when I am being pushed to the outside. But there is some truth to it. My California was all north, but not San Francisco or Napa. I grew up in the grass and oaks of the Mother Lode foothills in Calaveras and Amador counties, ranching and logging country, in thinly settled hills with towns of 1,500 or fewer. I spent my college years in the upper Sacramento valley among rice fields and orchards.

Most of my California life was rural, redneck, agricultural—not much different from what I see around me in Illinois. Gun racks on pickups, back-roads beer parties, 4-H, Future Farmers and Future Homemakers. "Sweet Home Alabama" and John Cougar Mellencamp were more familiar to me than Los Angeles new wave or East Coast disco. Calaveras County had two run-down movie theaters, but Amador County had none when I lived there; neither had a fast-food place, a chain store, a bowling alley, even a stoplight until after I left. A college friend from La Jolla thought I lived in Mayberry—even to other Californians, the picture is more middle America than fast-times California. In graduate school I discovered that one of my roommates and I had gone to the same jock-and-cheerleader high schools, only mine was in Sutter Creek, California, and his was in Middletown, Indiana.

So despite being a native Californian, I am much more comfortable in Greencastle, Indiana, than in San Francisco, just as Chicago kids have much more in common with kids in Los Angeles than in downstate Illinois, and mallrats in Indianapolis would feel at home in a mall in Sacramento. Certainly regionalism still lives, but in many ways the labels "urban," "suburban," and "rural" define cultural differences in the U.S. more accurately than "Eastern," "Midwestern," "Southern," or "Western."

Since my earliest days in the Midwest, I have felt a kinship with the overland emigrants of the nineteenth century, although my travels have been mostly in the opposite direction of theirs. I was raised near the end of the Mormon Emigrant Trail, crossed the same country on the same routes, and ended up settling near the trail head, or at least in the area where so many embarked from, the majority of the overland trail emigrants having come off farms in Indiana, Illinois, Iowa, and Missouri. (That most famous of emigrant companies, for instance, the Donner-Reed Party, said goodbye to the friends of the friends of Abraham Lincoln in Springfield, Illinois, just down the road from my Decatur, before heading west into infamy.)

Even today many of the folks in my part of California are only a generation or so out of the middle part of the country. Most of my friends were born in California; most of their parents were not. The dust bowl drove them out of the plains and southern states; wartime work and the golden prosperity of the '50s lured them off Midwestern farms. My mother's family, farmers from Arkansas, first came temporarily to California in the 1930s to pick fruit, then returned after the war to work in a Sierra lumber mill; my father's father, at one time a homesteader on the plains of eastern Montana, came to California to work in the Long Beach ship-yards during World War II and stayed after the war to work as a painter at an air base.

These folks brought their homes with them. My mother farms her city lots with fruit trees, tomato plants, and overflowing flower beds. In Sutter Creek we used the same dumb-guy hick accent to mock Gene Cutsinger's drawl that David Letterman took from Indiana. My high school girlfriend wasn't beneath playing the hillbilly with "ain't seen you in a coon's age" expressions. The Skoal ring on the back jeans pocket of farm kids around Illinois is familiar to anyone in Amador County.

And even this almost-flat landscape is not as alien to me as Midwesterners might believe. When my wife and I drive the Sacramento Valley on visits to my family, one of us inevitably trots out another standard joke: "Looks like we made a wrong turn—I think we're in Moweaqua." You won't find a flatter, more fertile stretch of farmland anywhere between the Rockies and the Alleghenies than you see between Redding and Bakersfield. I knew about fruited plains long before I saw the central prairies.

But standing on the top of Blue Mound, I am struck not by similarities to my home country but by differences. I consider "place" to be a locale's landscape, people, and history of both, and of those three it's Illinois' landscape that keeps me feeling out of place the most. That California prairie? It's a fraud—when the wind is blowing the fog or haze out of the central valley, it's easy to see that the fruited plain is running right up to purple mountain's majesty east and west. It's easy to remember that over those coastal mountains the sea is crashing against rocks, and that to the east the snowy peaks keep a desert at bay. In the middle of the Illinois prairie, on the other hand, I know that soybeans are on the other side of the corn. Tall grass gives way to short grass to the west and dense woodlands to the east. Nothing higher than the Sears Tower between me and the North Pole.

My California world went up and down. Every bike ride, especially on a Schwinn Sting-Ray with a banana seat but only one gear, was an exercise in cost-benefit analysis: Is the fast free ride down worth the long walk back up? We never had to hunt for a hill to sled down (though the sledding was more often cardboard on dry grass than toboggan on snow). San Andreas chopped off the top of a hill to make a little league park. Football fields throughout the Mother Lode League are cut into hillsides—there are no flat spots big enough. On one of our houses, the front deck must have been thirty feet higher than the street.

This horizontal world has upset my equilibrium. Consider, for instance, the elevation of Decatur: 629 feet above sea level. (This I discovered by looking in an almanac; unlike in western towns, elevations are not printed on town signs next to the population around here.) So the water in the Sangamon River that flows through Decatur will run west and north to the Illinois River, then south to the

Mississippi and down to the Gulf of Mexico, maybe 1,500 miles, and in the entire journey drop only 629 feet. This astounds me. If you hiked just two hills east of the house where I grew up, you'd be more than 600 feet higher than where you started. By the time the water in the Mokelumne River reached our neck of the woods, it had already dropped some 5,000 feet—from its headwaters about 75 miles away.

A vertical world reads differently from a horizontal world. In all my tramping all over Northern California, on foot, by car, over miles and miles of unfamiliar territory, I don't ever remember being really lost. I might not have known where I was, but I always knew which way to go. The mountain ranges run north and south, easy enough to see from down in the valley. Rivers and their canyons run east and west. The land gains elevation to the east, not falling away for good until the top of the Sierra. When I was working with a surveyor in the Sierra, he once directed me by walkie-talkie to "go northeast—toward Lake Tahoe." I knew exactly what he meant.

In the Midwest, without a good low sun or a familiar highway, the points of the compass seem random. I have driven around cornfields—straight, right angle; straight, right angle—until I have circled back around to where I started. Once when dark overcame us while my wife and I were wandering Parke County, Indiana, looking for covered bridges, we realized we had no idea how to get home. Off on the horizon we saw an orange glow and figured it had to be Terre Haute. We headed toward the glow as best we could, even though Terre Haute was forty miles in the wrong direction. At least we knew where it was.

At first the lack of elevation bothered me more than anything else, particularly in Illinois—the worst derision I could heap upon the place was that it was so *flat*. Flat was beyond boring; flat was aesthetically unacceptable. Flat offered no hundred-mile views, and every Californian knows a home is nothing without a view. ("If you get up just three feet," my father told us ten times one day when we were inspecting a lot he was trying to talk himself into buying, "you can see Mt. Diablo.") We spent summers in Yosemite, the Florence of this vertical world, with neck-straining cliffs and sequoias, soaring waterfalls, immense domes. . . . Where in the Midwest was the spectacle, the drama of my California vertical world?

The flatness sends me instinctively, desperately seeking places like Blue Mound. When I drive my daughter down to visit her friend, I detour to the hill just to look at it for few minutes, sometimes climb it just to get a view, just to see where I am.

II

Why do I ache for this place that isn't home
That is my home? It is always the same,
Coming home late and out of place
Studying every weed and road for wisdom
Or whatever happens at this time of harvest.

—Dan Guillory, "Lost Gardens"

Staying this long in the Midwest was not part of the original plan. I had always assumed I would return to California, and in fact at one point I was within a week of loading up my books for the drive west. It has taken a long time to shift my thinking from "when" I return to California to "if." Even after all these years, when I see a perfect red barn surrounded by nothing but black upturned earth, or when I feel the bite of a subzero day, or someone asks, "Where you from?" I am still surprised: *Illinois? Illinois? I live in Illinois?*

But attachments I hadn't anticipated—jobs, marriage—altered plans. And those attachments led to others, to attachments more surprising and perhaps more important: a feeling of belonging. Or at least a need for a sense of belonging, a wish for rootedness. And a fondness for this country. Goddamn it, I like prairies.

To live in an alien place without feeling out of place often means adopting a new aesthetic. To come from the west and learn to love a prairie, one must abandon the European tree-and-mountain worship that shaped so much of our thinking about our American environments. I have recognized the necessity of learning to read a more subtle text. Landscape that defies comprehension in its vast horizontal sweep can be as awe-inspiring as ground that soars skyward. Little of the original grass-lands are left, but in restored patches here and there, such as at Rock Springs Cen-ter in Decatur and Midewin Tallgrass Prairie near Joliet, you can get a glimpse of the grandeur that amazed and befuddled early settlers. With its rich diversity of grasses and forbs, insects and birds—blue aster and bluebirds, cordgrass and clover, bobwhites and butterflies, coneflowers and sunflowers and blazing star—with its roots twelve feet deep that gave way only and finally to the self-scouring steel plow, a prairie is every bit as complex as a forest and has an understated beauty that asks you to look closely and pay attention. Big bluestem and Indian grass higher than my head, higher than my baby's head when she's on my shoulders, rippling red and brown in an autumn breeze—it ain't no sequoia grove, but it's still a stirring sight. And even that damn sea of chemical-fed corn that has replaced most of the origi-nal grassland—I can't help but marvel at it every summer.

I had to learn that small variations can have meaning, even drama. I've learned that these few little knots of hills are kames, deposits of gravel left behind by re-treating glaciers. Blue Mound was left by the Illinois Glacier, and from the plat-form on top you can look down 175,000 years. The back half of the mound has been gutted—a sharp loose cliff drops from the shelter into a gravel pit dug out for New Deal roads, opening a window onto the Ice Age.

If a more recent glacier had advanced past Boody a few miles to the north, Blue Mound would've been leveled. Looking north and east, I can see a slow slope from one horizontal plane to another, perhaps sixty feet over a half mile, easy to miss in a car: the Shelbyville Moraine, marking the farthest advance of the Wisconsinan Glacier, a mile-high sheet of crushing ice. When it retreated 12,000 years ago, the dirt and rock melting out of the ice left the land fifty to two hundred feet higher where the glacier had been, the dark loess making some of the richest soil in the world. Blue Mound is no Mt. Shasta, to be sure, the moraine line no Yosemite Val-ley, but they are quiet wonders just the same.

The weather here is the one feature my concerned Midwestern friends are sure I cannot possibly abide. The weather *has* been disorienting—it's lush and green in the Midwest when it is brown and dry in California, and vice versa. I am embarrassed now to remember my reaction to my first late summer thunderstorm in Indiana—*September seems a bit early for the rains to be starting, but I guess winters are longer here.* . . . But the weather in the Midwest is one of my newfound loves—here is the gaudy, eye-popping spectacle that the land lacks. The flatness underneath the big sky overhead has created a theater of weather to rival the theater of land in California.

I had known the grace of grass flowing in the wind from my California days, had come to revere the delta breezes that made the nights bearable after 110-degree days. What I didn't know was the wind's demonic other: tornadoes. I have become a tornado junkie, enthralled by the whole idea of these monster winds, transfixed by news footage, dreaming of twisters many nights, desperate to see one myself before I leave the Midwest or die. Like the rest of the male population of the Midwest (and some of the female), I can't keep away from the windows when the sirens go off. So far, I have bagged two benign funnel clouds but no roaring twister. I didn't see either of the two tornadoes that exploded through Decatur in consecutive nights a few years back, but witnessing the aftermath of splintered homes and lives has left me more wary of twisters. Still, I would like to see one skipping across the open prairie. . . .

I keep telling my eastern-born wife that we did too have four seasons in my part of California, but I have to admit that *hot, cool, rainy,* and *warm* don't take you on the spiritual roller-coaster that the spinning seasons do out here—and the key to the whole ride is a deep, brutal winter. Though I grew up skiing in the High Sierra, I didn't know the daily crush of winter until I moved here. When I've come to Blue Mound in midwinter, there's a nearly arctic barrenness stretching around me—wispy snow in tiny waves curling across the empty fields. It's easy to despair in such a landscape, but I've come to find it exhilarating, necessary—the world cold and bare, stripped down, riding out the worst the indifferent universe can bring.

When I moved to Decatur, I puzzled for a few minutes in the fall at the plastic orange fences that sprouted around open fields on the outskirts of town. Drift fences, it turned out. But "drift" is such a graceful word, and "whiteout" so pretty, neither accurately describing what the wind does to the snow. One snowy January day when the wind was stiff but harmless in town, I set out for the college outside of the city, and with one ill-advised turn I left the protection of houses and trees and found myself in a howling horizontal hell, a wall of snow blasting across the road, cutting off visibility beyond my bumper. I had driven in zero-visibility fog in the Sacramento Valley, but those silent blankets had none of the ferocity of the wind-driven demon that shuddered my car. Luckily the road—like most around here—was straight and flat, so I crept forward nervously, hoping no overconfident, seen-it-all, shoulda-been-here-last-year grain truck driver was barreling toward me in either direction. Californians measure Sierra snow in feet—three feet per storm, fifteen-foot base, the poor Donners and Reeds stranded in twenty-four—but three or four inches out here manages to make itself quite spectacularly terrifying.

Here in March exhilaration gives way to enough-already anxiety and the sting of cruel teasing as the temperatures rise and fall. Today from the top of Blue Mound I see the brown fallow fields still ragged with last fall's stubble, the little islands of white barns and empty trees still hunkered down against the wind. But from the little wetland at the bottom of the hill comes a creaky porch-swing chorus of peepers. A female cardinal calls sweet and sharp and confident—*frrrrr-weet chr chr chr*—in the brush behind the shelter. O west wind indeed.

And of course there are also the ice storms and electrical storms, the fireflies and fall leaves, the snow so dry it won't make a decent snowball, the air so cold your boogers freeze with the first sniff or so thick with heat and humidity and the pulsing screech of cicadas and tree frogs that it seems the land is panting on you—none of this had I known in California. All of this I am coming to appreciate more and more. And all of this is getting harder to imagine giving up.

III

> Somewhere, despite the tall
> Protection of skyscrapers (or mountains)
> You learned what these farmers know.
> To stay here you've got to be tied
> To something.
> —Lucia Getsi, "Woman Hanging from
> Lightpole, Illinois Route 136"

On an uncommonly bright and warm January day in 1996, I found myself in an Ozark graveyard with my family, sorting through years and years of circles and journeys.

My Uncle Grant had died. He was a lean, soft-spoken farmer, the oldest of five O'Neals, a father to my mother and the younger children after their father died young. In 1942 he bought a 160-acre farm with his wife Doris, out on South Mountain near Marshall, Arkansas.

In 1954 he moved to Northern California with Doris and their three children to work in Barry's lumber mill in Pipi Valley, El Dorado County. His mother, his youngest brother and sisters, and several cousins had come out before him. It's a beautiful spot, Pipi Valley, deep in pine and fir some 4,000 feet into the mountains. Grant operated loaders and other equipment with the usual expertise of O'Neal men, and he made good money. But he had no intention of staying.

In 1956 Grant and his family returned to their farm next to the Red River, adding on to the small house piece by piece to accommodate growing kids and then a rush of grandchildren and great-grandchildren who spent much of their summers at Papa's. There he lived until his death at age seventy-six, more than fifty of those years spent in the same house.

Uncle Grant is buried in Rambo Cemetery a mile or so from his house, on a cleared hillside overlooking the river and the woods and hills, next to a dirt road he traveled every day of his life, just down a piece from Aint Ellie's place—which was Grandpa Griffith's—and Uncle John's, a little further from Granny's last farm and the one-room school they all attended, within a few miles of the house where he was born. His grave is near his mother and father's and all of his grandparents' and other O'Neals' and Griffiths' strung together in tangled ancestral webs.

The contrasts were striking and painful. Those with me—my mother and father, my wife and my daughter—had come from many hundred miles to this spot. Each of us had been born in a different state; none of us live in the state where we were born. I couldn't tell you where any of us would be buried. But Grant had come only a few miles, and every day when he passed this place he knew that there was where he would rest.

Next to that fresh mound of red dirt I faced the sad truth of my life: no place like this is waiting for me. Uncle Grant had heard—answered, even—the siren calls of California and the rest of the world but chose to live his life in a place on earth so much a part of himself he will never be separated from it. That there are many more like me in our country than like Grant doesn't lift my spirits much. Scott Russell Sanders, that wise Midwestern advocate for staying put, writes, "A footloose people, we find it difficult to honor [a] lifelong, bone-deep attachment to place."

So what are those of us to do who find ourselves in a place where we have no history, no family, no instinctive affinity for the landscape, no bone-deep attachments? Sanders's advice: Dig in. Become inhabitants, not tourists. Learn: "We need to know where we are so that we may dwell in our place with full hearts." Tie yourself to something.

I'd love to do as my friends the Throneburgs have done out by Assumption: build on to a hundred-year-old farm house with salvaged barn timbers and fresh-milled lumber from local trees, heat and cool it all with the sun and wind and local fuels, replant acres of native grass and trees around it, reconstruct a wetland for wildlife and swimming. Do it all by hand. And root it all into a plot first worked by grandparents, every inch familiar from childhood.

That ain't gonna happen. My rambling old house here in town is already beyond the limits of my time, skills, and money.

But I've stumbled upon an oddly effective alternative, coming to me from left field: base ball.

Seriously. But not just any ol' baseball. Real old two-word base ball, "vintage base ball," it's called. For seven years now I've been toiling in the heat of the summer in long pants and a long-sleeved white shirt with a snappy blue-trimmed bib buttoned on the front, playing base ball with my bare hands for the Rock Springs Ground Squirrels. Teams from historical sites from New York to Colorado have taken up the game as it was played in the 1860s—no gloves, no walks, no over-running, no sliding, no spitting, no swearing. Balls caught on the bound are out. Uniforms and bats are modeled after nineteenth-century versions. We're not quite as obsessive as Civil War re-enactors, but we do try to re-create the feel of a different time. While we knock the nineteenth-century snot out of the ball.

It's all good-natured, goofy, three-huzzahs fun, which I first took up for a little recreation. Along with it came good-ol'-boy camaraderie with gentlemen like Root Hog and Droopy Drawers. And in some ways this base ball has brought my own past not only into the future but across the continent: Though I have loved the game since I was old enough to read a box score, I hadn't played since I was twelve, and now here in Illinois, of all places, I was channeling back San Andreas little league.

But I found in the game of vintage ball recreations and connections even more important. We play our matches on a stretch of mowed prairie in the conservation area outside of Decatur. During our leisurely early-evening practices, swallows dip low along the field, darting for bugs. Pheasants call back and forth from the tall grass across the road. Red-tailed hawks circle over. White-tailed deer bound across the prairie behind me. The sky opens with red clouds. The wind bends wave on wave through the grass. I'd come stand in this outfield whether a ball came my way or not.

But base ball does seem to be a fitting employment for this flat open place. I don't buy much of all that gooey field-of-dreams hokum, but for a game that was city-born it seems more fitting for a land that rolls off to the horizon—no boundaries, no time limits, ever-increasing space. And what did we do when we dropped out of the trees and came to grasslands but run long-legged across it and chase and throw things. From my spot in the outfield, base ball strikes me as a hunting game—the ball first as flying prey to chase down, then as a weapon to strike down fleeing quarry ("hands dead" we call outs) as they scurry from safe spot to safe spot. When I'm legging down a soaring fly ball or chugging around the bases, this seems like a—dare I say it?—*natural* thing to do here. Even with our goofy hats.

Our base ball program is an extension of the Rock Spring Center's living history program centered on the Trobaugh-Good Prairie Homestead Farm, a tidy restored farm from the 1850s just down the path from our ball field. The good folks who work and volunteer at the Homestead make their own period clothing, demonstrate cooking over a woodstove, fashion household items in the woodshed, and tend an impressive garden with heirloom seeds and tools. The Homestead sits in the middle of thirteen hundred acres of woodlands, restored prairie, and river bottom, maintained by naturalists who know every leaf, feather, and scat in the place. The Rock Springs work from woods to homestead is a family enterprise shared by grandparents to grandchildren—the Slider-Longbons clan, the Torgersons, Stickles, Quintenezes, Harveys, Sampsons, Brickers, Tishes . . .

Add "Grindys" to the list. At ease and beautiful in her pigtails and simple nineteenth-century dress, my daughter demonstrates grace hoops, corn-cob checkers, and other children's games at the homestead. My son pitches in as bat boy for the Ground Squirrels and has even taken the field when we've been short-handed, recording a bare-handed foul-tick out from the behind position in his latest foray. Our modest historical play-acting is not in the same league with the work and expertise of the rest of the Rock Springs folks, but I am thankful it has allowed us into their neighborhood, a neighborhood of full-hearted people who know where we've been and where we are. Bringing my own family into their company has gone a long way toward making us feel at home in Decatur, Macon County, Illinois. It's not just the base ball, of course: my children have known no other home; I have buried friends in this town; every third person I meet has been in my classroom. But base ball has been a way to be on the land, with the people, and in touch with the history of both, to be in place in this place. The final surprising knot. I'm tied.

Like a reluctant lover afraid to commit to matrimony, I'm still trying to figure out what this means. The Midwest and I have been shacking up for nearly twenty years, but now I'm saying we've tied the knot? Did we say 'til death do we part? I just don't know.

But I do know this: as long as I live here, I will scope out every island of trees in the distance to see if the land rises under it.

When it does, I'll climb, gladly.

When it doesn't, maybe there will be a good spot nearby to get up a game.

Workers

Still on Cortland Street

ANNE CALCAGNO

There's a bridge at 1440 West Cortland Street where I like to stand and pretend I have fallen into the late nineteenth century. Half a mile from Clybourn Avenue—probably the most gentrified real estate plumb line of Chicago—with its back to the city skyline, this curlicued maroon bridge leans over a slow piece of dark green river, its banks bedraggled with untended trees. Looking north, a small crane lifts industrial waste onto one or two barges, and usually no one is about, which of course makes my metaphorical plunge that much easier.

The site is historic; it is the first double-leaf trunnion bascule bridge of its kind to have been completed in the U.S., which earned it an easier nickname: "Chicago style bridge." Of Chicago's fifty-two movable bridges (forty-three of which are apparently in operation), this is the oldest. It literally opened to water and sky on May 24th, 1902. But I didn't come to this bridge knowing this.

A friend suggested Cortland Street as an alternative route to nastily congested Fullerton Avenue. Those of us Chicagoans in the "know" regularly zoom angled patterns of smaller streets to get to the heart of Lincoln Park (for work, restaurants, home . . .). An enormous photographic banner was my first view as I came off the rise of Cortland Bridge. "Two Million Trees Planted in the U.S." What? Why? In fact, a lovely landscaping job of trees, bushes, and flowers defines Cortland Street. Elegant replicas of nineteenth-century city street lamps punctuate the route, their tall black silhouettes echoing the low black wrought-iron fences that protect the landscaping. The oddity of this bucolic effort is that it beautifies not a real estate opportunity but a steel manufacturing company: Finkl & Sons Co. To offset the carbon dioxide generated by manufacturing, millions of trees have been—and continue to be—planted in Illinois and Wisconsin. As the reverse side of their overhead banner proclaims, Finkl cares to be "Forging A Fresher America."

Men in overalls and electric blue hard hats (Finkl's logo color) amble back and forth past the bobbing black-eyed Susans. Seeing these blue-clad laborers, I'm jolted by how rare their public presence is, at least in my usual line of vision. Near Northside Chicago is a white-collar phenomenon, with most of its corporate and retail rear-ends netted to swivel chairs in downtown skyscraper upon skyscraper.

Downtown, in the basements and side hallways, janitors and physical plant services process their operations unobtrusively. The heartbeat of labor pulsates from the buildings; in the grids, ducts, pipes, wiring, cables. But the men (and women) who set up and run these physical systems appear in the city as sojourners, temporarily out of their environments. We know, and forget, that much of what we depend on is determined by them. A white collar gal like me can easily never enter one physical plant facility, manufacturing factory, or steel mill. True, when the economy's good, construction sites mess up the landscape with their promise, for a while. Muscular bare backs, hard hats, and foul language gleam behind temporary protective walls. But Finkl Steel is permanent, and has been since 1879. It set out to save itself, and the place of urban manufacturing, when it took over Cortland Street.

Just as Carl Sandburg would have willed it:

> Tool Maker, Stacker of Wheat,
> Player with Railroads and the Nation's Freight Handler;
> Stormy, husky, brawling,
> City of the Big Shoulders . . . .
> Come and show me another city with lifted head singing so proud
>   to be alive and coarse and strong and cunning.

—"Chicago"

And perhaps Walt Whitman, too:

> Sure as the most certain sure, plumb in the uprights, well-entretied,
>   braced in the beams,
> Stout as a horse, affectionate, haughty, electrical,
> I and this mystery here we stand.

—"Leaves of Grass," sec. 3

In the last decade of the twentieth century, manufacturing jobs in the United States, many right in the heartland, staggered and fell. Since 1998 alone, thirty-two U.S. steel companies in the United States have filed for bankruptcy, a fair number in the Midwest. As I sit, writing about "my" Heartland, it's the year 2002, and President Bush has just decreed a thirty percent increase in tariffs on imported steel to stave off a crisis in this industry. On April Fools' Day, an article in the *Chicago Tribune* quotes Richard Dowdell, who has just been laid-off after thirty-eight years in the steel industry: "People in Washington, they have coverage. But the people who work in the sweaty mills, they don't have anything." This loss of jobs, benefits, and belonging is the gritty reality against which Finkl & Sons have fought for their place. Officially called the North River Industrial Corridor, Finkl & Sons has given rise to a small miracle, or perhaps an infectious solid possibility.

A bridge symbolizes union in its physical and conceptual state, but the gap that Cortland Bridge was restored in 1997 to connect—the laborer and his city—is more than historical. I grew up in Europe, in Italy specifically, and my continued counter-Atlantic perception is the snotty but numerically accurate conviction that there are a hell of a lot more historical artifacts back over there. All this to say that I was hungry over here in this big city more new than old. I was waiting to be given some equivalent: the ideal American gaze. And all of a sudden I think I found it. Why is it ideal? For one, to find a centrally located and operational urban site this left alone, this stripped down to an earlier landscape, in Europe you might have travel back three hundred years. Second, this bridge and the road it propels downtown clasped a tradition hard enough to make it generate an innovation. That seems to me very American: history valued especially when its gets made anew.

The steel industry needs water for cooling, processing, and transport, and the Chicago River and the Great Lakes could always promise that. So the Finkl Steel foundry built its home along the river, and stayed, and changed and changed. The river is no longer any kind of dumping space. It has reverted to quiet scenic abandon, something of a stray, through which a barge now and again washes. Voluble about its aims, Finkl installed a few diamond-shaped informational kiosks, which court a walker like me going down Cortland Street. One nineteenth-century photograph shows men in the rubble, post–Chicago fire, and the chisel Anton Finkl created uniquely adapted to clean fire-tumbled brick. Another kiosk explains a nearby 300-ton press, built in 1937 and now retired. Another describes Finkl's mission to become "one of the most progressive recycling companies in our industry."

Still, even with the kiosks, I am a loner in my attachment, thrown strange looks from time-conscious runners, hard-hat employees, and recycling truck drivers as I stand in position, either along the river falling into the nineteenth century, or at the melt shop entrance to this twenty-first-century steel foundry. But I'm fanatic with my loves, and each of the past three years I've walked students in my "Discover Chicago" class here, to this vision of the Midwest.

"How can we be in the nineteenth century if the bridge was built in 1902?" they ask.

"Pragmatists!" I cry back. Pretend, pretend, I urge.

"The heat is unbearable," they resist as I still them in front of the infernal heat of metal being poured from a vat the size of a Volkswagen.

So I read to them from Rebecca Harding Davis's turn-of-the-century account, *Life in the Iron Mills:*

> By day and night the work goes on, the unsleeping engines groan and shriek, the fiery pools of metal boil and surge. . . . The mills for rolling iron are simply immense tent-like roofs, covering acres of ground, open on every side. . . . a city of fires, that burned hot and fiercely in the night. Fire in every horrible form; pits of flame wav-

ing in the wind; liquid metal-flames writhing in tortuous streams through the sand; wide cauldrons with boiling fire, over which bent ghastly wretches stirring the strange brewing; and through all, crowds of half-clad men, looking like revengeful ghosts in the red light, hurried, throwing masses of glittering fire. It was like a street in Hell.

I say we are reliving Carl Sandburg, Walt Whitman, Rebecca Harding Davis. But not only that, we're on the crest of the wave; this hot site is where the wealthy hip—patrons of the arts, the environment, hospital capital campaigns—mingle. In the last five years, Finkl has turned its warehouse-huge spaces into free—wonderfully dramatic—sites for charitable events, temporarily clearing out stored steel and operations at its own cost and inconvenience. Finkl now masters the art of cutting-edge neighborhood and charity relations. Rugged and hip, so hot and so cool. How pragmatic and Midwestern to connect brawn with beauty, muscle with belief. The Midwest has rarely concocted good deeds as effete; they're plain as bread, and good nourishment, too. I wish it had not taken me ten years to come to this view.

A long time ago now, I came to Chicago because I couldn't bear to move back to New York City. There, I had discovered I do not possess nerves of steel. Here you could actually find an apartment and a job, and not every restaurant cost as much as a monthly mortgage payment. Here, three corners in Chicago—stretching less than a mile—configure the steel industry, urban planning, a historic registry, and a renewed environment, all interdependent. Cortland Street spans a century, carrying and awakening me to matters I dearly love: sweat, poetry, hope, water, labor, gardens, the raw elements, and the magic of transformation in a devoted dance between (wo)man and nature.

The Pluses and Minuses of Life in the Midwest

JON ANDERSON

The top brass at the newspaper where I now work decided to build a $187 million printing plant on the banks of the Chicago River. That way, they reckoned, newsprint could come in by boat from Quebec and be offloaded right beside the presses. Nobody thought to check the river. The sludge on the bottom was filled with chemicals. No way could they stir it up, a branch of the federal government said. The plant got built, but with railway sidings for ninety boxcars a week.

I was born in Montreal, the city from which the early French explorers set out for the Midwest, looking for a way to China. One of them, Louis Jolliet, paddled all the way to Chicago and back in 1673 only to have his canoe flip over in the Lachine Rapids, a dozen miles west of Montreal. His diary fell in the water, with a complete loss of notes. I was twenty-seven when I came to Chicago by airplane, landing at O'Hare on June 15, 1963, at 5 P.M. I was a reporter for *Time* magazine, with an eye for details. I was s'posed to be here, grounding myself in the most average part of the U.S., the Midwest, for a year. Then, they said, we'll send you to Paris.

I'm still here.

CHICAGO, 1966

I sat on the bed with the mussed covers, and I had a strong feeling that I shouldn't be there. It was a young woman's bedroom. I swung my head like a camera, catching the title of the novel on the night table (*Other Voices, Other Rooms* by Truman Capote). The teddy bear on a shelf had a trail of red ribbons pulled tight around its neck. On the dresser were two smiling old people in a silver frame, and a postcard from a boyfriend that said, "It's lonesome without you." The closet bulged with frilly dresses and the blue uniforms of student nurses. "I know this place," I thought, my mind flashing back to the first Christmas when we came home by train from college to Montreal. "It's just like Beverley's bedroom."

A dozen Chicago police cars parked in the street. I was in the first group of reporters into the townhouse. Out front, another fifty journalists stood around in groups on the grass, shuffling, waiting. Downstairs, a detective called up at us. Hurry. The hall rug upstairs was sticky under my feet. My white sneakers were splattered with wet blood. I sketched what had happened for the map man in New York, putting an "x" where each student nurse had fallen. I wanted to use the bathroom, but instead I wrote down that red drips of blood hung from the blue tile walls.

I went back to the *Time* office in the Equitable Building, pulled the blinds shut, and typed, weaving in the coroner's description of how each body looked, the way that "Pam" had been bound by her wrists and stabbed in the heart, about the stains from the side of "Gloria Jean" I had seen on the brown cushions of the living room sofa. Pages of scribbled notes. I knew which one of the murdered nurses was getting married, and who was joining the Peace Corps, and who had landed a job at Children's Memorial Hospital, and who was queen of the spring dance, and who had made the water ballet team.

"Merlita," I wrote, "brought a pair of clacking poles from Manila and often did a dance at parties." I was crying.

Someone pushed my door open.

"Don't come in," I said. The door closed.

Nurses, to me, meant Beverley. Her father was a doctor. She trained at the Montreal General while I studied law over the mountain at McGill. Once, when her parents were away, we snuck down into her father's clinic in the basement of her house. It smelled of antiseptic. We leaned against the examining table, leather and chrome, and necked standing up until she shuddered.

Two things happened Saturday night.

I was cooking dinner by myself in my studio apartment on the top floor of a building in Sandburg Village. My furniture had been left behind by a previous tenant who had skipped on the rent. My hash was browning when the phone rang.

"Hi. A few small points," said the researcher from headquarters in New York.

"The one that was getting married? Mary Ann? Was she the one that was stabbed five times, once in the right eye?"

"And which one was the swimmer?"

The sentence, actually the tone—the bored stance of the harried journalist—got to me, but I told her. Then, two hours before midnight Saturday, which was our deadline every week, the Chicago police caught the guy. My story had an ending—and all those details nobody else had.

The first copies came in from the printing plant Monday morning. The story of the eight murdered nurses was there, under "Crime." The two-head was "One by One."

Above my map, the words "House of Death" were written, in red. Across the second page were the head shots, eight nurses in graduation caps that they never really got to wear. Buried in the story was a paragraph that said, "The girls, one observer noted, were good people, the daughters, sisters and sweethearts of other good people."

I was the observer. But not for much longer.

I typed a letter to Dick Clurman, the chief of correspondents. I told him I was quitting journalism for a while. I slid it into the overnight packet to New York. I wouldn't be going to Paris.

That's the down side of living in the Midwest: Creeps.

When I came back to journalism, a year later, I decided to focus on good people. The best man in the Midwest, I found, was Henry Betts.

CHICAGO, 1983

I wrote:

Each morning at 7, in a hospital on Chicago's Near North Side, about 160 patients begin a day of hard work. They dress (or are dressed). They feed themselves (or are fed). Then they spend hours, as one puts it, "trying to fit into a world that isn't set up for us." Some are learning to use gloves with adhesive straps so they can hold spoons. Others clean their teeth by rubbing them against a mounted brush. Women put on makeup and lipstick by leaning against specially designed containers. Many type, putting long sticks in their mouths and hitting keys at up to thirty words a minute. Others sip and puff through bent straws to work up to sixteen devices, turning book pages, operating TV sets, opening doors, switching on lights. A black box strapped to a leg helps some to walk. Its electrical impulses cause the leg to drop, improving the gait.

The goal is independence. Reaching it can be a very difficult struggle.

Few outsiders can deal easily with what they see: the reality, the mystery, and the fear of physical disability. It is a building where visitors often feel awkward. "I went to visit a friend of mine who had a stroke," says one. "But I walked through the halls with my hands shielding my eyes." Yet, for its patients and outpatients, it is by design a nurturing place of hope and spirit. Most stories about medicine tell about breakthroughs, dramatic recoveries, or miracles. This is not that kind of story. Rather, it is about the Rehabilitation Institute of Chicago, whose goal is a better life for some thirty-five million Americans who are disabled by injuries or such afflictions as stroke and arthritis.

Until the middle of this century, care for the disabled was seldom more than custodial. The Rehab's mission has been to radically change that approach with medical insights, technology, psychology, and an expanded social vision. Starting with nothing more than ideas, the Rehab has become a world center for the treatment of the problems of the handicapped, not the least of which is society's attitude. Making that happen—in Chicago—has been an obsession to its builders, among them its medical director, Dr. Henry Betts.

His reward?

He talked about that when the Chicago Press Club chose him as Chicagoan of the Year. People often told him, he said, that "it must be depressing to do your kind of work." His response: "The remark angers me. What do people think life really is? Won't each of us be disabled at some time? And die eventually? Can we remain depressed about these disabilities? I know I can't. To see people use strengths they never knew they had, to see them triumph and live with such glories really is exhilarating. It's the ultimate reward. I witness it every day."

I've had many other adventures in the Midwest. I keep them private. They kept me here.

My Father in White, Above the Royal Blue

DOUG HESSE

The night Cooper's Royal Blue and the Western Auto burned down, I watched with half the town of DeWitt. At nine-thirty, when volunteers carried Drs. School's and Frommelt's records from their offices in the adjoining Spikins building, it looked like the whole half block might go, interior brick walls chimneying the flames. At ten-thirty, when the blaze breached a second-floor flaw in the fire wall, police moved the crowd. Too much paint thinner in the Western Auto. Exploding aerosol cans punted toward us, scatting along ice from the hoses. It was December, a week before Christmas, and I was fourteen.

Even in 1970 small-town Iowa, Cooper's was an anomaly, a grocery in a main street storefront, a narrow alley behind and parallel parking in front. Though not yet supermarkets, Barnes' and Skeffington's groceries at least had lots. Years earlier Walker's department store had quit the grocery business to concentrate on clothing. So the Royal Blue was the last of its kind. It belonged to an age when Main Street (Sixth Avenue, really, U.S. 61) sold everything from Maid Rites to insurance to a tire change, a time before the Lincoln Highway became U.S. 30—before the four-lane bypassed DeWitt altogether.

Mom never shopped there. We lived nearby, too, also on Sixth Avenue, a block north of The Crossroads of America, the intersection of 30 and 61, and I would sometimes join my cousins there for candy or Popsicles. But trips that ended with boys carrying brown sacks to the car began at Barnes' or Skeffington's. Who shopped Cooper's was never clear. Aside from Mrs. Schrader, the Lutheran pastor's widow, I knew no one who lived downtown, and I guessed Cooper's got by on deliveries and the fact that people could still charge a pound of hamburger there. At a time when other groceries ran full- or double-page spreads, any sort of advertising by Cooper's is curiously absent from back issues of the *DeWitt Observer*. From working summers on the back of a garbage truck, I knew firsthand it had far less trash than the other stores.

I cared about the burning Western Auto in a way I couldn't about Cooper's. On junior high Friday nights—the only time stores were open past five—Vance Tech and I browsed every worthy store downtown: Williams' and Tillman's dime stores, buying malted milk balls or peanut clusters from glass bins. Gambles' and Coast to

Coast, where we sighted shotguns and flexed fishing poles. Skeffington's for *Hot Rod* magazine and *Creem* and, way back on the top shelf, *Playboy* and *Penthouse*, which fit neatly into *Life* for safer scrutiny. Kleinsmith's for Creedence Clearwater albums. Our last stop, by custom and convenience, since it was closest to my house, was the Western Auto.

The store filled two fronts, each with its own door. Al Almond and Charles Thompson had opened it in 1952, Almond, married to Thompson's sister, living in an apartment upstairs. As in many other shops downtown, the owners were its only clerks, though bigger stores hired a few grownups who worked full-time. In 1970 Dennis Frey's father could support his family by selling men's slacks at Walker's.

Toys covered half of one wall in the Western Auto, and half of these were plastic model kits. Vance and I would study the Corvettes and '57 Chevys for twenty minutes on a Friday night before maybe choosing one. Airplane glue was fifteen cents a tube; you supplied your own pin to punch the tin foil seal. Varnish and shellac, vise grips and inner tubes, headlights and plumb bobs, mixers and toasters: this is how I remember the store. That and dark hardwood floors, sealed not with polyurethane but spilled oil, burnished by work boots and hard-soled shoes. The whole store was seasoned kindling, saturated with "accelerants," as the newspapers would later observe. When it went up, the volunteer fire department didn't have a chance. It did have the responsibility for seeing that the post office didn't burn down.

The fire chief and his deputy, elected by their peers, wear white coats in 1970, the other firemen black, the better to find a leader during conflagrations. As I stand that night across from the Western Auto, I watch two white-coated men atop the Spikins building abutting the blaze. They direct truck placements and hose streams, pointing broadly, a *pas de deux* in smoke. The chief is my father.

And as I watch him dance through embers shot by burst timbers, I wonder how much heat weakens mortar and whether, if the building collapses, he will feel long the flames. "Fire never kills people," he had told me a few months earlier, when fourteen-year-old Billy Youngstrem died eight feet from his front door, having gone back in to save a dog, "the smoke always gets them first." And somehow that reassured me. But now there is too much smoke and fire. He and Fred Behr, the deputy chief, shimmer white in white and yellow against the night.

When you're fourteen and your father is forty, he cannot die. Maybe after a long cancer when he's old and you're old, too. But because you cannot imagine yourself at thirty or forty, you cannot imagine your father dying. Or at least in 1970 you cannot. Perhaps today's eighth-graders, poised for a service world of downsizing, have learned to consume the present, too, opening space for a future that includes the deaths of fathers. But such spaces did not exist for kids born into the small-town fifties and sixties.

Here the Central Sabers played football Friday nights, and you could count on cars nosed against the end zones at the old junior high field by the late afternoon, their owners to return during the sophomore game at six. You could count on the bank closing at three-thirty and old men playing sheepshead at Hap Smith's Shell station and manure spreaders shucking corn cobs sprinkled with pennies onto Ninth Street each Ridiculous Day. For big trips, downtown Davenport had department stores and shoe and stationery, Sears and the rest, and each Christmas Petersen's set up motorized scenes in its store windows. Northpark Mall would not open until 1973.

It was all an aberration, of course, for even small-town America is movement and change. A coal seam plays out. The bridge is built ten miles upriver. The new interstate turns highway to market road. Farms blow away. Fathers get killed by freight trains. That was Willis Hesse. Dad was seven. It was Christmas Eve, and he waited at a family party for a father who would never get there. When they brought Dad home from the hospital, an uncle took him up to his parents' bedroom to give him the double-barreled BB gun he'd wanted. And so Dad lost his father and Santa Claus the same night.

Fictive stabilities can never be seen from within their own time. Like Wittgenstein's fly, we can't see our bottles until something shatters them. And then we circle the shards, piecing them together in our minds, trying to see what we cannot know, the bottle's shape before the blow.

The call goes out to Grand Mound and Low Moor, and their companies arrive to knit hoses into the canvas and brass quilt. In twenty-degree weather the streets become glare ice. Hose pressure scoots firemen backwards. Sand is spread. I circle behind to the post office lot and watch the buildings settle, revealing third stories across Sixth Avenue, then second. Now the flames are hottest and brightest. Floor joists and plaster lath concentrate the heat, the imperfect collapse having left scores of air tunnels.

At midnight Iowa Electric's boom truck manages to snag the Royal Blue's hammered tin facade, and Peters's heavy wrecker pulls it into the street. The building stands in cross-section, two apartments' rooms above, a flaming doll's house. For the first time firemen don't have to shoot through windows, and steam replaces smoke. The crowd begins to realize the night air is cold and slowly starts to bed. I go finally, too, knowing that the Spikins firewall, later praised as eighteen inches of 1882 brick, has held and tonight my father will not die.

Thirty years later I look at the *DeWitt Observer* from December 10, four days after the fire, the first of the twice-weekly issues to cover it. In addition to the front page picture and story (continued on page three) are two full facing pages of photographs. Those not of the fire itself catch groups of people, women serving coffee and sandwiches in city hall, onlookers playing to the camera, firemen talking with helmets pushed back. In a small picture nearly lost in the bound volume's gutter is my father above the Royal Blue, only the store is now but smoke. His right hand is raised, but except for the identifying caption, he could be anyone. The *Observer* story quotes policemen and townspeople but attributes only a minor bit of information to "a fire department spokesman," who I instinctively know would never have been Dad. There is a shot in *Batman* where Michael Keaton stands preposterously high above dark Gotham City, ready to swoop down—but only when becoming public is absolutely necessary. Vengeance motivates Batman, transforming Keaton's sometimes goofy Bruce Wayne. I am not sure what enticed my father to wear a white coat, but I cannot imagine what he could possibly have needed to avenge. I do know he was happier on that roof than he would ever have been on the ground, though happy is not quite the right word. Less troubled. The night of the fire, Dad got home around four A.M. By the time I woke for school, he was already gone to work on the back of the trash truck he owned with Fred Behr. Smoky clothes piled next to the washing machine.

A new building eventually replaced the Western Auto and Cooper's. It's an orange brick and single story, the main street no longer valuable enough to warrant building up, the age gone in which people can even imagine living in small-town downtowns. Before the early seventies DeWitt had a single apartment building, all other rentals atop stores and in carved-up houses. As apartment buildings went up, upper Sixth Avenue decayed. Chuck Green razed the former DeWitt Hotel and built a squat Ben Franklin variety store. The Tower Building, its second- and third-floor windows plywooded for years, came down a few years later. The lot has been for sale since, a park bench and some yew bushes now joining the realtor's sign; from Thanksgiving to December, Santa's workshop shares the space.

The cores of Kansas City and Minneapolis and Chicago may gentrify, but not those of Mechanicsville, Calamus, or DeWitt. Even when the towns still grew, good jobs building tractors in Moline and Rock Island didn't lend themselves to life above a dime store. Then DeWitt no longer grew. There is no clear single agent for what happened: the two grain elevators bankrupting, Walker's folding, and Eclipse Lumber, Peters' Motor, Coast to Coast, the Ford dealership, DeWitt Hardware, and so on until you could buy neither a pair of pliers nor pants on Sixth Avenue. But had DeWitt read the fire right in 1970, it might have seen all of this coming. Don Cooper did, quitting the grocery business for good. But Thompson and Almond's Christmas Eve message in the *Observer* talked warmly of new stock in a new store early in the new year. By the decade's end, that shining new store would hold a pizza carryout and, for a few Decembers, when brown paper didn't shroud its windows, a holiday fruit basket center.

The last time I was in the "new" Western Auto was a Thanksgiving I was home from college. On Saturday the weather turned cold, and the battery in my old Mercury wouldn't hold a charge. When Dad and I walked into the stores, ribbons trimmed the toasters and toboggans. The floor shown whitish linoleum, the lights bright on a gray afternoon. We bought a battery from the back room where car parts were kept, out of sight of housewares. At home putting it in, Dad observed that Charley Thompson hadn't scratched the purchase month and year from the battery's sticker, hadn't started the thirty-six-month warranty. In a gesture emblematically my father's, for whom fairness, duty, and self-denial tightly interwove, with a screwdriver he plucked off the plastic "November" and "77" ovals.

Dad certainly read something in the fire. What he saw in the smoke I can only guess, though I'm sure he'd seen it before. Perhaps it was the futility of saving a burning past, the town and time's, his own. Perhaps it was a life of double jobs and self-employment and six kids, a childhood of moving, fatherless, from farm to farm and whichever relative could use him. He didn't run for fire chief again even though others lobbied him strongly. And while he stayed on the department until the mandatory retirement age of fifty, he didn't often play poker in the clubrooms above the police station. I read something, too, in the double vision of myself watching my father. At the end of *Field of Dreams* Ray Kinsella meets his younger father, whom he'd know only as a man broken by time. On our main street in 1970 I first saw my father's mortality. Looking back now, I also see his ending youth and wonder which building burns for me and when.

A Hard Saw

RICHARD HOLINGER

In 1935 my grandfather bought a small farm outside Chicago near Plano, Illinois, a town famous for its tackle boxes. Since then, the farmland's been sold to foreign investors, and my cousin Willie Cade bought the house where we spent our childhood weekends away from the city. The land today looks pretty much the same, about five hundred acres of cornfields, and fifty acres of the most beautiful floodplain woods in the state.

Two years ago lightning toppled an oak tree that townspeople reckoned was over three hundred years old. Once downed, its branches spanned nearly half an acre of tallgrass prairie, and one or two limbs sank deep as an oil drill into the earth.

Not long ago on a warm fall weekend, Willie and I strolled around the stricken tree admiring its girth and inhaling its bitter scent. I remembered Boy Scout campouts beneath its leafy canopy, my father pointing out warblers and wood-peckers, and walks beneath its shadowy dome while hunting rocks and turtles along the banks of Big Rock Creek.

Then we noticed that about halfway up the trunk someone had cut clean through, leaving a flat ivory surface wide as a dining room table.

"I'd love to have a slice of this." I ran my hand over the surface rippled by a chainsaw blade. "How about we go at it with that two-man saw up in the garage?"

I didn't take to chainsaws, first because of the noxious noise, and second because my father, who'd been a doctor, had told us gruesome stories of what a broken chain could do to a person's face.

A smile spread over Willie's face; as kids we'd used the saw when directed by our fathers to cut up dead trees into fireplace logs.

Because it was too late in the day to start, we agreed to meet the next Sunday. Before I knew it, I was walking beside the riding mower that Willie was driving downhill, a squeaky trailer carrying the saw and the space for our two cross-sections, in our imaginations already cut, varnished, and fitted with legs for our living rooms.

Four pickup trucks were backed up to the tree, their payloads half-filled with fireplace-ready logs and stumps to split later. The farmer's son-in-law and five other men in sweatshirts, jeans, and heavy rubber boots hovered about the jungle gym of limbs, chainsaws buzzing like giant bees above flowers. When they saw us haul out our saw, they turned to watch.

"Whatcha gonna do with that?" one of them asked. "Take a year to getcha a log?"

We took off our jackets and put on our work gloves. I'd worn my oldest, rattiest denim shirt over brown pants with frayed cuffs; at least I looked the part. The gray fall sky and cool brisk wind gifted us with a solemn, serious atmosphere, appropriate for our undertaking.

"Geez, Tick," Willie said, using my family nickname inherited from Kipling's character Riki-Tiki-Tavi, "the saw's not even as long as the cross-section we wanted."

He laid the saw against the span of trunk to show me that halfway into the tree we'd run out of blade to push and pull. We made our way down the trunk to below where the branching widened. Its waist there slimmed to two and a half feet.

Willie rested the saw on top of the bark and ran a bottle of oil along its edge, the thick, brown liquid slipping down the rusty blade. "Here we go," he said.

I grabbed the knob on the saw's far end and we were off.

We sawed for a good half-minute before stopping, both of us breathing hard. We'd barely broken through the inch-thick bark.

"You pushing or pulling?" he gasped.

"Both," I wheezed. "I think."

He poured on more oil, and we see-sawed some more.

"Why was it we wanted to do this?" I asked, next time we paused. "Oh, yeah, to get back to nature, to relive our past."

Back and forth, back and forth.

"There's no sawdust coming out my side," Willie shouted, the sweat coming in rivulets down his brow.

"You're not pulling hard enough."

His upset look turned into a smile, and then he was laughing so hard he had to stop sawing. "You got me."

One of the chainsaws strolled over. "How you boys doin'?"

"Getting there," answered Willie.

"Wood's hard," Chainsaw said. "Wet, too. And green."

"Thanks for the encouragement," I felt like saying, but changed sides instead, now on the handle side.

Half an hour and twenty rest periods later, I looked at our progress. "We're not even halfway through."

"We're darn near halfway through," Willie coached.

"That's why you're a successful businessman," I laughed, "and I'm an unsuccessful cynic."

We got back to it, oil oozing out the sawed fissure like maple syrup running down pancake bark and snowflake sawdust.

Willie stopped sawing. "I've had it," he admitted. "The tree won."

"We didn't lose," I insisted. "Being out here, giving it a go, is victory enough."

Willie revved the tractor mower and was rumbling toward the hill when I spotted a two-inch diameter tree on the forest floor.

"Hang on." I grabbed the saw and lopped off a log in a trice. "Just wanted to see if I could still do it."

"Here." Willie rolled a stump underneath. "Get a couple more. I'll hold."

Boilermen

RICHARD NEWMAN

> He is the grimy caryatid upon whose shoulders
> nearly everything that is not grimy is supported.
> —George Orwell, *The Road to Wigan Pier*

The Boilerman will never elbow his way to the same mythical status as the American Cowboy, the Westward Explorer, or the Sergeant in the Trenches. Like these other American male icons, the Boilerman is a loner. Like them, he possesses a gritty masculinity, a quiet stoicism, a sense of mystery. Like the others, the Boilerman is also extinct.

But let's face it: the maintenance department doesn't carry much romance, and the boilerman's days are too mundane, his duties too proletarian, his work all minutia and repetition. He toils as a handyman, a jack of all trades, as if he pored over secret male-only repair lore in the sooty recesses of the boiler room. He trudges ignominiously behind walls and under floors, gnome-like and unseen, for the greater public good.

When I mention boilermen, my friends' grade school boilermen spring to mind, recalled almost sadly along with their names, usually ones like Otis or Enoch. I saw my first boilerman in first grade: Mr. Klahnheimmer, a grizzled short man with a huge gut bulging between his suspenders like a gorilla bending the bars of his cage. He had only two teeth, and they grew tusklike from his bottom jaw, a tongue-breadth apart, behind a bottom lip with a perpetual surly curl. He was bald, with two white tufts of hair on either side of his head, which, despite the sparseness of follicles, were imbued with fantastic electrostatic powers to attract an assortment of debris: paper, wood shavings, sawdust, and mysterious dark matter which probably came from the wondrous boiler itself. Considering the immaculate cleanliness of the entire school grounds, we easily pictured Mr. Klahnheimmer as something of a living mop wending his way through the halls, classrooms, and gymnasium.

Mr. Klahnheimmer bore two particularly fascinating physical characteristics. The first was the color of his skin: gray. A dull grayness seemed to exude from his pores, as if his skin cells had begun to adopt the very darkness of the boiler room or permanently acquire the frequent smears of black grease across his hands and face. The second trait was a striking sense of squareness: his squat, squared frame;

his short, squared fingers with black grease embedded in short, squared fingernails; his large, squared head inset with those two small, square teeth.

And for some reason we called this man Zorba. Zorba Clodhopper. Though I can't begin to recall how or why we chose the name Zorba, it had the adhesive quality of inspiration: it stuck, perfectly.

I ran with a crowd of troublemakers, juvenile delinquents perhaps, and Zorba constantly foiled our best mischief. Once two upper-classmates had done us some grievous injustice, so during their gym class we sneaked into the boys' locker room, gathered around the locker they shared, and peed (we weren't old enough to piss—we peed) on their street clothes. Mr. Klahnheimmer had an odd, intuitive grasp of all our troublemaking, because in midstream I looked up to see his fierce beady eyes and two-toothed jaw jutting angrily through the locker room door. "Zorba!" we shrieked in panic, "It's Zorba!" and we ran through the back door of the locker room and into the woods, spraying ourselves with more urine in the process than we ever got onto the offenders' clothes.

Zorba was also the object of our mischief. More than once we crammed as many of those red gumdrop-colored balls as possible, dozens of them, all varying in size, into his gym janitor's closet and laughed ourselves silly imagining Zorba floundering in their midst when they spilled out. Someone else once wrote a dirty Zorba limerick on the bathroom wall, soon followed by a crude illustration. We were cruel boys, and just as unbelievably cruel to each other as we were to Mr. Klahnheimmer. In grade school it was safest to travel in a pack, tearing into the self-esteem of our peers, but at any minute the pack could turn on one of us. Finally, we found someone well outside the pack and peer group on whom to focus our blissful cruelty: Zorba.

What did Zorba think of our cruelty? What did Zorba even think of his re-given name? What did Zorba think about anything, that impregnable mind working like too-well-oiled machinery?

One day, during third- or fourth-grade class, two rows of lights went out, and I was instructed to go down to the boiler room and inform Mr. Klahnheimmer. The boiler room loomed just off the main hallway behind a thick metal door. On this occasion it was open, and I stepped into the darkness. A few metal stairs descended to a concrete walkway that led to the boiler itself. To my immediate right there was an area for hanging coats and coveralls, a few lockers and janitorial supplies and a desk, dirty and worn, but stark-free of any clutter. As my eyes adjusted to the room, I could see the little walkway traveled alongside the huge belly of the boiler, warm and humming, and on the other side I could see a red glow reflected off the far wall, and beyond that—nothing. Darkness. The deep, sooty blackness of the boiler room.

"Mr. Klahnheimmer?" I called.

There was silence, nothing except the hum or stirring inside the big black belly. I waited for what seemed like several minutes.

"Mr. Klahnheimmer? Mr. Klahnheimmer?" I tried again, louder, and then, certain he wasn't there, tentatively, in almost a whisper, "Zorba?"

I went back to class and reported that Zorba was nowhere to be found and thought that was the end of it. Later that afternoon, however, I was called to the principal's office. I was often called to the principal's office, and that call was always accompanied by a sick feeling in the pit of my stomach, as if I'd swallowed my own rapidly pounding, spoiled little heart. I was a professional troublemaker—I knew to take the direct, "sincere" approach to dealing with my trouble by promptly confessing and "reinterpreting" what I had done, but in this case I wasn't sure which act of mischief they'd happened to find out about, and I didn't want to confess to something they hadn't discovered yet. The principal, Mrs. Vanderay, had me cornered, and spin control would be limited.

"Mr. Klahnheimmer mentioned this morning that you've been calling names into the boiler room when he's trying to work," she said.

I explained what had happened.

"I didn't think he was in there, so I did say 'Zorba' once," I said pitifully.

"Mr. Klahnheimmer is a dear, sweet man with severe heart trouble," she said, "and he doesn't need children calling him names and making his blood pressure go up."

"I'm sorry," I said, truly repentant. The heart thing kind of got to me. A shadow of a third dimension was beginning to form on his character. "But one thing, I'm curious—if Mr. Klahnheimmer was in there the whole time, why didn't he answer?"

"Obviously, he was working."

"Oh," I said, but this wasn't obvious at all. What was Zorba really doing in there? Looking at dirty magazines? Worshipping dark boiler room gods? At this time of my life, I was obsessed with Greek mythology—I'd once matter-of-factly reported to my stricken Sunday school teacher that I didn't even believe in all this "God and Jesus crap," that I believed in the Greek myths. I privately worshipped my two favorite gods, Aries and Hermes, troublemakers both, and I remember musing *if a boilerman worshipped a god, he would doubtless worship Hephestus, the smith of the gods. But Hephestus is the kind of god who wouldn't care about being worshipped. He wouldn't want to be worshipped at all. The only way to worship a god like this is to keep your mouth shut and get to work.*

That's what I imagine Zorba doing—lying inside his hot furnace, sweat bursting from his forehead and spilling into his eyes while coals glowed impossibly hot beneath him, fixing the thermostat or stoically clearing the vent shaft, so all the schoolchildren, both the good ones and the rotten ones like me, could stay warm in their classrooms during the winter.

A few years later I moved to a different school, called Stringtown Elementary, where I saw my second boilerman. His name was Floyd, and, like Zorba, he was bald, but he was exceedingly tall and stooped, with long hands and forearms dangling uncertainly at his sides, as if he never knew what to do with them unless they worked on something. Also unlike Zorba, Floyd had no teeth at all, and his epidermis was entirely pink—a bright pink, a cartoon pig–colored pink, particularly his shiny pink bald head—and of course we called him Pink Floyd.

Like Mr. Klahnheimmer, Floyd possessed a quiet melancholia, only much more so, as if Edvard Munch's Screamer had screamed itself out, then sunk into inexorable sadness and lethargy. It was almost too much to bear—his dark mouth, gaping mournfully, the pink brow continually wrinkled in consternation, and, well, the proverbial deer-in-the-headlights gaze. And also like Zorba, I never once heard him utter a single word.

Indeed, the only thing that seemed to give Floyd any pleasure at all was ice cream, which our school cafeteria served every Friday, and which, without fail, he would eat with such alarming zest, spoon plinking repeatedly against the bottom of the bowl, that he'd give himself a headache and sit with his round pink head in his great pink hands for several minutes before shuffling down to the nurturing black womb of his boiler room.

Floyd also tinkered, and as we walked past his dark room, we could see him at his lighted workbench, large pink hands lumbering over a school bell or classroom clock, which he always managed to take down and repair without our ever seeing him on a ladder, while we were at lunch or gym or recess, and then we'd find, upon returning to our room, that the clock was working again, or, suddenly, at the end of math class, the once-broken bell would ring us out of our math-naps.

It took less than a week to fall into the troublemaker crowd at Stringtown Elementary. To my dismay and relief, kids were just as cruel here as they were at my last school. Here, however, Floyd was too easy prey. Picking on Floyd would have conveyed weakness, and only the bottom of the schoolyard pecking order would have pecked on Floyd. At this new school, students had to be prepared to stand up to the toughest kid in the class—picking on Floyd would have been akin to kindergarten worm-torturing.

Sometimes, however, a joke seemed too good to resist. As we filed down the hallway from one class to the next, Floyd often leaned against the thickly painted cinderblock wall, mop in hand, waiting for us to pass before he continued his work. I can still see the fear and bewilderment on his face as every one of us boys calmly deadpanned to him as we passed him one afternoon, "Pink Floyd, 'Another Brick in the Wall,'" a top-forty hit at the moment. Another time we chanted, with zombie-glazed eyes and bad British accents, the song's mantra, "We don't nayd no educaytion / We don't nayd no thought control." The effect was to scare the bejesus out of Floyd, who abruptly stopped leaning against the wall and shuffled downstairs to his lair until we were safe in our classrooms.

In the twenty years since I left eighth grade, I've come to realize that both of these boilermen were everything I'm not. For one thing, Zorba and Floyd were decent men. In some sense, they are my opposites. No doubt they got up early in the morning. They put in long, hard days of manual labor. They knew how to fix things. They never complained. They were incapable of lying. They probably never even exaggerated. Did they even speak? And they never once exhibited a vindictive streak in retaliation for the generations of cruelty we as children and adolescents inflicted on them.

The last boilerman to influence my life I never actually saw. For years, *River Styx*, the literary magazine I edit, rented an office in what was originally the head-quarters of some large insurance company. Erected in 1911, it was once a beauti-ful building in the Spanish Mission style, with stucco walls and a red-tiled roof. The building was replete with several stained-glass windows (a distinctive feature of St. Louis architecture), spiraling marble staircases, Corinthian columns, a labyrinthian layout, several enormous vaults, two beautiful wood-paneled rooms, a few mammoth fireplaces, and even a small library.

Of course, much of the building had fallen into disuse. The place was filthy. Electricity was unpredictable. In the summer we sweltered, in the winter we froze. One particularly cold winter the owner was vacationing at her other home in Florida, and it fell upon me to go downstairs to the old boiler room and light the pilot light in the furnace. Few people had descended this far into the bowels of the old building, and when I pushed open the huge, rusted door to the boiler room, I was met with a horrible stench. After fishing around for a light switch for what seemed like hours, I was astonished to see the floor littered with dead pigeons. Dead pigeons covered every square foot of surface area. There were hundreds of them, all a mottled gray-green, splayed across the concrete floor as well as on top of shelves or draped over an overturned trash can.

Death had been packed in that room for at least a year. The stench was similar to the time I de-boned a dozen chicken breasts for a dinner party one hot St. Louis summer and afterwards left town for a week, forgetting to empty the trash. As I picked my way through the dead pigeons, I couldn't help but notice how the old boiler dwarfed the gas furnace next to it, also built before I was born. That old boiler took up most of the room, like the carcass of a brontosaurus, filled with undigested pigeons, and you could hear the air rushing through its rusting belly.

The pilot light on the smaller furnace was off. As per the landlady's instructions, I lighted it, and, in a few moments, the furnace fired up again with an exuberant whoosh. It was that simple. Even I, a veritable Luddite, a technological quadruped, could do it.

On my way back across the pigeon field, I noticed a small desk in the corner, covered with dust, a few pigeons, and crumblings from the walls. On the desk was one item—a small desk calendar featuring Classic Burlington Northern Freight Trains. *Of course*, I thought, *steam engines—boilers on wheels*, and I looked at the picture, dated May, 1972, a steam engine spanning a long bridge. I imagined that poor bastard boilerman staring into the month of May, 1972, the day finally come after fuel oil replaced coal, and gas replaced fuel oil, when a mechanical incom-petent like me could flick a switch and heat up the whole building and render him obsolete, and janitors were no longer salaried but rather subcontracted out by "housekeeping" companies that didn't even pay a livable wage. Zorba and Floyd at least had pensions.

A friend of mine, after graduating from college, once worked for a custodial company, and he usually cleaned schools. He came in only at night to clean the rooms and floors and never even saw the kids—lucky for him. He made minimum wage, worked "part-time," and received no benefits. In all the office buildings I've ever worked in, cleaning never came with our rent. If we wanted it clean, we could hire a weekly housekeeping service or do it ourselves. Always, we opted to save money and do it ourselves, which meant not cleaning it.

And so I hadn't thought about Floyd or Zorba in twenty years. Surely they were both long dead, as was their mode of menial labor and stoicism. Had they safely retired with their pensions before becoming obsolete? Were they survived by family members? Did they come home at the end of each day to tell their families of our cruelty? Certainly not. Unfortunately, it often takes death and guilt for a person to bloom into a whole person before us.

For some reason, standing in that pigeon-littered boiler room, I remembered another very male, boilerman-type figure from my youth: the dour seventh-through-ninth-grade football coach who chain-smoked on the sidelines and prayed before every game and after every practice. Daily prayer was one of the many reasons I quit football, and once, during that portentous silence immediately following the amen and before the whistle, I asked with what I hoped was a tone of obvious false naiveté, "Coach, does God really like our team better than those guys?" And after all the inane praying to some Aries-like football god, the coach always concluded with the words, "Dear God, grant me the serenity to accept the things I cannot change and the courage to change the things I can."

Where did he get this bullshit? I wondered. What couldn't anyone change? I was a young man facing a lifetime of changes, all of them mine. Accepting things you couldn't change, I thought, was a spineless surrender. Years later I learned that the words are part of "The Serenity Prayer," minted on the backs of Alcoholics Anonymous medallions. For whatever reason, our coach had also left out the last line: "and the wisdom to know the difference."

Today I look back and cringe at my youthful cruelties, littering my past like all those stinking dead pigeons, and wince at what heartless words I'm still capable of. I certainly cringed in that boiler room, after not thinking of Floyd and Zorba for so many years. Football inanities and AA clichés aside, the past and our own capacity for cruelty are two things we can't change—and two things we could accept with courage and sadness if not serenity. Taking one last look at the Burlington Northern, that boiler on wheels chugging into the horizon, I tasted both the cruelty and compassion rising up in the back of my throat and swallowed, learning a little bit more what it might mean to be a man before I shut the boiler room door again on those dead pigeons.

Bits of Glass

JENNA M. POLK

Eddie collected glass bottles. He stuffed a mahogany cabinet with blue bottles, red ones, orange, and opaque brown. A few depicted dramatic scenes—Indians slinging arrows at cowboys, women sashaying across a ballroom floor, a saint reaching her hands out to a grieving crowd. He kept old wine bottles on the top shelf, leaving glass cars, owls, and palm trees in the reach of children. Mythical creatures scampered across his bottles, forever poised with their mouths open and arms raised. The bottles never changed.

"Eddie is going senile," my mother confided to me in the car. We were making our yearly trip to his house in Cornell, Michigan. I stared out the window as we drove by an abandoned school. The metal skeleton of the playground remained, though anything wooden like teeter-totters had been used for firewood long ago. "Eddie and Viola are lonely. They don't have visitors very often," she said. She had packed the trunk full of vegetables from our garden, to fill up their fridge and make up for the time between visits.

When we arrived, Mom and Viola made for the kitchen. Eddie guided me into the living room and unlocked his cabinet. "You wanna see something? It's a secret," he winked. I nodded, and he took a flashlight from his back pocket. Peering over his shoulder, he saw Viola stirring soup in a big silver pot. She laughed at something Mom said and slapped the wooden spoon against her thigh. She wasn't paying us any mind. Satisfied with our privacy, he pointed the flashlight at his bottle collection, and rainbows blossomed. He waved it back and forth, and light sparks darted across the back of the cabinet. "Sometimes I do this for hours," he whispered. His hands trembled.

Eddie turned to me: "You like my bottles, don't you? You can have one." I shook my head, smiling. "Go on, take one from any shelf but the top one." He placed his hand on the small of my back and gently nudged me forward.

"I could tell you a story about each one," he boasted loudly.

"Don't even get him started!" Viola called from the kitchen.

I smiled and grasped a peacock-blue bottle by the neck. "Do you remember where this one comes from?"

He took the bottle from me and turned it over in his hands. "Yes," he breathed, "yes, this is the California bottle." He turned and walked into his bedroom—which was across the hallway from his wife's. I followed.

"This bottle is from when I used to work in California. I worked for a company that did odd jobs on rooftops." He sat down and patted the bed. I sat down next to him, and he took a photo album from his nightstand. Showing me pictures, he prattled on about "the guys" and the beautiful weather. "They got palm trees the way we got pine. It's not like up here—nine months of winter and straight into summer. One time, we stretched a 240-foot banner across the front of a building. Goll', now that was a task." He indicated a picture of the banner, which read: **Presenting the 1962 Buick!** "The 1962 Buick was *the* car to see at the World's Fair."

Eddie showed me more pictures from the World's Fair, including a bulletin board that read, **Welcome to the World's Fair: the space age of 1962.** I giggled.

"What are you laughing at?" he grinned.

"The 'space age' of 1962."

We laughed together.

Eddie took pictures from rooftops all over California. Skyscrapers, sports stadiums, huge sculptures—he scaled them all. One picture showed him at the top of a forty-foot-tall ladder, putting the star on a massive Christmas tree. "Were you scared?" I asked, remembering my fear of heights.

He laughed, "After a few weeks on the job, I could scamper along a railing this big." He held out his hands less than a foot apart.

At the back of the album, there was a photograph of a crowded basement. Garlands hung from the rafters, and everyone had a drink in hand. In the center, a man sat on a pool table. He was dressed in an expensive suit, but his trousers were curiously absent. A woman's head loomed in the bottom left-hand corner, her hair an elaborate twist on the crown of her head. An out-of-focus man dangled mistletoe in her face. "This was the Christmas party. My whole crew went there, and everyone was pretty far gone." He took the peacock-blue bottle and uncapped the lid, placing it beneath my nose. A thick, gingery scent tickled my nostrils. "I bought this aftershave just for the party."

I closed my eyes and breathed deeply.

"Viola said that they're moving to a nursing home in three months," my mother told me on the drive home. She leaned forward over the steering wheel, stretching her back. "They're going to auction off their things and buy new furniture with the money."

"What about Eddie's bottles?"

She shrugged. "They'll probably get sold or recycled."

I uncapped the bottle and traced its mouth with my finger. Savoring the scent, I pictured Eddie at his party. Back straight, eyes bright—he danced. He held a young woman close to him, steady hands around her waist. She pressed her cheek against his, and he breathed in the perfume of her hair.

"All those bottles sold to a stranger," I muttered.

"What?" Mom asked.

"Nothing."

During winter, I heard that Eddie had auctioned off his bottles with a starting bid of $20. He wrapped them in newspaper and stored them away in boxes. No one bid on the bottles at first, and Eddie seemed bemused. A middle-aged woman broke the silence and upped the bid to $30. Finally, some man in a neon orange hunting hat bought the collection for $65. He packed up his pickup with the boxes, and the bottles rattled as he drove down the icy road.

Once, Eddie dusted his bottles every day and kept the cabinet polished. He fussed over them, angling each bottle to show off its best side. There were so many memories stopped up in the glass; he had a story for each one. The new owner bought the collection for $65 and probably kept it in his basement, waiting for the day the bottles would be worth something.

Eddie passed away a year later, after the Christmas of 2001. The doctors thought something was wrong with his heart—perhaps an aneurysm. In the end, he simply fell as he walked to the bathroom. His heart ruptured, and he died. I was nine hours away and couldn't attend the funeral; Mom told me about it over the phone. During the service, Viola sat with her hand pressed to his casket and said, "Thank you, Eddie. Thank you for so many wonderful years." If he had lived until January, they would have shared their fiftieth anniversary. But Eddie passed with the old year.

I'd known he was sick. Earlier that summer, Mom had made the annual visit without me. She brought them fresh zucchini, cherry tomatoes, snow peas, and cilantro. She also brought lilacs from our garden. "They look older, especially Eddie," she told me. "But they're happy in the nursing home. You should go visit them. They would really like to see you." I nodded, promising myself that I would visit. Eddie told wonderful stories, and I planned on getting them down on paper. We'd talk, and I would take notes—maybe even bring a tape recorder.

"Did you know that he kept two of his bottles?" Mom asked.

"No, what did he keep them for?"

She shrugged. "All I know is that he kept an old milk bottle. I don't remember what kind the other one was—you should ask him."

I never quite made the trip out to see Eddie. That summer I moved in with my dad in Illinois, trading up pine forests for cornfields. The Upper Peninsula of Michigan was just too far away from everything; Milwaukee, the nearest city, was six hours south. I was tired of being snowbound during the never-ending winters. I needed to get out.

My dad's home was thirty miles outside of Bloomington, a sizeable university town that became my stomping ground. There, I spent hours in the local bookstores, getting lost in the maze of categories. In Michigan, the nearest bookstore had two aisles, and most books were under the "Hunting and Fishing" category. I tried new restaurants and even acquired a taste for Indian cuisine at a local restaurant, the Taj Mahal. Bloomington wasn't a cultural center, but it was bigger than anything I had ever known.

The summer after Eddie's death, my family moved into an old farmhouse. We worked at making our house a true country home, putting lace curtains in the windows and old crockery on the kitchen counters. I unpacked the bottles that Eddie had given me over the years: two glass cars, a lady's boot, and the California bottle. I set them out on my windowsill.

My stepmom lugged a heavy box into my room and then sat at my desk. She watched me dust the bottles. When I set the peacock-blue bottle down on the windowsill, she reached for it. "Is that an old Avon bottle?"

"I think so."

She studied the bottle, holding it up to the light. "The label is in perfect condition! It's very old and well-preserved." She turned to me. "You know, honey, this is probably worth quite a bit."

I looked at my bottle. "Like thirty dollars?"

Handing the bottle to me, she said, "More like three hundred." She wandered into the sitting room and began hanging decorative plates on the wall.

I uncapped the bottle and smelled the aftershave. But I was afraid the scent would escape, and I closed the cap tightly. I left it on my windowsill. The bottle looked beautiful in the light.

Artists

In Hyde Park: Momentary Stay against Confusion

MARTHA MODENA VERTREACE-DOODY

As I write the first draft of this piece in the Office of the Chaplain at the University of Chicago Hospital, my husband Tim answers a page. As chaplain in his green lab coat, he responds to referrals from the staff. He brings communion, or prayer, or a Bible, or his ears and broad shoulders, to anyone in need. He walks with families facing life/death decisions, especially when he is on a twenty-four-hour on-call assignment. Designated a Trauma One hospital, it receives many of the critical accident and intensive care cases. His ministry is as much a part of him as his being Swedish. If I asked him why he does it, he would say, *Because I have to*.

Near my house, young people from the Baptist church at the corner hung dozens of prayer balls in the maple trees. Called *Prayers for Peace*, each clear plastic ball holds a scrap of paper inscribed with a prayer. At night, the streetlight reflects its glow off the stained glass into the prayer balls, swaying in a cold autumn wind. Somehow, in troubled times, I need to believe that prayers and wishes and dreams are more in concert than not. Participants also painted a large mural whose various scattered images bespoke both catastrophe and hope, incorporating secular and religious symbols presenting the reality of death, yet the hunger for peace. While the overwhelming spate of artistic reaction has few precedents, my own attempts to write in response to those events produced only silence, which heretofore baffled me.

I find myself challenged by my own inadequacy in the face of such great unknowns. Left with my poetry—or with a blank page—I have little confidence in my voice as a mouthpiece for world concerns, as a vehicle for social change. There are writers who can and do speak words into action; writers whose ability exceeds mine. I only hope that, if I am true to my own stirrings, to whatever is given me to speak, then somehow I give someone else the confidence to travel farther than I, to take more risks, to dare to achieve more.

When I thumb through several poem fragments, chaotic drafts which I hope to coax into poetry, I think of my husband, whose paper for his class in homiletics focuses on the impact that the terrorism of September Eleventh had on patients in crisis-care situations and their families. I realize that none of my poems prevent more terrorism. I cannot fool myself into believing that my words can wick the fear that has seeped into every neighborhood, into every household.

While writing is not a ministry, perhaps it is a vocation, a way of life to which writers are called. I know that I experience my own voice keenly when I share my work, when others share themselves with me in response. If my husband, or anyone else, would ask me why I write, why I try to get the stuff published, I could only say, because I am driven to hear my voice in the clear light of day. *Because I have to.*

When my husband and I married in midlife, our friends, although happy for us, never seemed to pass up an opportunity to chide us for all we missed. Married a year after we met, after a two-month engagement, we are well aware that a first marriage of twenty-year-olds raises the expectation of children. But for us, our first project is a house, not progeny.

We are a bi-coastal couple. A California dreamer from San Francisco, Tim sees bricks as objects that fall on people during the San Francisco Earthquake. Born in Washington, D.C., I spent my childhood wrapped in received memories of a Midwest city of frame houses burning in the Great Fire. We chose Chicago, where we met, as the city in which we stake our claim, midway between two coasts. Our challenge: to combine East and West to make Midwest.

Our neighborhood, Hyde Park, was a township, later annexed to Chicago. Although close enough to the Loop to make shopping and entertainment easily accessible, nevertheless the neighborhood retains its particular charm, its personality, its identity. Fortunately it takes less time to travel the seven miles to Chicago's Loop via Lake Shore Drive than it did a century ago. The speed of change in an evolving neighborhood can be dizzying. My father's sister remembered when the primary mode of transportation was horse and buggy; when people wished on the moon, not walked on it; when letters were sent in envelopes, not cyberspace. As she grew old, and older, the world outpaced her ability to adapt. She died a happy, albeit confused, woman fifteen days after her one-hundredth birthday.

Our parents knew wartime. During World War II, Tim's father served on Okinawa. My father, a chronic asthmatic, tried several times to enlist. When he made his last trip to the recruiting office, my mother had dinner waiting for him when he returned, as she knew he would be rejected yet again. Only reluctantly did my father ever show me his draft card, with his 4-F status. Our marriage springs from the foundation of what our parents accomplished for a future which they could not perceive, a different kind of war—a war in which the adversary does not march in ranks, or wear easily identifiable uniforms.

One hundred years ago, the Columbian Exposition conquered the area, necessitating landfill along the lakefront for the Ferris wheel, the lagoon, indeed all façades creating the White City, so named for the gleam of the structures. The Irish provided a firm foundation for our church, Saint Thomas the Apostle. Designed by Francis Barry Byrne, its duplicate stands in Cork, Ireland. Completed in 1890, with its wide high-roofed hall, unsupported by pillars or arches, the church is considered the first modern American Catholic church, according to the booklet available for sightseers, and is listed in the National Register of Historic Places. Housing, too, arose at that time, including a row of modest bungalows unique to the area. We had wanted to buy one, nestled along Dorchester Avenue, but no one was selling.

Finally, our agent took us to Greenwood Avenue, lined with honey locusts, cottonwoods, and oaks whose topmost branches wove above the street. The plaque on the corner house read:

Built in 1903, this city block of semi-detached rowhouses from 5200 to 5400 South Greenwood is considered to be the original Professors' Row of the University of Chicago. Samuel Gross Developer.

This brick and gray stone house is our first home purchased together. Our inheritance made possible in large part our financing the purchase—a bittersweet reality in that our parents will never see the fruit of their long work handed down to us. Tim's parents were both from San Francisco. My mother was born in Somerset, Kentucky, and my father, in Jeffersonville, Indiana. Other relatives come from Ohio, Michigan, Sweden. For me, settling in the Midwest has become a familial homecoming as much as settling in the area that would give me the key to my writer's voice.

The house became our dream as we avoided terms like *money pit*, a favorite term with which my brother Walter describes his graceful vintage home in Philadelphia, choosing instead the word *character*.

My husband and I met by pure happenstance. Before meeting Tim, I loved a wild Irishman, James, whose relatives lived in Hyde Park for over fifty years. Because James lived only three blocks from me, we walked all over our neighborhood. Our feet owned every square inch. Hyde Park was our playground. We got fat in all the eateries, saw the best and least of theaters, boutiques, and delis wax and wane. Although we never married, the *we* that we became produced a wonderful, enduring relationship that only his accidental drowning could sunder—a fainting spell, a tub of running water, a blocked drain. My world ended that early May morning when I lost my partner, my best friend for over twenty years.

My co-op filled with cards and dishes of food from concerned friends who also knew and missed James. A friend gave me a copy of Donald Hall's *Without*, his extraordinary collection of poems based on the illness and death of his wife, Jane Kenyon. I devoured those poems. I read every word in every card or letter, as if by immersing myself in words I paid a poet's price, the ransom of my partner, who would then call saying it was all a mistake, that my words could bring him back if I promised not to look back through the shadow of death.

I pored through mysteries, especially stories whose central characters were plagued with the unchangeable reality of the beloved missing. *Without*. Ian Rankins's John Rebus, Colin Dexter's Adam Dalgleish, and Peter Tremayne's Sister Fidelma provided hours of escape from James's sudden death as I entered into the twisted, tangled world where violence lurked just around the corner, along the strand, in the next town.

I wrote dozens of poems about James's death, then fell into a deep silence. Meeting my husband helped me recover the sound of my poems in my own ears before

I had the courage to set them to paper as I had done before. The ancients believed that, in the shamanic power of the poet to make or break fortunes, the poet's work manifests the physical embodiment of the self and grants the metaphysical certitude of life after death. Well before Shakespeare wrote *So long lives this, and this gives to thee*, the Egyptians carved their names in stone in order to assure themselves of the afterlife of memory, and scratched out the names of their enemies in order to erase all traces of their existence.

Yet, for the first time in my life, I was no longer sure that I could trust my voice to possess the strength to speak of my life with James without becoming trapped in a cherished but idealized past. I held no illusions about personal immortality gained through the pen; nor did I hold out much hope for making a widely read contribution to the general discourse of writers.

Because I felt the power of words to underscore the tragedies of experience, I decided, one Sunday in January, to attend the 8:00 mass rather than the 10:00, which James and I had always attended. Not hearing him sing the responses with me, not having him harmonize with me—his strong baritone to my squeaky soprano—was disheartening. At the early mass, I heard Tim proclaim the readings as if he owned them. The pastor who introduced us officiated at our wedding in December.

I knew, however, that if I were going to open myself to a new relationship, especially so soon after James's death, I would have to write my way through profound grief, seek healing, and then celebrate the joy of my marriage. And so the poems came—at first as letters to Tim—haltingly—but they came: poems which celebrated our walks to Botany Pond, the floating garden of lily pads and ducks on the campus of the University of Chicago; poems which remembered our treks to find mummies at the Oriental Institute on campus; poems which reveled in long meals at the Medici Coffeehouse.

And so the poems came—some good, some not. Some published, some not.

I then wept for the friends and relatives of those killed in the terror of September Eleventh. I wept for my brother, whose firstborn child and only son, Bryan, was murdered as he sat in his car. I wept for James, whose like I did not think I would see again. Finally I realized that I had to struggle to regain my speech, to free myself from my silence. The United States Poet Laureate Billy Collins notes that after tragedy, *What we want to hear is a human voice speaking directly into our ear*.

While turning the soil in the garden for the first time after my husband and I moved to our new house, I found a 1903 Indian-head penny in the garden near the sunflower seedlings. I could imagine a craftsman working the land, preparing the lot for one of several houses in that block. I could imagine his consternation at losing the penny, which probably was worth more to him than a dollar is today. After planting and watering sunflower seeds which I had soaked all night to quicken, I found two four-leaf clovers in a backyard patch.

Dangling from a rope line that my husband strung between our house and garage, the bird feeder with its loose seeds sways next to the seed bell. Our modest garden fills with passing birds, seldom scared away by the pounce of a stray cat. Cardinals alighted, and sparrows and robins, blue jays and monk parakeets, warblers, wrens, chickadees, and doves and pigeons—the usual city dwellers. In flowerboxes, which my husband built from scrap wood, I grew petunias, marigolds, pansies—a riot of color for the back porch and the occasional hummingbird.

A small green room facing the backyard garden is my favorite writing space. When silence emerges in the face of catastrophe, patience is the stance that the writer assumes. This silence is not the popular notion of a writer's block, when nothing seems forthcoming. Rather, the writer is besieged by so much stimulation, such an onrush of ideas, such an emotional turmoil, that the writer feels paralyzed, unable to begin. When ideas drag in coming, or when memories come too fast, I go out into the backyard to wrestle with my daimon.

At dusk the neighborhood raccoon patrols garage roofs into the trees linking our yards like a lifeline. Poetry seems to dance in and out of my life like the fireflies nightly exploring my backyard I see from my bedroom window.

Tim's voice rises above the din of cicadas, whose nymphal skins I find drying on leaves of tiger lilies. As he invites me to share in his treat of California apricots, I remember that adult fireflies have only one thing in mind—finding other adult fireflies.

The Poet as John Nachtigal

KEITH RATZLAFF

For ten years I've carried around an old tin can key, the kind you used to find soldered to the bottoms of coffee cans. I found it hanging on a nail in the old railroad depot in Henderson, Nebraska, the place where I grew up. I took the key then to remind me of John Nachtigal—the man who had lived there and who had died not long before—even though I had never talked to him and really didn't know much about him. Even now I still don't know much, and what I "know" is so embellished that it's hard to find the truth. It's at least partly true that he deserted the Russian Army, probably the Forestry Corps; just when, I'm not quite sure, although it must have been around 1920. Supposedly he was afraid that Russian spies would find him, drag him back across the Atlantic, and press him into service again. Maybe that's true, but maybe it's just talk. I know he was a carpenter who built a bungalow on North Main Street; supposedly he lost the house in a card game. I don't remember ever seeing him talk to anyone. My mother says with assurance that my grandmother was frightened to death of him.

By the time I was growing up in Henderson, the railroad was long gone, and Nachtigal had been living in the ramshackle depot on Front Street since I could remember. Front Street is Henderson's main artery—the only angled street in town, skewed against the grain of the street grid, since it follows the line of what used to be the tracks. The depot stood just outside the business district in one of the most prominent places in town. There John Nachtigal gardened a little, kept bees, threw his cans in a pile outside his door, and burned his trash in the weed patch between the depot and the high school.

I have in my head only two clear pictures of him. Picture one: When I was little, I went with my mom to deliver a food box to him at Christmas. I remember the cans and weeds, the swaybacked steps of the lean-to porch that Nachtigal— or somebody—had tacked onto the depot. The red paint had peeled and worn to pink. I think I remember him wearing a yellowed BVD shirt with brown pants and suspenders, but maybe not. Maybe this is all a composite of other times and I'm inventing and remembering as I go. I remember a yellow and white cat. Picture two: I was walking home after dark. I looked in his curtainless window and saw

An earlier version of this essay was published in *Mennonite Life* 46, no. 4 (December 1991): 22–23.

him reading a newspaper under a bare yellow bulb hanging from the ceiling. The shadows were hard, and his eye sockets and the outline of his jaw were dark. I remember feeling at that moment both sorry and ashamed for some reason I couldn't—and still can't—name.

I suppose I keep the coffee can key to remind me of where I come from, as a kind of memento, a word that capitalized is part of a prayer in the Catholic Mass, and uncapitalized is a strangely old-fashioned, frilly word that simply means a reminder of the past. Where I come from is a town at the edge of the Midwest, dominated by three large Mennonite churches and the school (now consolidated). The closest I've come to explaining this place to my coastal or European friends is to evoke America before World War I, when people inherited farms and businesses, died or were disfigured in farming accidents, married within the church, didn't divorce, still spoke a little Low German, ate big meals, knew their cousins. All of this for better or worse. But in a culture that believes in the transience and marketability of everything, from consumer goods to marriages to world events, my key is a reminder that to have grown up when and how I did is to be able to look back and find, if not permanence, at least continuity. In a culture that cannot account for death, it's good to have a souvenir, a memento mori.

I've also come to see John Nachtigal's role in my hometown as a kind of allegory of the role of the poet in the larger world, as an answer to the question of whether art and artists matter. That Nachtigal lived in the very heart of town, not on the edge of it or on a farm by the river, forced us to think differently about ourselves. We had to include him because he lived with us, and we had to account for what it meant to include him. We didn't have to like him or look at him or talk to him, but he made us think inclusively—as a community, not a tribe.

Richard Wilbur in "Poetry and Happiness" says "it is possible . . . to write out of one's private experiences of nature or God or love; but one's poetry will reflect, in one way or another, the frustration of one's desire to participate in a corporate myth." Poets can write without audiences; there's nothing inherently communicative about a creative act. But the urge to make is still the urge to account for being human. Artists embody their cultures; they can't help it. That's different from being useful, but doesn't preclude it. The basic connection between artist and community isn't reciprocal or commercial or utilitarian; poets aren't plumbers (and in my case thank heaven for that). At its core the relationship is holistic and mystical, the kind of symbiosis you get between the shape of hills and the sky you see them against, or the inseparable bond in the way a curve bends a road. Whether John Nachtigal liked any of us or not I can't say. But he bought his groceries at the IGA and was buried in the church cemetery. If he was ours, in another way we were surely his.

When I was first learning how to write poetry, I wrote a number of poems in what I thought was the voice of John Nachtigal. The earliest were romantic paeans to rural life and the satisfaction of farmers and carpenters. But gradually his voice—my voice, of course—became that of someone more solitary, almost always trying to justify himself. Oddly, or maybe not, that voice seemed more at home, more connected to people and place in the ambivalent ways Midwestern towns are actually tied together—by the accident of immigration, the hard work of farming, by church or the defiance of it, by knowing each other's lives because, as someone has said, we are each other's stories:

Out Here

As a rule there's nothing here
to see. Our fences ride away
on land that couldn't care less.
We wait for something to stop
and defy the horizon,
somehow for the roads to come back.

When the starlings left last fall
we thought about swallows,
the way they know the straight lines
of geography and year. All winter
we prophesied, but birds
straggled in all spring, miraculous
as weeds and we didn't see.
We did not believe they could cheat us.

The only train here in the last ten years
killed Marlow and an out-of-town girl
while they pried into each other's clothes,
the car hidden on rails under the sumac.
The girl probably said: Marlow.
Honey, there's a train coming. And he,
with the certainty of our lives, probably said:
I doubt it.

It's like that. When we talk about the river
we mean water running away. When we listen,
it's for the one cracked second
when the clapper hits the church bell
before the sound loses itself
toward whatever direction God is.

That's not a romantic voice, but I hope it's a real one, a Midwestern one. There was nothing romantic about Nachtigal's life, unless being alone is a romantic state, and I don't believe that. Nor is living in a cold depot, or having kids vandalize your beehives because the plaque the bees secrete ruins the finish on the Camaros in the high school parking lot.

During the part of my life I spent growing up in Henderson, John Nachtigal didn't produce anything, like Duchamp, who "retired" from art to play chess for the rest of his life—which in the end was Duchamp's ultimate artistic act. Nachtigal was our paradox. He wasn't needed, but he was necessary. His squalor kept us from seeing ourselves as too good, too holy. He didn't tell us anything we wanted to hear. We knew "Nachtigal" meant "nightingale," but we'd never heard one; and we didn't know that it was and is an old-world bird that only sings at night and alone.

Midwestern Dramas

DAVID RADAVICH

Drama and the Midwest—isn't that an oxymoron? It sounds like one to many who do not live in or know this part of the country, and even to many who do. The Midwest has a reputation of being the "not" place—not the impassioned South, not the establishment East, not the romanticized West. It seems to fall between, an absence that stays the rest of the country, that holds other regions together like a gluing block in carpentry.

Nobody was even clear until fairly recently about what the Midwest is. The boundaries aren't distinct; they shade or seep in all directions: to the East in mid-Pennsylvania and West Virginia, to the South along the Ohio, to the West in the Ozarks and Great Plains. The Midwest has become at last an area marked by Great Lakes and great rivers—the Ohio, Wabash, Illinois, Mississippi—providing astonishing fertility and crisscrossed with railroads and waterways like nerve patterns in a highly developed brain.

When thinking of this region, one instinctively latches on to Illinoisan Frank Baum's *The Wizard of Oz*, with its Kansas farm and folksy lifestyle twisted by storms and taken, astonished, through animated fields to a city of glittering skyscrapers. It's hard to improve on this insightful juxtaposition of some of the Midwest's most salient dramas: flamboyant weather, the tension between wanting to stay rooted in home and soil or to escape for adventure, the aliveness of nature which can aid or torment, the sharp, glistening verticality of cities rising insistently from flat or rolling landscapes. These are quintessential dramas of the Midwest, which remain fixed in our imaginations from an astonishingly small number of books and movies, among them *State Fair*, *Field of Dreams*, and *A Thousand Acres* (all, interestingly enough, set in the archetypal state of Iowa).

But these are more generalized conflicts, and not many would think of the Midwest in connection with *theatre*—plays written about, performed, acted out in and of the country's midsection. That honor, we assume, belongs to Broadway, Hollywood films, maybe Tennessee Williams's Mississippi and New Orleans. I used to think that way, too, deceived by the seeming comfort Midwesterners evince in their outwardly uneventful lives. The surface of the Midwest seems placid and reliable—its preferred trope a litotes that diminishes extremes and softens rhetorical edges—the service it performs in the American psyche being stability and reassurance, the canvas against which more colorful palettes can be applied.

In the past few years I've begun collecting Midwestern plays and playwrights. At first it began as a kind of fossil hunt: I expected to undercover a few rare birds whose bones might still be preserved in the muddy riverbeds of history. As I searched I found more and more and more specimens, until my collection includes perhaps the greatest array of dramatists from any region in the twentieth century. William Dean Howells, the first important dramatist from the Midwest, is now remembered mostly for his fiction and his mentoring of younger authors like Mark Twain and Hamlin Garland (Midwesterners both). William Vaughn Moody and Booth Tarkington are mostly unremembered except by a few diehard fans. But what about Tennessee Williams, who launched his career in St. Louis and Columbia, Missouri, where he acted and wrote over a dozen plays set in that area? What about Arthur Miller's early work in Michigan? Thornton Wilder? And then there are all those wonderful African-American dramatists: Langston Hughes, Lorraine Hansberry, Charles Gordone, Adrienne Kennedy, and August Wilson, among others.

Why are we missing this remarkable picture? David Mamet's breakthrough plays were set in the Midwest—*Sexual Perversity in Chicago, American Buffalo*—but he's since moved on to Hollywood. David Rabe arose out of Dubuque, Iowa, and has found himself in the East. Even Lanford Wilson, with his impressive canon of works set in Missouri and Illinois, now writes of New York and California. Why are these writers all but invisible as Midwesterners? What kind of cultural silencing refuses to hear their voices, or if it does, fails to recognize their origins in the centerfield of American life?

This is a perplexing question I have confronted as playwright and poet living and working in the Midwest. Is it better to move to New York or L.A. to find actors, theaters, fellow dramatists to interact with and feel nurtured by? Or will one get lost and trampled, like William Inge, the "dean" of Midwestern playwrights, who, after four smash Broadway hits in the 1950s, transferred to Manhattan and ended up committing suicide in 1973? Midwestern playwrights face the same dilemma—to stay in comfortable but unrecognized anonymity or to seek the more beguiling glamour of fame and fortune elsewhere—that many other Midwesterners face.

The decision for me was easy. Though not a Midwesterner by birth (Boston) or upbringing (Oklahoma and Idaho), I've taken to the elemental conflicts of my adopted native land with the passion of a convert. Ferreting out the hidden dramas of the Midwest—overturning those rocks of anonymity and dismissal, finding what's on the underside, what provides the foundation for this mostly unknown and unseen part of the world—has become my particular vocation. Such are the conventions of Midwestern society, which diminishes its own truth, understates its own history and accomplishment, that most denizens of the region don't recognize their own cultural markers, the layers of Native American, European explorer, multivalent immigrant past. A seeming homogeneity of Midwesternness, refracted onto itself by Easterners and Hollywood, obscures the textures of cultural soil in the country's midsection that many here have been brainwashed to believe.

For that reason and others, native theatre has not flourished much in the Midwest, despite thriving metropolitan centers like Chicago and Minneapolis, despite the many exported Midwestern playwrights working throughout the country and abroad. Saint Louis, a city of over 2.5 million, offers astonishingly little innovative theatre, despite world-class institutions for music, art, and opera. The preference goes to sanctioned imports mostly from the East Coast or Britain, for musicals and dinner theatre. The story isn't much different in, say, Indianapolis or Columbus, though pockets of committed playwrights, actors, and directors struggle in each of these cities to create interest in, and support for, new theatrical work.

The truth is, even now, with the dispersal of Broadway-level talent and enterprise to almost every corner of the country, fame and fortune for a Midwesterner is apt to be found elsewhere. I once heard a persuasive paper arguing that the Midwest was "colonized" by Easterners and that the prevailing trope of silence and understatement represents a form of cultural "resistance" to what has been perceived as Eastern glibness and trickery. Whatever the final intricacies of this argument, the Midwest suffers from its own invisibility, to itself and to others, and a lingering inferiority complex.

I had a telling experience of this when my one-act play *Wake Me No Wake* opened Off-Off-Broadway in 1996. The play had been produced three times in Illinois and Saint Louis, all very satisfying to both author and audience. But the starry allure of Broadway is such that I summoned all friends I knew in the greater New York area and arrived at the theatre full of hope with my wife and a claque of supporters for my very first Off-Off-Broadway production.

What an awakening! Despite good actors and acting, the performance was much worse than anything I had witnessed in the Midwest. The director simply misread the play, didn't understand, or care to understand, it. Was this a matter of cultural myopia? That's hard to say, as I've had four subsequent Off-Off-Broadway productions of other plays, with varying degrees of performance quality. I can, however, testify that Midwestern productions of my plays have been as good as any I've had elsewhere in the country, though they receive little notice, not much community support, and precious little funding, corporate or otherwise.

What does it mean to live and write in the Midwest, where the magic of words is mistrusted and overt conflict avoided? Why do Midwestern readers turn instinctively to the coasts for experience, two regions which habitually regard Midwestern home turf as quaint (at best), boring, backward, or simply irrelevant? A big factor, certainly, is East Coast control of publishing and the West Coast lock on popular media. But the issue goes much deeper, into the psyche of Midwesterners, who take virtually all their information and much of their predilections and assumptions not from the life around them but from outsiders. As a region, the Midwest has been taught to distrust, even denigrate, itself, despite rich traditions which clearly indicate the opposite.

To be sure, a wonderful, stubborn strain of defiance does operate under the plain-spoken surface. When I lived in vibrant, enjoyable, hilly Lawrence, Kansas,

our mantra to outsiders passing through and dismissing Kansas as flat and uninteresting was: "Keep on driving!" Many people enjoy their lives in the Midwest
without feeling particularly deprived of glamour and Dean & Deluca's. But that
rarely articulates itself as Midwestern pride, nor does it prompt much support of
the local arts (though Ohio seems to manage this better than most, through its
energetic state arts network). In Illinois, we suffer from "the Chicago complex,"
in which the overwhelming metropolis tries mightily to ignore the five-sixths of
the state below I-80 and to dismiss its more rural values. Like many other aspiring
cities, Chicago is a wannabe New York or London, looking outside the agricultural
Midwest for approbation and applause. The same is true of the state's flagship university, the University of Illinois, which takes as its mandate not serving the state's
population but reaching outside the region for news-magazine validation of its
world-class reputation.

What, again, does it feel like to write in the Midwest? To confront regional invisibility in the outside world, and cultural indifference at home? Why would
dramatists, particularly, stay when other regions offer more audience interest and
institutional support? Those are difficult questions to answer, but I believe many
of us find the anonymity invigorating, certainly challenging, maybe comforting.
Maybe we Midwesterners feel more comfortable waging artistic battles at home
rather than emigrating and become other than ourselves. On some days, I revel in
the prospect of subterfuge, knowing that writing plays in East Central Illinois, one
of the *least* auspicious theatre locations in the country, may lead to the most radical art. Not radical art as the bi-coastal establishment would have it, but something more elemental still: a striking Midwesternness that has not been voiced,
not seen, and scarcely can be recognized.

That and taking comfort in the enduring dramas of the Midwest which nurture
all who live here. The conflict of wanting to live rootedly where we are known
without pretensions for who we are versus the desire to escape, to seek adventures
and overturn our confining selves and contexts. Circularity of seasons that offer
constant theatre against the backdrop of years unfolding like rows and weavings
of corn, soybeans, fruit trees, cemetery headstones. The flatness of many landscapes, softened by hills, punctuated in sharp relief by perpendiculars: soaring
trees, silos, skyscrapers, all the more dramatic against horizontal soil that radical-
izes our attempts to stand up and keep moving.

And, of course, the rich drama of harvesting what we sow, enjoying fruits of our
labors in time, but also punishing ourselves through pollutants, both physical and
moral, we casually discard in water, soil, and air and then consume. The Midwest
may be the most karmic region of the country, where we live intimately with our
own acts and the good and evil consequences of ourselves. We literally eat and
drink from our own efforts; we inhabit fertility and its potential waste. Living
here, we can't escape destiny; we can run away and try to forget and re-create elsewhere, but the honesty of living with consequences provides the central Midwestern drama, which sustains and calls to many of us in our struggle with invisibility.

Lest one think of the Midwest as unrelentingly rural, it is important to acknowledge the great cities of our region, their muscle and magic. That wizard pulling levers behind the curtain in Oz is most likely an Easterner, from Wall Street, perhaps, or Washington, D.C. Or if he's a Midwesterner, he's performing for the outside world his dance of glittering hopes. Midwestern cities, unlike their coastal counterparts, lie not on the edges but between, in the nodes, nourished on all sides by confluences of water and soil, trade and gathering wind. When you pull aside the curtain, the voice of the Midwest reveals a horse of different colors: solid economies, lively arts, striking architecture, enterprise of vigor and value. Names of Indians—Cincinnati, Peoria, Chicago, Milwaukee; names of explorers—Detroit, Columbus, Lasalle, Marquette; remakings of the past—Lebanon, Cairo, Versailles, Toledo—bespeak our hidden glamour and variety.

Living in the socially defined Absence of mid-America is rich and full. The face we Midwesterners present to the world keeps us largely unknown, perhaps unknowable: we can move freely in ourselves, in nature, in lively communal rituals, without outsiders knowing of our means and purposes. Even our cities hide their manifold nature. The masked drama of the Midwest thrives on seeming simplicity and restraint, while sending embassies to all corners and continents, protecting sources, investigating possibilities, renewing continually its abundant spirit and energies. To live here means to participate in enactments of life that others can only turn into cliché, our silence understood by the seeding, radical ground we know.

Being Midwestern

DAN GUILLORY

On a preternaturally sunny day in the early summer of 1974, I visited a 125-year-old Illinois farmstead, owned by one of my senior colleagues, a fellow who had helped to farm this rich bottomland near the Illinois River during the grim days of the Depression. He volunteered for the Marines in 1942, entering college and the academic life after the war. Ted Barton, as I shall call him, had inherited this land from his great-grandfather, who had served in the Mexican–American War of 1848 and was awarded this parcel of farmland as part of his "mustering out." Ted and I were bent studiously over our fishing poles, trying to hook bluegill in the deep green pond on what had once been the Military Tract of the Illinois Territory, land originally set aside as payment in kind for Army veterans. We fried the fish, we picked ripe blackberries, and we waded through sandy-bottomed creeks where silver-backed shad flashed in the shallows. The day began to compose itself with the neatness of a poem. I met Ted's brothers, sisters-in-law, and numerous cousins. We fired up an ancient John Deere tractor and cleared thick brush on the crown of the hill. At evening we stood overlooking the Illinois River Valley and watched the sun go down on Dickson Mounds, site of a state museum and one of the largest burial sites of the Mound Builders, whose culture stretched up the Ohio and down the Mississippi all the way to Louisiana.

A small college creates its own bubble-like environment, and I had made little real contact with the people or the land of Illinois until that day with Ted and Muriel, his schoolteacher wife. As we walked through the woods, I spied a strange plant on the forest floor. "Jack-in-the-pulpit," exclaimed Muriel. And what was that odd little assemblage of twisted leaves? "Dutchman's breeches," she explained. Growing up on a rural farm, she had pressed countless leaves and flowers into scrapbooks, memorizing the names, especially the folk names, of the plants that grew on the prairie, including big bluestem, little bluestem, coneflower, prairie dock, mayapple, wild carrot, chicory, and rattlesnake master.

She and Ted could point out honey locust, black locust, post oak, river birch, bush pine, red oak, white oak, burr oak, shagbark hickory, and all the common trees of prairie groves and river courses. They loved the environment on a first-name basis, including the avian realm of brown and green hummingbirds, scarlet tanagers, flickers, indigo buntings, purple finches, red-tailed hawks, Canada geese, and even the odd bald eagle soaring over the willows and sycamores of the bottomland in late fall and winter. In medieval culture, schoolmen and churchmen used the Latin term *plenitudo* to describe the abundant richness of the created world. Since the time of my arrival in Illinois, I had craved a certain fullness, something to compensate for the agoraphobia induced by the dizzying 360-degree horizons. In the ecosystem of the prairie, Ted and Muriel helped me discover an analog to the ecologically dense world of the bayou. They were my guides and gurus to "prairieland," the quaint term used by early visitors to describe this vast and rolling terrain.

Many of my East Coast peers in the groves of academe also suffered agoraphobia on first encountering the vaulted skies and long horizons of central Illinois. But, having grown up in a bilingual home in the Cajun bayou country of southern Louisiana, I experienced a special kind of cultural displacement, a yearning for the spiciness of Creole phrases and the rich gumbo of drawls and accents. The open skies and rolling landscapes of Illinois seemed strangely overpowering, and I desperately missed the familiar green canopies of live oaks festooned with tropical vines and wispy Spanish moss.

After several visits to the Barton Farm, and after hiking along the banks of the Sangamon River, I slowly acquired an intuitive sense of the land. I returned again and again to a bluff outside Decatur where the Lincolns cleared space for a one-room cabin in the summer of 1830. One of my good friends from Louisiana actually described the spot as "beautiful," a term I had previously reserved for every locale except Illinois. By precious increments my personal prairie space was becoming populated with living things. I was beginning to hear the faint murmuring of history and the softer whispering of prehistory. Without realizing it, I was succumbing to the blandishments and seductions of Middle American culture. Today, when I hear the Midwest dismissed as flat, dull, boring—or "flyover country"—I am profoundly offended, because I had to study the landscape and learn to love it. This process may have been a survival tactic, or it may have sprung from the deepest of all American needs: a craving for a sense of place. In the Midwest, place seeps into your bones and being. A few years ago, I spent part of a pleasant autumn in the Lake District of northern England. After weeks of stone cottages, picturesque lanes, hills, and lakes, I found myself scanning the horizon, like a submarine captain at his periscope, searching at dusk for the archetypal red barns, spindly windmills, and silver-capped silos of the prairie, the fundamental icons that have been wired to my consciousness.

I am not the first outlander to fall prey to the siren song of the prairie—nor the first to write about this curious process. In the 1830s many English, Scottish, and eastern American travelers trooped through Illinois, marveling at the giant sunflowers, the swaying prairie grass, and the majestic Indian mounds, still untouched by farmers, looters, or road-builders. In the same decade, poet William Cullen Bryant left Massachusetts to visit his two brothers in Jacksonville, Illinois. During the visit he had ample time to explore the Illinois prairie at his leisure, and in 1833 he published "The Prairies," calling them "the gardens of the Desert." He noted the uniqueness of the place "for which the speech of England has no name." Eliza

Farnham, an upstate New Yorker with transcendentalist and progressive leanings, was also taking copious notes on Illinois life and culture at the same time, a little farther north near Peoria. She did not publish her work until 1846, when her classic *Life in Prairie Land* appeared. Farnham was remarkably candid about the hardships and beauties of frontier life. She catalogued the pains (malaria, wildfires, blizzards, frostbite) and the pleasures (wide prairie vistas, the cornucopia of fruits and flowers, and the joys of rural hospitality). So contemporary writers, I suppose, must likewise take the good with the bad, the broad green bands of corn and beans, the meandering creeks and streams, the flaming autumn foliage—and the hideous strip malls, the ugly landfills or slag heaps, and the urban blight of boarded-up houses and rusted-out factories. The urban sprawl of Chicago now extends ninety miles westward from the Loop. But there is still much to savor in the transparency and regularity of everyday prairie life, a social and personal richness still accessible in hundreds of towns, counties, villages, and townships across the Midwest. The overwhelming impression one receives—when flying overhead in spring and summer—is that of a broad expanse of green fields, rich, fertile, and beautifully organized.

The orderliness of things is palpable—not merely the mathematical precision of fields, the angularity of barns and outbuildings, or the neatly platted grids of typical Midwestern towns. There is a reassuring sobriety and decency in human relations, a sense of moderation and social optimism that sustains even the smallest transactions and accounts for generosity on a heroic scale, especially during natural disasters like the great flood of 1993. There is a kind of social gyroscope that keeps things upright. Aberrations like the Springfield race riot of 1908 (witnessed by poet Vachel Lindsay) become models of shame, and the perpetrators are forever anathema. In his masterful study of early Illinois culture, *Frontier Illinois*, James Davis makes the point that, alone among the Midwestern states, Illinois had no early history of internal conflict on a major scale because social consensus was always the goal. Ray Bial, a friend and distinguished Midwestern author-photographer, once shared with me his belief that the essence of the Midwestern personality is moderation. Outsiders may understandably mistake that quality as evidence of apathy or inertia. But the cultural evidence shows otherwise. This same region became the cradle for Frank Lloyd Wright's revolutionary Prairie Style of architecture as well as the Chicago Renaissance, including the University of Chicago, the Art Institute, *Poetry: A Magazine of Verse*, the poetry of Vachel Lindsay, Edgar Lee Masters, and Carl Sandburg—and the novels of Sherwood Anderson and Theodore Dreiser.

So the harvests of Illinois have always included cultural and agricultural productions, poetry and red barns, skyscrapers and hybrid corn. American poetry and architecture, both dependent on strong, simple lines and honesty of expression, owe their modernist beginnings to prairie culture. Filmmakers routinely evoke Midwestern icons as symbols of the heartland and basic American goodness, as in the recent *Road to Perdition*, where young William Sullivan is rescued by an anonymous Illinois couple whose poor farm is located in a beautiful montage of straight highways and neatly demarcated fields. Young Michael's experience echoes that of another fictional character, Huckleberry Finn, who is treated wisely and humanely by Mrs. Judith Loftus when he crosses over to the Illinois side of the Mississippi River in the improbable disguise of a girl.

The whirling cultural changes of the Reagan Years—downsizing, Yuppies, corporate mergers, globalization, personal computers, and MTV—battered the Midwest like a giant tornado. Yet the heartland might have survived with its farms and culture intact if it had not been for a fundamental shift in the economic structure of the region. The Midwestern crash was part of a larger scenario of global wheeling and dealing over the turbulent decades of the '80s and '90s. This dreary saga featured sleazy entrepreneurs, junk bonds, crooked CEO's, multinational corporations, and fraudulent earnings reports that ultimately pushed the Dow-Jones Average over the 10,000 mark until the cascade of 2002, when the paper empires of Enron, Tyco, WorldCom, and others began to blow away.

But the fundamental damage had already been done; the basic wealth and industrial plant of the United States never really recovered from the decade of the '80s, in spite of the successes of Silicon Valley and the sale of SUV's and overpriced real estate in the nineties. Detroit and its Midwestern allies in auto production continued to be downsized (General Motors) or co-opted (Daimler-Chrysler), as they fired trained workers and lost more and more market share to Japan (Toyota, Honda) and Korea (Hyundai). The automobile industry had always been concentrated in the Midwest, so the workers in the heartland were naturally hit the hardest. Steel-producing plants and other forms of old technology were also concentrated in the Midwest, and the massive closing of foundries and mills gave the region a new nickname—the "rust belt." The loss of all these high-paying, skilled factory jobs was catastrophic, but this blow was only the beginning in the erosion of Midwestern identity.

Many of the petrodollars accumulated during the 1970s and 1980s were being used by OPEC investors to buy farmland in the Midwest, often on a large scale. In central Illinois, for example, foreign and domestic speculators drove up the price of prime land from around $700 to $5,000 per acre. At the same time, the Reagan administration, through the Department of Agriculture and the Production Credit Association, encouraged farmers to buy additional acreage, oversized tractors, combines, and other agricultural technology, like high-tech hog farms. Most of these purchases were in the six- or seven-figure range. By the mid-1980s the combined effect of global economics and over-investment at the local level resulted in a catastrophic decline in the number of family farms, especially in Iowa and Illinois. In spite of the heroic efforts and populist idealism of John Mellencamp and Willie Nelson through their Farm Aid concerts, the process seemed inexorable. The '90s were as disastrous as the '80s in this respect, and the decline continued, part of a larger historical shift that has been occurring since the 1920s and the advent of the modern highway system. But the loss of the family farm is the single biggest blow to Midwestern culture and identity, because the farm is the physical and psychological seat of the defining values, like the family, the work ethic, the land itself, and a certain kind of stoicism.

All of these values naturally suffered during the accelerated decline in the number of family farms during the 1980s and 1990s. The first signal change in attitude was a marked preference for the "sun belt" as opposed to the "rust belt." Many of the aging factories in places like Clinton, Iowa, or Flint, Michigan, or Anderson, Indiana, or Decatur, Illinois, closed their doors or abruptly gained new owners whose headquarters were perhaps in London or Osaka. And the new owners often renamed, sold, consolidated, or downsized their American operations, a trend quite visible in Decatur, as shown by the fate of Borg-Warner, Firestone, and A. E. Staley, taken over respectively by Zexel, Bridgestone, and Tate and Lyle. Off-season and supplementary factory jobs that had silently kept the family farms afloat began to vanish. Farm children, who in the late 1960s and early 1970s, armed only with a high school diploma, could land high-paying factory jobs in nearby towns, now found themselves out of work and out of luck. Hence they began the exodus to the sun belt, especially the counties clustered around metropolitan centers like Atlanta, Dallas, Houston, San Antonio, Denver, and Phoenix. In the 1980s the population of Decatur, Illinois, actually declined, while an eerie scenario of real-estate and consumer-goods deflation began to play out. A house that would have cost at least a half-million dollars in the hyperactive Southern California market would go for a tenth of that in central Illinois. When I first moved to Decatur (in June of 1972), all of the following everyday items cost significantly more than they did in my hometown of New Orleans: a quart of milk, a gallon of gasoline, a new washing machine, a visit to the dentist, or even a ticket to the Roxy. By the 1980s that ratio was diametrically reversed, and I was shocked to discover how expensive New Orleans had become. Even today Chicago and St. Louis appear to be bargains by comparison to Boston, say, or New York, or San Francisco.

Economic changes always have far-reaching cultural consequences. Midwesterners became poorer in dollars but poorer in spirit, too. A certain sense of inferiority began to express itself. The work ethic suddenly seemed a lot less chic in the waning days of Blue Light Specials. By bumper sticker, billboard, T-shirt, and the yadda-yadda of daily conversation, Midwesterners joined the national chorus of complaint about the drag of working. Closely linked to what Robert Hughes calls the "culture of complaint" was a radical change in attitude toward the weather. Generations of Midwesterners were conditioned by working in freezing weather, driving wagons and cars through blinding "whiteouts," and generally trying to keep warm. Swedes and Norwegians chose to settle in the upper Midwest precisely because of its freezing winters. Now Midwesterners who couldn't physically participate in the migration to the sun belt began to openly repudiate their defining blizzards and ice storms. This new attitude amounted to a kind of cultural treason, because if anything separated Northerners and Southerners, it was the weather. Temperature and temperament seemed closely linked, at least in the popular mind.

During the late 1970s I lived through a series of apocalyptic Illinois winters, a time when people actually bragged about their natural ability to withstand the cold. "Give me the cold because I can't stand the heat!" was the mantra of the day. In 1978, snow accumulated on the ground for six weeks in southern Illinois, and at the other end of the state, in Chicago (where I was trying to work on a fellowship at the University of Chicago), eighty-one inches of snow fell, making that the worst winter on record, temporarily forcing the closure of O'Hare Airport and Lakeshore Drive. I walked through trenches and tunnels of ice to reach my office on Fifty-Eighth Street. Today, I often observe students who have lived all their lives in the glow of planetary warming. In their preferred style of dress they have symbolically moved to the sun belt, making no distinction between winter and summer wardrobes. And they are usually decked out in T-shirts, shorts, and sandals at the first hint of spring. Many of these hot-bloods do not seem to own anything heavier than a sweatshirt. One day in late March of 2002, I watched from my office window as Frisbees were tossed in the air while a late snowstorm zoomed in from Iowa and dumped six soggy inches of white stuff on the incredulous athletes, burying the Frisbees and all vernal exuberance for the rest of the afternoon.

Of course, global warming and unpredicted meteorological quirks only contribute to these skewed perceptions of weather. Although Americans possess critically short memories, some may recall that in 1993, a once-in-a-thousand-year flood engulfed eleven states of the Midwest, including every single county in Iowa, a state which had already lost the largest number of family farms. The most visible archetypes of the culture seem to be slowly disappearing, the snowy fields beloved by poets like Robert Bly, the ship-like barns, and the little white farmhouses with "gingerbread" trimming on porches and gables. Can the Midwest thus maintain its identity as it loses its weather and its most trusted images of itself?

A deeply rooted sense of place has always characterized Midwestern life, and at a certain point culture *is* place. What happens when the place is being systematically reconfigured because the weather waffles or invisible corporations bulldoze family farms to create giant green factories that profit from the much-lauded "economies of scale"? Ironically, I find myself worrying about the loss of Midwestern identity at the same time that I have belatedly found it. In spite of county fairs and active local history organizations (many of which raise funds to save old barns and preserve other historical sites), the younger folk seem to have missed all the poetry of the place. Two of my brightest graduates (both from farm families) were delighted to be "getting out," having found good jobs in San Antonio and Denver. The exodus continues.

While I was writing this essay, squadrons of green and gold Japanese beetles landed to digest the leaves of my elm trees, blackberry bushes, redbuds, crabapple, apricot, and tea roses, free-standing evidence of my Midwestern love of gardening. Of course, people garden all over the world, and admittedly the English, French, and Japanese do so with a special verve and artistry. But in the Midwest, gardening is a common and general practice, occupying a good deal of the population's free time between Easter, say, and Halloween. Gardening was the first behavioral clue to my changing identity in this part of the world. Although I don't aim for champion blue-ribbon pumpkins or giant ears of corn, I do grow organic tomatoes, beans, peppers, herbs, okra (a concession to my Southern roots), and blackberries, as well as marigolds, tulips, irises, tea roses, gladiolus, coneflowers, and wisteria. My acre of good black Illinois soil is populated with numerous trees and lilac bushes, and the seasons follow a more finely tuned clock now that I am surrounded by hundreds of planted bulbs and flowering trees that bloom in succeeding weeks of the springtime. Winter whiteness sharpens the eye and makes one appreciate the tiniest show of green. My first winter in Illinois seemed so melancholy and gray that I treasured every blade that pushed up through the crust of ice—spears of crocus and snowdrop, and the tiny emerald shoots of bluegrass and rye. Gardening is a passport to social acceptance—at least in rural Illinois—and it offers an instant topic or icebreaker for neighborly chitchat. When I first moved to rural Shelby County, where I now live in a 107-year-old farmhouse, my retired farmer-neighbor came over to supervise, inquiring suspiciously, "Are you doing that there *or*-ganic gardening?" He and his wife have been gone for years, but he gave me a stand of deep pink hollyhocks. And this summer they are in splendid bloom, in spite of near-drought conditions.

To garden is to monitor the climate and the weather, and there is an abundance of both on the prairies. I have experienced drought, flood, tornado, blizzard, ice storm, and earthquake, each one several times, in my tenure on the prairie. Here, weather talk is richly nuanced and endlessly varied, the Midwestern equivalent of all the good-old-boy yarns, the verbal winks and nods of Southern tall tales. Like my neighbors, I find myself spinning endless variations on weather topics, especially the actuality or probability of rainfall. "What we need about now is a good *general* rain," the old farmers will utter with oracular certitude, and usually they are right. Or they will offer highly specific coordinates for a rainstorm or tornado: "They got about two-tenths of an inch at Pruitt's Farm, and we ain't got nothing." Or, "Twister followed the hard road all the way from Chatham to Springfield." I think Illinois farmers and woodsmen should go on "walkabout," like the Australian aborigines who identify distinctive landforms and sing the land back into being. Rain talk and weather talk are perhaps popular and profane examples of the same sacred urge.

The grandfather of all weather clichés in Illinois must be this old saw: "If you don't like the weather, just hang around because it's bound to change." And so it does. The mercury can plunge 45 degrees in a single afternoon. At this latitude, we've experienced 110 degrees Fahrenheit in high summer and 25 below in the dead of winter. I speak of actual temperatures here without all the folderol of the "misery index" or "wind chill factor." Perhaps I have grown abnormally sensitive to variations in light, wind, temperature, and the pressure gradients that build like a palpable wall as a new front inevitably moves in. I read clouds. I adore space—the same cavernous skies that terrified a bayou boy used to the small-scale snugness of bayous and lagoons. I cannot imagine the Midwest without that sense of

space, and it is always a relief to return to the middle world after the mountains
and deserts of New Mexico, the swamps and bayous of Louisiana, or the glass and
steel megalopolis of the eastern seaboard. Rightly or wrongly, I feel the Midwest
occupies the physical and spiritual center of the country. It is a great, breathing
organ to which everything else is attached, like a series of appendages.

I have mastered the small rituals which organize the pleasures of life on the
prairie, like raising the index finger from the steering wheel to salute and greet on-
coming motorists without unseemly waving or shouting. Dressing for my part, I
now own work boots, field coats, and a dozen or so baseball caps, some bearing the
logos of hybrid seed companies. I have even learned to listen, not an easy skill for
a loquacious Cajun to acquire, especially one who grew up in a household where
everyone argued vigorously and everyone was always right. Like a Japanese host at
a tea ceremony, where the object of the ritual is to make the other person feel
comfortable, I have patiently introduced subjects that would allow my guest to
speak confidently. Talking purely for the sake of talking seems to come naturally
to Southerners, but Midwesterners engage in the practice hesitantly and with
some obvious twinges of guilt: "I better stop gabbing and let you get back to work."

One of my village friends is Shelburn, the local mechanic and handyman. He
is an excellent, dedicated craftsman, and I love to watch him work. Actually, I
love to hear him talk *while* he's working. He can ramble on endlessly about cars,
contraptions which he's worked on for over five decades. He'll point to the leak-
ing gasket, the snaggle-toothed gear, the frayed wire, and deliver a homily on
failed transmissions and short-circuited headlamps. In between the automotive
talk, he gives short elegies on departed friends, or rhapsodizes about the golden
days when the village had three cinemas and two car dealerships. I hear the ca-
dences of Kentucky in his speech, but I also hear the precise diction of the automotive engineer. One day he stunned me with a little digression on the temples
of Japan, which he had visited during his Korean War service. As one of my Eastern friends is fond of saying, "Midwesterners may be slow to open up, but once the
dam breaks, look out!" I still miss the saltiness, puns, and hyperbole of Southern
speech—to say nothing of its torrential flow. But I have also come to savor the
trickles of plain Midwestern talk, especially its habitual indirection. Rather than
tell a penny-pinching farmer that he must install a new transmission on his farm
truck, Shelburn might say, "A fellow could still get a whole lot more use out of this
truck with maybe a little work, like a new gearbox."

Home can become a tricky concept, as I recently discovered when somehow my
old home of New Orleans began to feel distinctly more foreign than my adopted
home of Illinois. Further reflection on this paradox made me also cope with the
fact that I have actually lived longer in Illinois than anywhere else on the planet.
Thirty years can dramatically alter cities—and lives. Now I pass for Midwestern,
even though the Midwest itself is changing under my feet. And the home I made
here is not merely physical but phenomenological, a place of the mind. I have
lived in any number of prosperous American cities without experiencing what

Gaston Bachelard loved to call the "poetics of space," or what Martin Heidegger liked to refer to as "the ground of being." But my home is precisely that sense of grounded space, here on the prairie.

I cherish certain defining Midwestern moments. After a few days of blustery snow, when the world is locked in ice, the glaring sun hangs in a postcard-blue sky. Everything has been turned to whiteness, save the vertical order of things, telephone poles, weathered boards, rusted-out water pumps, and the fragile vanes of windmills. The light is acetylene, blistering the eyes, and every image is cut sharply into the consciousness, as if by laser scalpel. In such moments I am always fully alive, redeemed, and awakened. Tonight, I am reading under the ash tree, and the heat of July is retreating in slowly moving waves. A gold and magenta sunset is simmering along the horizon. High above, a crescent moon rises over the little ember of Mars. Suddenly, the cicadas erupt in a deafening cacophony, and I gaze slowly over the rows and rows of hybrid corn, undulating as the ground gently rises and falls, as far as the eye can see.

Rural Writers

ROBERT HELLENGA

I grew up quite happily in Three Oaks, Michigan, a town of 1,800 people, so I have no instinctive fear of small towns or of the rural Midwest—the kind of fear you sometimes sense in new faculty members at Knox College, in Galesburg, Illinois, which is where I teach. I mean the fear of being cut off, isolated from large cultural events: symphony, theater, museums. Growing up, I never had a sense that Three Oaks was a backwater, never had the sense that it didn't count for much in comparison to Chicago, which was nearby, or New York, which wasn't.

I've also lived in university towns: Ann Arbor, Chapel Hill, Princeton, and it was in these places that my intellectual identity—ancient Greek civilization/Middle Ages vs. Renaissance/Romantic poets—was shaped. I've never felt much attachment to any of these university towns, however. They are not places I go back to. They are not locales that I turn to in my imagination when I'm writing fiction.

We moved to Galesburg in 1968 and have lived there ever since. In Galesburg I experienced a new awareness of place: a sense that Galesburg did not rank very high in the hierarchy of desirable places to live in the world. I was more aware of this in others than in myself. After all, Galesburg was more than fifteen times larger than Three Oaks, my home town. But I didn't like it when people spoke of being "stuck" in Galesburg for the summer—or even for life.

It's an insidious problem; it's the problem of the prestige address, and it's hard to escape it. In one of my favorite *Seinfeld* episodes, for example, Elaine gets a new phone, and a new phone number, and a new area code. It's not 212! This drives her right up the wall. She's talking to a very attractive guy; they exchange phone numbers, but when he sees her number, he's baffled. It's not 212. She tries to explain that it's still in Manhattan, but he's no longer interested in her. Her sense of who she is is bound up with a sense of place. Manhattan. Not Brooklyn or Queens or the Bronx or Staten Island, but Manhattan. Area code 212. A charmed circle. Just to be there is enough. To be outside the charmed circle is to lose your self-esteem, your sense of self.

I certainly can't endorse Elaine's identity-dependence on area code 212, but I know what she's talking about. When I'm in Manhattan, which is not very often, I have a sense of being at the center of things, of being where everyone else wants to be. I think it's important to resist this sense, but there's no point in denying it.

Since moving to Galesburg, we have lived in Chicago—across the street from Ann Landers—when I was directing a program at the Newberry Library; and then in Chicago again—in Hyde Park, right across the street from the Museum of Science and Industry—when I spent a year on an NEH Fellowship at the University of Chicago. And then we spent a year at 31 Borgo Pinti in Florence, Italy, where —sheerly by a stroke of luck—we rented an absolutely fantastic apartment. I've also lived in Bologna.

Chicago, Florence, and Bologna are all great cities, though for different reasons. I have worked hard to claim them for my own by studying their history, by poring over maps and guidebooks, and by participating in their daily lives. In Bologna, in fact, I have on two occasions marched with the families of the victims of the terrorist bombing of the train station in the big demonstration which is held every year on 2 August, the anniversary of the bombing.

In my first novel, *The Sixteen Pleasures*, the protagonist starts out as a book conservator at the Newberry Library in Chicago. Then in chapter 2 she goes to Florence, and she winds up staying there. At the end of the novel she finds herself in Piazza Santa Croce, and this is exactly where she wants to be.

In my second novel, *The Fall of a Sparrow*, Sara, who narrates part of the novel, winds up living in Hyde Park and working at the Museum of Science and Industry. Her father, the protagonist, goes to Bologna to attend the trial of the terrorists who bombed the train station seven years earlier, a bombing in which his oldest daughter was killed. At the end of the novel he, like Margot, has no plans to come back to the States.

In my most recent novel, *Blues Lessons*, the protagonist lives in Hyde Park, in what seems to be the same apartment building that Sara lives in in *The Fall of a Sparrow*, and which is very similar to the apartment building my daughter—the daughter who worked at the Museum of Science and Industry—lived in. No one goes to Italy.

What about the rural Midwest? Why am I talking about Chicago and Florence and Bologna?

To begin with: when it comes to the rural Midwest, I speak as a native. I don't need to work to "claim" it. I've never studied it, the way I've studied Chicago and Florence and Bologna. I've never even read the Sandburg autobiography about growing up in Galesburg, though I have two copies. I've just lived here. And secondly: as I've already mentioned, it was when we moved to Galesburg in 1968 that I first felt a kind of uneasiness about my identity as a rural Midwesterner. I realized that when someone says that "X is a good place to raise a family," that's code for "X is not a very interesting place to live." It wasn't a major issue for me personally because Galesburg is in fact a good place to raise a family, and we had three daughters. We were able to buy a fantastic house for $18,500. I can walk to work. And the society in Galesburg has been as witty and funny and supportive as any I've ever encountered. On the other hand, why am I talking like this? Why do I feel this need to justify myself geographically (so to speak)? What is the problem?

The "problem" is laid out in Willa Cather's My Ántonia, which I read for the first time last summer. For the first two-thirds of the novel I experienced what I call "neutral affect." It seemed to be a nice enough book about pioneer life in Nebraska, the sort of book that tells you how things were in the old days. It's only when the narrator, Jim Burden, leaves the small town of Black Hawk and starts to look back that the book becomes meaningful for me. At the university in Lincoln, Burden studies Latin with a gifted teacher, Gaston Cleric. One night he props his book open and stares listlessly at the page of the "Georgics" where the next day's lesson begins: "It opened with the melancholy reflection that, in the lives of mortals, the best days are the first to flee. 'Optima dies . . . prima fugit'" (263–64). A few pages later Burden applies this to his own childhood—the world of the farm and of the small town—and as he goes on to study at Harvard and to become a widely traveled, broadly cultured man of the world, he continues to look back to the rural Midwest as his *optima dies*, his best days; and at the end, when he goes back to visit his childhood friend, Ántonia, now a farm wife with twelve children, there's a kind of sadness—a sadness that could easily have become sentimental but doesn't—about the road not taken, and about the old values that are going to disappear over the horizon.

Like Jim Burden, I've gone off to faraway places. (Like Willa Cather, too, I might add, who lived in Greenwich Village.) And I think I've come to understand what he understands in the end. There are two differences, however, between my experience and Jim Burden's.

The first is that although I've gone off to faraway places, I've come back. I live in the rural Midwest. It's my home.

The second difference is not so obvious, but it's more important. It's the most important thing I have to say in this essay, maybe the only important thing.

Unlike Burden, and unlike Willa Cather, I refuse to accept the dichotomy that runs through My Ántonia between the values of the high culture exemplified by Burden's study of Latin and the values of the down-home, salt-of-the-earth Midwestern culture exemplified by Ántonia and her twelve children. I'm not going to deny that there is some substance to this dichotomy; this dichotomy, in fact, was probably inevitable in 1918, when Cather published My Ántonia. But it's not inevitable now; and I'm going to resist it in every way I can.

I see now that this dichotomy is a problem that I've been struggling to clarify ever since I moved back to the Midwest after spending three years at Princeton. What I think I see clearly now reminds me of one of the points Henry Louis Gates insists on in Colored People: there are a lot of different ways to be black. There are a lot of ways to be a rural Midwesterner, too. The stakes may not be as high, but the principle is the same: do not allow yourself to be contained by stereotypes, or by other people's expectations. When I'm in Italy I try to do as the Italians do. I'm not a native, but I try to act like one. But when I'm in the Midwest, I don't need to try to act like a native. I am a native. Whatever I do is Midwestern because I'm a Midwesterner, a rural Midwesterner.

Actually, as a writer I think I figured this out a long time ago. The protagonists of my first two novels are both Midwesterners—it's very clear that they're not New Yorkers or Californians—who go to Italy. They both wind up staying in Italy. But they remain Midwesterners—innocents abroad, open and trustful in their dealings with a variety of cosmopolitan types who try to take advantage of them, but resourceful, sophisticated in their own ways, able to hold their own in an older, more cynical society. They are able to do so because they refuse to accept the dichotomy that pits "sophistication" (a frame of reference that includes Italian folk tales, *The Lord of the Rings*, and classical languages and literature, Iranian as well as Italian culture, international as well as Italian politics) against "salt-of-the-earth" culture (the rural setting in *The Fall of a Sparrow*, with its cornfields and soybeans and long freight trains and functional families). And that's the way I like to think of myself: non-dichotomous.

I want to conclude by briefly addressing a more practical concern. As a writer it probably doesn't matter anymore where you live. It's not necessary to be in physical proximity to New York agents, etc. We have telephones, FAX machines, email, attachments. Actually, I'm not sure that it was ever necessary for a writer to be close to New York. There was always the post office, after all. And a photocopy of a manuscript is just as good as the original. You can make eight photocopies of your first novel and send them to four agents and four editors simultaneously, which is what I did.

I don't know much about the other arts, but surely it's harder to be a rural Midwestern painter or sculptor or potter or musician or dancer than it is to be a Midwestern writer: you can't just stick your painting or your sculpture or your pot or your symphony or your dance in the mail; and a slide or a cassette or a video isn't as good as the original. If you're a visual artist, you need galleries where people can see your work; if you're a musician or a dancer, you need places where people can come to hear or see you perform. Especially if you want to make a living at your art.

Each of these arts has a different structure of economic rewards and incentives. I don't want to speculate about these differences, however, but to point instead to one thing that all artists and writers need, and that is the need for community. I've been fortunate to work at Knox College. I've often thought that the small liberal arts college is the smallest unit from which you can reach out to everything else in the universe. You've got scientists; you've got people teaching foreign languages; you've got historians who can take you all the way back to Sumer. You've got literature people. You've got political scientists and anthropologists. People come to visit from all over the world. And when you die . . . if you've been there long enough, the college will put on a terrific memorial service for you.

This has been my life. I can't imagine it otherwise, can't imagine how I would function outside the world of the liberal arts college community. My first novel was never published. There was a reason for that. But the second novel, *The Sixteen Pleasures*, promised to be different: I'd won prizes; the first two chapters had been published in the Chicago *Tribune* and in *TriQuarterly*; my agent said he'd have no trouble selling it. Nonetheless, it was turned down thirty-nine times over a period of three years. I was fortunate to be living and working, during this time, in a community where I felt valued in spite of these rejections, and where (I might add) I still feel valued in spite of the novel's subsequent success!

But what if you're a rural Midwestern writer who is *not* part of a college community? What if you're on your own? Where do you find the kind of support you need to keep going? The answer, I think, is that you turn to state and local arts councils, to classes at the nearest college or university, to writing groups (even if you have to form your own). But this isn't so bad. Now that I think of it, in fact, it's exactly what you'd have to do if you lived in midtown Manhattan.

Houses

Alcoholism and Family Ritual

BY PETER SELF, M.C.

The importance and power of rituals in primitive societies or in religious groups is well known. Rituals reinforce the shared beliefs and common heritage of those who take part in them. With their prescribed form and unchanging content, rituals help those who perform them make sense of their particular universe. Contrary to the common perception that ritual is of no account or is even entirely missing in the chaotic environment of the alcoholic household, we have found that alcoholic families in fact do have very well defined rituals which they respect with a fervor no less intense than that fervor which prevails in non-alcoholic families.

We divide the types of ritual here studied into two dominant categories: the everyday or Quotidian Ritual and the special or Epiphanic Ritual.

For example, let us consider Subject Family 421.

[This was, in fact, as was well known within the amused community of The Elixir, the Castorp family. The original referral to the Castorp family was provided, again in bold fact, by Hans's cousin Ricky's mother, who had herself participated in an earlier study called "Snatch Time: Alcoholic Wives and Immodesty: A Cross-Referential, Diachronic, and Reverse-Regressive Study of the Stability of Moral Signifiers: Drunkenness, Libidinal Profligacy, and 'Exposure.'" The Elixir clinical staff had coined the term "Snatch Time" to indicate those moments when an alcoholic woman's intoxication crossed that always mobile line which allowed her to sufficiently lose touch with her culturally conditioned "modesty" (a term that the staff struggled mightily with, suspecting that it had little if any power to mean anything in this context) so that publicly exposing her breasts or genitals became, as it was said, "no problem." The study's particular focus on "alcoholic wives" rather than "women" was a reflection of the fact that in a good many instances the wives in the study were the wives of residents at The Elixir, which fact added a certain "aggregate" to the findings. The term "aggregate" itself is also worthy of some comment. The men of The Elixir (a cross-section of Central Illinois' men, and so on the whole a "rough" bunch) imported the term from the system of grading used for various coarsenesses of sandpaper. So, if one were to say, "That's a forty grit on Tom's nose," for example, this was a very humiliating and painful experience on the "aggregate" measuring rubric. Thus, the resourceful thinking of the study de-

This is an excerpt from *America's Magic Mountain* by Curtis White.

sign team allowed them to measure—however qualitative and anecdotal the mea-surement—not only the extremity of the drunken wife's conduct during "snatch time" but the appropriate degree of humiliation for the husband (coarse, medium, and fine, or 40, 80, and 120 for the aficionado) as measured on the "aggregate" scale. It is significant to note that The Elixir would hardly have been interested in the issue of, as Mayor Jesse put it, "drunk women airing their privates" if it hadn't opened up avenues for investigation among the male residents of The Elixir (his-torically 80% of the population). It was in fact a "coarse" interpretation of one Ricky Castorp's mother's conduct with a group of Catholic high school boys in the back of a pickup camper that led, eventually, to his own plan of treatment at The Elixir. Bluntly, Ricky had joined a line of boys from St. Ignatius in which a "train" was being "pulled" by a drunken woman. When it was Ricky's turn, he heard laugh-ter and whispering outside. "Oh my God, Ricky's doing his own mom." This was 20 grit, floor sander, off-the-chart quality "ouch" on Ricky's young nose. The Cas-torp family on Hans's side, upon learning of this incident, had forbidden future contact between Hans and Ricky and had generally ostracized Ricky's family. It was thus with a touch of vindictiveness that she (Ricky's mom, Hans's aunt) had suggested "those nice Castorps" to the study team.]

The quality of so-called Quotidian Ritual consists of three measurable variables: location, variation, and synchrony. The study team carefully mapped the Castorp home for its available spaces and entered them on a grid. The available spaces were living room, dining room, kitchen, master bedroom, second bedroom, bathroom, front porch, front yard, backyard, and hamper. (Note: The team was obliged to add "hamper" because on several relevant occasions young Hans [thirteen at the time] got into the dirty clothes hamper and closed the top down on himself, in which place he stayed for as much as several hours at a time or until a particularly nox-ious scene could be concluded.) Then, by adding a diachronic scale along the bot-tom of the grid, a measurement of family movement could be gained which would range from "lethargy" to "extreme agitation." Hence for Hans Castorp's father:

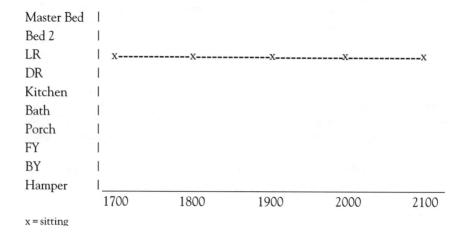

x = sitting

However, for Han's sister, Gretel, the graph looked like this:

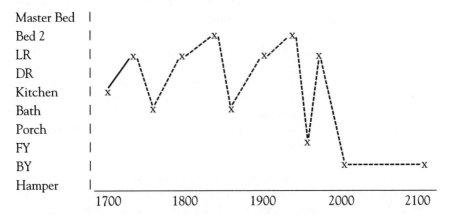

Hans's father and sister perfectly define the extreme clinical states of "lethargy" and "agitation." (Note: Some critics of this study have suggested that in fact in most of these evenings Hans's father was in fact passed out drunk and is for that reason an acceptable example of no particular pattern of "behavior." One waggish clinician went so far as to suggest that since Castorp *pére* appeared never to have moved a muscle on any night of the study period, he had in fact died.) Let's take a look at young Hans's graph on a typical evening just to get another snapshot of what the "ritualized" family routine might have looked like in the Castorp family circa 2016.

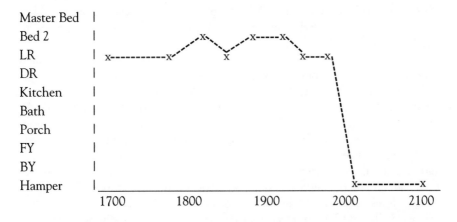

Young Hans's graph, by comparison, has a relatively healthy rhythm in its progression. It is neither lethargic nor agitated. One should note, however, that as the evening progresses, a troubling pattern, not unlike his sister's, emerges in his increasingly rapid movements between the living room and his bedroom. The qualitative researcher would certainly be tempted to comment that the living room space contains a classic "mixed emotional signal" for the boy. It has, on the one hand, the calming and entertaining presence of the television set, and, on the other, the disturbing presence of the drunken father with the television remote. Thus, his mild agitation is caused by the infrequent but unpredictable interruptions in the television programming caused by the troubled waking of his father, who invariably mutters, "What's this shit?" Since Hans had no recourse or appeal to his father's intoxicated whimsy (short of taking the radical and patricidal option of claiming the remote control device for himself), he was left, psychically, in a disconnected, always unfinished nowhere, to which unhappy state he would respond by retreating first to his room and then, ultimately, to the dirty clothes hamper where he stayed until 2300 hours. At that point he came out only in order to go to bed.

The large question for measurement, diagnosis, and therapy remains: Is there an essential difference between the behavior of Hans and his sister? One might suggest that the only real difference is that Hans had what the research team called "pockets of retreat" from family space while his sister, Gretel, seemed for unknown reasons not able to define or identify such spaces for herself. Unless, of course, one would wish to say that her ultimate retreat to the backyard, festooned with the family dog Poochie's excrement, was a "pocket of retreat." (The research team considered and rejected this possibility.) On any descriptive scale, the simple fact that she seems to have fallen asleep out there would make categorizing it as such a "pocket" untenable.

Final note: The measurement instrument that we have employed here does in fact have a rubric (x) indicating "verbal exchange," but we have left it out of this graph because, simply, so-called "verbal exchange" was not a part of the Castorp family's "Quotidian Ritual." The only exception here, as already noted, would be the father's occasional dark commentary, directed, for all ostensible purposes, to the TV itself.

Next, we move to the "Epiphanic Ritual." This is what is commonly called "Special" time in most households (i.e., Christmas and other holidays, but especially Christmas). Here, the Castorps were no different from others. The Castorp family ritual had nothing to do with elaborate preparations for Christmas stretching back for weeks and involving decorating the house, gift buying, and the endless mutual congratulation of friends. Rather, the Castorp Christmas ritual consisted of one forty-five-minute-period on Christmas morning when the family would gather round the Christmas tree to open presents. This, obviously, is a scene repeated in millions of American homes on Christmas morning. Since, however, the Castorp household was also an alcoholic household, their Epiphanic Ritual had one decidedly unique twist. During the course of this Special morning, father Castorp (a hungover father Castorp on a statistical probability of 99.9%) would ignore the drinking of cocoa, the eating of rolls, and the opening of presents and insist instead on his need/right to watch the football game on the television set which loomed above the family like an ominous teetering rock. At a certain point each year, one of the family members (this richly symbolic role was passed from member to member each year) would suggest, "Dad, why don't you turn off the TV for a little while? We're opening presents." To which Dad's ritual response was invariably, "God damn it, I'm watching the goddamned football game, and if you don't like it you can all go in the other room." This apparently straightforward comment was treated, by the family, as oracular and enigmatic. There was usually no direct reaction to it. Rather, it was pondered by the rest of the family as if it were a rune. ("What do you think Dad meant?" "Why did he say that?") This is not unusual. In ritual space, the ordinary becomes the extraordinary; in ritual space, plain speech becomes enigmatic. The family members—excepting the children, to whom I will return—exchanged looks which asked, "How can we understand the expression 'Go away, I'm watching TV' to mean 'Merry Christmas, I love you all, and what did Santa bring you?'" This was the sort of riddle that gives classical mythology its life. The children, on the other hand, were not capable of such a cognitively sophisticated translation or arrangement of expression. For them, the effect of Father Castorp's pronouncement was to add heat to their already simmering psyches. Very gradually, like gently rising heat in a pan of popcorn, they began to rise and fall with increasing vehemence, finally reaching a point where Mother Castorp was trying to hand Hans a present as he bounded three to five feet in the air on the family sofa. To which Father Castorp's response was, following ritual formulation, "Can't you guys keep the goddamn racket down?"

By these marks are families known.

In the year following the study, the original test families were revisited by the clinical/diagnostic teams in order to test the effects of introducing into well-established ritual patterns (both quotidian and epiphanic) a so-called variable. The variable in each case was a well-trained and long-term resident of The Elixir. This variable, in the case of the Castorp family, was one Professor Feeling. Professor Feeling's peculiar (one wants almost to say "alien") presence was injected into the midst of family ritual with unpredictable results, all of which confirmed that—*left to themselves*—all households, whether dry or alcoholic, have powerful regulating family rituals. When that ritual organization is disturbed by the introduction of a foreign element (a very apt description of Feeling's presence), nothing is as it "ought" to be. For instance, during the time of Feeling's introduction into Castorp Quotidian Ritual Reality, the following state of mind was described by Mr. Castorp:

"I can't sleep. There's something ominous and threatening in the house. It's going to get me. I have to stay awake. I believe the house is possessed."

In addition, Mr. Castorp identified the following "uncanny" events:

- the television remote was repeatedly "lost" and just as inexplicably "found";
- Hans's hamper was discovered on the street curb on garbage night;
- Gretel began sleeping in her bed.

All of these eventualities were described by Mr. Castorp as "spooky."

Since it has already been broadly reported in both professional and popular criticism of this study, we will acknowledge the report (if not the fact) that on at least one night Professor Feeling actually slept with either Mrs. Castorp or the daughter, Gretel. (The observer's reaction to this particular variable was the hand-tied gnashing of clinical teeth.)

Mr. Castorp was ultimately confronted with the idea that a member of the clinical team had slept with his wife or daughter through a report that appeared on the program *America's Most Humiliating Home Videos*. He is described as rising from his couch, tripping over the coffee table, falling across it, and landing heavily on his shoulder (the right). From this painful, awkward, and—again—humiliating posture, he is said to have tried to invoke the ritual protocols and language of the "Wrath of Dad." Professor Feeling is said to have acted as if he were a dog rolling on the ground "laughing to see such sport."

The children, for their part, acted as if their hair were on fire.

On the morning of the Epiphanic Ritual—that is to say, Christmas—Professor Feeling crouched on the floor with the family members and enjoyed hot cocoa and sweet rolls. Being a little tightly wound by nature, he was even a little more inspired by the sugar and cocoa than the children were. His "variable" presence yielded predictably "special" (or exaggerated, explosive, chaotic, accelerated, and even demonic) results. Understand, as a clinical variable, it was Professor Feeling's responsibility to introduce destabilizing or simply challenging irregularities in the flow of regular ritual activity. In this way is the strength of ritual practice tested. This variable moment occurred when it came time for Dad to make his epic pronouncements vis-à-vis the importance of the football game. Now, "Dad" was already rather tensely aware of Professor Feeling's variable presence by this point in the study. As we've had cause to mention, the Professor had spent many long hours clad in the rags of Castorp family quotidian ritual with prominent results. Thus, no sooner were the hierophantic words "Goddamn it. I'm watching the goddamn . . ." out of Dad's mouth than Professor Feeling jumped to his feet, threw his long and flamboyant scarf around his neck, and shouted, "Did you say football? I love that fucking game!" He then stood in front of the TV and, worse yet, in front of Mr. Castorp, bouncing up and down like a possessed puppet. When Mr. Castorp began yelling that he couldn't see the game, Feeling said, "Are you too far away?" Then quickly and powerfully he lifted the TV from its stand and carried it over to Castorp the Elder and dropped it in his lap, rather heavily, thus pinning him in the "father's chair" as if he were some wriggling bug on a pin. For their part, the family members went quickly from "shock and dismay" to epic glee and back again, all depending on which was more striking, Dad's curses and threats or the amusing spectacle of him pinned in his favorite chair beneath the TV.

The "Feeling variable" achieved considerable notoriety in clinical circles because he was the first such variable to "go autonomous." That is, the force of his variable character was so pronounced that his original variable function began to seem to all concerned murky at best. Meanwhile, the centrality of his role in the family system—challenging and usurping the alcoholic father—was crystal clear. It might be added that, from the perspective of The Elixir's concerns in the study, this was an "okay" result. The consultants, however, who had designed the study's empirical tools were very unhappy about the conduct of the "variable," and they were furious that the "variable had gone autonomous." They denied that the notion of a Variable Gone Autonomous had any scientific legitimacy. They made particular reference to a) the possible displacement of the father to the streets, b) the destruction of the family TV, and c) the utterly unacceptable possibility of a variable-gened offspring incubating in Mrs. Castorp. The consultants at last received a court order returning Professor Feeling to The Elixir complex, at which point, with an enormous sigh of relief, the Castorp family was able to resume its habitual ritual practices.

No Queens on Pickett Street

MARTHA MILLER

Greg Young and Liberace died the same year, albeit of different causes. Greg was murdered, and Liberace died from AIDS. To this day, neither perpetrator has been arrested. I remember being struck by the timing, because in 1987 I put to rest something of my own. I stopped trying to be a straight woman, stopped trying to live a life that I'd known for many years was all wrong. Of course, queens had been murdered before in Springfield, and I knew as much about AIDS as the next person. Rock Hudson was already gone. A close friend was diagnosed with HIV; at the time we figured he had ten years—he had six.

Greg Young's stage name was Natalie Nichols. Opening the *State Journal Register*, I found a big write up about his murder. The paper elaborated on the glamorous women's clothes squeezed tight in his closet; his anxious poodle shut in the bathroom. The implication was that because of his lifestyle he asked to be stabbed repeatedly; he couldn't expect better. Of course, Liberace's sexual preference, the worst-kept secret in Hollywood, sold tabloids for several weeks. Like Greg's, his death was his own fault. He charmed the socks off all those old women, but it wasn't they who infected him.

I was living in Laketown then. The house was a small Cape Cod that my parents had sold to my husband and me when they retired to Florida. We'd moved our little family into it in the late 1970s.

Laketown began after World War II when a contractor named Barker-Lubin bought some farmland and put up tract housing priced for returning servicemen. The tiny houses were the same size and one of three or four floor plans. When I was a child, in the 1950s, the neighborhood was full of kids. The yards were huge and shady. In the summer our mothers watched *Queen for a Day* on boxy black-and-white TV sets, then lay side by side on a blanket in the afternoon sun listening to a radio through an open window. My sisters and I played jacks on cement porches that held the heat of the sun and played war with green plastic army men in the dust around the roots of the shade trees.

The basement had a huge coal-converted furnace that looked and sounded like a ticking octopus in its center. In the winter, we put on roller skates and skated in circles around it, using up our youthful energy, often ducking damp laundry that my mother hung on plastic clotheslines.

I made my children a playroom down in that basement. I coated the walls several times with white, and I painted a huge purple and gold butterfly near their toy box. My sons slept upstairs under the eaves where my sisters and I had slept. The children were young; that house was probably the only one they remembered.

We lived there eight years before things came unraveled. I was newly sober and looking at my life through a new set of lenses. Ending the marriage turned out to be very expensive—the cost no doubt increased by the woman I chose for my lover. After the divorce, my sons and I stayed in the house on Pickett Street, but it didn't take long for my ex-husband to turn on me.

A *Queen for a Day* contestant, who is thinner than my mother, has one six-year-old son. She has been married five years. The moderator says to her, "Are you a widow, then?" She says, "No, I had my son before I was married." The 1954 audience gasps. I quickly ask my mother, "How did that woman get a baby without a husband? Why is everyone so upset?" My mother tells me that you can have babies without husbands, but only if you are bad. The people now know the woman was bad. Later I plan to rob a bank as soon as I am big enough to get a baby without a man.

The "bad woman" contestant does not win. She will not be queen. Her wishes will not come true.

I sit in a lawyer's office, my butch lover at my side. The attorney is a lesbian who could lose her job if that knowledge became public. "My advice to you is to stay out of court, whatever it takes," says the attorney. "Try to talk to him. See if there is some compromise. You could lose everything in court."

My oldest son goes to live with his father; the youngest stays with me. We stay out of court, a place where even as a mother I no longer have rights. I pack my firstborn's clothes, toys, and books in plastic garbage bags. I tell him I will pick him up on Sunday to spend the day with him. I watch his father back slowly out of the drive, his eyes watching me watching our son. Once I had children, it never occurred to me that someone could take them away. The rest of the evening at the house on Pickett Street is quiet. We choke down our supper, trying to ignore the empty chair.

When I was a little girl, my bedroom was about six by eight feet, a hallway to another room, really, with a slanted ceiling and varnished hardwood floors. I extended the room by putting a bookcase on the landing to the stairway. There wasn't any door to close between my sister's room and mine. When I was sixteen, I started filling my bookcase with alcohol, behind copies of Nancy Drew and Trixie Belden, a pint at a time. By then I had a hi-fi and 45 RPM records or the latest hits. I liked to dance. I spent countless hours alone in the cool, gray basement. I set up an easel down there and painted on stretched canvas with oils, dreaming about how I would leave Springfield and go to New York and live in Greenwich Village and be an artist. I had a thousand dreams. But the only painting I would do as an adult was a butterfly in my children's playroom, ironically in the same basement, in the same house.

My butch lover and I walk through the state museum one rainy Sunday afternoon. We are dressed in blue jeans and T-shirts. My little boy runs ahead of us to see the Indian relics. We do not touch, but see men and women hold hands as they stroll along. I hear a child say the word "homos." Later an older male in an audible whisper says, "All she needs is a good fuck."

Limited war targets the military only. That's the difference between total war and limited war. Terrorists have no problem hitting non-military targets and civilians. My neighbors, I'll never know how many, waged a campaign against my family and me. They aimed this calculated, collective meanness at us. Collateral damage was incurred as the lives of innocent civilians, women and children, were shattered. And the reason—the reason was something so small, so private.

One night I wake to the sound of the phone. "You're going to get AIDS," says a voice that must be a child's. I hang up. The call is only the first of many. My sons learn the hard way that there are now things they cannot share with even their friends. Of course, my relationship with a woman isn't a secret to the neighbors. Foolishly, we do not try to hide anything.

Another evening, after the supper dishes are done, we take a walk. It is warm. The sunset is red and orange. A few blocks from home we pass Jack LaHart walking alone. He is the aging father of a woman I played with when we were children. He lives five houses west of us. I nod to him, but he looks right through me. I turn and find him glaring at us, a grim look on his face.

We were poor, me living and paying bills on half the income I had during my marriage, my lover looking for work. We went all through August without air conditioning because we couldn't afford to fix it. When things broke, there was no money for repairs. But we could have held on if it hadn't been for the neighbors who were openly hostile toward us. A dog upset a trashcan, and we were turned in to the city before we could get it cleaned up. Often we found trash in our yard that wasn't ours. The night I saw Jack LaHart, I realized that this was an organized effort. He was the president of the Laketown Association. I had visions of them discussing us at their meetings as something they had to "take care of," like the sewer problems, potholes, or the X-rated movie theater that had opened in the area. My ancestors came to this country from Germany in 1740. I'm eligible to be a member of the DAR, for Christ's sake.

My lover and I go to Smokie's Den to be with our own kind. Smokie is taking up a collection for a small granite angel and a headstone for Greg Young's grave. His parents had nothing to do with him; we were his family. A line snakes in and out and around the tables while the song "That's What Friends Are For" plays over and over. The gay people of the Springfield community raised a lot of money for a dead drag queen that night. I dance in the soft, warm arms of my lover and feel sad, for Greg, for Liberace, for all of us.

It does not matter what my neighbors do to us; there is no law against wanting a queer out of your neighborhood. I cannot count on the community to which I've paid taxes for help. People who do not even know me hate me. I realize with a new clarity that we are alone.

We sit in the park eating peanut butter sandwiches for supper because we can't afford McDonald's. Our table is under a tree. Rain beats down around us. My tow-headed son is wearing a coat, eating a sandwich with one hand, holding the dog next to him with the other. He is shivering. When we finish eating, we sit in the car with the heater going, trying to dry off. A realtor is taking a prospective buyer through the house. This scene is repeated several times in the next three months. I have to get at least what I owe on the house, and I cannot. Repairs need to be made; interest rates make the house payments too high. As the harassment escalates, I consider walking away and letting the bank take the house.

Later at home, my little boy tucked snugly in his bed, I make two cups of Earl Grey tea.

"We don't have to do this," my lover says. "We can stay and fight."

I think of my son, shivering in the rain, a brother he sees once a week, friends that tease him at school. I shake my head. "No, we will not fight."

She waits until I sit across from her. "I'm just saying that somebody has to fight."

I say, "No" once again, and the discussion is over. I have decided to start looking for an apartment. If I can't sell the house, I will leave it to the bank. I am not totally dispossessed; I have too much to lose in a fight, and it is impossible to battle hate while simultaneously suffering from its effects.

At the last moment, I found a woman interested in buying the house. She called me, in fact, shortly after the realtor sign came down. I think she may have been supplied by one of the neighbors (a friend or relative, perhaps), but I'll never know for sure. I told her she could take over the payments and pay the closing costs and the house was hers. Interest rates went down a few years later. If I had been in a position to wait, I could have gotten the ten thousand dollars in equity I had in the house. But I was in no position to wait. Some things are more precious than equity.

The moving truck waited in the driveway. I stood at the upstairs window through which the morning sun, always a little too bright, woke me, the same window I'd talked my eight-year-old sister into crawling out of (I'd told her I'd go next) so she could slide down a plastic clothesline rope to the ground, the same window from which I watched my son, his head down, get off the school bus and slowly walk toward home. I'd turned to the attic, where my sisters and I had played during the day, making forts between old suitcases, and avoided at night, when it became a dark, cold place behind the clothes rod. In all my years, I'd never seen the attic empty. Stripped of its contents, it looked small and innocuous. It smelled dusty. Only as I write this do I wonder about my own children. Had they played there? Had they been afraid at night, too, or had the ghosts of my own childhood been exorcised? My sons remember the good times in their home on Pickett Street, but though I did my best to protect them, they still carry scars from wounds inflicted at the end. And they will probably never understand that it wasn't me who did something bad.

I walked around the basement, remembered the easel when I was a teenager, the dreams of New York, my children's playroom. Those walls had contained my life for almost thirty years. I can see the purple butterfly now; like other things in that place, the image is sharp and painful and clear.

Today my children are grown. Greg Young rests in peace, as do countless victims of AIDS. Human lives were lost and justice never served. A museum in Las Vegas, where you can't take pictures, has a cold-mirrored Liberace collection. But in my heart, a spotlight finds him, strikes his silver hair as he smiles, then turns and spreads his glittering rhinestone wings. All these years later, the perpetrators have never answered for their actions. And I live in the same city, but I do not drive by the little house on Pickett Street, nor do my children.

How Does It Feel?

MARY TROY

It's the question that makes us groan, the newscaster shoving a microphone in someone's face and asking, "How does it feel now that your home has blown away in Hurricane Natasha?" "How did it feel when the truck came through your living room wall?" "How do you feel about the man who killed your baby?" We wince, turn away, press *mute*. We don't want to hear the sad response. Or we shout at the television, "How do you think she feels, you idiot?" "What a question!" This is what they call investigative journalism, we snort to ourselves or our loved ones beside us on the couch. Some of the bereaved and terrified are rude: "Get out of my face." We cheer for those. It's a question normal people—i.e., non–TV talking heads—and sane people never ask, not in real life about real, non-TV, tragedies.

We had a party to commemorate the one-year anniversary of my father's death. I say we, for my parents' children helped plan and execute it, but it was my mother's party, a part of her grieving, an official marker. Her grief was deep and permanent, but she had ways of coping. Not me. The party was a smaller version of the one a year earlier, the cocktail buffet for hundreds that served as a wake. I remember the crush of bodies, remember a priest I knew leaning against the kitchen sink in my parents' home as I stood beside him, a glass of wine in hand. We were bumped against, jostled, and squeezed. "We need to unionize," he told me. "For the sake of justice." He spoke not about being a priest, but about being an adjunct instructor at the University of Missouri. At that time, I was also an adjunct, not at the University of Missouri, but at two other universities in town. It was our bond that evening. One of my sisters-in-law asked if I thought the platter of beef or the bowl of artichoke rice salad or something like that needed refilling. I nodded. Everything always needed refilling. The husband of a friend of my brother's told me he would be changing jobs soon. People talked of the Dixieland version of "When the Saints Go Marching In," played as the casket was being taken from church—the only part of the service that Dad had suggested. "Nice touch," they said. Some spoke of my parents' near-legendary love, their undiminished delight in each other. One of my parents' neighbors told me that if my mother had truly not wanted to be a widow, she should have married a man at least twelve years her junior. Her problem had been in the planning, he explained. She had not understood the laws of probability.

By the second, tamer version of the party, no one talked about Dad. But at the first one, many guests/mourners told me they knew how I felt. They would not be crass enough to ask.

A person's life tests him, but his death tests those left behind. I failed that test. By the time Dad's colon cancer was discovered, it had already spread to his liver. And I was already suffering from what I thought of as a low-grade depression. "How does it feel to be you?" a TV head could have asked. "Bad," I would have said. Or, "Dead." Or, if trying to create a mood, "OK."

My husband and I, at almost forty, late bloomers, just recently out of graduate school and underemployed, bought a house. It was nearly one hundred years old, give or take a decade, and had its original three-inch-thick oak door with an etched glass panel, its original oak staircase, a double-sized kitchen and butler's pantry renovated in the '50s. It was on the south side of the city of St. Louis, only three miles west of the Mississippi, so it was inexpensive compared to most of the metropolitan area, much less expensive than dwellings beyond the city limits. My brother had bought a home about one-half the size of ours for more than twice what we'd paid, but his was in a storybook kind of suburb, full of what the politicians were just then calling "family values." We thought he was foolish.

Why did we want a house? Now, that was a question we should have asked before we bought, not after and endlessly, never coming up with a satisfying answer. We were too old for children. We didn't even have a dog yet. Well, my husband is artistic, but I, though a fan of beauty, do not have a decorator's soul, any sense of design. What I wanted was neighbors. I pictured myself belonging to a group without rules or meeting times or dues. I imagined people imbued with that real Midwestern sense of helpfulness, neighbors dropping in or gossiping over the back fence, no doubt joking about my growing a few flowers in amongst the weeds.

Our new neighbors were shooters.

Well, OK, not those on either side of us, but the guys catty-corner across the back alley, maybe sixty feet from our gate. They sat on their back stoop on summer evenings and fired their guns, mostly up into the air, but sometimes at things. Many in the neighborhood called the police, deciding not to put up with such behavior in this old and formerly nice neighborhood, but the shooting was over and the shooters gone by the time the patrol car arrived. Every time. As a result, we seldom used our back yard or our patio that first summer. Older residents said the neighborhood was "changing," and pointed to the other signs—cars parked on the streets had their windows smashed; litter filled the alley and our front yards; grizzled but not truly old men leaned against the garages, walked into our yards, stopped traffic. One once tried his key in our front door lock, perhaps convinced it was his house. When my husband told him it was not his, that we lived there, he shrugged and walked away, but kept a watch on us from across the street for a few days.

We had a neighborhood meeting about the shooters, invited our alderman. Before we went to the yard a block away for the meeting, my husband and I joked with each other. "A vigilante group," we said. "Should we carry torches?" We wanted to accept insanity, wanted to be broad-minded and let the beaten-down roam our streets, put up with the confused trying to get into our homes. We were English majors, after all. We had gone through a rigorous graduate school, had worked on our writing and on analyzing literature, both skills few wanted or valued. So we knew all about not being part of the mainstream, felt comradeship with the economically disadvantaged, even with those who had not done it so deliberately to themselves as we had. But we wanted to get rid of the shooters.

It turned out the shooters were renting from a landlord who owned much property in the city but who himself lived in a "family value" suburb. Since the shooters, a couple of young white men—the main troublemaker had red hair and freckles that gave him an impish look—could not be caught, the alderman said we could at least get the landlord to evict them, make them a problem in some other ward. He would put pressure on the landlord the only way he knew how—with the dreaded city inspectors.

Within days, the city inspector was seen cruising the neighborhood. He may have cited the target house for sundry violations, but he got lots of us, too. Our tin cornice up at the top of the house, above the second floor and beside the hidden flat black roof, needed painting. Rust was visible against the white. Others had garage doors in need of attention, missing handrails for the front steps. We had recently had our plumbing redone because of a serious leak that developed the week we moved in, a leak that meant a new floor in the bathroom, a new toilet, and a new ceiling in the butler's pantry, so we could ill afford more home maintenance costs, especially for a home we already felt uncomfortable in, one with a back yard we were afraid to use.

The aldermanic brainstorm did not remove the shooters. They got themselves removed the natural way. One of them, the redhead, finally shot someone, and not a random someone after all. He shot his girlfriend and was tried, rumor had it, as a juvenile. Reports were he was only seventeen.

Well, OK, a mean kid had been our neighbor. But he alone was not the problem. The vagrants and broken windows were not what I had hoped for. Coming home from an evening class, I was often afraid to get out of my car in the alley, afraid to open the sliding garage door and then pull into the garage fast to get the door closed behind me before any of the alley loafers, who, I reminded myself, may have been harmless, saw me. I stopped using my garage. A young couple from a few houses down grew afraid to let their children play in their own yard. A bullet ripped through another neighbor's front window, lodged in the plaster above their couch. It had been fired from a passing car. Someone tried to jimmy our basement door lock. The old woman on one side of us rented her upstairs to a man and woman who operated a burglary ring. One of our car windows was smashed in. In my dreams, our house collapsed; the walls tumbled and brick dust swirled about as I slept. I woke up shaking each time.

We heard shouts and screams at night. Years earlier, I'd heard the story of a woman in New York City, Kitty something, who was killed outside her apartment building; people had heard her screams but had not helped. It was horrid. Reportedly the people had not wanted to get involved. Now I had a different take on their so-called apathy. Were the screams we heard coming from the front or back? From two doors down or a block away? What did they mean? "Was that a call for help?" we would ask each other. "Did you hear a shot?" We called the police a few times, but could tell them nothing. I learned to ignore the sounds of trouble and pain. I developed great ignoring skills.

OK, so what I had was not true depression—clinical and chemical and causeless. Mine had a cause, a problem I was not able to cope with. Not effectively. I did cope: I smiled; I became a Pollyanna, even around my husband, who I guessed needed his spirits kept up; I accepted all, said out loud that others had it so much worse. I despised the things that came out of my mouth. I grew more cheerful week by week.

We had been there less than two years when we said it out loud to each other: "Move. Let's move." We tried "by owner" a few times, and in the nine years we were there, we went through four real estate agents, one we used twice. Over the nine years we lived there, my husband made some amazing renovations to the house—exposing a brick wall, removing old linoleum tile and refinishing oak hardwood and pine floors, rebuilding a wall and adding another wall and a walk-in closet, putting in ceilings and toilets, replastering and painting, removing tons of cement from the back, laying a brick patio, and stripping and patching and painting a wooden vestibule. He did much of this while working two jobs, and some of it while teaching seven composition classes a semester for three colleges. But as the house was made prettier, more livable, indeed more elegant, the neighborhood grew uglier and meaner.

We tried not to consider it hopeless.

When we told friends or my family members, suburbanites all, that we were trying to sell, we were not asked why, or how we felt about living there. Problems in the city were well documented, and yet the city, always spoken of as if with a capital C, was a cause, championed and discussed and defended by people who did not live in it. Yes, it was full of magnificent structures, architectural marvels, historic mansions. Yes, it had a rich history from fur trapping, to Lewis and Clark's base, to a stop along the Native American forced migration route, to a once booming industrial town—"First in shoes, first in booze"—and finally to the Gateway Arch tourist stop. People nodded at me when I said I was selling my house (a wishful statement: I was trying to but not selling), but did not want to listen to me tear the city down. I knew because they changed the subject, or told me about friends of theirs who loved the city life. Some friends told me they themselves would love the city for the different ethnicities, the good restaurants, the blues and jazz clubs, the symphony, blah, blah, blah, blah, would live there if not for their children. The city had such bad schools. It was all code. The bad schools meant race to some people, poverty combined with bureaucratic incompetence to all. The word "changing" in "changing neighborhood" could mean race, too. But even as those with the opportunity were getting out, one family moving fast and in the middle of the night, we all knew it was not as simple as race.

Twelve years of the trickle-down Reagan method of funding the rich first meant little money for cities, along with high unemployment and low minimum wage. The trickle seemed to have evaporated before it got to most of our neighbors. Oh, sure, there were a few pockets of wealth in the city limits, a few more areas of middle-class money, usually cordoned off with barrels and gates and one-way streets, but most of the city was poor, a fact that seemed perpetually to escape its planners. It certainly escaped the attention of its cheerleaders—most of whom, as I said, lived in the suburbs, drove in for football games at the new stadium the city could not afford and that its residents were not allowed to vote on.

The last weekend my father was conscious, my brother came in from Texas for what he and Dad knew was a final visit. Mom asked why we didn't come by, too. I had been over often, of course, Dad a true friend and one of my favorite people to talk to, to joke with, to listen to. I was with him and Mom for a few bad-news doctor visits, the last one making him crabbier than I'd ever seen him when the doctor talked to Mom and me. "The chemo's not working. He has only a few months. We'll try to keep him comfortable." "I'm here," Dad said, and on the way down in the elevator, "Asshole!" This time, I said no. I had a wet, dripping kind of cold, but I promised I would be by early the following week. When I did get by on Tuesday morning, Dad was on the floor beside their bed. He had been strong enough to drive my brother to the airport on Sunday evening, but was not able by Tuesday to stand when he got out of bed heading for the bathroom. Mom was waiting for me to help lift him, but though not unconscious, he was confused, not able to help us. He was at the most 140 pounds by then, but the two of us could not manage. We had to call my other brother, the one who lived in town. All that week, my brother, my sister, and I took turns staying with Dad and Mom in case she needed help. Dad was not talking, but early on, he may have been aware. On Thursday when my sister arrived and I prepared to leave, he blew me a kiss as I walked across the room to tell him good-bye.

By Friday evening, he kept his eyes closed and would not eat. On Saturday, his kidneys failed, and we stayed over that night. For a few hours early Sunday morning, we all slept, Mom by his side, holding his hand, and he used that time of peace to go.

Through the initial days of the funeral and wake, then the first few months of getting used to him not being there, many said they understood. Dad died on a warm Sunday in late February, but by the Wednesday of his funeral mass and cocktail buffet, a winter storm hit. I was warmed by the presence of two good friends who'd known Dad only through my words but who drove through hours of snarled traffic to offer me comfort.

People put themselves in my situation. They understood I was overwrought. They knew the stages of grief. They knew I was strong. They knew I would come out of it. They knew so much, my life stopped being mine. I breathed in and out. I nodded. I smiled. I cried. On cue. I did not have to do anything, certainly not say anything. My experiences were everyone's. "We're all in this together" became a lonely slogan, and I was disappearing.

My siblings and I did not draw together to say how we felt. Some of us, a brother and a sister-in-law, worked by planning, cooking, arranging, and being the host
and hostess of both cocktail parties. That may have been part of their grieving. My
sister had problems to deal with in her own marriage. I had my habit of silence. I
understood all just as I was understood. I felt my smile twist my face.

The summer after Dad died, a gang of men, some white and some black, living
in the same apartment the shooters had occupied years earlier, broke into our
garage and smashed the windows of the car my husband had been brave enough
to park there, burned the passenger seat, pried some of the metal trim off, took the
radio, cut the battery wires. We knew who had done it, for we watched them come
back the following night to get the car they thought they'd disabled so well. My
husband had replaced the wires, and we had removed the car, but as he watched
them come back across the alley, he called the police. That group of thieves and
vandals had a scanner, though, and scattered before the police showed up. The
ringleader, at least the one I guessed was the leader, rented the place with his wife
and two children—a precocious seven-year-old and a seemingly afflicted and backwards boy of five or so. I had bought Girl Scout cookies from the daughter earlier
that year, had invited the woman and her children in, offered them sodas when
they came selling.

The car was a high-mileage ten-year-old Volvo station wagon. It was in good
shape, though, and we washed and waxed it often when we first had it, feeling almost rich, at least middle-class, when we drove it through town. Though it was
bronze and from the top looked like a casket, it was the first car we'd owned with
both a working radio and an air conditioner. Perhaps our pride in it, our care of it,
had created envy. Maybe it had simply seemed an easy job—our sliding garage
door locking with just one bolt from the inside, and the door into the garage from
our yard not locking at all.

Meanwhile, we were on our fourth real estate agent, and lucky to get her. Many
we called said sorry, but they would not take property east of Grand Boulevard—
we were half a block east of Grand—and some said nothing east of Kingshighway,
a major thoroughfare about four miles west of us. One agent told us our house had
been for sale too long, was no longer "fresh." He took only fresh property. We
knew that if we sold, it would not be enough to clear our mortgage, and with com-
mission and inspections, and very likely some improvements mandated by the city
for safety—we would have had to have all our woodwork stripped and repainted
to get rid of the old lead-based paint—we would lose money. In some estimates,
nearly $20,000. Property had gone down that much.

The following summer, I was at a party at my sister's house in the far west of the
county, not a storybook neighborhood, but a new "bedroom" one for people mainly
from elsewhere in which the subdivisions were called meadow-something or field-
something and the homes had cathedral ceilings and decks as big as tugboats. One
of my sister's friends, a woman I knew from other of her parties, sat beside me on
the deck, both of us in webbed folding chairs, drinks in hand. It was growing dark,

and lightning bugs began to show off. I don't remember what we were talking about, but she put her hand on my arm and asked what it had felt like to lose my father. "How does it feel?" she asked. "Then and now." I told her. I started to cry, but stopped before anyone could see. I told her I had passed up the chance to spend one last afternoon with him because of my cold. I said it was like I had swallowed a rock. I said I talked to him in my mind all the time. Nothing I said was profound, or even interesting. I said thanks for asking.

The following winter, after most of our neighbors had moved, taking losses and getting out while they could—one couple had such a bad reaction to city life, they ran all the way to cold and sparsely populated Montana as if it were the promised land—our back door was kicked in. Our easy-to-carry-and-fence electronics—TV, cordless phone, boom box—a few pieces of costume jewelry, some clothes, a woven couch throw, and our laundry basket to carry it all in. It was noon on a snowy December Friday, not a time both of us were normally gone, so we knew we'd been watched. Our dog had been maced and was cowering in the bathroom when we got home. The following Monday, the same thing—hard kick and quick grab—happened to a house across the street, and two days later, to another home in the hood. A few days later, the eight-year-old boy next door, Billy, did not wake up. Even after the autopsy, there was no understandable cause of death. The world seemed impossibly cruel and cold. I visited the dead boy's home, took food into the wailing and weeping, but did not ask what I knew someone should—How does it feel? A stupid question after all, I rationalized. The wailing was eloquent enough.

Two weeks later, we started packing, going somewhere but not knowing where. This was our life, we said. Loss or not, we could not stay attached to this dying city. Let it go. Cities rise and fall, and this one can fall without us. Maybe we had not been strong enough, maybe we had expected too much, maybe we were too easily frightened. What I learned about myself was I would not have joined up with Daniel Boone. I would have abandoned the Alamo. But we were strong enough to go, and, maybe a first, both of us were willing to act at the same time. It was the beginning of our efforts at crawling out from under our depression and inertia, stopping the pretense of hope, no longer having to talk ourselves out of despair over and over. So we left. We did not sell. We just left. "How does it feel?" I asked myself as I drove the damaged station wagon I now hated, leading the moving van to our new rental home in a safe, indeed storybook, suburb. "How does it feel to run away?" "Great," I answered. "Flight does not deserve its bad rep."

We talked about Dad often. My husband admired him as much as I loved him, and we talked about what he would have said or done were he still with us, what he had said or done. I told stories about him, like how he'd helped a former grade school classmate who'd escaped from prison and needed money. Dad met the convict in secret, gave him money and food. Or the story about the woman shop steward who'd wanted to arm-wrestle him for a raise instead of negotiating. He declined that challenge. My sister and I talked, too, remembering our visit to

Osceola, Arkansas, where Dad had a rental house he spent four nights a week in, commuting back home for long weekends for more than a year. When my sister and I visited, both of us in our mid-twenties by then, he gave us a dinner consisting of a large rare steak and a bottle of wine. And I talked with both my brothers, both sisters-in-law, and often with my mother. But it took a question from a woman I did not know well, someone who did not claim to know how I felt, to keep me from vanishing.

Years ago, I was watching TV at my parents' home, still my home then. I may have been in my late teens. My younger brother was there, too, and others I don't remember. We sat on the family room couch and saw a report on a tornado, an interview with people from the mobile home park whose possessions had been picked up and pitched into the next county. "How did it feel when the tornado came through?" the woman with the microphone asked. We groaned. Her target was an overweight young man with a puffy face, a crooked nose, a somewhat stupid look on his face. "Well," he said. "'Course I was in the bathtub when it started." We laughed, my brother and I. "Yes, it was Saturday night," we said. "Guess that kept the tub from moving," we said. What a simpleton! Didn't he know that was not part of the question? She had not asked about his hygiene. We found it funnier as the interview went along. He imitated the sound of the approaching tornado, like a train whistle, shook all over to demonstrate how his mobile home had rocked. We laughed harder as he repeated himself. "I would have to be in the tub."

If I saw that now, I would laugh again, knowing his answer was unique to him but still not important, knowing that most times the words are inadequate or meaningless to the listener, maybe even to the teller. But when the interview was over, he may have said, "Thanks for asking."

Near the end of my city experience, I joined a church as part of a last-ditch and desperate attempt at sloughing off what I still called depression. I did not stay long. The congregation was too cheerful, and I knew there was not that much to smile about. Besides, I was thinking about guns. We had two guns Dad had given my husband, one a shotgun and one a rifle, both antiques of sorts from Dad's old relatives. I could not tell rifles from shotguns, did not know what ammunition they took, and that told me I was not ready to shoot. Fine by me. I knew I would not shoot another person, no matter what. I never would be able to.

But sometimes I wanted to. In my fantasy, I would have the weapon—rifle? shotgun?—by my side. (What good would a concealed gun do?) I'd park my car in front of my house in the city and get out, bag of ungraded essays in hand, gun at my side. As happened every now and then, a man, sometimes two or three, would come up and ask for money. They would be young and muscular. One in the group would have a story that was almost plausible about his desperate need. In my fantasy, I would not be afraid. I'd reposition my gun, move it a bit so they couldn't miss it, would keep their distance. Hell, I thought, I may even give them money, the two or three dollars I usually had in my purse. I didn't care about that.

Dad had had a soft spot for those of us who end up on the wrong side of the law, a great disregard for authority. We even had a train robber in our past, famous for being stupid enough to rob the train and then ride it to his destination, and Dad laughed about him often. After Dad retired, he devoted most of his time and zeal to helping people who could not pay their bills, needed food or clothes, the hopeless kind of people I lived among. I wasn't that good. I wanted a gun by my side, though I reminded myself I would not shoot. I could not harm another living person. I said that, yet I knew what virtue untried was. Absolutely nothing.

J.W.

JOHN MCCLUSKEY, JR.

So long as I can remember, those in the closest family circle called him "The
Old Man." I never knew where that came from. Neither did my parents—his older
son and daughter-in-law—nor my Uncle William, whom we all called "Sticky."
How long the name went back, they could not say. Surely, though, the father
could not have always been "The Old Man." The search for his youth through
thickets of legend would surely be an adventure. Yet there are no pictures of him
as a boy. He very rarely talked about growing up in the South, as though his life in
Ohio was the real life he created and lived.

He was James William McCluskey—or to a few, "James Willie"—before he
started north from Statham, Georgia, Gwinnett County, to Middletown, Ohio in
1921. To most he would be simply "J.W." throughout his life. When he talked
about that trip, a long, slow ride on the Louisville and Nashville line in an over-
heated Jim Crow car with a floor littered with cigarette butts and bread crumbs,
he did not talk about what prompted it. At least most of the time he did not. He
did talk about the glorious train station in Cincinnati and the brief mingling with
others who were a part of the Great Migration to Northern cities during and after
the war. Generally males, most of the workers fled the depressed agricultural economy of the South for the steady jobs in Northern factories. He often said: "I arrived in Ohio with a dry bologna sandwich that was two days old and nine dollars
to my name." Though the amount of money would shift in the telling over the
years, he always remembered it in single digits. The bologna sandwich on flaking
bread remained the same.

From Cincinnati he traveled the thirty-five miles north to Middletown, where
the mills were booming and painting the night sky red. He promptly found work
at Crystal Tissue, a paper product manufacturer. He rented a room, bought a bicycle. He bicycled the three miles to work every day and saved every dollar he
could, slowly building a base to buy a house and move his wife and firstborn son,
still an infant, from Georgia. He was a thrifty man, later called "stingy" and an
"eagle-squeezer" by friends. He paid for everything in cash. He would loan money
to relatives, the extensive and extended family in southwestern Ohio, but to the
surprise of the borrowers—often migrants from the same region in north Geor-

gia—he always kept a tally of the principal and slowly accruing interest. He always collected.

J.W. invested in a pickup truck, with which he did odd hauling during his off-hours from the paper mill. By 1930 he had bought another truck, and by 1945, with three trailers and two dump trucks, he incorporated his business as J.W. Mc-Cluskey & Son. (Uncle William was serving in Italy and would join the corporation upon his arrival home.) The small trucking firm was the first Black-owned business in the city. The trucks hauled scrap steel from area foundries and plants to Armco Steel, where it was melted down and recycled for use in the heavy manufacturing plants—automobiles, refrigerators, farm tractors. The drivers also hauled coal from the mines along the Ohio River to Middletown, where loads were sold to private homeowners. The work was steady, and the firm could always use good workers. Early on, the company gained a reputation for putting new migrants from northeast Georgia to work while they waited for openings at Armco Steel. At the same time, J.W.'s front porch at 511 17th Avenue became the site where men talked of labor, the transition to the North, and sports. Several stories have made the rounds over and over again since the late 1940s, often nursed with a bottle of beer or three fingers of bourbon in a sparkling clean used jelly jar.

One young man, fresh from Gwinnett County, complained to J.W. after his second day on the truck. "J.W., you from Georgia same as me. What I can't get over is everywhere I look I see steel. Down home the rakes and the forks got wood handles and we handling hay and cow shit and so forth. But here the handles on the tools is steel and we throwing steel all day. It make me homesick real quick."

Once, another Georgia refugee climbed out of the truck's cab and stepped proudly. It was his first day on the job as a helper. The truck was scheduled to bring ten tons of steel shavings from a manufacturing plant fifty miles away back to Middletown. Twenty thousand pounds would be shoveled up over the side boards of a trailer by two men. The new man did not know that the shavings often melded and would have to be broken up with a pickaxe. Eager to the task, however, he walked and crunched his way from the truck in a landscape that must have seemed lunar. "O.K., J.W., we here now. Where's the iron at?"

J.W. must have snorted before he added: "Hell, you're standing on ten tons. Get your pick and shovel and let's go!"

Certainly the texture of technology changed for all those who came north to the factories. Changed, too, were the work choreographies. In the fields fathers and sons might work side by side, as wives and daughters might also in or outside the houses. In the steel mills that was unlikely, since so many of the men came up alone at first, with very young families left behind. Attitudes about labor, authority, and pride gained by working at a parent's side were important. No sermon need be given; simple observation was enough. Both of J.W.'s sons worked with him on the trucks in those early years. After his retirement and when other men worked with my father or Uncle Sticky, they soon learned that the phrase "You want me to carry your sweat all day?" was a warning to keep up.

When younger and in elementary school, I was not privy to the talk on the porch at 511. After completing some errand that brought me to my grandfather's house, I was dismissed with a nickel or dime for my efforts. But I heard much about the feats of Satchel Paige, Joe Louis, and Ezzard Charles, the heavyweight from nearby Cincinnati. I also heard about the initiation ritual of the snipe hunt, where a new arrival was given a burlap bag and told to stand over a manhole cover spouting steam from its holes. He was told to start his vigil at midnight and stand however long it took for the imaginary snipe to emerge. "Best eating north of Georgia, I'm here to tell you." And tastiest when caught deep in a cold winter night away from the guffaws of those safely warm in their houses.

By junior high school I was permitted more time on the porch. I could notice then my grandfather laughing along with the rest, the knot of workers nostalgic for home and relatives off the day shift at the mill. He married and was widowed three times during his long life. I remember the second wife, Arva Lee, sometimes standing behind the screen door laughing softly with the men. He could joke and laugh at a joke on himself. In their company my grandfather would utter lines I assumed he had fashioned. "Never pay sticker price." (He was a car and heavy appliance negotiator extraordinaire. He always dressed humbly when he met with a store or car dealer manager to close the deal.) "The graveyard is full of fools who mistook kindness for weakness." (He was known as a "character" who liked his whiskey. At the end of any night of drinking and joking, he could recall exactly how much money he had agreed to loan. He was also known to have a small gun collection. As I said, he always collected on his debts.)

I remember his front porch in other ways. Across the street from my grandfather's house stood Booker T. Washington Elementary School. My father, my younger brother and two younger sisters, and I attended the all-Black school. On the east and west sides of the school were two spacious fields. Through our respective high school years, my brother and I would work out in the much larger and sunken area on the west. We picked the hottest part of a summer's day to jog around what was always referred to as "The Schoolground Bottom." Our logic was simple and yet (we felt then) exquisite. If we could do a forty- to fifty-minute workout complete with windsprints under a blazing June and July sun, then the two-a-day August drills in full football gear would be easy. Our grandfather found flaws in such logic. He would sit on his front porch and occasionally shout at us. My brother and I agreed years later that we could never hear complete sentences, but certain nouns and phrases would ring clearly. "Hospital," "heart attack," "gon' fall out" came to us as we went through our paces. Afterwards, we the forgiven would join him and often sip ice-cold water from a sweating Mason jar half filled with ice cubes. He would sit with a fly swatter, his lower lip protruding from a pinch or two of snuff. Five years older than my brother, I can remember him listening to a baseball game telecast by ticker tape with no crowd noises. Baseball was a passion that claimed him upon his move north. The capacity to listen to and enjoy a full game read mostly in monotone by a lone announcer in a studio was a feat of love and imagination.

It was on that same porch that we would assemble before the drive down to Crosley Field in Cincinnati to watch a doubleheader. A variation of that Sunday's excursion forced its way into my novel manuscript, "The River People." It was the day I saw Jackie Robinson steal home and the day my grandfather played a deadly highway game of "chicken."

My grandfather always drove to the games, and I sat next to him in the middle, his right elbow catching my shoulder on occasion. My father always sat next to my right at the door. In back was surely Uncle Sticky and two other men, perhaps my Uncle Sleepy and Red Crawford. As a seventh and eighth grader I had hunted rabbit and pheasant with that same group of men. Late as usual, we would tear off to Cincinnati. About ten miles from the park, the long lines of traffic would start. Motors would overheat and the front hoods would go up. We would start moving so slowly I could memorize the Burma-Shave signs (The big blue tube's / just like Louise / You get / a thrill / from every squeeze / Burma-Shave). Impatient at the wheel—he hated to be passed on the open road!—Grandpa pulled out to pass as many cars as he could to get us on down the road. On one stretch we must have passed a dozen cars before we spotted something heading toward us far down the highway. He floored the accelerator, passing more cars. My father might have given him a quiet but firm warning that something was approaching ahead. Still my grandfather sped on. The shouts grew as the vehicle—now clearly a pickup truck—approached. There was no shoulder left of the road and the line of cars to our right was still bumper to bumper. "Stop it, J.W., stop it! You gon' kill us!" someone shouted from behind. I did not move. I could see the front grille of the truck, the face of the white man at the wheel, gesturing wildly with one arm. At what we would all remember as the last second, he found space in line as the truck passed. The passengers in the car ahead looked back in terror as we missed their back fender by just inches. It would be a while before the nerves would settle and Uncle Sticky would chuckle and chide Grandpa for acting like a child at the wheel. Grandpa would only shake his head. "Got to see Jackie. Got to hurry on down and see what Jackie gon' do today." It would be the only time I saw and heard grown men plead for their lives.

The parking lots nearest the stadium would be filled and every entrance blocked with a "parking lot closed" sign. We passed these, weaving our way through the crowd making their way to the park. When I mentioned to Grandpa that all the lots seemed filled, he smiled, patted my arm, and said nothing. We stopped in front of a skinny man leaning on one of the signs and counting dollar bills. He chewed on the butt of a cigar and grinned when he saw the car and Grandpa waving. We got out, and Grandpa paid the wide-mouthed man he called Slim. I noticed that he gave him a generous tip. I learned later that for a slight fee, Slim could always find a space for "his good buddy J.W."

For me a root beer and grilled Kahn's hot dog with brown mustard was the goal of the drive down. The men would buy hot dogs and a beer before we took our seats. Around us in the stands were Dodger fans (or, more correctly, Junior Gilliam, Don Newcomb, Roy Campanella, and especially Jackie Robinson fans) who had driven over from Kentucky or Indiana or up from Tennessee to watch the Dodgers and the Reds. They brought along their greasy brown bags of fried chicken and hardboiled eggs. In or out of the dugout, every time Jackie moved someone would cheer. The South and North picnicked together around the Crosley Field green for six hours on that bright Sunday. All plaints of low wages and overwork were suspended for a time.

Jackie's miracle steal was practically anticlimactic given the drama on the highway. He was on third base in the first game with the Dodgers behind by a run. As the pitcher's arm started forward, Jackie Robinson started his pigeon-toed run toward home plate. He got to the plate just after the ball, but the pitch was low and outside. Jackie was already into his slide before the catcher could gather himself. The dust flew, and the crowd was hushed for a split second until the umpire crossed his arms at the wrists. The stadium exploded: Black strangers hugging one another; white fans of the Cincinnati Reds puzzled by the loyalty for a team based hundreds of miles away. How the game ended I cannot say. I suspect like the rest of the Black fans I took a little of Jackie and the Dodgers back home with me. I could brag at school or on the playground. Grownups could boast on their jobs. We had seen our hero steal home.

On that same front porch I mentioned to my grandfather that I wanted to go south for a year, doing what I did not know. I was on summer break from college, and it was the early 1960s. Stories of the civil rights campaigns were in the newspaper every day. At the same time I was growing curious about the circle of kin in Georgia on both sides of the family. I had heard descriptions of red clay and thick pine forests and houses with wraparound porches ten miles down a bumpy dirt road. Occasionally during my summers in grade school, my family had driven to Georgia, but I had stayed behind due to the pressing concerns of Knothole League baseball during those earlier years. When my family returned, I wondered at the red dust on the car mats (how can dirt be red?). I wondered, too, at the tales of large family picnics held outside, the adults eating first while the children fanned flies. Quashing any impulse toward nostalgia, earned or not, my grandfather would shake his head, perhaps lean to spit snuff juice into a soup can serving as spittoon, then say, "South no good." He never elaborated, but just before I graduated from college I would learn from my father what lay behind his father's reticence.

"The Old Man" had come north following an armed assault on his family. I had heard the accounts growing up, but the stories always seemed to be distant background, a shroud over ancient history. Perhaps I was not ready for the details of the story until the age of twenty or so. There were several versions, differing only slightly when told by male or female or by members of the Detroit wing of the family versus the Ohio wing. A version is also available in Benjamin Mays's *Born to Rebel*, though it sounds a note of pathos missing in the family oral accounts. Essentially, white landowners in north Georgia coveted his father Asberry's rich and productive four hundred acres of land. When Asberry refused to surrender any portion of the land, he was told that the land would be taken from him by force. He quickly gathered relatives from the surrounding counties, and these armed men encircled his home. They were there for days, but nothing happened. Eventually they had to return to their own farms and slowly left. Still sensing the probability of an attack, Asberry sent his family members back to live temporarily with kin. For the next few days he kept vigil with a teenaged nephew.

The guess is that someone leaked word that the homestead was protected by only two people then. At any rate, the house was attacked. With the nephew loading the guns, Asberry went from window to window, dodging shots fired from outside and firing himself in turn. The confrontation lasted minutes. When it seemed that he might lose his life, he told the nephew to escape through the back door. He covered for him as he ran toward the woods and to safety. The Klansmen finally retreated, however, carrying away several of their men. Asberry left for Atlanta for a few days, then returned. He kept his land and was never attacked again. Again some of the details are very different from the Mays text, which quotes liberally from Will Alexander's *Seeds of Southern Change*. What is common to both, however, is the violent attack and the standoff.

An intriguing sidebar to this story was that my future maternal grandmother was a young woman living with her family over two hundred miles from where the incident occurred. She said that even without telephones the Black farmers in her area somehow heard about the incident within hours. For the next three nights family members were instructed to turn down their gas lamps, expecting the Klan or its allies to ride throughout the state and strike arbitrarily.

My grandfather left Georgia soon after the attack and ever afterwards would link the South to violence. He rarely returned except for funerals. Yet even his return for Asberry's funeral in 1948 was not without incident. Stopping by a store along the Dixie Highway with my Uncle William and one of his Georgia nephews, my grandfather had planned only a quick purchase. The white proprietor warned the young men not to read the comic books unless they planned to buy. My uncle, a war veteran, leafed through one of the magazines and was still deciding about a purchase when the proprietor moved up to him. Apparently some words were exchanged, and the man was about to strike my uncle when my grandfather appeared with a drawn revolver placed to the back of the man's neck. The story goes that my grandfather said nothing, only shook his head in silent warning against the absurdity of even thinking about striking his son as he and his charges backed slowly out.

In the spring of 1967, when I decided in Palo Alto, California, to accept a teaching position at Miles Collge in Birmingham, Alabama, it was met with much puzzlement throughout the family. Why Birmingham? Atlanta or Nashville, maybe, but Birmingham? To the family, it was a hopeless sahara. As I made ready for my cross-country drive in early June, I received all kinds of travel advice from the family. My grandfather passed along the word that he was sending me a gift. Though I stayed west for an extra day waiting for his gift, it did not arrive before I left. On the last day of the trip, a warm Sunday, I negotiated two-lane highways through western Kentucky and Tennessee toward U.S. 65 in Nashville, where I would speed on to Birmingham. Along the way I passed a small church, pristinely white in color. In front Black families were spreading blankets and appeared to be making ready for picnics. I remember someone, a young woman, waving. Her waving was taken up by someone near her. I waved back. It all took place in less than five seconds. In the years that have passed, I have wondered if their waves were in fact more than a salute to the passing stranger, but a beckoning to share their food and stories. What is unmistakable is the strong sense of peace and community in that instant. It was not until I stood on the bridge at Carbretta Creek at Sapelo Island, Georgia, at sundown or slept next to the Colorado River in the Grand Canyon many years later that I experienced so aching a moment of peace.

A week after I had arrived in Birmingham and started my first teaching job, a package arrived. It had originated from Ohio and had been forwarded from my address in Palo Alto. Inside was my grandfather's gift—a .38 caliber Baretta automatic with a full clip. No note, no card. I had never owned nor handled a handgun, just a .20 gauge shotgun for hunting rabbits, quails, and pheasants. I understood his message, his warning, his plea. Yet I could not doubt that he had witnessed at least a moment of peace in north Georgia as I had that Sunday in Tennessee. Perhaps he chose to erase it from his memory.

Years later we would chuckle about his gift, which made it through x-ray machines at post offices, about possible prosecution for sending firearms through the mail. He said the risk of a violent racial encounter was greater than the legal risk. "You don't want to be anywhere unprotected." He was not a violent man, nor was his father. Both believed fiercely in defending land and family. My grandfather would live long enough to hear about changes in the South, especially the cities, though he would never accept the changes as genuine or long-lasting.

He died in a nursing home in 1991, away from his Concord grape arbor, away from the porch, quieter by then. It was the porch to a house less than a mile from the Miami River, flowing leisurely to the Ohio, then the Mississippi, and train tracks that carried a freight north late every night. These connections of the ironies of geography have arrived only recently. He needed around-the-clock care by then, and it was a difficult decision for the family. He had said many times that he would not live long away from his house. He was right.

I know of only two photos of my grandfather. One is a studio portrait. The other is the one I like best, the one my father has taped to the wall over his work desk. J.W. is standing next to a well-used pickup, a dent in the back fender, a spare tire bolted to the side and resting on the running board. Perhaps there was an AM radio inside that broadcast the Reds games. (My own truck is sleeker, allows for CDs and FM.) In the background are skinny and bare trees, which means late fall or winter. J.W. stands with his hands behind him in a plaid shirt, perhaps wool and not neatly tucked—he defied nattiness. Beneath the plaid shirt is a dress shirt and a neatly knotted striped tie. His fedora sits straight on his head, no "rakish angles" for him. His slacks are at full break over knob-toed shoes. He looks directly at the camera, directly at you, probably eager to get the session over with and go back to work.

The Baby Shower

PHILIP GRAHAM

DON'T FORGET YOUR BATHING SUIT, the invitation to the baby shower read. A joke, I thought, or an attempted one, at least—some feeble connection between shower, water, bathing. Who knew?

I still needed to negotiate the right tone for Midwestern humor. Soon after moving to Illinois from New York, my wife and I had encountered on occasion various people who expressed curiosity that Alma and I had different last names. Were we *really* married? seemed to be their unspoken question. I always answered, "Well, when we got married, I decided to keep my maiden name," a mild jest that, back east, managed to squeeze out a chuckle or two. But here in Illinois, the response was invariably either a look of incomprehension or a careful nodding of the head. I began to suspect that most people thought I'd simply misspoken and meant Alma's maiden name, and they were too polite to correct me. For this and other reasons, I had some theories about why some folks in the heartland seemed a bit shy in the presence of irony. The kindest was that they suffered from a fresh fish deficiency.

So I set the invitation down and said, "Bathing suit, ha ha. Funny, I guess."

"No," Alma replied, "it's no joke. Laurie's parents have a pool."

"So? We're in the middle of winter."

"Pete says his in-laws have an indoor pool, connected to their farmhouse."

Laurie, a local girl from the nearby town of Fisher, was married to Pete, one of Alma's colleagues at the university. They were expecting their first child, and Laurie's mom and dad were hosting the baby shower. I'd known for a while that this bash was brewing and had been trying on various reasons why I wouldn't be able to go. Not that I didn't like Pete and Laurie. I was afraid to drive to Fisher.

Not fear, actually. Dread was more like it. Urbana, the town where Alma and I had lived for the past year or so, though smack dab in the middle of some of the flattest flatland the Midwest has to offer, is a nationally recognized Tree City U.S.A. Trees grow here, there, and everywhere, conveniently blocking out any view of the surrounding countryside—very helpful if one doesn't want to dwell on the fact that the town is indeed and undeniably smack dab in the middle of some of the flattest flatland the Midwest has to offer.

The flatness was what I dreaded. Driving those twelve or so relentlessly horizontal miles from Urbana to Fisher. Any time we had to drive outside the town limits, the flatness made me long—no, ache—for the rolling hills and varied seashores of my childhood on Long Island. The flatness made me quietly frantic: with no outstanding topographical features to help mark my way, I could imagine losing myself in a maze of corn and soybean fields and never getting out. The flatness made my chest tighten, a sort of reverse claustrophobia: all that open space suddenly felt like the smallest windowless room. The flatness was quietly deforming my sense of fairness, breeding in me a growing, disturbing contempt for people who lived in such a landscape.

But an indoor pool connected to a farmhouse? I'd risk my dread of flatness to see *that*.

So when the day came, Alma and I arrived at the home of Laurie's parents and parked beside the other cars lining the edge of the gravel driveway. I regarded their farmhouse with disappointment. Its raised porch and two-story, white-shingled facade seemed indistinguishable from the scores of other farmhouses we'd passed on the harrowing—to me, at least—drive through the countryside. Some kind of farm equipment, a thresher perhaps, sat like a huge mechanical insect between the house and a barn. A few cats roamed along the side of the porch. A biting cold wind cut across acres of stubble field.

No sign of a swimming pool.

I sighed, and followed Alma through the front door.

We were among the last to arrive, and so most of the guests sitting on the floor in the living room, circling the pile of presents, had clearly already accustomed themselves to their surroundings. But Alma and I couldn't help gaping at the fake palm tree in one corner of the room, the fake thatch eaves lining the top of each doorway. And then there was the meticulously detailed mural of a Polynesian beach filling the full stretch of one wall: a painted stand of palm trees swaying above an inviting curve of white sand flecked with seashells, and a serene blue water's reflection of stars in an evening sky.

The other walls, however, were inexplicably lined with carpet patches, one square foot after another, mirroring similar patches on the floor and, of all places, the ceiling. Each of these patches displayed its own color and design: red stripes, green and blue plaid patterns, orange and yellow checkerboards—I had no idea there could be so many commercially available, tasteless variations of carpeting. Blessedly, some of the patches confined themselves to simple, single pastels, yet still I felt dizzy waves beginning to pass through me.

"Hi, everybody," Alma and I managed to squeak out, and we settled ourselves on the floor.

Only then did I notice that one of the doors to the living room was made of glass, misted-over glass. So it was true, there was an indoor pool here, a *heated* indoor pool. How could I ever have doubted it? Sitting in the middle of this South Sea carpet patch heaven, I'd be willing to entertain anything.

Laurie's mom and dad began making speeches about how pleased they were that we'd all been able to come, and how happy they were that they'd soon be grandparents, but their words faded in the background while I simply stared at them, these very ordinary-looking people responsible for decorating this very peculiar living room. Laurie's balding father, roundish in his jeans and checked shirt, and her mother, obviously wiry even in her shapeless dress, with long slack hair just beginning to gray, could have been any of a thousand fellow shoppers I'd pass by in the mall back in town. Who'd suspect? I couldn't stop thinking.

"Who'd suspect?" I whispered to Alma, and she shushed me.

The time to open the presents had arrived, a sweet ritual of scattered wrapping paper, oohs and aahs, and heartfelt thanks for a car seat or a set of plastic rattles. This was an inherently interesting process for Alma and me, since we were on the verge—the thrilling, hesitant verge—of deciding to take our own plunge into parenthood. My eyes kept drifting, however, to that tall papier-mâché palm tree in the corner, its green paper leaves dangling above us. They truly seemed to sway in the wind, but this must have been a disorienting side effect of those crazy-quilt patches.

I could really do with a swim right now, I thought. Some of the other guests had already made their way through the misted glass door, their gifts having been opened and appreciated, and muted splashes and squeals of laughter drifted to the living room. Bathing suit in hand, I walked through a thatch-eaved doorway and down the short hall in search of a bathroom where I could change.

I hesitated before opening the door, uncertain of what new decorating marvel might be awaiting me. Sand and conch shells in the shower stall? A statue of a surfer on the curve of an endless wave? No, I walked into an utterly ordinary bathroom—except for the thick brown weave of shag carpet on the floor.

So I went about the business of changing into my bathing suit, unprepared for the sudden appearance of a cat, or rather a cat's head, rising from that shag-carpeted floor. Its whiskers twitched, its eyes glinted at me for only the briefest moment, because I let out a sharp yelp at the shock of this unlikely sight, and then it disappeared.

I stood there, my heart its own rhythm section, my bathing suit around my ankles, and stared at the floor. Ugly brown carpet, nothing more. Could I have imagined this? Might this be another optical illusion brought on by my prolonged exposure to that bizarre mish-mash of colored patterns on the living room's floor, walls, and ceiling? I pulled up my suit and then knelt on the rug, one hand tentatively reaching to where that possible cat had seemed to appear. My fingers probed among the spaghetti-like tendrils of carpet until I felt something metallic: a ring-like handle that lifted when I pulled, and up rose a trapdoor.

I peered down into its darkness, listened for the pat-pat of cat's feet. Nothing. Still, at least I knew that I hadn't been hallucinating—I'd indeed seen a cat, even if it had vanished down a hole in the floor.

I returned to the living room, questions reeling. The presentation of gifts was still in full swing, so I gave Alma a wait-until-you-hear-this look and made my way to the glass door.

Harriet, another of Alma's colleagues, was on her way out, her damp hair gleaming, and she asked, "A pretty wild place, huh?"

"If you only knew," I replied, and stepped through the glass door.

Another mural. Similar to the one in the living room, only much larger, and filling *two* long walls, with even more painted palm trees, more sand, more shoreline. The pool itself seemed to stretch on forever—how had I possibly missed it when we first arrived?—and I didn't wait more than a moment before jumping into the inviting blue water.

So warm, the water, so cleansing, and all this in the middle of winter! Within a few minutes, Alma jumped in beside me, and we swam together, her eyes widening as I told her of my bathroom adventure.

"What in the world do you think that's all about?" she asked, but my eyes were already drifting away, toward some strange patterns in the water I hadn't noticed at first. Yellow, green, and red currents seemed to pass beneath us, so I ducked my head under water.

Colored light gleamed from a glass porthole just below the water line. I swam closer and saw a fan in the porthole, its slowly turning wire blades wrapped in crinkly colored paper and lit from behind by a lamp. My mouth gaped open and I rose to the surface, coughing water.

"Check it . . . out," I gasped, still recovering, and Alma, her eyebrows arched quizzically, sank beneath the surface.

I'd never before visited any house as strange and marvelous as this one. Yet here it was, in Fisher, Illinois, of all places, its exterior so nondescript it wouldn't warrant notice. And I still didn't know why the bathroom had a trapdoor for a cat.

Alma's head bobbed up, water streaming from her face. "Amazing! It's . . . it's psychedelic down there!"

I laughed and agreed, and we swam in circles together until Alma, gliding closer to me, added, "Y'know, Laurie tells me that her mom uses the pool to give swimming lessons. She even offers a class for babies."

Infant swimming lessons? Of course—why would anything about this house be ordinary? Already I could see myself and Alma in the perhaps not so distant future, treading water in this pool and watching Stella guide our as yet hypothetical baby through the steps for the doggy paddle, then the breaststroke, then—

Someone opened the glass door from the living room and yelled, "Cake!"

Alma and I dried off and changed, and I showed her that trapdoor, *proved* it to her, actually, because I think she hadn't quite believed me.

In the living room I made sure I sat next to Pete, the expectant father, hoping I could get the straight dope from him about his parents-in-law and their strange house.

I poked a fork into my slice of gooey chocolate cake and asked, "Um, Pete, have you been in the, y'know, bathroom lately?"

"Sure. Why?"

"Well," I half-whispered, "there was this cat, and I found a trapdoor, and—"

"Oh, *that*," he laughed. "Stella and Jack have the whole system worked out, don't they?"

"System?"

"Yeah, for the farm cats. Forty of 'em, last time anyone counted."

"Forty?"

"Probably more by now. Keeps the rodent population down, big time. Stella likes the cats to come in the house, especially in the winter, but Jack can't stand them underfoot, so he built the tunnels."

I simply stared, waiting for him to go on.

"They connect all the rooms on the first floor. You never know when a cat'll pop up."

"Huh, tell me about it."

We dug into our slices of cake, but still something bothered me, something I still didn't understand. "Um, what's with all these carpet patches?"

He laughed again. "Wild, huh? That's for the cats, too. They'd wreak havoc on the furniture with their claws if left to their own devices, so Stella came up with the idea for the patches. They can sharpen their claws to their hearts' content, and when one patch is ruined, it's simple to replace. They can even climb the walls, if they want."

The ceiling, too, I thought, looking up. I could imagine Stella and Jack alone at night in their living room, bathed in the soft glow of the television, surrounded by insistent little scraping noises coming from the dimly lit corners, while above them the dark shapes of cats clawed their way slowly across the ceiling, like clusters of storm clouds.

"Eh, Pete, what are your in-laws like?"

"Oh, they're great." His eyes roamed around the living room. "Don't ya think?" Pete, like me, had been born in Brooklyn, and he looked as happy as a clam.

"Yeah, great." I let my eyes roam, too. The winter afternoon light was dimming, and though it was getting a bit dark inside, no one had yet bothered to turn on a lamp. That's when I noticed that the shells on the beach in the mural, the stars in the sky and their reflections in the water, must have been touched up with phosphorescent paint, because they were glinting, positively *sparkling* in the growing darkness.

Was there no end to surprises? I wasn't sure I could take another. I turned to Alma, a look passed between us, and we stood to go.

We said our good-byes, accepted thanks for our present, and I made sure before we left that I shook hands with Stella and Jack—somehow I needed to touch these people who had created this odd masterpiece on the prairie. I looked at them steadily, trying not to be rude—Jack's eyes were slightly rheumy, and Stella's nose and cheeks were dotted with freckles—but saw no overt sign of genius.

Outside, the sun was starting to set. Rather than dwelling on the warm glow cast over the landscape, I turned to take in Jack and Stella's house one more time. Not a single weird doodad poked out from a shingled dormer; the porch railing sported no surrealistic filigree: no clue to what riches lay hidden within. True, the handful of cats wandering in the yard now looked strange to me, but that was only because I knew their secret.

So we drove home, and what was once flat now seemed far more contoured, a slight ridge here, a bit of a roll there, these subtle variations now curiously dramatic. How had I missed them before? I thought, flushing with shame. Then the whole sky gave up its final flare of orange, red, and purple streaks and washes, with nothing on the horizon standing in the way of this spectacular show. Here and there, dotted among the fields, were farmhouses much like Stella and Jack's, and I couldn't help wondering, How much *were* they like Stella and Jack's? Could they all be false fronts for an unbridled imagination? I had to resist the urge to stop and knock on the door of one of these homes and invite myself in. Show me, I imagined pleading, show me all your secrets!

Again, shame cut through me—I'd written an entire book of short stories that tried to limn the quietly spectacular lives thriving within ordinary homes. So how could I have allowed my dread of the flat landscapes around me to obscure what I thought I already understood?

As the sunset dimmed its last display, Alma and I chatted away about our remarkable day, and nothing, absolutely nothing I drove past—whether a distant silvery silo or a clutch of trees beside a brook—appeared ordinary. My eyes unusually alert, I found myself speeding up the car, not wanting to miss any of these Midwestern vistas before the dark set in.

Rewind

Remembering Canute

SHARON DARROW

1

sandy red dirt   apricot seeds   dry Oklahoma garden
     walking with my young uncles to the apricot tree
  the field to the south of the house   stone arrowhead we found there

The dustbowl had resettled itself by the time of my birth, and by the early 1950s, the windbreaks had grown tall and dense enough to seem to a child like mail order samples of forest dividing one small farm from another on the high plains.

The day I remember before all others was the day we found what I've always called "the arrowhead," a slender triangular stone with diagonal stripes of yellow ochre, white, brown, and two strong slashes of dark blood red. I hold it in my hand now, removed from my mantel in Chicago where it rests alongside my half of the stone-polished pottery from the pueblos of New Mexico. Photographs of our three daughters, and orange and blue remnants from the fallen Berlin Wall. Over the years I have seen other arrowtips in museums, most no longer than an inch or so with a fierce and frightening point. This one is at least four inches long and about one-and-one-half inches at its widest, the point broad, the sides knapped into a balanced taper—a spearhead, perhaps.

I want to believe that I remember holding Uncle Loyd's hand as we walked around the edge of the field Grandpa had plowed for the hundredth time that year, that we found the chiseled stone at our feet in the same spot we'd stooped to pick up split-open apricot seeds. Whether we found it together that day or he simply gave it to me, suddenly, miraculously, it appeared in my palm, a connection to something hidden, ancient, and hitherto unsuspected by me, barely more than a toddler at the time. The mystery: Others had been there before us, before my great-grandfather, James Darrow, had brought his family by covered wagon from Tennessee via Texas, stopping in Bowie long enough for his wife, Virginia Vashti Turney, to give birth to my grandfather, William Floyd—and perhaps my Great-Aunt Eva, although she may have been born after they homesteaded near Canute in western Oklahoma and built their half-dugout soddy. Nearly seventy years later, Grandpa, homesick and plagued by emphysema, sat in the humid garden of his new home in Arkansas and told me how scared he'd been in the night as he lay on his little cot next to earthen walls papered with newsprint, and listened to the centipedes skittering beneath it. He remembered wildfires across the prairie, plagues of grasshoppers, and sandstorms so thick his mother had tied a wet cloth over his mouth and nose to keep him from choking. When those calamities passed, they left blackened fields or stripped foliage or everything gritty and pink, even the feathers of the white chickens.

I remember *this* clearly: we walked through the plowed south field one day, the sand clumped together and dark red from the rainstorm the night before, and the rangy, tough apricot tree was no longer there, just a peeled-back stump, lightning-struck. But I wanted apricots, I wanted the walk with my uncles, I wanted Grandma's fried pies. Most of all I wanted the tree back, and it was gone. A hollow opened in my chest—my first grief—as I tried to replace the vision of the black-ened trunk with that of the green and living tree. Awareness of memory was born in me in that moment of irrevocable and somehow inevitable change that had come upon us. Years later, as I watched my grandfather fight for breath on his deathbed, clinging to the chrome bed rails with his bruised and worn hands, hold-ing tight as if to life itself, I saw it again, as vividly as that day when I was, at most, three years old—the storm-ravaged apricot tree.

2

feathers on the ceiling   blue marble   blue Ford   roaring down a red
   highway
      the cellar door's tinny rattle   chickens roosting in the cedars
     galvanized buckets filled with cement

When I was born, my nineteen-year-old Uncle Loyd lived with us in our new house in Elk City. It had a living room with gray feathered paper on the ceiling, a kitchen, two bedrooms, a tiny central hall, and a bathroom whose door had locked behind my mother once. She couldn't get out. For a long time I waited outside, needing in there, torn between fear she'd never get out and fear I'd wet myself, hardly aware of a difference in the tragic consequences of either. My hero daddy climbed in the bathroom window, took off the doorknob, and saved us.

On weekends I packed my red metal suitcase to go visit Grandma and Grandpa on the farm. Loyd, with Doris, his girlfriend, beside him in the front seat, drove his blue late '40s Ford fast, the wind blowing through the open windows and the red dust boiling up behind us, through the fields of full summer. The red furrows and green cotton plants bright in the sunlight, I had to shade my eyes as I stood on my knees in the back seat, straining for the first glimpse of the barn around the last corner and down the lane past the buckshot-riddled mailbox. Loyd could turn that car on a dime, and never have to take his arm from Doris's shoulders, his fist clutched around a bright blue marbleized steering knob he'd attached to the wheel specially for one-handed driving.

What joy to arrive in a whirl of red, roll across the yard covered with last year's cotton boll husks, and stop at the back door. In all the years I traveled to that house, I never once entered the front door, unless I'd already come in the back and, for novelty during the cousins' games, decided to exit the front just to see how it felt to come in that way.

Once when I was around nine or ten, a man drove up, got out of his car, and approached the front door between the two overgrown cedar trees the chickens liked for shade to roost in on hot days. The cousins hushed and waited. He knocked and we looked at our short, round Grandma, whose face had grown tense with this blatant evidence of strangerhood. No one she knew even the slightest would come to her front door. This could be trouble. The cousins drew back and watched from the shadows of the living room while she went to the screen door, her arthritically bent fingers reaching in secret to secure the latch. We, who lived in towns in other states where vacuum cleaner salesmen and preachers and sometimes even panhandlers interrupted our mothers' workdays, stood in confusion and curiosity, ready to leap to our grandma's defense. We heard a note of distance enter her voice, a tone so foreign to our ears we'd remark on it later as we sat on the arched cellar roof, the cool, dank air rising from its concrete chimney vent, and watched the stars come out and the oil rig flares glow on the dark horizon. The night wind brushed across the hairs along our forearms, chilled from a source that could only be the deep well whirling above us, and raised goosebumps of recognition. It brought visions of those other travelers, the spear-makers who'd crept by this spot a hundred years before, two hundred, maybe more. They'd sat on the flint rock boulders and watched the dipper crank around the north star, and, huddled near a small fire, they'd planned to marry and raise children, chosen their work in the tribe, and prepared for hunting and gathering. Then, singing down the moon, they'd fallen asleep to dream a world nothing like the one we knew by daylight, incandescent light, or the blue light of the television set. Only through the ancient dark, the sacred wind, and the still-warm earth could we touch them. And so we did.

3

a cappella music   the preacher's shouts   seven minute icing   lost
    in a forest of legs
& glowing cigarettes   stuffed white dog   fireworks in the front yard
    petunias & scratchy wool jacket   orange toboggan

Other early memories: aunts and uncles, brides and grooms cutting their wedding cakes on kitchen tables in tiny houses like our own. I stared into the mirror to see if I looked anything like those brides, but my round little face just frowned back, and I couldn't see anyone there but me.

Uncle Glen and Aunt Dorothy's and Uncle Loyd and Aunt Doris's weddings
have merged in my mind as if they had come one Saturday after the other, or
maybe all on the same weekend, though in truth they were about six months
apart. The grinning uncles in their suits, their Brylcreemed waves atop their heads,
their starched shirts and ties; the young aunts in their light-colored tailored suits
with gloves and tiny hats, their faces shining and happy; the laughter; the cake!
My memories may be based on the sepia-toned wedding photographs I saw each
time I visited my grandparents' house, but in them the brides and grooms were all
normal-sized. My memory tells me that everything except me was large—the people, the tables, and the chairs I had to climb on to get a good look (and a lick of
icing). The houses were filled with forests of legs, just like at church. I got lost in
that forest, my heart beating louder than the talk high above me. Although I tried
my best to keep the panic from pouring out, I cried, "Mommy, Mommy," until my
parents found me there among all the skirts and trousers, picked me up, set me in
the highchair where the voices had faces again, gave me a dish of cake, and I could
smile and think about being a bride, too, someday. Then I drank some milk,
rubbed my eyes, sucked my thumb, and got carried to the bedroom for my nap. As
they tucked the blanket around me, they said, "Sweet dreams."

4

the dream:

       leaving Oklahoma   red roses on a white trellis   gumbo mud &
crawdads   mother (on her way to the mental hospital) & baby sister
asleep in the back seat, curled together, fetal
       reading road signs & maps before school books   trailer parks
across the south
two schools a year   lynching in the Mississippi headlines   black leather
jackets & duck tails   bullet in the top of my head, out my
feet, splitting like particles of light   oaks & Spanish moss

At first we rented houses, then, after my mother's illness, Daddy bought a small
trailer house we could pull behind our car whenever his job transferred him to another city to build oil refineries. I liked the wood-paneled walls arching into the
low ceiling, the foldaway table in front of the couch, the two extra chairs for my
sister and me, the bathroom that was all shower stall with toilet and tiny corner
sink tucked inside it. I didn't like the pop of the butane heater burner several seconds after the hiss of gas, and the influx of cockroaches when we moved to Mississippi. When we got home from church at night and turned on the light, they
ran for cover. My sister and I kept the nightlight on in our room to keep us safe.

    About that time Daddy and Mama bought a brand new trailer house with their
bedroom in the front and their bed under a sloping window they could lie under
and watch the stars at night. This larger trailer had a permanent table and four

chairs and a special shelf over the refrigerator for the TV. My sister's and my bed-room was in the back, and all was well until we moved to Beaumont, Texas, and switched from butane to fuel oil, and we had to have the tank up on stilts just out-side our back window. I had always been afraid of fire, and when someone shot a bullet through our bedroom wall just about a foot above our sleeping heads one New Year's Eve, it took me years to realize how close it had come to killing one of us, but only seconds to imagine it entering the fuel drum about a yard to the right. The explosion would have wiped out all of us, all the children, the white kids on this side of the fence and the black kids on the other, the trailers here and the shotgun houses there, all the moms and dads, brothers and sisters, aunts and un-cles, even the person who'd fired the handgun. I imagined his surprise as we all floated up over Sabine Pass, then the ship channel, and away.

5

> *Tangee, Galveston Beach, sunburn, high heels   drag race on*
> *mountain highway drag race in the Panhandle   prom date loses eye*
> *& arm to Viet Cong   hellfire & brimstone in Arkansas   college*
> *boy sweetheart   sewing white velvet & lace   homebaked wedding cake,*
> *licking the icing bowl*
> *   borrowed veil & something blue as TV light*

He was a freshman in college and I a junior in high school when we met. We didn't like each other at first, but by Christmas of my freshman year in college, we were married. My parents owned a white frame house by then with a dining room. We filled the house with friends and relatives for our wedding reception, and hon-eymooned in Hot Springs, shaving cream and crepe paper streaming off his white Ford Falcon as we raced over the mountain highways eluding our followers. Nei-ther of us had been hungry enough to eat before the wedding, so we stopped at a hamburger stand just outside town, him in his new black suit and me in the most expensive outfit I'd ever owned, a wool knit suit and green velvet high heels with purse to match and coordinating off-white gloves.

6

clay pot, clay head, clay & paint
*   football, "RELAX," "BREATHE," pelvic tilts   the baby nearly dies*
voices off/ fingerspell/ repeat   the deaf baby nearly dies   nearly dies
40 days over 100 degrees in Fort Worth   (words)   tornadoes & fires
across the prairie (words)   photos of vacations out west   blue
northers   Expect a Miracle!
*   (words/words)*

In one of the vacation photographs I sat at the top of a rough log ladder in the mouth of a high cave, gazing up at the ceiling soot-stained from some long-dead Anasazi woman's hearth. Glad to be in the shade after the climb through the heat radiating off the white limestone cliff, I sat alone in her dwelling—only one person at a time allowed to climb the rope-lashed ladder. I was all alone until the ancient ones crowded around me just beyond my vision the same way they had risen in the darkness on the farm, just past the yard light, just past the glow from the windows, the flicker of the television. But this time I couldn't get out of there fast enough. I stepped onto the ladder and felt suspended between this world and some weird imagining, a fantasy life I suddenly could no longer distinguish from the real. Was the fantasy the time-echo in the cave? Or was the fantasy my life in the daylight world of children to clothe, husband to feed, household to run? Where could I go to sing down the moon?

I began the long climb down. But halfway through my descent, the world tilted and I seemed to be crawling backwards along a ladder laid flat over even ground. The only thing that made sense in that moment was to release my hands and stand erect. Just as I began to relax my grip, just before gravity took over, I saw my mistake. I grabbed the ladder and clung to it, my pulse pounding all the way into my fingertips. I had almost pitched my body backward and plunged to the path far below. Edging my way step by step back to the valley floor, I struggled to breathe the thin mountain air.

7

hero daddy succumbs to cancer after experimental treatment fails
   but first he charms the children by swinging on the backyard swing
leaving Texas   *(& words &)*   *the Sears*
Tower two-story suburban house   blue tv light/ voices off/ midnight
breath on a stranger's back

The dream went on for nearly half a century. I grew up, and my babies grew up and left home; my young husband withdrew into middle age, became the stranger, and finally drove his Explorer out of Illinois and back to Texas. Now, in my sunny Chicago living room, the divorce final at last, I hold the spearhead in my hand, shut my eyes, and see the dusty kiva where my husband and I took amazing photographs one summer, the Anasazi light perfect, the ancient air buzzing around us. I couldn't breathe there. But oh, the vacation photos were magic.

Sometimes I wonder what would have happened if my odd momentary perception on the cliffside had prevailed and I had remained convinced I was crawling along the ground. Would I have stood up, stepped off the ladder along the cliff wall—and walked away from this life around the curve of the hill, back into the depths of all I could have been, yet never had been, all I could have said, but didn't say?

I hadn't told my husband about the eerie sense of presence in the cave, and certainly not about the crazy notion of a world gone perpendicular to itself during that split second I had been sure my disequilibrium was the true orientation of the earth. Sometimes I wonder if that was what caused us to grow apart. The more I hid, the more I needed to hide; the less he saw, the less he wanted to see. When I started hiding myself from him, had I started a real process of fading away?

Perhaps I was the one who had become the stranger.

8

*the lake & taxicabs   he el to the Loop   children's books &
poems   baseball students with piercings, tattoos, bright blue hair   tall
white farmhouses, red barns
        cornfields   uncles and aunts   remembering Illinois*

I lived in the same house for nearly fourteen years in a Chicago suburb, and have lived in Chicago near Wrigley Field for two and one half years. I've felt like a Chicagoan for a while now, but a Midwesterner, rather than a Southerner? Only for a month. For years when I returned from visiting my family in the South and the interstate highway divided when we crossed the Mississippi River at St. Louis, I yearned to follow the Memphis sign instead of the Chicago one. Last month, however, I didn't feel that tug as I returned from the Darrow family reunion on Petit Jean Mountain in Arkansas, my car packed with fresh tomatoes and squash from my mother-in-law's garden. Those plain white farms, red barns, silos, and cornfields came into view, and I remembered the first time I'd driven that road so many years before with my children, a dog, and a cat in the back. Then I remembered all the other times, the children growing older, and now driving themselves back and forth across these borders. Memories. All we have left at the end of the day.

As I drove, I opened the windows to the smell of the country air, new growth, and the tilled soil, rich and brown, so unlike the bright red earth I knew as a child. I felt immense relief to be back. Born and bred in the South, my voice and language still heavy with it, I'd come to the Midwest by chance, and against my will and better judgment. I'd resisted it, wanted to leave it, but finally, when I did at last have a choice of my own, I chose it.

Now, in my own large apartment in a bright Victorian house, high in the treetops, I hold the spearhead, listen to my daughter, home for the summer before her senior year in college, as she meows to the cats while she works on a scrapbook of her recent trip to Northern Ireland. She's just returned from Dallas, where she attended another family wedding—her father's.

I place the spearhead on the mantel and ask her what she wants for dinner. She asks for a pasta dish I began to cook after we moved here, her favorite meal from her childhood, she says. I walk back to my kitchen, barefoot on the cool wood floors of this house I have chosen for myself, and I heat the water to bring back the memories. Here at the end of the day, we break bread, drink wine, and tell stories of when we each were children in our different worlds, and it all comes together, and we are home.

Positively 4th Street

MARY HELEN STEFANIAK

WHERE MOTHERS RULE

Where I grew up—in a working-class neighborhood on the south side of Milwaukee—mothers were not much like the mothers you see today, if you look fast enough to catch us before we drop the kids off and drive away to work, drinking our coffee or making last-minute phone calls as we go.

The mothers on 4th Street were like God: all-knowing, all-present, all-powerful, and most of the time unseen. Their most apparent role in the flow of neighborhood life was calling kids in. They called us in to eat supper, to go somewhere (like Sears on Mitchell Street or my grandmother's house), to practice (usually the accordion), to do our homework, or to take a bath and go to bed. No matter where we were—down by the creek, at the corner store, in the field behind John Greenleaf Whittier School, or in Judene Szweda's bathroom—our mothers always knew where to find us. If we strayed beyond the reach of their call, then somebody else would hear it and pass it along: "Hey! Mary Helen! Your mom's calling you."

After I grew up and went to college, I learned that the mothers on 4th Street (and across the alley on 3rd) were oppressed by society and by their working-class husbands, who demanded that women stay home, take care of the children, and have supper ready and waiting when the men got home from work. Growing up, I confess, I saw the situation differently. The way I saw it, men had to go to work, the same way kids had to go to school. Since I did not aspire to a job as a welder at Ladish Mfg. or a spot on the assembly line at Allen-Bradley—to be honest, I did not aspire to doing anything that somebody else told me to do for eight hours a day—it seemed to me that mothers were the lucky ones. They got to stay home.

At home, the mothers were in charge. The fathers were like visitors—only more exhausted and less polite. Fathers were significant chiefly as chauffeurs (since most mothers couldn't drive) and on their days off. Then they became repairmen, plumbers, carpenters, painters, window washers, lawn care experts (my Dad's specialty), or auto mechanics, each man according to his talents and the needs of the household, which were usually determined by the mothers.

And what did mothers do all day in the freedom and sanctity of their homes? That, of course, I paid less attention to, being busy at school or down at the creek or at the freeway construction site, where we zoomed on makeshift skateboards down the new concrete ramps. When I picture the mothers on 4th Street, I see Mrs. Fecteau at the Singer in her dining room, sewing up a summer's worth of shorts for her four daughters while keeping an eye on her favorite soaps. (Almost forty years later, Mrs. Fecteau is gone, but *As the World Turns* is still on the air.) I see Mrs. Shultis on her backyard patio, hanging paper lanterns. The Shultises had the only patio on the block. They threw parties—I remember spying on a luau with leis and everything—not just baby showers.

Mrs. Szweda I see sorting clean laundry on the table in her dining room. (Nobody I knew used the room for dining.) I see her hanging shirts on door knobs and drawer pulls of the built-in buffet. Either that or peeling potatoes. She had two grown sons and a husband in the house, truck drivers all. I don't think I ever came looking for my friend Judene after school without seeing her mother in the kitchen peeling potatoes and dropping them into a free-standing cooker the size of a laundry tub. It was like a Crockpot on wheels.

Most of the mothers on 4th Street were called "Mrs." but a few had names, like my mother, who was "Mary" even to some of my friends, and Pam Dragan's mother, Connie. Recently I noticed this: The mothers with names were the ones who had jobs. (Outside the home, as people used to say.) Both my mother and Connie Dragan were waitresses, Mom part-time at the Tasty Town lunch counter in Gimbels and Connie at *The Bay*, a restaurant run by *her* mother.

Working outside the home was a questionable pursuit in those days. One of the threats of World Communism, I recall from the 1950s, was that mothers would be forced to work outside the home and leave the raising of their children to state-run day-care centers. (Can you imagine?) My mother's job was acceptable only because (a) it was part-time, (b) my sister was old enough to babysit for us, and (c) there was no reason to suspect that my mother *liked* working at Tasty Town, where the tips were terrible.

Connie Dragan, on the other hand, obviously enjoyed her job. I'm sure some people pursed their lips at the sight of her running down the front steps to the car in dark stockings, red lipstick, and her crisp black and white uniform, looking far more energetic than was decent for a mother of nine (or seven or six or however many she had at the time), and leaving two or three little Dragans on the porch behind her, sad and forlorn, along with their babysitter (sometimes my sister), who looked equally forlorn.

What I remember best about my own mother getting ready for work was the way she smelled—a pleasant blend of Jergens lotion and Listerine (original flavor). Her Tasty Town uniform was a starched yellow jumper over a white blouse, with a little white apron on top of that and a white crown in her hair that made her look like Judy Garland in *The Harvey Girls*. My mother worked at Tasty Town for many years before she moved on to a fancier restaurant and better tips at the Boston Store downtown, and finally to Food Service at St. Luke's Hospital, where she worked until shortly after my father died, also at St. Luke's Hospital, in 1983.

(She used to send him treats on his dinner tray.) Now she volunteers there. Every year, around Christmas time, she puts some thought into what she'll wear to the Volunteer Recognition Dinner. Occasionally she buys a new outfit—something mothers seldom did during the years we lived on 4th Street. Lotion and Listerine she still keeps on hand.

Now that I think about it, Mrs. Szweda also had a job, on top of all the laundry and potatoes. She played the clarinet in a four-piece band that used to practice in her living room. They did weddings and anniversaries, Holy Name Society smokers, things like that.

Mrs. Szweda's name, I remember, was Irene.

CHICKEN MAN! HORNET WARS!

In the neighborhood where I grew up, a real can-do spirit prevailed.

Picture my father (whose name was George) standing in our front yard, girded for battle. He wears mechanic's overalls rubber-banded at the wrists and stuffed at the ankles into big black boots buckled right up to the top. His neck is swathed in scarves. His hands are double-gloved in rubber and suede. Over it all, he wears his black policeman's raincoat and a broad-brimmed hat covered with netting that hides his face and disappears into the scarves around his neck. With both gloved hands, he grips the brass nozzle on the end of our green garden hose. The hose snakes around behind him across the lawn to the side of the house, where my mother leans over the spigot, ready to turn on the water when he gives the signal. Crouching in the shadows at the side of our house, she seems to be hiding from the alien being in the front yard.

Stiffly, encumbered by his armor, my father lifts his arm. That's the signal. Water sputters, then shoots in a long, forceful arc from the brass nozzle.

It's summer, 1962. The first skirmish in my father's annual war with the hornets is about to begin.

The enemy resides in undetermined numbers in a nest in a pillar on our front porch. My father knows that when it comes to hornets, you can smoke them out or you can flood them out, and being personally acquainted with a man who burned his house to the ground smoking them out, he has chosen water over fire. He twists the nozzle to the off position and clumps up five wooden steps to the porch, dragging the hose behind him. My mother, having done her part, beats a hasty retreat toward the back door. My father is on the front porch now, approaching the pillar stealthily. A hornet or two (I'm imagining these) buzz in idle curiosity around his broad-brimmed hat and facial netting. My father aims the hose at the dark space where the corner of the porch roof rests on the pillar and twists the nozzle again.

Most of the kids in the neighborhood and a few of their mothers are gathered to watch from a safe distance on Uncle Bud's front lawn, two doors down from our house. From there, we see a white cloud of spray burst into being in the corner of our front porch. My dad stands fast, in spite of the dousing he must be taking as the water glances off the pillar and ceiling. All at once, the white spray of water turns dark. In Uncle Bud's yard, we take a step or two backwards. Hornets continue to pour out of the pillar. The black cloud of them is mixed up now with the water, my dad in the middle of it all.

Suddenly, a cry erupts from the cloud. "Son of a bitch!" we hear, and then, in rapid succession, "Ouch—ouch—ouch—OUCH!" My father drops the hose and runs. Straight for Uncle Bud's yard.

The crowd scatters—a disorderly retreat. My friend Judene, who lives in a house across the alley from ours, must not be thinking straight. She tries to make it home through our yard, a mistake that costs her two stings in what we referred to discreetly in those days as her seat, one for each cheek.

Judene and my father, who sustained a dozen stings, were the only two human casualties of that historic battle. The hornets fared far worse. When the air cleared, our porch was littered with tiny corpses. My dad must have wiped out a hundred of them. The remaining thousands took up residence for the summer in eaves and gutters at the Dragans' house and Grandma Karras's and Uncle Bud's, at the Westphals' and the Weslowskis' and the Fecteaus' across the street.

Mr. Fecteau was the one who killed chickens in his basement. He was a small man with a large Adam's apple that bobbed up and down in a way I found alarming whenever he swallowed or spoke. (His name was Larry, but I never heard anyone call him that.) Sometimes Mr. Fecteau let the neighborhood kids watch him kill the chickens, as long as we stayed over on the steps and didn't get in his way. I can't remember if he chopped or twisted their heads off—maybe I closed my eyes for that part—but I do recall that following the removal of its head, each chicken was stuffed into a cardboard box for a minute or two. ("To get used to being dead," my friend Pam's older brother explained to us.) The box had a lid with a weight on it that was supposed to be heavy enough to keep a thrashing, headless chicken inside.

One time, when we were watching, a chicken slipped out of the box before Mr. Fecteau got the lid on properly, and—you guessed it—that chicken ran around the basement with its head cut off. Like a fast-moving fountain, it led Mr. Fecteau on a gory chase around the big old octopus furnace and back out toward the basement steps (at which point we kids scrambled upstairs, shrieking). By the time we returned, Mr. Fecteau had the chicken by the feet and was dropping it into the big pot of water he had simmering on a stove down there. Soaking in hot water was supposed to make the chickens easier to pluck. That's what Mr. Fecteau said, anyway. The poor chickens, headless though they were, always made a sad little gurgling sound in their throats as they went into the pot.

When I told this story to my daughter recently, she said, aghast, "The guy killed chickens in his *basement?*"

I was surprised by her reaction. To me, the whole point of the story is the eyewitness proof it offers that chickens really do run around with their heads cut off. The location chosen by Mr. Fecteau to behead them struck me as a purely practical matter. Where did my daughter expect him to do it? In the garage? By the 1960s, in a city the size of Milwaukee, there must have been an ordinance against keeping, much less slaughtering, livestock in your garage. If Mr. Fecteau had killed and dressed his chickens out there, in plain view of the alley, a policeman—like my father, for instance—might have felt obliged to nab him for it. Mr. Fecteau didn't go to all the trouble of bringing those chickens in from somebody's farm out in Thiensville just to get collared by the cops.

Then my daughter said, not without a certain envy, "You grew up in a weird neighborhood, Mom."

It didn't seem weird to me. Fourth Street between Plainfield and Bolivar was about as ordinary an elm-shaded block as you were likely to find on the south side of Milwaukee. Summers passed in sun-speckled boredom. Notable moments—like the water fight that started with Tommy Dragan's squirt gun and ended with my father and his garden hose holding off half the neighborhood, or the time two dozen men carried Butchie Teidemann's one-and-a-half-car garage down the alley to our yard—these moments were few and far between.

"They carried a garage down the alley?" my daughter said. "In their bare hands?"

Not in their bare hands, I told her. They wore their workmen's gloves. Their steel-toed shoes, too, those who had them.

HALF A LESSON FROM UNCLE BUD

In my old neighborhood, a girl had only two choices: accordion lessons or baton.

Pam Dragan and I took baton. Once a week, we walked five blocks under a canopy of elms from 4th Street to Howell Avenue, where our teacher lived, brandishing our batons, indulging now and then in a march step or two, toes pointed, knees raised high. We shared our half-hour lesson with two chubby little girls—sisters—who, if memory serves me correctly, always wore their sequin-spangled leotards. Probably they only wore these outfits once in a while, but that's how I remember them, dressed for success. My friend Pam and I wore cotton-print jamaica shorts that came with matching sleeveless blouses. Our mothers bought us three or four of these shorts sets at the start of each summer. After a couple of weeks, I'd be wearing the yellow plaid shorts with the red, white, and blue sailboat top, setting up a rotation that left me mismatched for the rest of the season.

We practiced our baton twirling in Pam's backyard for at least a half-hour a day, no matter how bruised our elbows got. Unlike the sparkling sisters, Pam and I never twirled in a single parade, but we had our private moments of glory. There were times, for example, when we managed to do the horizontal over-and-under twirl at high speed, not once banging our elbows with our batons, which, on the count of three, we threw into the air *together* and then stood our ground without flinching, keeping our eyes on those batons as they went up like propellers flashing silver against the evening sky.

Sometimes we even caught them on the way back down!

When we did, we were often rewarded with applause from Uncle Bud, who lived next door to the Dragans and spent his summer evenings watering his garden or sitting on his back porch, smoke curling away from his pipe like a little gray banner.

We didn't know what to make of Uncle Bud—a bachelor, living alone on 4th Street, his house the only lannonstone ranch in a two-block stretch of wooden frame houses and Milwaukee bungalows. He was a guy our fathers' age with a round face, a salt-and-pepper crewcut, and a pipe stem always clenched between his teeth. We tried to imagine why he wasn't married, proposing various tragedies that might have robbed him of wife and kids and the chance for a normal life. Jealously we wondered what he did with the two spare bedrooms in his three-bedroom ranch. But most of all, we vied for the privilege of running down to the corner store for him, to pick up a can of shaving cream or a loaf of bread and keep the change.

Uncle Bud sent me to the store only once—an occasion I remember thirty-five years later in painfully sharp detail. One bright evening, when I was balancing my baton on my index finger in Pam's yard, waiting for her to come outside, I heard Uncle Bud whistle from his back porch. He waved me over. He was all out of Half-n-Half, he told me when I reached his porch steps. Could I run to the store for him? "Just get a small one," he said, and dropping a musical handful of quarters into my palm, he added the words I was waiting for: "Keep the change."

When I got back from the store, Uncle Bud was nowhere in sight, so I rang the bell and waited, my Popsicle dripping, my licorice ropes getting stickier by the minute, and a wax carton of half-and-half sweating in the crook of my arm. I rang the bell again. From somewhere inside the house Uncle Bud hollered, "Who is it?" and I yelled through the screen, "It's me."

"Who?"

"With the half-and-half."

A pause followed, then the muffled voice again: "Put it on the counter."

I transferred the licorice ropes and Popsicle to the hand that held the half-and-half, wiped my fingers on my jamaica shorts (sailboats today), and pulled the handle on the screen door. Inside, the house had what I thought of for years afterward as a bachelor smell: a blend of pipe tobacco, aftershave, mothballs, furniture wax, and Airwick Room Deodorizer. I took a deep breath of it, crossed the shining kitchen floor, set the carton on the counter, and scooted out the back door again.

I had gone but a few steps from the house when I heard the squeak of hinges behind me, followed by a quizzical "Hey!" I turned around. Uncle Bud was standing in the doorway with the one-pint carton of half-and-half in his hand.

"What's this?" he said.

It was like a trick question. I said, "Half-and-half."

He stood there, looking at the carton as if it were an artifact from another world, which, in a way, it was. Finally, I had to ask, "Is something wrong?"

He said, "I was hoping for tobacco."

For a split second I thought he'd answered me in Arabic or something. Then I got it. Tobacco. Uncle Bud was hoping for *tobacco*. I could picture packages of it behind the counter at the corner store, above the rows of cigarettes. *Half-n-Half Burly & Bright* ("A Cargo of Contentment in the Bowl of Any Pipe") was right there on the shelf, in a green and red package, between boxes of *Captain Black* and cans of *Prince Albert*. I had *seen* the tobacco. I had thought, "Do you have Prince Albert in a can? Well, let him out!" And then I had purchased a Popsicle, two licorice ropes, and a one-pint carton of the kind of half-and-half my mother would have sent me for.

The ground did not open and swallow me up in Uncle Bud's yard. It never does when you need it to. I had to run all the way back to my house and hide in the basement instead. We had a dungeon of a basement on 4th Street—wooden joists and heating ducts to bang your head on, dripping pipes, an old converted octopus furnace in the middle of it all. I stood down there in the former coal bin, watching tears of humiliation darken the dust on my tennis shoes and remembering Uncle Bud's chuckle. I looked down at my yellow plaid blouse and my red, white, and blue sailboat shorts. Like Eve discovering her nakedness, I saw for the first time how dumb I looked.

KING OF SCROUNGE

Among his film and video-making friends, my son Jeff has had a reputation since high school for coming up with special effects on little or no budget. Jeff can do things like turn a heap of broken calculators and molded styrofoam packing material into a convincing cyberman. (And when I say convincing, I mean that the cardboard tube wrapped in electrical tape on the cyberman's bionic wrist actually fired flaming projectiles that were, Jeff claims to this day, completely harmless.) My son's resourcefulness I attribute partly to his father, who's been known to reshape a Ford Pinto fender to fix the trunk of a Mercedes coupe; and to *his* father before him, a university professor and do-it-yourself plumber who once explained that the Ph.D. after his name stood for "Plunge harder, Dad." But most of my son's talent for scrounging comes, I believe, from my father, who died when Jeff was eight.

On the last afternoon of my father's life, I said the rosary for him. The idea was not to invoke heavenly intercession but to help him fall asleep. I said the rosary as lullaby, the decades droning on and on, one *Hail Mary* after another. My father was very weak by then, and it was hard for him to talk, but he finally managed to interrupt.

"I think you're keeping me awake," he whispered.

"Should I sing instead?" I asked him.

He rolled his eyes.

"Sorry," I said.

I would have liked to pick him up and walk him, the way he used to walk my children to sleep, cruising around and around our dining room table with Jeff or Liz or Lauren in his arms, singing the same lullaby—half Croatian, half non-sense—that I'd heard him sing to both my little brothers many years ago on 4th Street. *Spavaj sinco moj, lepo spavaj.* Sleep, my son, it means. Sleep well, sleep sweetly, beautifully sleep. "Of course it works," my mother liked to say. "They go to sleep so they won't have to listen to your father sing anymore."

There may have been some merit in her theory. My father didn't sing songs; he belted them out. Even lullabies. His favorite tunes were from the forties. (I have often surprised my husband by knowing the words to "Begin the Beguine" or "Glow Little Glow Worm" when the big bands play at Hofer's Danceland in lovely Walford, Iowa.) But Dad also liked beltable songs of a later era, like "Mac the Knife" and "Hang Down Your Head, Tom Dooley," which gave him goosebumps. "Look at that, look at that," he'd say, interrupting his song to show you the goose-flesh on his arm. "I'm telling you, I missed my calling. I could have made a fortune with this voice."

On 4th Street, there wasn't a kid on the block who would risk raising George Elleseg's ire—and thus his voice—by treading on his front lawn when he was seed-ing it, which was most of the time, or taking one of his tools without asking. The tools were in the garage that he and two dozen neighbors and cousins had lifted on the count of three and carried by hand down the alley from its former location behind Butchie Teidemann's house to our yard, where they lowered it gently onto the salvaged brick foundation my father had prepared for it.

Relocated, that garage became the hub of the neighborhood. Your bike had a flat tire? You asked George if you could use his air compressor. You wanted the seat lowered or, as my sister's friend Pat used to say, highered? George was sure to have whatever size wrench you needed. If a screw or a bolt or a nail was required, you peered through the bottoms of dozens of baby food jars whose caps were nailed in rows to the ceiling above his workbench until you found just the size and type you were looking for.

In a neighborhood full of scroungers and do-it-yourselfers, my father was the king. The garage was only one of many accomplishments. Both the stockade fence in our backyard and the privet hedge in front were scrounged—the latter nothing but sticks with roots when Dad picked them out of somebody's garbage cans and planted them along our lot line, deaf to the jokes of neighbors who then watched the sticks grow into a shoulder-high hedge so dense not even the skinniest kid could squeeze through it. Most of the lumber with which he ruined our dark and mysterious attic (by building two nice bedrooms and a walk-in closet) was sec-ondhand and full of silverfish. My sister and I squished torpedo-shaped bugs daily for years.

Like most do-it-yourselfers, my father preferred not to finish a project if he could start a new one instead. With the upstairs lacking only inconsequential de-tails (a track for the closet door to slide on, a handrail for the stairs), my father de-cided to build a go-cart that resembled a red Model T out of lumber scraps, sheet metal, and that most salvageable of items, an old lawnmower motor. While my little brothers sat up front and steered, my father trotted alongside, ready to hop aboard the rear bumper, flip a switch behind the driver, and drag one foot in the alley until the heavy car rolled to a stop. (The missing detail: brakes.) A few years later, following in my father's footsteps, my brother recycled the wheels and other choice parts of the go-cart to enter a soapbox derby. Later still, when shortness of breath made all my father's tools grow heavier, he and his friend Ralph Dragan used two of those same wheels to build a cart for the air compressor.

When it came to recycling, my father was ahead of his time.

After he died, the air compressor went to my soapbox-building brother, which means that Dad's still fixing flat tires on the south side of Milwaukee. A lot of his other tools—wrenches and saws, a pipecutter and threader—found their way into our garage and basement, where they have helped us build shelves (and cybermen), fix leaks, and keep a succession of old cars running long after they should have gone to their last reward. They've also taught us a lesson in immortality, offering proof, I think, of life after death, at least in my father's case. Once, in Iowa City, I was sitting on the porch when my husband came outside to pound some stakes in the garden with a hammer from my dad's old workbench. At the top of our porch steps, 265 miles and more than three decades from the garage on 4th Street, which, by the way, he'd never seen, my husband paused, lifted the wooden handle to the sky, and said, "Just using your hammer, George. Thanks."

The Basement

PAULETTE ROESKE

I am not black, although my dark complexion and frizzy black hair caused me to sulk famously as a five-year-old in the heart of America's Heartland, "I don't want to play with those old white kids out there," when games did not go my way. This was not a studied observation of the difference between me and my paler friends, but rather a riff on the tune my mother had taught me, the mother who called me "little nigger girl" to point to her opinion of my appearance, which also contaminated my every word and deed. In a skip-a-generation genetic dance, I resemble the dark side of the family, my much-loved grandmother, my father's mother, *come-from-god-knows-where-but-certainly-not-the-Germany-from-which-she-claims-to-have-set-sail.* My mother drags racial anecdotes into the present, I think, because she delights in flinging out the hard stone of each defamatory syllable: *lit-tle-nig-ger-girl,* she likes to say, repeating the phrase as the punch line while hiding behind the wide skirts of a past that permitted, even privileged, such language. After all, how can she be held responsible for words that are not hers but rather part of a script she is not at liberty to rewrite? Each repetition continues to identify me as the outsider, consigning me to a camp distinct from her own, one that, in her view, occupies a place in the foothills of the mountaintop where she resides.

If my appearance was my mark of Cain, the Great Depression marked my mother. One of six prematurely fatherless children, the only daughter of a woman who took in other people's wash, my mother became a fervent consumer as soon as she was able, even before she was able. Like the ill-fated house in D. H. Lawrence's short story "The Rocking-Horse Winner," our house sent up its chorus of whispers: *"There must be more money! There must be more money!"* A hypersensitivity to her rank on the low end of the socioeconomic scale alerted my mother to any evidence that could be used against her, such as a daughter who looked as if she had crept over from the wrong side of the tracks and taken up residence in the white part of town during a blink of racism's watchful eye. Even now I am not sure why I attempt to rationalize that the pain in her life led her to the unthinkable acts of bigotry she may have practiced to mitigate her own sense of dispossession. Sometimes I imagine my mother walking down the streets of Smalltown U.S.A., me clutching her hand, my brown fingers barred against her pale flesh. Tricked out in frills from bonnet to anklets, I was the sad testament to my mother's belief that clothes could effectively disguise the damage done by a renegade gene or two.

The balmy summer I turned ten, still smack dab in the middle of the Heartland and in a Walgreen's drug store managed by my father, I, underage and packing no work permit, was relegated to the basement, where I would perform tasks suited to my youth and inexperience for twenty-five cents an hour. My sole Saturday companion was Howard, the porter, his name stitched in fancy red script on the breast pocket of his standard-issue gray smock with the Nehru collar—*Howard*, over his heart. He was a light-skinned black man, quiet and kind. Gray-haired, older than my father, for forty years Howard had held the job for which he was hired and from which he would someday retire. Or, more likely, he was hired as a stock boy and promoted to porter, although the job description remained the same. Already he seemed too frail to lift the basement's oversized game pieces, the towers of boxes and crates he would stack and restack with the kind of magic Robert Frost describes in his poem "Mending Wall," where he says of the fallen boulders, "some are loaves and some so nearly balls / We have to use a spell to make them balance." Howard, the store's only black employee, and I—the two of us sequestered, although for different reasons, in the underground labyrinth of corrugated aisles, where we would be kept out of sight to silence the tongues of the local gossips. In my shorts and polka-dot halter, my skinny arms and legs were darker than Howard's hands and face. Perhaps his gaze fell on me as it would on a granddaughter while I worked under his forgiving eye, or maybe to him I was just the manager's kid, and he had long ago learned the proper response to that.

On Saturdays I arrived early with my father, who opened the store each morning, but Howard was always there ahead of us, lounging in a nearby doorway where he had been waiting long enough to look settled in, hands in his pockets, cap pulled down over his eyes. When he saw us he would smile, hitch his shoulders, and greet my father. "G' mornin', Mr. Roeske," he said, and my father answered, "Morning, Howard" to the man whose last name I never knew. When I echoed my father's greeting, Howard replied in his soft, easy voice, "G' mornin', Miz Paulette." I had no way of knowing what this ritual must have cost him. The year was 1955. In less than six months in Montgomery, Alabama, Rosa Parks would redefine the word *refusal*, speaking it for Howard as well as herself, and America's class structure would begin its slow horizontal shift toward a fulcrum and the hope for balance. Suddenly shy, I pressed against my father, who jangled his heavy ring of keys.

At night the basement lights were shut down to a fraction of their power. When my father unlocked the door to the stairs, it swung open on the dim shadowland that Howard and I would inhabit. We felt our way down toward the switches Howard would throw as we watched the basement wake one bright rectangle at a time. First, the seasonal stock in aisles crammed with boxes of collapsible lawn chairs, Styrofoam coolers, citronella candles in tin pails decorated with stars and stripes, portable grills on three short legs that required bending to tend, sparklers, blow-up life preservers that ordinary breath turned into dinosaurs or swans, and miniature discombobulated hula girls to snazz up the dashboard of your car. Aisle after aisle, the light resuscitated cartons of Kiwi, Brylcreem, and Burma Shave, Dippity Doo, Aqua Net, Spray Net, hairnets, hairpins for picking locks and truss-ing turkeys, paregoric, Dr. Caldwell's Syrup Pepsin, ipecac, Vicks VapoRub for your mother to slather on your chest and cover with a cloth warm from the oven, Epsom salts, Mercurochrome (the pretty orange one that didn't burn) and iodine (its sister that did), calamine, witch hazel, Queen Helene Mint Julep Masque, Chantilly, Shalimar, Midnight in Paris—whose enchanting blue bottles I recog-nized from the ten-piece gift set my mother opened each Christmas morning—Dreft, Bon Ami, Bo-Peep ammonia, 99% Pure and floatable Ivory, all of it shuffled and stacked by Howard like cards in a marked deck, all of it in the name of keep-ing America busy, beautiful, healthy, and clean.

The candy room's lights illuminated rows of shelves sagging under the weight of boxes of Whitman's Samplers, Circus Peanuts big as thumbs, Bit-O-Honey, Zag-nut, Jujubees, Orange Slices resplendent with sugar, miniature paraffin Coke bot-tles filled with sweet jewel-tone liquid, red paraffin kiss-me lips and paraffin moustaches and teeth to chew into waxy wads the size of walnuts, Beemans, Teaberry, Blackjack to paste across your two front teeth for a knock-out smile, and Clove—my father's favorite, the protruding tip of its burnt-orange package bright against the pocket of his white pharmacy jacket.

The exotic cargo of the adjoining tobacco room flashed images of the tropics when its lights blinked on. Equipped with blowers that circulated the wet air and turned the space into a giant humidor, the room was a hydrating bath for the red tins of Prince Albert; bundled five-packs of Wm. Penns, with the man himself talking things over with an Indian brave and maiden; Hav-A-Tampa Jewels and Muriel Air Tips, featuring on their boxes romance-novel women in headdresses and dangling hoop earrings, ropes of beads, Scarlett O'Hara waists, and gladiator boots with leather straps crisscrossing their calves; packs of Red Man and Cherry Blend; and cartons of cigarettes bearing their alluring geometries in the colors of the American flag. The rooms collaborated on their singular fragrance: a marriage between chocolate and tobacco spiked with an occasional rush from a smashed bottle of Old Crow emanating from a wire cage where the liquor overstock was stored. I found the cage mysterious, its door weighted with a padlock the size of my open hand, its solemn choirs of bottles in shades of amber or clear as water, these, too, shimmering now that the subterranean reaches were completely lit by the long fluorescent tubes, some of which flickered mightily overhead, a visual Morse code, an unsigned message from the powers above. Call it the spirit made flesh, the whole wonderful spectacle shining like Christmas in July, my own heart pounding at the abundance, the vulgarity, and its attendant desire.

In the basement's heart the conveyor belt churned, motor humming, rollers clattering under the weight of innumerable canvas baskets filled with necessities and the luxuries of summer's delightful inventory. Aligned like so many cars on a freight, the baskets traveled the length of the track, then tipped to begin their ascent to the selling floor, their cargo listing dangerously enough to cause me to hold my breath. But on they rolled, lifted toward the rectangle of light at the top that shone like the golden rays welcoming Jesus in a painting of the ascension. It was Howard who hoisted each heavy basket, sending up merchandise for America while the two of us craned our necks to watch the scissoring legs of the floor man who cadged the baskets with a long metal hook and dragged them out to fulfill the promises made by the store's gaudy advertisements rendered in red paint in my father's flashy hand to snag the shopper's eye and heart.

The goldfish were a popular Walgreen's special: two fish, bowl, plant, ceramic doodad, gravel—49¢ complete. My father needed extra help on the weekends that the store ran the fish promotion, so Howard and I worked as a team for the good of consumerism: he pried the lids off the big white plastic pails and skimmed the floaters from the surface while I turned my back on the dozens of little deaths that had occurred overnight. I never knew how he disposed of the evidence, but his discretion allowed me to pretend that every fish woke to swim the happy circuit of the pail's circumference.

After Howard returned to his boxes, I sat enthroned on an upturned bucket, queen to my slippery subjects, the tools of my trade arrayed around me. Glancing up from time to time, I glimpsed him in his gray smock before he vanished like a shade behind a row of plastic pop-up punching bags—a hook to Daffy Duck's goofy smile meant he'd come whanging back at you—and surfaced by the cartons of croquet sets he levitated and resettled according to an exacting but unwritten law of commerce. And so time passed as he worked his magic, appearing and disappearing. *Eenie-meenie-minee-mo, catch-a-nigger-by-his-toe* we chanted solemnly at our playground games.

My job was simple, but I gave full consideration to netting the two fish who would be pals for life, basing my decision on their size, markings, and personality. The gravel was a kaleidoscope of pinks, blues, and greens that I swirled across the bottom of each glass bowl, anchor for the fern I nestled in a hole I poked with my index finger. A miniature ceramic arch, mermaid, or deep-sea diver, one to a customer, completed each underwater world I created with patience and persistence, as surely as a poem, word by word.

Each bowl went into a canvas basket, perhaps twelve to a layer, the layers separated with sheets of cardboard to create an aquatic high-rise. As the day wore on and the baskets multiplied into a city, Howard lined them up on the conveyor belt. He waited until I had exhausted the pails before calling me over to push the big red button. This was, he knew, the moment I yearned for, when, with one determined press, the rollers would start up with a fish-sloshing lurch, the whole crazy contraption chugging to life under the thumb of a scrawny ten-year-old girl. How magnificent to watch the dozens of surfaces break and begin to shine as the black rubber flaps at the top of the belt parted like the Red Sea under Moses' rod to make way for this glittering cargo. I stood at the bottom squinting up into the light, waving them into the future, hoping for the best for them all, the pure orange, the orange and white, the orange and black, the tri-color, the rare albino, all of them blued under the lights' eerie florescence, as I waved them into happy homes where girls like me would feed and pet them and teach them tricks. Howard stood behind me supervising the ride, and I imagined him waving, too.

At dinner that night, my father, happy in his undershirt as he hunched over pot roast, mashed potatoes and gravy, and me, full of myself because I was a working girl, the time seemed right to beg my mother for fish of my own. I had my favorites, two jewels picked out and held back after a daylong debate with myself. Always, no matter how often I changed my mind, Howard confirmed that the ones I held up for his inspection were real beauties, the best of the lot. My mother, however, routinely denied my appeals for a pet, and she denied this one as well. Howard, I thought bitterly, would have let me have them. When I told her so, she first replied with several slow shakes of her head as proof of her incredulity and then remarked, "Just like a nigger to dirty up a house that way. Yes, just like a nigger."

In our house, the word *nigger* was sometimes uttered without malice, but it was always hierarchical. My mother used it to label everything that her five senses apprehended as being other than that which she had always known and understood. In short, on a good day, *nigger* meant *different,* and in my small Midwestern town, difference was not valued. It was not even tolerated. My mother, of course, had directed the word at my own precious self, although then I did not know I was precious. I did know, however, that Howard's approval of the work of my imagination manifested through my brand of fish bowl art *was* precious. At that moment, seated at the kitchen table staring down my mother's certainty, I intuited that difference was to be sought and cherished. Years later I would conclude that chronicling the differences within sameness was the work of literature, the source of story, without which the world would need only one story. On the page, my childhood's painful moments of difference alchemized into the brightest good, encouraging me to celebrate the periphery where often the best views are to be had.

Welcome to the Land of Freedom

RICARDO CORTEZ CRUZ AND RODNEY B. CRUZ

Contains a sample of Lakeside's "Fantastic Voyage"

"If you didn't come to party, what you come here for?"
—The Beat Boys in "Be Bop Rock," 1983

"When the mind is tethered to a center, naturally it is not free. It can move only within the limits of that center."
—Bruce Lee

INTRO (AND HOOK)

In any community, you'll never encounter one story at a time. Having said that, we feel you. We think that our re-creation of Decatur, Ill., is always (de)pressing because it singularly brings to light what was done in the dark by oppression.

To appropriate the research of Yale art historian Robert Farris Thompson, our story screens that part of black life "informed by the flash of the spirit of a certain people especially armed with improvisatory drive and brilliance." What we turn over is not memoir but rather a thick (very intense) record of unforgettable past events, which we continue to spin. We realize that our lives are happening in the face of a death in the community. Or worse, the story we spin is regarded as one big circle that plays in a terrible tone while the whole community itself dies. But we got to keep the faith, baby.

SECOND TRACK

We were born in 1964—as soul brothers (absofuckinglutely!), without a doubt, with our mothers always in our ear, talking brilliantly to us, stressing the importance of staying unpretentious and beautiful. We jibed/jived naturally in a flow where you didn't need a crew or posse to prove you had balls or a lot of heart. As we recollect, we didn't have to call women "bitches" or "tricks" or "black holes/hoes" to get some attention. We didn't need a stinking rap, never felt compelled to trip just to show off our muscle. Most important, we didn't need people to tell us how cool we was because we were never UNDER THE INFLUENCE like today's young "soldiers." We didn't need Cristal or Lucille Ball shouting "Now relax, Ricky" or a crystal ball to show us how to chill until the next episode.

Shoot, we had more on our minds than getting some ass. We liked cheese (a yellow or creamy complexioned person), but we was no rat. We liked meat on the bone, but not necessarily like that. Coming from the school of hard knocks, we discovered that chicken-heads (aggressively unpleasant women) could come in a variety of looks, like United Colors of Benetton. We didn't believe in putting down women or hitting on them. We got off on music, the soul/sole power that lay in the cut, the potency that hid in the uniquely different sounds which bended your ear.

We went with the flow until suddenly one day we started to go against the grain. Like we were black superheroes, we changed into "field niggers" working toward a better tomorrow. Now we always say, it's critical to reject the oppression the culture designs for us.

What's our motherfuckin' name? Maybe brand us "Trickster" because our road to success probably appears magical in light of the past. Value our vitality and inventiveness for their own sake. Let us show you our strategies for survival. As you might guess, we hail from the street corner, so po-lease let our broad talk today be rich in (s)language while we attempt to take community life apart and put it back together "through reaffirmation, through that special feeling of *communitas*."*

Ax black people in/about the Midwest, and they'll tell you frankly, like it is: It can be overwhelming trying to grow up in a region as white and dry as fine wine. Yet, as natives of Decatur and despite being residents of a Macon County place, we thought we had all the freedom in the world. One day, all of a sudden, D-town, what we knew as "Home of the Jheri Curl" (the hair/do that drove brown paper bag folks into a spraying frenzy as they dragged around the 'hood with activator bottles), blew up. Everyone, including us, boasted how fresh it was to be between the University of Illinois ("Chambana"), Illinois State University ("I-State"), and Springfield, the capital city, boy-y-y! We liked that Decatur was the birthplace of the Republican Party, that Lincoln made his first political speech in our hometown.

Back in the day, we loved the Midwestern space; we drank it all in. Indeed, we sucked up fucked-up Decatur; it was Everclear, Mad Dog 20-20, a California Cooler, or bad coke to us. The average resident really believed that a dependency on this smaller metropolitan area could/would make it better, all right.

But like the emergence of moonwalker Michael Jackson, we broke out and quickly turned into star quality. "Back the fuck up," we communicated in body language, "cuz I'm bad." People knew that we was real close, partners in crime living off the wall, with most people calling us "crazy 'n' shit" because we thought differently, out of the box. We'd be walkin' and squawkin', rapping and capping,

---

*With a license to ill/steal, we have taken from *Afro-American Folktales*, edited by Roger D. Abrahams.

about race matters like we thought we was Richard (W)right and Baby Huey (Newton).

JUMP INTO FIRE

The sweet breeze of Juneteenth (the 19th of the month, the date when the Emancipation Proclamation got signed by Lincoln, a.k.a. Black Independence Day) subdued any remnants of hot air left from an early day's heat wave. Saturday night's habitual walk to South Side Park seemed set to become a perfect backdrop for summer madness but proved to be an affair somewhat tame compared to the happenings a mere twenty-four hours ago:

We were carrying sacks of pop bottles to be exchanged for cold hard currency at Cloyd's Supermarket. Our conversation centered on talking smack about the ladies, crazy-ass white boys, and finding easier ways to make loot than lugging bottles to the store. A sudden quacking of a duck horn halted any chatter involving cash for bottles. Out of nowhere sped a green Dodge shaped like a late-model cab, wheels roaring down Packard Street. When the car got right beside us with that duck horn still blowing, we peered inside the sled and saw two white boys dressed in camouflage gear.

Then Kapow! Kapow! We heard a loud popping sound that was almost comic, as if the speakers were pointing their fingers at their would-be victims and saying the words. Glancing around, one of us was shot in the leg and the other just looked shot. Whitey had snapped, and we no longer considered ourselves photogenic. The bottles came crashing to the ground. Hindered by the glass smashing into many pieces, we finally understood what it was like to have an overseer, white boys continually watching us, honking at us. They were what Martin Luther King Jr. called "some of our sick white brothers."

WHEN YOU GROW UP IN THE STREETS (ON THE AVENUE OR THE CORNER WHERE THE BUSINESS TRANSACTIONS ARE MADE), THE SOBERING THOUGHT YOU'LL ALWAYS GET WHEN CONFRONTED BY A PAIN IN THE ASS IS "NO ONE CAN ESCAPE DEATH." *This time they fired a B.B. gun, fortunately. The wound stung, but we both agreed it wasn't serious, at least not yet. However, it was understood we had to act fast. Immediately we crisscrossed past the car, then zigzagged our way back, scurrying between backyards and alleyways like squirrels trying to get a nut, until we lost them. After that, we didn't want to go home. We wanted to Audi 5000 from Decatur.*

"You just babies," niggas said, but we knew the language of resistance: In a sort of B-movie, we'd find our blaxploitated selves strolling down the street—on Broadway. We'd be cracking up, Xtremely aware and sensitive of our own selves amid the bloody, spontaneous, protest-related riots, such as the struggles in Dixmoor, Illinois. Even in '64, Americans liked seeing violence on their wooden television consoles in order to view its subjects in black and white, to regard them as either good or evil. We fought that stereotype to death.

The revolution was not televised, but the denizens of Decatur, up south, still put us in our place. Subtle segregation, almost too difficult for the mind to grasp, and blatant discrimination said that central Illinois was not for the prosperity of minorities. The "Negro," as we were commonly referred to in the 1960s, stood out as the lowest subject, the most dispirited and downcast. And until Stokely Carmichael gave it *power*, the color black kept appearing more often than not as a sign of death, repeatedly signifying nothing or conveying to viewers the total absence of light. We tried to lift every voice and sing, but society still regarded us as bass/base. So the challenge became to find a way to sound out against the establishment.

MONEY AIN'T LONG ENOUGH
[TO MAKE US CHANGE OUR MIND]

It's no secret that a city's economic success translates into bountiful harvest for the pursuit of social enlightenment. For Decatur—miraculously still boasting (on its Web site) about its rank as one of 94 Best Places among smaller metropolitans by *Forbes* magazine—the mission to pursue noble goals has spiraled down like the city's property values. Nowhere is it more noticeable than at the park. The common ground.

In the early to mid-twentieth century, Decatur was a boomtown in terms of capital improvement, such as the transfer house connecting the city's trolley system, the Carnegie Library, Stephen Decatur High, all hallmarks for construction in central Illinois. Through the century, such projects lured big business, including Firestone Tire and Rubber, Wagner's Casting, A. E. Staley Manufacturing, Illinois Power, General Electric, Archer-Daniels-Midland, Caterpillar, and Borg-Warner (which reveled in a nearby sports complex being named after it). With industrious enterprises like these—bold new (ad)ventures—it was no small wonder that Decatur sat smack in the forefront in terms of city improvement plans or fancies. Decatur's recreational system was so outstanding that various parks were filmed and emulated by other cities nationwide.

Unlike other places of its size in central Illinois, Decatur's conceptual geography was a central downtown Mecca, lined with retail and professional offices, that functioned as the city's nerve center. As its downtown got encircled by well-conceived urban neighborhoods and hangouts, Decatur almost magically began producing project princesses and articulate black male leaders with mouths conveying messages like ghetto blasters.

MIXED MEMORY

As luck would have it, two decades later in the 1980s, we experienced a renaissance, the rebirth of the cool, coinciding with a journey into sound, the supersonic delving into our cultural beginnings. We didn't need songstress Janet Jackson to tell us that "we go deep." Social relevance transformed itself into something embedded inside a funky twist: The music we listened to issued forth courtesy of Prince and the Revolution (think *Sign o' the Times* and "It's Gonna Be a

Beautiful Night"), Rick James and the Stone City Band (*Street Songs*), Cameo's declaration "I just want to be what you want me to be," Lakeside (again, Dayton, OH), Ohio Players ("Love Rollercoaster" being their crossover biggest hit, but "Time Slips Away" possibly remaining as their most suggestive), The O'Jays (another Midwest group finger-pointing with "Backstabbers"), Motor City's One Way, electric funk, Jive Records, Def Jam, and Shannon's slammin' "Let the Music Play" on Emergency Records. Chicago's Earth, Wind & Fire and The Chi-Lites loomed in the twilight of their careers by smoothing us out during a clip (think "Fire!") when racism seemed under control, when it looked like skin was <u>everybody's sin.</u>

After the thrust and force of the black nationalistic movement, the '80s featured another astounding (but often less talked about or recognized) moment where we re-grouped for the greater good.

Firstly, George Clinton, the self-proclaimed "Dr. Funkenstein," and his cosmic big band Parliament/Funkadelic ushered in the encouragement of collective improvisation with *Mothership Connection* in 1975. Since then, no other group has influenced black music so dramatically. Clearly inspired by the intergalactic, Afro-Platonic avant-garde artist Sun Ra (who claimed to be a man not born, like Mary Shelley's Frankenstein), Clinton's raw, vaudeville style and irreverent black consciousness marked a new, fresh movement that made great music more purposefully/purposely Afrocentric and freakily used cultural identity as spiritual, soul-stirring strength. As a crucial note, we argue that music effects/affects community. Slave gave additional force to this profundity. The group formed in 1975 but, of course, was conceived in the mind since the beginning of time. From Dayton, OH, it debuted by going gold with "Slide" en route to becoming the premier masters of stellar fungk to rise out of the Midwestern dirt during the '70s.

However, credit Shy-town's Gil Scott-Heron, the true founding father of hip-hop, for giving black music an edge. He fed the poor in areas of urban decay with sentiments like "Whitey on the Moon," which justly criticized government spending on the space program. Certainly, the Midwest has played a key role in one giant step for mankind . . . at least until the big decline in quality kicked in.

In the pre-aids era, what we had in Decatur was sex and drugs, a "give it to me, baby" ghetto-life decadence amply enjoyed. We ate up Barry White's "Ecstasy" and Brick; for the record, we didn't want to sit down—we wanted to git down! Decatur eventually became a warped record that spun out of control in its quest to have some fun. We felt funkier than ever before, and with the groove our only guide, we had all been moved.

By 1983, we had graduated from high school crushes. The biggest development was that we found ourselves feeling more mature, w(h)ining and divining as we shimmied through the party line during some free time in the black-only clubs or speakeasies. Whenever we appeared in the nightlife, a variety of characters entertained us. "What's up?" we said to Graceland, against the wall. "Feelin' good, sellin' good, what more is there to life?" he responded while we walked on by. We shook our big heads and went down the stairway to heaven.

Surrounded by "Smoke" and "Little Boogie," we didn't ask for our propers, for a little respect, like Aretha Franklin did. We demanded it, drawing attention rivaling that of Louis Farrakhan when he exploded with the Nation.

One jookass cowboy, notorious for being strapped, had the nerve to call us "faggots" behind our backs because we didn't fool around, dabble in shit, or put ourselves in compromising situations where we could get our heads blown. Every time we put our faces in the after-hour places, we parted the waters like King, able to move the crowd because niggas didn't know what to expect from us. The only thing they knew was that we brought something different to the table.

Representin' motherfuckers, we stood out as each other's ABC (ace boon coon). Our jones (fix or compulsive attachment) was maintaining ourselves as radicals, the contemporaries that Malcolm said had a burden more so than any other time in history.

SISTER BREAK

In the meantime, black stallions and domesticated shorties on the side had a lot brewing at the crib, too. In the kitchen, ladies laid a slim (cigarette) on one another. And some of the soul sisters with hamhocks for legs and ankles started sass about James Brown saying it a bit too loud. Beloved black women argued that brothers had already spent too much time trying to "fight the power," as the Isley Brothers had suggested. "That's why they ain't got no job now," black women carrying baggage said. Others remained strong but silent, frying green tomatoes using cookware made in the U.S.A., and they found it hard to be proud. Many chopped onions until they cried, washed homegrown collard greens like it was dirty cash that black men made them launder, and served plastic cups of Kool-Aid with lemons in it to the playing children. Sometimes in deep frustration, they'd hack their finger with a stainless steel knife, losing their wedding ring in the sink and letting the love go down the drain. A Band-Aid and alcohol failed to help the situation. There is no quick fix for poverty and dueling identities.

Fortunately, the other half, our collective sistas, got some support from sultry singer Sade crooning/vocalizing "Hang On to Your Love," a huge hit encouraging the hip to gravitate to a more relaxed but sensual look. We got the impression from Sade that love was not necessarily a main man but the idea that a man could be mainly loved. As if wanting to live paradoxically, to show both grace and struggle, women started showcasing pretty ponytails and tender bare feet.

GHETTO THING

Glory be, we found salvation at the park. We declared one nation under a groove, people getting down just for the funk of it, and even the rooty-poot niggas and rookies tied red, black, and green ribbons around the old oak trees in a demonstration of unity. The wide open space gave brothers and sisters hope, time to get ourselves together! *Thumping music from porches lining the streets egged us on like cheers, and going to the park was like approaching a sea of spectators checking out a local parade. A group of kids ahead of us argued over who was Decatur's best "pop-locker" and "break-dancer." Somebody yelled "Big Ten is the best" before a voice sliced its way over the kids' conversation. "Hey! Aren't you them 'cruise' boys? Just because you got Injun/engine blood in your veins don't make you better than anybody else." Every word spoken to us was punctuated by hissing. We stepped through the grass, the weed all around us, and made a conscious effort to stay alert, to be aware of snakes that seemed to strike quickly. Some said we were "conceited" and "slick," watching us drib-ble a Rawlings leather basketball hard and fast between the legs to drown out the noise.*

We eventually learned to ignore the jawing. *We strutted past the stoops marking the way to South Side, laughing out loud, barely noticing when our destination had been reached.*

South Side, a.k.a. Mueller Park, was like a Universal Zulu Nation: The com-mon ground ushered in a new paradigm for youth culture where peace and survival went privileged. People ganged up in amusing groups, playing and swaying in a sweaty, rhythmic orgy. *When P.J. the D.J. stuck the needle to the record, Afrika Bam-baataa's "Planet Rock" broke out, people screaming and chanting while the MC "threw-down" (got busy).* Bam! We liked that shit!

The pigs would show up, but nothing ever happened, no arrests. Everybody got along. The suckers discovered no dangerous minds to lock up. There was nothing but a party . . . black people from the projects (Longview) and elite alike keeping cool, hanging out in the park, chilling with a bottle of jungle juice and/or smelling of fresh herb. Flygirls/hotties/slims wore Vanity lace, many of them wearing the same thing. Brothers held their joints out in the open, delightfully skied and de-liberately leaning over to show off their muscles by the basketball courts. They sported Kangol hats (with the kangaroo logo) and parachute pants, and sometimes drove their mopeds on the side. *When Teron Heron got his turn on the mike and turntables, he would scratch shit up. Smothered by niggas offering nickel-bags of funk and staring at women like they was having a crack-attack, we enjoyed the jam. Then we readied ourselves to ease on out, chewing watermelon-flavor Now and Later candy and scoping out the chicks with the I.D. bracelets. Exiting the park, you had Slick Rick lick-ing his lips while telling a moralistic children's story and Rod looking good to the ladies.*

We remember that not all African-American women hesitated to treat brothas nicely then. You could find a house full of warm Nubian queens, each extending her hand. And black men came across as much more playful (instead of simply wanting sex). They were each other's gun. *Most of the men's judgment was based on skin color; light was tight. Everything else was simply weed. We can still hear Rick blast-ing, "I'm in love with Mary Jane / she's my main thing / she makes me feel alright / she makes my heart sang [sing] . . . takes me to paradise!"* All kinds of folk would be styling out, slipping into the groove, nodding until it was pitch black. Talk was cheap then. You'd see couples acting freaky under the big top of the pavilion or swapping slop in the shadows. To outsiders, it probably appeared to be circus love, but to us it was greater than *American Pie.*

CUTIE PIE

Ms. Sweet-but-Street would sway to the big beat, kick the blue plastic sandals off her feet. She and her big lips would pretend to secrete as they rubbed us down, teasing with the promise of a sticky, nut chocolate treat. She stayed in front of us, relaxing by spreading her legs like honey butter, and what she was showing us was BASIC INSTINCT. *She started running her big, pretty lips, talking about how she could make a nigga cum just by tongue-kissing him. We could tell she was more than a little pregnant, but, dang, she looked good*

"Damn," she shouted, "oowee, this is the jam! I know somebody wants to dance with me! Shit, dance wit me, okay?" With her fingers exploring the deep pockets of our baggy pants, she acted like she liked rod.

Girl looked so fine she made us wanna holler, but we held back; her story was a tale of abuse, of a person that just didn't want to be lonely.

OLD FRIEND

We'd love to bring back the days of yea and nay, the little things about Decatur that make remembering it so bitter and so sweet. And while we could drink a case of it and still be on our feet, Decatur (its culture and counterculture) remains nonetheless intoxicating. Life in our hood is sometimes scary, edgy, or addictive, we know. But we dig the joy and pain. The sunshine. And rain. Visitors won't want to miss the purple haze and the mind-altering maze of the city. The community itself enjoys a history steeped in the drop of black blood/bile, black bodies swingin'. Decatur, population 83,000, is the Midwest in a microcosm. You must witness firsthand its inclination for anger, its melancholy and sadness, to believe that it exists. Get the picture?

ON YOUR TOUR, EXPECT TO FIND A DOUBLE-CONSCIOUSNESS MAPPING DECATUR, THE DUALITY THAT W.E.B. DUBOIS POSITED AS A MAJOR FACTOR WHEN CONFRONTING ISSUES OF RACE. Visit the Decatur Celebration in August, Illinois' largest family street festival (covering twenty-two blocks of downtown), and you'll discover that the death mask comes easy, by the dozens. Seems like everybody's got one or knows where to find it. Partake in sales from any of over sixty vendors, and you're sure to get some horrific stories, dark tales. For example, there's the tragic story about the sorry black teenage brother that got murdered, execution-style, by two other black teenage boys for merely thinking about dropping the dime to the police about the trio's robbery.

We stand for a generation of black people festering in the August heat, our wounds always/already too big to heal. But, shit, we tried: We sought to buffer the death threats sent to Malcolm X, to soften our brother's break with the Nation. As black men, we felt delivered when King, the ultimate dreamer, was awarded the Nobel Peace Prize on December 10. His "dream variation" was like a pacifier to us; it came as a joyous daybreak. Until then, before President Lyndon Johnson declared war on poverty, black mommas carried us. They were responsible for the welfare of the black community. They took us safely through the storms. They stomached our senseless kicking back—our sounding off and adolescent protesting—like we were nothing. They drew us close, pampered us, and told us that everything would be alright until LBJ twisted the arm of Congress at the White House and convinced government to pass a Civil Rights Bill banning The White Man from preaching that everything in America was equal.

BLUNT

For decades people in Decatur fired up one another. Then they started going out of their heads or ending up zonked.

STATE OF MIND

Flash forward to the present, and only a few of the original corporate suit(e)s remain, the rest replaced by other hoods, including Mr. Cocaine, Ms. Heroin, and Uncle Metho. The city has gotten rewarded with a shrinking tax base and philanthropic contributions, all drowned in a recently named manmade waterway called Lake Narcotic. DECATUR TODAY IS A MERE SHADOW OF ITS FORMER GLORY, A LARGELY UNILLUMINATED AREA MIRRORED BY HIGH UNEMPLOYMENT AND AN INABILITY TO ATTRACT BIG BUSINESS. In the past, Great-Grandpa could point to the old Stephen Decatur High project and say with pride, "I helped build that." Now it's likely that his descendants wouldn't even be involved in such an undertaking 'cause they a) lack technical expertise, b) can't meet the educational requirements, or c) failed the test for alcohol, drugs, good citizenship. In the old days, if you fucked up, Momma would make you tell what you did wrong, then send you outside in the cold/rain to think about it before she called you in and whupped your ass. Now, when kids get suspended from school, they ain't thinking about going back. And Opportunity refuses to give them second chance.

SWITCH

IN THE EARLY TO MID '70S OR POST–CIVIL RIGHTS, A PERSON COULD LITERALLY WALK OFF THE JOB AT ONE PLANT AND BEGIN WORK AT ANOTHER.

LOVE AND HAPPINESS

In the milieu, as a sign of the times or symbol, there was black heroism, Superfly, The Mack, fine female action heroes like Christie Love and Cleopatra Jones, working-class brothers dying for coffee/Coffy, that crazy nigger Richard Pryor all up in our faces with the N-word, Black Caesar, duking (fistfighting, especially on the street), and the Big Top (the Illinois state prison system that took some of our friends). Mister Softy looking to keep on truckin' with cool treats and a bell that called out to us like we were cattle [no worry about mad cow disease]. We frequented The Phase for an all-night party. Traditionally marginalized culture enjoyed *Cooley High*, anti-apartheid alliances such as that at Northwestern University, orgiastic free love, a dramatic rise in interracial marriages, *Black Enterprise*, and something fresh that began by targeting black collegiate women and ended up as *Essence*. *The Harder They Come*—spectacle/drama blending "advocacy, rebellion, and music," according to cultural critic Nelson George—turned out to be a huge hit. Graffiti marked a new day. "Papa was" indeed "a rollin' stone," but "wherever he laid his hat was his home," thanks to women like Donna Summer, who made fucking sure that there was "love to love you, baby."

CONFUSION

Alas, Sly & the Family Stone's pitch-black, depressing, acidic "There's a Riot Goin' On" was telling as well. The notion of black people wanting/seeking more seemed too difficult for Decatur residents to imagine and fathom. Frankly, the entire population appeared shell-shocked. The powers-that-be, the very pale and affluent, could hardly stomach it without getting upset. The down moment, worsened by the media blowing things out of proportion, was traumatic for the city, like a sinking into muddy waters. A slow fall where paranoia kicked in and people panicked to save themselves. Homeowners turned to automatic rifles and guns, staring out of their windows like Malcolm in that famous shot taken after his family experienced death threats. Residents looked to mow down the "hoochie-coochie men" and "mannish boys" in their neighborhoods. Statistics lay heavy on people's minds. People started to conclude that too much of a criminal element lay in the community—that there existed an upstart gang of black people, comprised largely of angry males, who had become perpetually dirty and uncouth, or too vulgar and common. A color line had to be drawn, Decatur concluded. Ironically, that's when a lot of black men began to pull the disappearing act with their lover or spouse.

[Scratches]

NEW EDITION, CRU-CIAL!

We continue to savor the *Good Times*, but ("damn, damn, damn") all we're saying now is, how can anybody oversight the fact that a lot has happened to Decatur to make it considerably less dynamite today?

Gone are those days for the subjects of Decatur. Economic conditions in the community, circa 2002, find your average folks lacking quality-paying jobs. After all, working at Cheddars just doesn't pay the rent.

One of the key components of a city on the move is its educational system. Currently, Decatur is saddled with a school district unable to adapt to the social-economic demands of its students. It seems doomed to be partly remembered for its debacle involving Eisenhower High School, where an infamous seven participated in so-called "felony mob action" at an intra-city football game, got expelled, and couldn't even be saved by Rev. Jesse Jackson and his posse, the Rainbow/PUSH coalition. African-American male students are dropping out of the system before graduation at an alarming rate. Minority (and traditionally marginalized) students make up more than half of the school district's population, yet there's no plan in place to curb this drastic decline in graduation rates. Throw in a rise in crime, and *it's as if these students are willing to drop* **dead.**\Think back to *Cooley High*, and it's so hard to say goodbye to yesterday. "Old school" has always been endearing. It, too, features black kids dropping out like it is nothing, but at least these teenagers had dreams.

LIVING IN THE BOTTLE

In reality we are family that prided ourselves on avoiding intoxicants, harmful addictions. We never liked the thought of being vulnerable. However, like that brother Shine in the African-American folklore "The Sinking of the Titanic," we did have to swim through the motherfucking water, that is, endure the flooding of Lake Narcotic, to survive our Midwestern town. Even today, with nothing but love for black mothers and children, we are happy to reminisce about our running days in Decatur. Maybe black musical artist T. S. Monk had it right after all when he sang: "Give us the bon / give us the bon bon bon bon vie / give us the good life."

Maybe it's <u>only</u> ironic that the musical group Inner City from Chicago followed that credo a decade later (by sampling it, being intertextual to convey that the beat goes on) with "Buena Vida (Good Life)" and "Big Fun." But we think the shit goes deeper than that.

We feel you, Inner City. We were always chanting: "We don't really need a crowd to have a party." We still believe the obvious separation of ethnic populations in the Midwest can make you stronger, if not better. Look closely at the Midwest—the bonfires and clearings, the stars with nothing in their way, the bluegrass, the apple pies and redbirds, the black berries ripe for the picking, and the dirt that gets easily spread, and suddenly you'll realize the dramatic impact that the region has had on its people.

WHAT WE HAVE TO SAY

All of America must take some responsibility for the niggers and niggerati that are no longer with us, the dead homies and uppity black people sadly victimized by black-on-black crime: the fancy-dancy, cheatin', playing international nigger run down on the street; the itchy, fidgeting huzzy who found herself continually ravaged after publicly admitting that she liked sucking Dick; the brother with naps who bit the dust during his interplanetary mission; the ruint Smack-man that turned into a servant for Mickey-mouse out of simple greed; any dude that got offed in the "Nigger War" (American Civil War, as seen by whites); the red bone rib or tar baby whose existence went ignored because she was either too light or too dark; the monkey in the cage; the black justice that poor community life has tapped out.

Langston Hughes wrote, "Bear in mind / that death is a drum," but "what we play is life" (as Louis Armstrong noted).

INTERLUDE: *LISTEN TO YOUR HEARTBEAT PLAYING THE RHYTHM OF OUR SONG*

The truth is, African-Americans, especially those forced to live within the confines/fields of the Midwest, are the real survivor; every television network needs to do a show about that. In the quest for black liberation, we've taken the good, the bad, and the ugly and learned to mix the shit into something positive. Moreover, we've maintained, certain that our account of the struggle for identity will continue to be heard through various speakers like rebop. Our efforts to redefine ourselves, reconstitute ourselves, will carry on like an ancient dusky river. We will explore the mainstream but always create our own flow as well. While the memories keep flooding back, we'll be like a jazzy harmony that is groovy, baby, and richly complex, and the beat won't/don't stop.

After all, there is, always has been, a message in our music and music in our (r)evolution. To boot, we find ourselves re-released because of the milieu.

With such a record of darkness, we are unforgettable—that's what we are. Like Kunta Kinte, the slave and the African, trying to go home once and for all. We are *Roots* redux, adults and tribal warriors, and our world is like clay, containing us, (in)forming us, feeding us, pushing us. As we grow, we lay bare the skeletons, what remains of genocide. [And we're sorry, Momma. We didn't mean to hurt you, so tonight we're cleaning out our closet.]

We are unforgettable—that's what we are, like King's trademark lit cigarette in a cigarette holder. We hope everybody else can at least dig that.

Our story is "to be continued."

A Menagerie of Mascots

MICHAEL MARTONE

MY FATHER TURNED INTO A MONSTROUS VERMIN

I was in Fort Wayne for the millennium's New Year's celebration. My mother was on the municipal committee that had planned the year's events that culminated with the fireworks launched from the top of the Summit bank building downtown. Freezing, the crowd below watched the display from the new park built with the proceeds derived from another recent celebration, the bicentennial of the city's founding in 1774. The park was a wonderful legacy. It had been built on an often-flooded floodplain with a design that recognized that fact. The flowerbeds were planted with ornamental grasses, yellow flag iris, bulrushes, and reeds that thrived in swampy conditions. The fountains produced a fine primordial mist, subtly lit, that floated over the marshy fields. In the cold of that night, the misting fountains created a crystalline landscape both old and new as the citizens of Fort Wayne greeted the turning of the age.

My mother had been on the bicentennial committee as well, and in both cases she had been instrumental in the development of the mascots. The bicentennial wasn't hard to figure out. Someone dressed up as General Anthony Wayne and made the appearances at the parades, beer tents, plaque dedications, and battle reenactments. Johnny Appleseed was a close second—he's buried in Fort Wayne —but the general looked better in uniform and lacked the cooking pot on the head. And besides, General Wayne came equipped with a horse. The millennium required more brainstorming. My mother, always the poet, finally rested on the notion that the millennium would best be represented by a millipede, a millipede she named, for no other reason than the alliterative, Millie.

A costume was commissioned. The millipede would be incredibly long. Most of it would be dragging along the ground. The segmented body suit in greenish velour and black velveteen piping had oversized antennae, bugged-out eyes, and a butterfly's coiled proboscis. The multiple pairs of legs, only two pairs of which would be operable, were connected together in order for all of them to simultaneously move, marionette fashion, as the operator walked along.

My mother volunteered my father to be the bug. I teased her when I called home about the symbolism of the committee's mascot being a verminous scavenger.

"They're herbivorous," she replied.

"But hard to make cuddly, I bet," I said.

And what about having my father, her husband, appear for a year as this creepy crawly thing.

"No one will know," she said.

I had recently moved south, below the bug line as we like to say, the climatic zone where the winter wasn't cold enough to kill off insects. Infesting our new house, we discovered moving in, was a hatch of millions of millipedes, or what we found out were millipedes once the county extension agent duly identified them. I have grown somewhat familiar with the flying roaches and the grasshoppers as large as small cats.

"You'd be surprised," my mother said, "about how cuddly your father is, milli-pede or not."

"You might have at least called him Milton or Mick the Millipede."

My father was good-natured about it all, suited up and crossed genders. My mother sent pictures of Millie in the parades, at the ribbon cuttings, in front of the huge numbers counting down on the official digital clock. I received a video of the ceremony in the park, the burial of the time capsule. I saw my father as the giant creature wave his many hands at the camera, inch his way through the festive crowd with the gold-plated shovel. He looked like a bad special effect, a monster from a Japanese Godzilla film, his dragging tail cutting a swath of destruction through a twig and tissue paper city.

By the time I actually saw him in costume in person on New Year's Eve, my fa-ther's tail had worn dramatically thin from the continuous friction of his various civic duties. They had taken to wrapping the nether region up over one shoulder of the upright upper half. The result was a commingling of legs or, now more ac-curately, arms that seemed to emanate from the lime body at every angle. That night the committee had sponsored a carnival for children at the Fine Arts Cen-ter to help them stay awake for the fireworks at midnight. The building was lousy with screaming kids doing spin art, singing karaoke, and having their faces painted. My father, as Millie, moved through the crowds. The children were strangely calmed by the hulking figure, magnetically drawn to hold one of its many hands as it slithered along. It led a little parade over to the park, the children still attached. Millie seemed to undulate through the ground-hugging fogs the foun-tains produced, lugging its cargo of limpid limpets. It stopped and turned dramat-ically to face the sound of the first exploding bombs going off above the city.

WE DIDN'T SPEAK OF REDI KILOWATT

My grandfather worked as a meter reader for the municipal electric utility, City Light and Power, until it was sold to the regional for-profit company, Indiana and Michigan or I&M, in a deal he regarded as shady.

I&M had always had a presence in Fort Wayne. That company owned the elec-tric interurbans that ran all over Indiana early in the century. I&M maintained the high-tension transmission lines that brought much of the electricity into the city to be sold by City Light. There was a billboard near I&M's building, shielding the lot where it kept the hulks of transformers, generators, and cable spools. The billboard was by the corner of Spy Run and State, and my grandfather had to read its meter. The sign, of course, was lit all the time, and sometimes parts of it moved. The billboard, advertising the advantages of electric power, utilized a character named Redi Kilowatt—a stick figure made up of a skeleton of lightning with a lightbulb head and a lightbulb nose and socket outlets for ears.

My grandfather despised Redi Kilowatt, and we weren't to speak of him. Not that we would have even noticed his existence without the focus of my grandfather's rage. Redi Kilowatt would have been just another cartoon on the landscape of cartoons I wandered through as a child. Still, we knew the days Grandfather read the meter on the sign. He would come home restless and unsettled, drink an extra Pepsi on the back porch to facilitate his belching.

After City Light was bought out and he retired, my grandfather took elaborate routes through the city to avoid passing the sign. This was a difficult thing to do, since State was the main east-to-west thoroughfare on the north side of town. There were times that passing the sign was unavoidable and the traffic light at the corner of Spy Run and State always stopped you. Grandfather seethed in the car as Redi Kilowatt, his crimped kinetic arm waving back and forth, loomed before him.

Stopped at the same light on our journey across town to visit my grandparents, my family contemplated Redi Kilowatt, who might then be wearing earmuffs for winter or sunglasses during the summer, promoting electric heat or air conditioning. My mother always mentioned, her father not being present to hear, how Daddy was looking more and more like that Redi Kilowatt—the wiry frame, the round, mostly bald head with the tiny white shock of hair at his crown. "Don't tell him I said so, please!" she said as the light changed.

HOOSIER DEFINES ITSELF

My uncle went to graduate school at Tennessee to study health. He got a government grant to run a study in the hope of demonstrating the validity of his thesis: that to know the deleterious effects of obesity would aid in weight reduction. He had two groups of dieters. The control group simply followed the menus and exercise suggestions provided by a national weight-reduction company. The subjects in the experiment also had to follow the diet and in addition complete a rigorous course detailing graphically and statistically the dangers of fat. To his surprise, my uncle proved that while the control group modestly lost pounds, the educated group effortlessly gained a ton. Traumatized by the detailed information they were receiving, they nervously ate in order not to think about what was happening to their bodies as they ate.

While in Knoxville, my uncle sent me a poster I hung on the wall of my bed-room. The drawing depicted a team portrait of the mascots of the Southeastern Conference, their eponymous heads bobbing above the various team football uni-forms. There were two Bulldogs, a Hog, and several military combatants—Missis-sippi's Rebel, Vanderbilt's Commodore, and Tennessee's own Volunteer. Alabama's Tide was, strangely, an Elephant that would make no sense until, years later, I moved to Tuscaloosa and learned that it derived from the historical confluence of a Rose Bowl game and a local luggage company. Right after my uncle's gift, my fa-ther gave me the complimentary poster representing the Big Ten, and I taped it next to the first one. I liked to think of the two portraits as my uncle's two groups of dieters.

The head of the Hoosier was rendered as that of a bumpkin, the dictionary de-finition, after all, the same definition that Dan Quayle, on the floor of the United States Senate, once argued to legally change. The Hoosier on the poster showed up as a yokel, a rural rube with a fraying straw hat atop his rusty head of hair. He had vacant blue eyes and freckles, big lips, and buckteeth that gnawed on a bent straw of a wheat stalk or weed stem. This Hoosier, even wearing a big-shouldered football uniform, not the requisite blue denim bib overalls, didn't look very com-petitive surrounded by the vicious menagerie of Wildcat, Badger, and Wolverine.

There is a whole class of mascots that suffer in this modern era of corporate cor-poreal identity. Look at the Buckeye, looking like an eyeball with eyes. Adjectives get attached. Hurryin' was wed to Hoosier. Or weapons are issued, a pitchfork, say, that arms the Hoosier as an animated American Gothic. For a while there, the In-diana mascot metamorphed into a bison. I believe it derived from the state's seal, where a pioneer with an axe fells a tree while the silhouette of a bison lights out for the territories. In the end, Hoosier is just what it is. It is the word itself, its own mascot. One year, perhaps the same year native son Quayle rose in the Senate, the state tried to change the motto on the license tags from Hoosier State to Heritage State and was met with near insurrection. No one really knows what a Hoosier is, but not knowing, as my uncle proved, has its own logic. A Hoosier is a Hoosier is a Hoosier.

THE STATE DRINK OF WISCONSIN

The state bird of Wisconsin is the robin. The state flower of Wisconsin is the wood violet. The state tree of Wisconsin is the sugar maple. The state animal of Wisconsin is the badger. The state wild animal of Wisconsin is the white-tailed deer. The state domesticated animal of Wisconsin is the dairy cow, and the vari-ous breeds—Holstein, Brown Swiss, Guernsey, Jersey, etc.—take yearly turns. The state fish of Wisconsin is the muskellunge. The state insect of Wisconsin is the honeybee. The state mineral of Wisconsin is galena. The state rock of Wisconsin is red granite. The state soil of Wisconsin is Antigo silt loam. The state symbol of peace of Wisconsin is the mourning dove. The state of Wisconsin is undecided on the state of Wisconsin's drink. The legislature continues to argue the issue. Beer could be the state drink of Wisconsin. Milk could be the state drink of Wisconsin. Or both beer and milk.

TOUCHDOWN JESUS

My father liked to take me to football games at Notre Dame. He liked to point out how gold the gold on the helmets of the Fighting Irish was, how they were as gold as the gold on the dome of the big building on the campus we could see from the stadium. Navy's helmets were gold and Pitt's helmets were gold, but not as gold as Notre Dame's gold helmets. I saw O.J. Simpson play in South Bend. We always sat in the end zone and I remember watching him hauling in the kickoff ball and starting his sprint up the field right before us. I saw Roger Staubach and Navy in a snowstorm. Crushed tight together in the stands, everyone wore heavy wool coats before the coming of down parkas and Gore-Tex. I was there when Dan Devine's team changed its uniform to the green jerseys from the blue. The entire stadium went crazy seeing this brand new team emerge from the tunnel. And I remember when Notre Dame built the library beyond the other end of the stadium and finished off the nine-story facade with a mosaic of a beatific Christ, His arms raised above His head, in the jubilant gesture of the referee signaling a score. He hovered, it seemed, above the goal posts, above the thronging crowd, above the teeming stadium, the Goodyear blimp drifting above His head, exhorting us all. Touchdown! Touchdown! Touchdown!

We always got there early. Sometimes we stayed by the car and tailgated in the parking lot, eating our lunch from a cooler in the trunk. But more often, especially when we were with some of my father's old high school teammates, we would all drift over to the field house to look at the names of the lettermen on sacred plaques, admire the immaculate cases of memorabilia, trophies, and photographs of the old great and holy teams. My father had gone to Central Catholic in Fort Wayne. They had been the Fighting Irish, too, and in his senior year, his team had won the mythical state football championship. My father, who had been quarterback, and his old backfield would recite the names on the plaques, remind each other of games they'd played in or seen.

Most of all I liked it when we went to the far end of the stadium before the game, to the locker room door. A crowd had always gathered to wait and watch for the Notre Dame players to emerge alone or in small groups, threes or fours, from their campus dorms and drift toward the stadium, wading through the crowd into the locker room. The players were huge. None of them had necks. They were stuffed into the insignia-dripping letter jackets of dark blue wool with glossy blue-black leather sleeves.

Touchdown Jesus looked down on us all gathered in the plaza before the locker room door. Look, there were some more coming our way! Often, just by the door, there was a boy—it was never the same boy—about my age, waiting in his wheelchair or leaning on his crutches, his body mangled into a cast or contorted or quaking with palsy. The players had been tipped to his presence. The crowd parted as they approached. The players tolerated the back-pats and the praise as we moved to make room. We just wanted to touch them, to get a word in. They said "excuse me" politely, didn't stop for us as they made their irresistible journey toward the door. But when they spotted the kid by the door, they were drawn to him and to the football that miraculously appeared in the folds of his hospital blankets, in the crook of his traction-set arm. We all watched as each player stopped and took the ball to sign it, signed it, and handed it back to the bandaged kid, saying a few inaudible—to us—words and then tousling his hair with their beefy hands before disappearing into the changing rooms to be transformed for the game.

MY MOTHER INVENTS A TRADITION

At our dining room table in the house on Clover Lane in Fort Wayne, Indiana, my mother made it all up. She was the Dean of Girls at Central High School. The city school system had announced Central's closing and the busing of its students to the six other high schools in the system, two of them, Northrup and Wayne, just being built. Mom would be going to Northrup, and her job now was to manufacture the particulars of the new school's identity. There was a committee, a group of students and teachers drawn from the constituencies of Central and the two north-side schools siphoned off by the expansion.

I remember the group listening to records of marching bands playing fight songs and alma maters, the words absent, in our living room. They rated the melodies on graph paper on a scale from 1 to 10. "This is 'On Wisconsin!'" my mother would say. And one evening the band uniforms and cheerleading costumes were modeled and judged there, too, but that was much later. My mother had to do the heavy lifting of the task force, actually writing the words to the songs the band members would play in the future. She would also narrow down all the choices of styles and colors in the catalogues she gathered from the wholesalers of academic garb, the purveyors of embroidery and emblems, the flag-makers, the jewelers, trophy stores, yearbook printers, decal suppliers, and fundraising companies. Then she would guide the committee to her favorites.

At the dining room table she had to get herself in the mood for her creations. For this new school she was constructing a nostalgic past out of nothing. It was named for a former superintendent, no help there. So she relied upon the stored memories of her own high school, the images of high school created in movies she saw while she was in high school. There had been ivy on the red brick walls and a senior door only seniors could walk through. Every year the graduating class planted a climbing rose bush along the fences of the stadium, and the trowel used for the job was handed down to the next class at a ceremony in the spring as the roses budded and began to bloom. Northrup had none of these rituals as of yet, was being built in a scraped-flat cornfield on the northern edge of town. The excavation left a few trees from a woodlot nearby, and mother mused to me that perhaps that could become a lover's lane. She imagined the moon over the copse of trees. "The students," she wrote for the students in the new handbook, "call this spot Lover's Lane."

I was in high school then, at North Side, my mother's high school, the one she waxed about with nostalgia as she worked at the dining room table. At North Side now no one remembered why the seniors gave a garden trowel to the junior class. The rose bushes had been torn out during a renovation before I started there.

She went with orange and brown for Northrup's colors, presented them to the committee as a *fait accompli*. It was the early '70s, and those colors were hot. Our sofa was orange and brown striped. The other new high school, Fort Wayne Wayne—I know, it is a very funny name—was forced into red, white, and blue since its mascot, the General, followed from the name. Mom had more leeway and went with the palette of the moment. She trusted that her words for the school songs, the cheers, the student codes, and the orientation materials would give the colors a patina, age them in a tea of her own emotional past.

The mascot would be a Bruin. This seemed more sophisticated than the simple Bear, and perhaps it fit the same logic of euphemism left over from Central, the school that was closing, where the team mascot Tigers had also been known as the Bengals in the sports pages. Bruin went nicely with the earthy tonic expressed in the newly selected colors, rhymed with ruin, and suggested the whole conceit for student publications. The newspaper, she decided, would be called *What's Bruin*, and the yearbook would be known for years to come as *Bear Tracks*.

At the dining room table she wrote the poems that became the fight song and the alma mater. I have no notion of the words themselves. They survive to this day, sung at assemblies and home games. I went to a different school and never had to learn them. I can remember her singing, though, trying to fit her words into the scansion of the appropriated songs. As I watched her sing a few bars, then stop and erase, then sing a few notes more, I was making this memory of my mother creating memories and the myths of memory. A few scraps of cloth. A totem or two. Some new arrangement of the same old words hooked to a persistent jingle.

A CYCLONE OF CARDINALS

Midwesterners like to think a tornado is the region's official natural phenomenon. It's their pet weather, their special storm. The twister in the black and white Kansas of the movie is more powerful and magical than anything in glitzy Oz. The citizens of Xenia, Ohio, where all the tornado alleys empty, speak nervously but with a kind of pride about their repeated visits of destructions. With its precision and its paradoxes, a tornado fits organically into the landscape of open plains and cleared spaces where its victims can see the funnels dancing on the horizon, chase them across the checkerboard of the farm fields and feed lots.

I lived for a while in Ames, Iowa, where Iowa State University adopted the Cyclone as its mascot, the "V" of the vortex twirling on the sides of football helmets, stationery letterhead, sweatshirts, and baseball caps. But in Ames, for some reason, those graphic depictions were eclipsed by an icon of an angry cardinal. The designers had worked hard to make the bird look angry. Its beak curved into a permanent snarl. Its black eyebrow crooked above its glaring, staring eye. They had named the cardinal Cy, the name the umbilical back to the official atmospheric logo, I guess. It was, when I arrived, a mystery to me. Cartoon cardinals were everywhere, adorning outdoor advertisements, adhering to side panels of cars and trucks, decorating the facades of buildings where the more placid and real pigeons roosted in the flexed fiery combs on the heads of the giant representations. I gathered that any animal species made more sense to those people who orchestrate motivation. A bird, any bird, was more inspiring to rally around than a mere organized wind. Maybe. Maybe it was only symmetry that propelled the choice—the cardinal a kind of mirror image, an avian match for the cross-state rival Iowa's golden hawk schematic that stood for the Hawkeyes, whatever a Hawkeye was.

I discovered that Ames was an outlet for Collegiate Pacific, a company that manufactures licensed trademark apparel. I discovered this when I was taken to one of the factory's open houses, where we locals were invited semi-annually to come in and take the mistakes and misprinted items off their hands for a significantly reduced price. And that had been another thing I noticed about my new town. While the official cardinal had been the predominant mascot fauna, I couldn't help but notice the eclectic nature exhibited by the populace upon their casual wear. Lions, tigers, bears. All manner of birds. Spartans, gladiators, Trojans. Fighting thises and thats. Pirates, cowboys, devils—blue, red, and green. Indians, chiefs, redskins, warriors, braves. Tarheels, Yankees, Rebels, Hoosiers, Buckeyes, Hawkeyes. Bulls, Browns, Bees. You name it. It was a kind of United Nations of proprietary images, teeming with team identity.

On closer inspection you noticed the flaws at the sales and on the street—the ghost images of the double exposure, the smear of a misaligned silkscreen registration, the misspelled words, the missing letters. I loved the mad juxtapositions of multiple printings that created hybrids of logos and language—"University of University" or "ate State." Here on someone's back was, what? Here were the Jabberwocks—a swirling cloud composite of swords, lightning, and horses' hooves. Someone else displayed the Chimeras—a bestiary of eyes and beaks and the 4-H cloverleaf.

At the outlet sales the whole town rummaged through the mountains of rejects. Short- and long-sleeved T-shirts, sweatshirts with hoods and without, pullover sweatshirts, sweatshirts that zipped and those printed fleece-lined insides facing out, ponchos, sweaters, cardigans, windbreakers, blankets, towels, hats, caps, scarves, even the old felt pennants on a stick. I liked the rubbery feel of the paint on cloth and all the Latin of the upside-down-printed school seals. The open books, the oil lamps, the olive branches, the oak leaves and acorns, the palm fronds, the bells, the crosses, the earth, the moon, the planets, the stars.

It turned out that Collegiate Pacific also made a line of outfits for mascots, the kind with the foam rubber body suits and giant heads. I was told they had had a surplus cardinal suit lying around. Maybe the school that ordered it failed to take delivery, or they came up short with the payments and the company repossessed the bird, donating it to the hometown team. Besides, the architecture of a comparable Cyclone suit seemed impossible to construct with the available technology. Where would you put the eyes? Should a Cyclone even have eyes? It would keep coming out as an odd-looking cloud—dirty gray, nebulous, amorphous, simply wrong.

THEN YOU HIT THE ARCHER
OVER THE HEAD WITH YOUR UKULELE

I wouldn't do it. I wouldn't take part in the rally's skit my mother had written and choreographed. I was five and in the habit of accompanying my mother downtown, where she taught freshman English at Central High School. I had my own desk at the back of her classroom, where I drew pictures of the Trojan War and Odysseus sailing home, the books she was teaching. She was also the faculty advisor for the booster club, and I helped her sell candy, popcorn, and pop in the concession stands during the games. She spray-painted the spirit posters too, the message emerging in the burst of paint as she pulled away the masking letters. It also fell to her to run the weekly pep sessions. During basketball season they were in the tiny gym. I sat up by the drummers in the band, who taught me Central's signature rhythm, a backbeat syncopation that made the marchers skip on every fourth step. I liked to watch the Tiger on the floor, acting in my mother's morality plays. The Tiger suit consisted of the furry orange and black striped footed pajama that zipped up the belly and a papier-mâché head I had helped my mother repair and paint. The head was very large. I could fit completely inside it curled up. It was hard to breathe wearing it, so the student inside would lift the head like a knight's visor to gulp in some air between cheers.

South Side, Central's arch rivals, were the Archers, represented by a green leotarded Robin Hood. The Archer, in elf shoes, patrolled the sidelines with a longbow and a quiver of arrows. My mother had written me into her latest creation vanquishing the Archer. In it there were vignettes representing the history of the rivalry. I was supposed to be in the scene from the '20s. Dressed in knee socks and knickers, raccoon-skin coat, and felt porkpie hat, I was to hit the Archer, who had tied up the Tiger with his own tail, over the head with my ukulele, freeing Central's mascot. Later in the sketch, all the historic characters did the Twist, then wildly popular, around the supine green body of the defeated foe.

For some reason I can't begin to remember, I didn't want to do it. I do remember my mother and her students pleading with me during the rehearsal, telling me how cute I was and would be. It was hot in that coat. The Tiger had his Tiger head off completely. It wasn't that I was shy or I didn't know how to twist. I understood the concept of the piece. I didn't have any lines to memorize. Perhaps I felt too re-sponsible. What if I performed and the magic charm of that performance failed to work, the strings of my enchanted ukulele no match for the strung-taut bow of the green archrival.

It had been just that fall my parents had taken me to Ball State, where my uncle was a student, to see the grand homecoming parade. Suddenly one of the Roman slaves, a fraternity pledge drafted to haul his house's float, broke free of his chains and ran right to me in the crowd. "You must save me," he cried. "Save me, please!" until his brothers, dressed as Legionnaires, dragged him back to the float. I must have been thinking of that incident months later in the Central gym. All these costumed people begging me to help, urged me to save the Tiger who stood there patiently, headless, happy to have this moment to catch his breath.

THE WAR DANCES OF REDSKINS

I was a Redskin. I was a Redskin for three years when I attended North Side High School in Fort Wayne. Before that, in junior high, I had been a Chief. This was in Indiana, of course, a state named to honor, with the inaccurate name of In-dian, the people killed, expelled, or assimilated in order to create a state named Indiana. The Miami mainly. Little Turtle's grave is just down the river from where my high school sits. The excavation there uncovered the remains of the sword presented to the chief by George Washington, etc. It was another excavation, however, the one on the sandy riverbank to lay the foundation for North Side in 1926, that suggested the future name of its mascot. That dig uncovered an ancient midden, relics of teeth and bone, worked stone, a few beads, remnants of fire, maybe even a grave or two, and led to the honorific of "Redskin" attaching to the athletic teams of the new high school built on top of the site. The evidence of that excavation, its meager catalogue of artifacts, a residue of an indigenous Pre-Columbian, perhaps, inhabitation, is today used as justification by those who want to retain "Redskin" as the mascot in the face of the occasional efforts to change it. See, the supporters say, there is a reason, a history, a tradition for the appellation. They miss the point, of course, of using this particular epithet, its particular nu-ance of that history and tradition. But never mind.

The name came with a character, a student in costume who danced before the start of football and basketball games. The costume was buckskin chaps and shirt with the leather fringe on the sleeves, a beaded breastplate and full-feathered headdress, more a plains get-up than the more accurate woodland outfit. But then what did we know. And the dance and the music that accompanied the costumed character were all Hollywood, too. It was supposed to be a war dance, we imag-ined, with a lot of rhythmic bowing, hands outstretched, moving with a step that was both shuffle and skip in the inscribed outline of the tip-off circle. There might have been a hatchet or a lance.

A kid named Kevin was the best of the three students (there was a yearly competition) who held the position during the time I went to school. All arms and legs, Kevin added a twirling dervish turn to the movements, took his shirt off even during the late football season, danced around the lance (yes, there was a lance) he ceremoniously thrust into the ground. There was war paint, too, on his face, red and white, the school colors, grease-based makeup streaked under each eye. The war paint had been applied over an initial coat of cooper color he sponged onto all his exposed very white and freckly skin. Often the finish was splotchy, dappled.

Kevin didn't have enough time to get into makeup during the big riot. This was my junior year, the year the school system closed Central High School downtown where my mother had taught English and been the dean of girls for nearly twenty years and bussed its mostly black students out to the six white high schools around the city's edge. This was in the early '70s. The integration hadn't gone well, with every high school experiencing protests, beatings, fights, vandalism, and bomb threats. This was even true at the two new high schools, Wayne and Northrup.

At North Side the alienated black students staged a boycott of classes, and a school-wide assembly was called by the fretting principal hoping to talk things out. We met in the gym. The football team and the cheerleaders were there, already clustered on the court with the frazzled administrators and coaches. The teachers patrolled the stands. Those squads on the floor had a semblance of harmony and order, having had to work together through practices in the summer. Kevin burst in, running half-dressed in his outfit, feathers flying, to his spot in the center of the floor. He was very white, I remember, without his makeup. He seemed to glow, reflecting the bright light of the new mercury vapor lamps just then reaching the peak of their illumination, having been turned on in haste as the crowds of students poured into the gym from all around the building. They shoved a microphone into his hands urging him to speak, and I remember thinking this breaks some unspoken code to which mascots adhere. The mute mascots were to remain silent on the sidelines as if they had appeared in our midst from some preverbal land where only pantomime, pep, and pumping fists were allowed. They are to always be illustrative in their stoic silence. Indians even more so.

But our Indian said something. Did he say to the throng of angry and frightened students packed into the bleachers that we were all Redskins? Did he say it? "We are all Redskins!" I hope he said it. And then he did the dance. Yes, he did the dance. A skeletal band had been mustered, the drums beating the tom-tom and a trumpet blaring that warning staccato. We watched Kevin dance the dance.

I don't remember what happened then, but we ourselves all ended up dancing on the gym floor. Marvin Gaye was on the speakers. The Stones. Carole King. We were studying *Tapestry* in Mrs. Neuhaus's English class.

The cheerleaders reminded us to take off our shoes before we ventured out onto the gym floor. We filled that floor. We were on the edge of a riot, on the verge of a party. The administrators began to look relieved. We didn't talk. What could we say? Dancing seemed like the thing to do at the time. We were so many, nearly 2,000, we couldn't do much more than mill in time to the music that didn't stop, it seemed, for hours. We danced that way, in a kind of trance, until the buses came.

THE MOTHER'S MARCH

I went with my mother when she went door to door in the neighborhood, collecting for the March of Dimes. She let me push the doorbells. I liked the illuminated ones that blinked out when I depressed them. Mother and I would visit with many of the neighbors, who invited us in for a chat and for something to warm us up. This was after the polio vaccines. We had all just taken the sugar cube the summer before. The charity had altered the focus of its appeal to birth defects, but most often my mother and our neighbors shared memories of polio—the closing of the river beach, the braces and the iron lungs, Roosevelt. I drank hot chocolate and sometimes got to play at playing someone's piano. At home, my mother would let me separate the big pile of coins we collected into smaller piles of pennies, dimes, nickels, and quarters.

"The first thing I did when I saw you for the first time was count your fingers and toes." She had been knocked out completely for my birth. I had been delivered with forceps. I picture her groggily counting my fingers and toes. They're all there.

Years later, I came to realize that during those treks through the neighborhood my mother regarded me as a kind of mascot. I was an emblem of her luck as a mother, both the charm that embodied the wish and the body itself charmed into existence. I was illustrative of the charity's objectives. See, all his fingers tickling the keys of your piano, depressing the buttons of your doorbells. I was no cartoon, no stylized rendering of the talisman, not even a poster child. I was just her son, but that was enough for metaphor.

The Basement

MAURA STANTON

When the tornado siren goes off, I drop my book on the bed where I'm propped with pillows, and jump up to search for my two cats. Olive is sleeping on the bed in the guestroom. Oleander is curled up under the coffee table downstairs in the living room. I'm glad my husband is teaching this afternoon. He's in a huge limestone building that always feels safe during storms.

I lug the cats and the weather radio into the kitchen, and unlock the basement door. I drag the cat carrier down the steps, and set it in the middle of the messy storage room where we keep everything we seldom use but can't bring ourselves to throw away. Here is a black and white television not hooked up to cable, and a computer that uses old 5$\frac{1}{4}$-inch floppy disks. Shopping bags filled with Christmas paper rolls sit on top of a metal file cabinet stuffed with ancient tax forms. Under the stairs we've stored twenty years' worth of cardboard cartons and boxes, just in case we ever move again. Our first couch, made of wicker, sits in a corner, piled high with stacks of damp literary magazines. Some metal shelving contains extra kitchen stuff that won't fit in our cabinets upstairs, greasy roasting pans, an ice cream maker, an extra blender, and a dish drainer from the days when my husband commuted to a job in another state.

I don't like my basement, and never come here except on quick foraging trips to locate the right size box for something or other, or to grab an article stored here that I suddenly need. I hate the damp and the spiders and the small, high, unwashed windows. I hate the gloom that seems to seep like a gas from the limestone block walls. And yet I would never live in a house in the Midwest that didn't have a basement, for I'm terrified of tornadoes.

So here I sit, on a blue dinette chair with rusting chrome legs that used to belong to my mother-in-law, trying to soothe my cats, who can't understand why I've locked them into the cat carrier but haven't put them in the back seat of the car. I'm afraid to let them out down here, for who knows what scary holes or crevices they might scoot into. I wouldn't want spider webs or beetle casings to get stuck in their fur.

The rain is beating mud against the high windows. The lights flicker. Panicked, I remember that I forgot to bring a flashlight, and I dart back up to the kitchen. Now I can see how bad the storm is, for though it's only three o'clock, it's pitch black outside, and I can hear the wind howling. Lightning flashes, illuminating the tortured shapes of the trees outside. I grab the flashlight out of the junk drawer in the kitchen just in time. The power goes out.

I follow a circle of light back down the basement stairs, closing the door behind me as if I thought it would make some difference. I sit on the lowest step, and train the lights on the cats, who blink and meow. I train it on a bookcase in the corner, filled with battered mystery novels and unread Christmas present books. I rake the light over the old darkroom equipment, over the ice cream maker, and over a battered cardboard box that contains all the stuff I wrote in college.

And suddenly I remember that I began as a writer in a Midwestern basement. This gloomy place is both warehouse and womb.

I lived in a small house in south Minneapolis with four brothers and four sisters. Very early I learned to concentrate so that I could read in the living room with the TV blaring, or out in the backyard hammock with kids throwing balls or blowing soap bubbles all around me. But I needed quiet and privacy for writing. My father had an office in the basement, and when he was out of town, which was most of the time, I could work down there. It was cool in the summer, and in the winter I could turn on the gas logs in the fireplace just long enough to take the chill off the room, but not long enough to eat up all the oxygen, something my father had warned me about.

My father couldn't afford a real desk. There were too many other things his family needed. So he had taken over a folding metal "game" table that no one used any longer. The table had a checkerboard, a backgammon board, and a Parcheesi board enameled onto its surface, along with boards for other games we'd forgotten how to play. The center drawer was supposed to hold checkers and chessmen and other game pieces, but these had been lost over the years, and now the drawer was filled with Bunn-o-Matic pens and pencils.

My father sold institutional Bunn-o-Matic coffee makers, and was on the road Monday to Friday. To pass the hours in lonely motel rooms he bought books, and the walls in the basement were lined with metal shelves crammed with hardbacks and thick paperbacks. During his free hours on the road, he haunted bookstores in Denver, Minot, Omaha, Kansas City, and Milwaukee, and when he came home on Fridays, exhausted from driving six hundred miles across the prairie, or through a snowstorm from Rapid City, he always had half a dozen new books in a brown bag. Books were his only extravagance.

He liked history, philosophy, and biography the best, but he also bought novels and poetry. He owned a copy of *Finnegans Wake*, which he had tried to read, as well as the thick Ellmann biography of Joyce. Many of the books, like his set of Proust's *Remembrance of Things Past*, he hadn't yet read, but was saving for his retirement. When I needed *The Good Soldier* and *A Passage to India* for an English class, my father found them for me down in the basement.

He usually piled the new books on the old bumper pool table in the middle of the basement. No one used it any longer because the cue sticks were broken. He had an easy chair and a bright pole lamp right beside it, and that's where he went to escape the noise of the house on weekends when he wanted to read.

That year, my senior year, I spent a lot of time in the basement, but I was too unhappy to write. I'd go downstairs, roll a piece of scrap paper into my father's typewriter, and just sit there feeling paralyzed. The year before, I'd been cheerfully writing a suspense novel set on the Riviera, but it seemed false to me now, and I couldn't go on with it. I'd never been out of the Midwest, and I knew nothing of jewel thieves. I'd just taken my first creative writing class with Vern Rutsala, and my eyes had been opened. Now I wanted to write poems and stories that told the truth. I wanted to go to the Iowa Writers' Workshop, which Vern Rutsala had told me all about, but I didn't have enough money.

I felt trapped and frightened. At twenty-two, I had a vision of my life as a narrow box with a lid that was about to shut, and I didn't know how to escape. In March I'd been offered a job on the newsletter in the county courthouse, but the idea of spending eight hours a day inside the thick, gray walls of the castle-like building, watching handcuffed men and women being led down the halls to this or that courtroom, filled me with horror. I'd turned the job down, telling the hearty, kindly boss, who'd given me a tour and taken me out to lunch, that I was going to Iowa.

And Iowa had admitted me, in both poetry and fiction. But they hadn't given me an assistantship, and the government loan I'd applied for covered only the tuition, not the money for room and board in the dorm. My father had been struggling to support us for years, and had no savings out of which he could loan me the money.

So it was impossible for me to go to Iowa. I knew that. But yet I hadn't given up. I'd filled out all the papers, and even requested a room in the dorm, just as if I were really going.

But I'd also signed up with an employment agency. I took a battery of tests, and interviewed for jobs at banks and insurance companies and at General Mills, where I took more tests. The jobs I might get depressed me, but I knew I'd have to take one when it was offered because my student loans would come due in a year. I'd taken five years to get through college because I'd switched majors, and in the fifth year I had to take out an extra loan in order not to have to work a part-time job.

I saw myself sitting at a desk in a shoulder-high cubicle in a modern glass tower, typing reports or punching an adding machine. I'd always be too tired to write when I got home. Eventually I'd save enough money to get my own apartment. Then I'd probably have to take a weekend job to pay for the furniture, like a friend of mine who had graduated last year.

The only alternative was to join something. I filled out forms for the Peace Corps, and also for an overseas Library Service run by the Red Cross and attached in some way to the Army in Korea. It wasn't really the Army, I told myself. In the brochure a woman in a snappy blue serge uniform was handing a book to a soldier. They were both smiling and looked happy. I knew nothing about Korea except that it snowed a lot, and that during the Korean War my uncle had been shot in the thigh. He had once shown me his wound.

Then I graduated from the University of Minnesota, one of so many thousands that they didn't even announce our names. We just filed past the stage set up in the football stadium in our caps and gowns to receive a rolled-up blank piece of paper. But nothing changed. I no longer went to class. Occasionally I went downtown on the bus for a job interview. And most of the time I sat down in the basement, pretending to write but really reading my father's books on existentialism.

My father had books by and about Sartre, Teilhard de Chardin, Kierkegaard, and Heidegger, and I felt that if I could only grasp the concepts, and learn how to live an existential life, I would be saved. All I had to do was accept the fact that I was condemned to be free, and all would be well.

I didn't feel the least bit free, but Sartre seemed to have covered all my objections. He explained that wishing myself out of the basement and into Iowa wasn't enough, I had to do something. That even if my actions were ineffectual they would still count because I would be trying to achieve my end. I was supposed to give meaning to my surroundings by my projects. The trouble was, I didn't have any projects.

I'd been in love earlier that year, but it had ended badly, and I blamed myself. I'd been afraid of a commitment. And though I'd gradually ceased to believe in God, I was still going to Mass every Sunday in a cowardly fashion, partly so as not to hurt my parents, but partly because I didn't like the idea of being an atheist. It depressed me to think of all the years and effort I'd wasted praying, and I kept hoping I'd get my faith back.

And now I had one precious summer in which to write before the years of grim work began, and all I did was sit in the basement, thumbing through my father's books, waiting for the humidifier to turn itself on and off.

One day, when I was hanging out laundry on the line for my mother, Mr. B., who was working on his lawn mower, called me over to his yard. He was a retired executive at General Mills, and was rumored to have invented Bacos. He had lived in the little stucco house next door for thirty years, and knew everyone in the neighborhood.

"The FBI's investigating you," he said.

"What? The FBI?"

"I thought you should know." He laughed. "I gave you a good report."

"But the FBI! Why?" I wondered if they had seen me the one time I'd marched in an anti-war demonstration across campus. Could they have picked me out of the crowd? Anti-war demonstrations at Minnesota were low-keyed compared to the demonstrations at Berkeley and Madison. It was a commuter campus. Most students lived at home and had part-time jobs.

"Something to do with Korea—some quasi Army organization."

"Oh!" I said. "It's the Library Service in Korea that I applied for. But why would the FBI be interested?"

"North Korea is a Communist country. They like to check up on people, just in case. I think they've talked to the people across the street, too." Mr. B. smiled, and turned back to his machine. "It sounds like you'll be accepted if things have gotten to this stage."

I finished hanging the laundry. The sheets felt cold and clammy in my hands as I spread them out along the line, and they dampened my blouse. I felt chilled, even though it was a lovely day in the '70s, with bright, puffy clouds in the sky.

I carried the laundry basket down to the basement, left it on top of the washing machine, and went into my father's office. I sat down in his chair without turning on the lamp, hugging my arms and shivering. I didn't know what oppressed me more, the thought that the FBI was building a file on me, asking the neighbors questions about my life and drawing conclusions that would be permanently part of a secret record of who I was, or the thought that I might have to go to Korea. Because if I was accepted, how could I say no? I had absolutely nothing else.

I got up and began to pace back and forth, noticing that the window wells, which had been packed with snow back in March, were beginning to fill up with weedy crabgrass. My mother hadn't gotten around to pulling it up yet, and it made a sinister image against the glass as its ravenous stalks and seedy tips struggled up toward the sun, beginning to block the daylight from the basement so that the room seemed shadowy and dim.

I thought of men in suits in Washington reading the reports on me, and I was filled with revulsion. The idea of choosing to accept a job that they had to approve, a job that would take me thousands of miles from the authentic life I wanted to lead, struck me as impossible. If I could stay down here in the basement until September, until all the other young writers I envied were sitting around tables talking about stories and poems without me, then I might be able to accept my fate. But I couldn't embrace it.

I ran upstairs and brought down the brochure with the address of the Library Service. I stuck a clean sheet of paper into the typewriter, and wrote a letter withdrawing my application. I stuck it in an envelope, took one of my father's stamps, and dropped it in the box outside the drugstore that afternoon. My heart didn't stop pounding until I saw it fall through the slot.

A few weeks later, my father came home early one Friday and found me sitting in his chair in the basement. I was reading *The Magic Mountain*, a book he'd bought only recently. I'd found it in the stack on the bumper pool table. I jumped up at once and kissed him on the cheek.

He put his briefcase down on the desk. He was frowning. "Your mother says you're spending all your time down here. She's worried. Why don't you get out more?"

"It's cool. And I like to read."

"It's not good to close yourself up like this."

"I guess I'll go for a walk around the lake," I said. I put the book down, in case he was reading it, too, and climbed the stairs to the back door. My mother was just coming into the kitchen with the mail. She handed me a letter, then went down to the basement to give my father his mail.

It was a letter from Iowa, confirming a double room in Currier, the graduate dorm. The paper seemed to burn my fingers. I dropped it on the counter, next to the pitcher of iced tea my mother had just made.

It was a dazzling day, but I felt like some kind of phantom as I crossed the park where girls were suntanning on blankets and children were tossing Frisbees. Why couldn't I just accept the fact that I wasn't going to Iowa, and get on with my life? I knew that somehow I was thwarting myself whenever I had a job interview. I'd tell personnel directors that my hobby was writing poetry, or answer their favorite question about how I saw myself in five years (a question the employment agency had trained me to reply to by enthusiastically insisting that I saw myself as a manager with a lot of responsibility) by saying that I hoped to have written a novel. I'd take satisfaction in watching the interviewer's face go blank, but at the same time I knew I was only hurting myself.

The sidewalk went up a little hill on the far side of Lake Nokomis, and I could see the Foshay Tower and the tops of other downtown buildings floating in the distance. I kept walking, past the little beach where teenagers played loud rock music, and the big beach where pregnant mothers sat in lawn chairs at the edge of the water, watching their toddlers. I passed the spot near the bridge where divers had found the body of a woman who had drowned herself one June, and the birch tree where I'd been kissed back in January on a snowy night. I'd been in love and full of hope for the future.

When I got back, my parents were both sitting in their armchairs in the living room, drinking iced tea. My little sister Ellen was playing with her Lego set in the middle of the floor, and I had to be careful not to step on any pieces.

"Get a glass of iced tea," my mother said. "We want to talk to you."

I poured myself a glass of iced tea, and sat down on the couch.

"If you really want to go to Iowa that badly," my father said, picking up my letter about the dorm room from his end table, "I could ask Dr. Coan to lend you the money. I've never asked him for anything before. I feel funny about it. But if it means so much to you—"

"It means everything," I burst out. "I'll pay him back! Of course I'll pay him back!"

Dr. Coan was an old friend of my father's from AA. They'd met in Illinois years ago. My father had not had anything to drink in many years, but Dr. Coan sometimes broke down, and had to fly up to Minnesota for a few weeks at Hazelden. My father would visit him there, and sometimes he came out to the house for dinner. They often talked on the telephone. Dr. Coan had been the one to discover my scoliosis, and had made sure that I got the best treatment available.

My father looked tired. I knew that it must make him feel a little sick inside to ask for money from an old friend, even if it was for his daughter. It was a blow to his pride. But this was one time in my life when I felt no remorse or guilt. Any flicker of self-sacrifice was overmastered by my radiant desire.

"Will you ask him, Dad? I swear I'll pay him back!" I was sitting on the edge of the couch cushion, leaning toward him, afraid he would take back his offer.

"I'll call him tonight," he said.

And one week later I had my future in my hands in the form of a small blue check for $1,000 made out in my own name.

I had a million things to get ready for graduate school, so it wasn't until a few nights before I was to leave for Iowa that I found myself in the basement again. I'd gone down to look for a book, but when I turned on the lights in my father's office, the gloom that I'd been feeling all summer was still in there, like a cloud of gas, trapped underground. I felt a sudden terror that I was only dreaming that I was about to leave home, that nothing had changed. I ran back upstairs and into the sunshine, gasping. But a few years later, when I brought my new husband home to meet my family, we had to sleep on the pull-out sofa bed in the basement. I didn't think it would bother me, but I had trouble sleeping, even with the humming lullaby of the dehumidifier, and in the middle of the night I started sweating, and sat up in bed in a panic, afraid my life wasn't my life.

But of course it was. I had only to reach out and put my hand on my sleeping husband's back to know that I'd escaped from the basement long ago.

Now I train my flashlight around this other basement, looking at the flotsam and jetsam of the life I've been living now for many years, the life I chose, and I'm amazed.

Editor

Becky Bradway's collection of essays, *Pink Houses and Family Taverns*, was published by Indiana University Press in 2002. Her work has appeared in *DoubleTake*, *The Encyclopedia of the Midwest*, *E: The Environmental Magazine*, *Creative Nonfiction*, *North American Review*, and elsewhere. She teaches creative nonfiction at Illinois State University and lives in Normal, Illinois. Her latest project is a nonfiction novel about American modernist poets. Her Web site is http://bbradway.net.

Contributors

Ben Alvey recently graduated from Millikin University with a BFA in Acting and a minor in Writing. He grew up in and around Columbus, Indiana, until he was eighteen years old. Ben now resides in the Chicagoland area. He hopes to visit Columbus often, but not too often. Ben is proud of that fact that he has memberships to eight different video stores. This is his first published work.

Jon Anderson has been a staff writer for the *Montreal Gazette*, *Time*, and, for the past twenty-five years, the *Chicago Tribune*. He was awarded the 1999 Studs Terkel Award by the Community Media Workshop of Chicago for his reporting on Chicago's diverse neighborhoods. He lives in the Edgewater neighborhood of Chicago.

Anne Calcagno was raised in Milan and Rome and is both bilingual and a dual national. She came to the U.S. to attend Williams College, and remained. She now lives in Chicago, where she is an assistant professor of English at DePaul University. For her short story collection, *Pray for Yourself*, variously set in Italy and the U.S., she won the James D. Phelan Award, a National Endowment for the Arts Fellowship, and two Illinois Arts Council awards. She is currently at work on a novel about Italy and Eritrea during World War II. Her travel writing has appeared in the *New York Times*.

Bonnie Jo Campbell is the author of the novel *Q Road* and the story collection *Women and Other Animals*. She won the Associated Writing Program award for short fiction, had work included in *The Pushcart Prize* anthology, and was chosen a Barnes and Noble Discover author in 2002. She received an MA in mathematics and an MFA in writing from Western Michigan University. She lives in Kalamazoo, Michigan.

Maxine Chernoff is the author of six books of poetry, most recently *World* (2001), and six books of fiction, three novels, and three books of short stories. *Some of Her Friends That Year: New and Selected Stories* (2002) includes stories set both in Chicago and California. Her novel *A Boy in Winter* is being made into a film for Showtime. She is Professor of Creative Writing at San Francisco State University and chairs the department. She edits *New American Writing*. Since moving to California from Chicago in 1994, she has lived in Mill Valley with Paul Hoover and their three children.

Ricardo Cortez Cruz was born August 10, 1964, in Decatur, Illinois. He is the author of *Straight Outta Compton* and *Five Days of Bleeding*, novels "short and funky." His new novel is *Premature Autopsies: Tales of Darkest America*. He teaches English at Illinois State University. His recent publications include the creative nonfiction piece "My Flesh and Blood," in *Not Guilty: Twelve Black Men Speak Out on Law, Justice, and Life*, edited by Jabari Asim.

Rodney B. Cruz was born December 17, 1964, in Decatur, Illinois. He is a graduate of Illinois State University. The *Indianapolis Star* published his editorial on NBA legend Kareem Abdul-Jabbar and black history. He is currently employed in the Department of Content Data Analysis for AdminaStar Federal, a subsidiary of Anthem Insurance.

Sharon Darrow has published poetry, stories, and three books for children and adolescents: *Old Thunder and Miss Raney, Through the Tempests Dark and Wild: A Story about Mary Shelley*, and *The Painters of Lexieville*. Her poetry has most recently appeared in *ACM*. She teaches children's writing at Vermont College.

Stuart Dybek is the author of two short story collections, *The Coast of Chicago* and *Childhood and other Neighborhoods*, and a collection of poetry, *Brass Knuckles*. His poetry and fiction have appeared in numerous magazines, including *The New Yorker, The Atlantic Monthly, Harper's*, and *Ploughshares*. He has received the 1998 Lannan Award, the 1995 PEN/Bernard Malamud Prize, the Academy Institute Award in Fiction from the Academy of Arts and Letters in 1994, four O. Henry Prizes, and the Whiting Writers Award in 1984. Dybek teaches at Western Michigan University and is a permanent member of the faculty of the Prague Summer Writers Workshop.

Sonia Gernes is a poet, fiction writer, and professor of English at the University of Notre Dame, where she teaches Creative Writing, American Literature, and Gender Studies. She was born in Winona, Minnesota, and grew up on a dairy farm nearby. She has published one novel, *The Way to St. Ives*, and four books of poetry: *The Mutes of Sleepy Eye* (1981), *Brief Lives* (1982), *Women at Forty* (1988), and *A Breeze Called the Fremantle Doctor: Poem/Tales* (1998). She was awarded an

NEA Creative Writing fellowship in 1999. Her current projects are a collection of nonfiction and a fiction/painting collaboration with a visual artist.

Jaimy Gordon's third novel, *Bogeywoman*, was on the *Los Angeles Times* Best Books List for 2000. Gordon has been a Fellow of the Fine Arts Work Center and the Bunting Institute. Her second novel, *She Drove Without Stopping* (1990), won her an Academy-Institute Award from the American Academy of Arts and Letters. She teaches creative writing at Western Michigan University.

Philip Graham is the author of a collection of prose poems, *The Vanishings* (1978), and two collections of short stories, *The Art of the Knock* (1985) and *Interior Design* (1996). He co-authored a memoir of Africa (with Alma Gottlieb), *Parallel Worlds: An Anthropologist and a Writer Encounter Africa* (1993), and is author of a novel, *How to Read an Unwritten Language* (1995). Graham has twice been a Fellow at both the MacDowell and Yaddo artists' colonies; he has received an NEA Fellowship, two Illinois Arts Council Artist Grants, an NEH Grant, and the 1992 William Peden Prize in Fiction.

Robert Grindy grew up in the Mother Lode area of Northern California before enrolling in the MFA program in fiction at Indiana University, Bloomington. After receiving his degree, he worked at *The Saturday Evening Post* in Indianapolis, then taught writing and literature at Franklin College and DePauw University. He now lives in Decatur, Illinois, with his wife and two children and teaches at Richland Community College.

Dan Guillory has published *Living with Lincoln: Life and Art in the Heartland* (1989), *The Alligator Inventions* (1991), and *When the Waters Recede: Rescue and Recovery during the Great Flood* (1996). His awards include grants from the Illinois Arts Council and the National Endowment for the Humanities. He is a professor of English at Millikin University in Decatur, Illinois.

Robert Hellenga is author of the novels *Blues Lessons* (2002), *The Fall of a Sparrow*, and *The Sixteen Pleasures*. His short work has been published in the *New York Times Magazine* and *Crazyhorse*. He is a distinguished professor at Knox College in Galesburg, Illinois.

Doug Hesse was happily raised in DeWitt, Iowa, and its surrounding farms, timbers, and creek beds. He was educated at the University of Iowa. Professor of English at Illinois State University, he is past president of the National Council of Writing Program Administrators and is chair-elect of the Conference on College Composition and Communication. He publishes essays about the essay and has guest-edited an issue of *College English* devoted to creative nonfiction.

Richard Holinger teaches English at Marmion Academy, a college prep school in Aurora, Illinois. Degrees include an MA in English from Washington University and a PhD in English with a Creative Writing specialty from the University of Illinois at Chicago. His poetry, short fiction, creative nonfiction, and book reviews have appeared in magazines such as *The Texas Review*, *Midwest Quarterly*, *The Southern Review*, *Boulevard*, and *Another Chicago Magazine*. His column "View from Geneva" appears in his weekly hometown newspaper, the *Geneva Sun*.

John McCluskey, Jr. teaches in both the Department of African American and African Diaspora Studies, where he has just completed a six-year term as department chair, and the Department of English at Indiana University. His publications include the novels *Mr. America's Last Season Blues* (1983) and *Look What They Done to My Song* (1974) as well as short stories in several journals and anthologies. He is working on a novel titled *Chicago Jubilee Rag*, a fictionalized account of Frederick Douglass and other historical figures at the 1893 Chicago World's Fair. He has co-edited, with Charles Johnson, the collection of voices, stories, and poems *Black Men Speaking* (Indiana University Press, 1997). Currently he is also co-editor of and a contributor to a volume of cultural history, *The Chicago Renaissance: Literature and Politics, 1935–1960*.

Erin McGraw is the author of three books: *Bodies at Sea* (University of Illinois Press, 1989), *Lies of the Saints* (Chronicle Books, 1996), which was a *New York Times* Notable Book of the Year, and *The Baby Tree* (Story Line Press, 2002). She teaches writing at Ohio State University.

James McManus is the author of four novels, a collection of stories, two books of poems, and *Positively Fifth Street*, an account of Ted Binion's murder and the 2000 World Series of Poker. His work has appeared in *Harper's*, *The Atlantic*, *The Paris Review*, the *New York Times*, the *Boston Globe*, *Best American Poetry*, *Best American Sports Writing*, and *The Good Parts: The Best Erotic Writing in Modern Fiction*. He teaches at the School of the Art Institute in Chicago.

Michael Martone is author of *The Blue Guide to Indiana* (2001), *The Flatness and Other Landscapes* (2000), *Seeing Eye* (1995), *Fort Wayne Is Seventh on Hitler's List* (Indiana University Press, 1993), and other books. He has edited or co-edited three books: *Scribner's Anthology of Contemporary Short Fiction*, *Townships*, and *A Place of Sense*. His fiction and essays have been widely anthologized and published in literary journals. He is a professor in the MFA Program at the University of Alabama-Tuscaloosa (but remains an Indiana boy).

Cris Mazza's forthcoming novel is *Homeland*. She has published *Indigenous/Growing Up California*, a memoir (City Lights, 2003). Other novels include *Girl Beside*

Him (2001), *How to Leave a Country*, *Dog People*, and *Is It Sexual Harassment Yet?* She is also co-editor of two anthologies of women's fiction, *Chick-Lit: Postfeminist Fiction* (1995) and *Chick-Lit 2 (No Chick Vics)* (1996). She was an NEA fellow in 2000–2001. Since 1993, Mazza has lived west of Chicago. She is a professor in the Program for Writers at the University of Illinois at Chicago.

Martha Miller has published two mysteries, *Nine Nights on the Windy Tree* and *Dispatch to Death*, and a collection of short fiction, *Skin to Skin*. She has had four plays produced and won an Illinois Arts Council fellowship for fiction. She is the mother of two grown sons and teaches English at Richland Community College. She lives in Springfield, Illinois.

Richard Newman's poems, essays, and stories have recently appeared in *Boulevard*, *Crab Orchard Review*, *Southern Humanities Review*, *Southern Indiana Review*, *Story Quarterly*, and many other periodicals and anthologies. His *Greatest Hits* poetry chapbook was recently published. He edits *River Styx*, teaches at St. Louis Community College, and reviews books for the *St. Louis Post-Dispatch*.

Rosanne Nordstrom grew up in Wisconsin and graduated (BA and MA) from the University of Wisconsin. In 1980 she moved to Chicago, where she worked at the City Colleges for almost a decade. This selection was from a memoir, *My Life with Paco*.

Jenna M. Polk studied prose and poetry writing at Millikin University in Decatur, Illinois. She is working on a master's degree in literature at Illinois State University. This is her first published work.

David Radavich's poetry collections include *Slain Species*, *By the Way: Poems over the Years*, and *Greatest Hits*. His dramatic works have been performed across the U.S., including five Off-Off-Broadway productions. Radavich has published a variety of essays on poetry, drama, and contemporary writing. The recipient of numerous writing awards, he was named an Illinois Distinguished Author in 1995.

Keith Ratzlaff is Associate Professor of English at Central College in Pella, Iowa. His books of poetry include *Man under a Pear Tree* and *Across the Known World*. His poems and reviews have appeared in *Poetry Northwest*, *The Georgia Review*, *New England Review*, and elsewhere. He is the author of two chapbooks: *Out Here* and *New Winter Light*. His poems also appear in *Poets of the New Century* (2001) and in the forthcoming *A Cappella: Mennonite Voices in Poetry* (2003).

Paulette Roeske is the author of four collections of poetry, including *Anvil, Clock and Last* (2001). She is also a fiction writer; her collection *Bridge of Sighs: A Novella and Stories* won the Three Oaks Prize in Fiction. Recognized by fellowships from the Illinois Arts Council, the National Endowment for the Humanities, and the Japan Foundation, Roeske teaches at the University of Southern Indiana.

Sheryl St. Germain is on the creative writing faculty at Iowa State University. Her work has received several awards, including two NEA Fellowships, an NEH Fellowship, and the William Faulkner Award for the personal essay. Her books include *Going Home, The Mask of Medusa, Making Bread at Midnight, How Heavy the Breath of God,* and *The Journals of Scheherazade.* She has also published a book of translations of the Cajun poet Jean Arceneaux, *Je Suis Cadien.* Her book of lyric essays *SwampSongs: The Making of an Unruly Woman* is forthcoming.

Scott Russell Sanders is the author of eighteen books, including *Staying Put, Hunting for Hope,* and *The Force of Spirit.* He explores the landscape and culture of the Middle West in *Writing from the Center.* For his work in nonfiction, he has won the Lannan Literary Award and the John Burroughs Essay Award. In all of his books he is concerned with our relation to nature, issues of social justice, the character of community, the implications of science, and the search for a spiritual path. He is Distinguished Professor of English at Indiana University. He and his wife Ruth, a biochemist, have reared two children in their hometown of Bloomington, in the hardwood hill country of the White River Valley.

Reginald Shepherd was born in New York City and raised in tenements and housing projects in the Bronx. He received his BA from Bennington College and MFA degrees from Brown University and the University of Iowa. His first book, *Some Are Drowning,* was published in 1994 as the winner of the 1993 Associated Writing Program Award in Poetry. He is also author of *Angel, Interrupted* (1996), *Wrong* (1999), and *Otherhood* (2002). Shepherd has received a Discovery/The Nation award and grants from the NEA, the Illinois Arts Council, and the Constance Saltonstall Foundation.

Sharon Solwitz has published two novels, *Blood and Milk* and *Bloody Mary* (both by Sarabande Books). Her short stories have been widely published in venues such as *Triquarterly, Crazyhorse, Ploughshares,* and *Boulevard.* She is a winner of the Carl Sandburg Prize for Fiction, among other honors. A longtime resident of Chicago, she teaches in the MFA creative writing program at Purdue University.

Maura Stanton has published four books of poetry: *Snow on Snow, Cries of Swimmers, Tales of the Supernatural,* and *Life among the Trolls.* She has published a novel, *Molly Companion,* and a collection of short stories, *The Country I Come From.* Her poems and stories have appeared in many magazines, including the *American Poetry Review, Poetry, Ploughshares, The Paris Review,* and *The New Yorker.* She teaches in the MFA Program at Indiana University in Bloomington.

Mary Helen Stefaniak, a native of Milwaukee, is a writer of short stories, novellas, and personal essays. Her work has appeared in *Redbook, The Iowa Review, EPOCH, Short Story,* and several anthologies, most recently *New Stories from the South: The Year's Best.* She is Director of Creative Writing at Creighton University. Her collection *Self Storage and Other Stories* received the 1998 Banta Award for Literary Excellence, and her novella "The Turk and My Mother" (2000) was short-listed for the O. Henry Prize.

Mary Swander's latest book is her forthcoming memoir *The Desert Pilgrim: En Route to Mysticism and Miracles.* She is also widely known for her memoir *Out of This World* and her book of poetry *Driving the Body Back.* Swander is a Distinguished Professor at Iowa State University and lives in Ames and Kalona, where she raises organic vegetables, geese, and goats.

Mary Troy is author of two collections of short stories, *Joe Baker Is Dead* and *The Alibi Café and Other Stories* (2002). She has won a Nelson Algren Award from the *Chicago Tribune,* and has published her work in *Boulevard, Ascent, River Styx, American Literary Review,* and other well-known journals. She directs the MFA program at the University of Missouri-St. Louis and is at work on a third collection and a novel.

Martha Modena Vertreace-Doody is Distinguished Professor of English and Poet-in-Residence at Kennedy-King College, Chicago. Her several books include *Second House from the Corner* (1986), *Under a Cat's-Eye Moon* (1991), the children's book *Kelly in the Mirror* (1993), *Oracle Bones* (1994), *Cinnabar* (1995), *Light Caught Bending* (1995), *Maafa: When Night Becomes a Lion* (1996), *Smokeless Flame* (1998), *Dragon Lady: Tsukimi* (1999), and *Second Mourning* (1998). She lives in Chicago with her husband, Tim, and her cats, Bon-Bon and Fred.

Curtis White is a novelist and critic living in Normal, Illinois. His most recent novel is *Requiem.* He has two forthcoming books, *The Middle Mind: From the Poverty of the American Imagination to the New Sublime* (Harper's Books), and *America's Magic Mountain* (Dalkey Archive). He is also the editor of *Context: A Forum for Literary Arts and Culture.*

S. L. Wisenberg lives in Chicago in a 100-year-old building that lies between the Sheridan and Addison stops on the Red line. She grew up in the land of cars, freeways, and newness (Houston), and has spent most of her adult life in the Midwest (the Chicago area and Iowa City). She is the author of a short-story collection, *The Sweetheart Is In* (Northwestern University Press), and an essay collection, *Holocaust Girls: History, Memory, and Other Obsessions* (University of Nebraska Press). Her Web site is www.slwisenberg.com.

Janet Wondra is a poet and essayist who teaches at Roosevelt University in Chicago, where she heads the creative writing and film studies programs. Her poetry has appeared in such publications as *Witness, The Southern Review, Denver Quarterly,* and *Exquisite Corpse.* Also a filmmaker, she has screened her work at art museums and film festivals internationally, including the European Media Art Festival (Osnabrück, Germany), Darklight Digital Film Festival (Dublin, Ireland), Mill Valley Film Festival (Calif.), East Lansing Film Festival (Mich.), and International Women's Film and Video Festival (Austin, Tex.).